SOCIAL-SCIENCE COMMENTARY
ON THE GOSPEL OF JOHN

SOCIAL-SCIENCE COMMENTARY ON THE GOSPEL OF JOHN

BRUCE J. MALINA
RICHARD L. ROHRBAUGH

FORTRESS PRESS
MINNEAPOLIS

SOCIAL-SCIENCE COMMENTARY ON THE GOSPEL OF JOHN

Scriptural quotations, unless otherwise noted, are from the New Revised Standard Version of the Bible, copyright © 1989 by the Division of Christian Education of the National Council of the Churches of Christ in the United States of America.

Grateful acknowledgment is made to Sadan Publishing Ltd., Tel Aviv, for permission to reprint illustrations 2, 3, 6, 9, 13, 19, 23, 28, 29, and 31 from *Following the Way* by Bruce E. Schein.

Cover art: *The Banquet*, a Fourth-Style painting from the dining room (*triclinium*) of a Pompeian house, whose owner is portrayed with his guests, attended by young slaves. Reproduced by permission of Museo Archeologico Nazionale di Napoli.

Library of Congress Cataloging in Publication Data

Malina, Bruce J.
    Social-science commentary on the Gospel of John / Bruce J. Malina
    Richard L. Rohrbaugh
        p. cm.
    Includes bibliographical references and index.
    ISBN 0-8006-2992-2 (alk. paper)
    1. Bible. N.T. John—Commentaries. 2. Bible. N.T. John—Social scientific criticism.
I. Rohrbaugh, Richard L., 1936- . II. Title.
BS2625.3.M29 1998
226.5'077—   98-24813
                                                                              CIP

The paper used in this publication meets the minimum requirements of American National Standard for Information Sciences—Permanence of Paper for Printed Library Materials, ANSI Z329.48-1984.

Manufactured in the U.S.A.   AF1-2992

02   01   00   99   98   1   2   3   4   5   6   7   8   9   10

For Dean Philip F. Esler,
of the Divinity School, University of St. Andrews, Scotland
Indefatigable, brilliant, and insightful
Context Group colleague and friend

CONTENTS

Contents

PREFACE

The Gospel of John is a New Testament writing that continues to command wide interest. In his best-selling and much reprinted *The World's Religions*, Huston Smith describes Christianity and its founder almost exclusively in Johannine colors. The "Power for Living" program of the Arthur S. DeMoss Foundation, publicized during the 1983 Super Bowl, is fundamentally rooted in John's Gospel, with its "First Law" beginning with John 3:16, the popular banner unfurled behind football goalposts right to the present. The message of Campus Crusade for Christ, which presents Jesus as the individual's personal Lord and Savior, is largely of Johannine inspiration. And most U.S. college students, if they know the story of Jesus at all, know it quite well in terms of John's Gospel: Jesus' meeting with the Samaritan woman and his attitude toward women; the need to be born again; Jesus saying, "I am the Way, the Truth and the Life"; the saying about casting the first stone; the raising of Lazarus; Jesus washing the disciples' feet; the waving of palms at Jesus' triumphal entry into Jerusalem; the inscription on the cross; the mother of Jesus at the cross; the piercing of Jesus' side with a spear; Mary Magdalene's visit to Jesus' tomb; Jesus as the Word of God; the identification of Jesus as God purely and simply. For usually unexplained and unexplored reasons, John's Gospel seems to have the greatest appeal to American individualists. We see this borne out every semester in undergraduate students who enroll in our college courses in New Testament writings. This social-science commentary on the Gospel of John has been written with such undergraduate students in mind. Our goal is to present a historically sensitive, cross-cultural, comparative set of lenses with which to hear (or read) the Gospel of John as its original audience did. The success of our previous *Social-Science Commentary on the Synoptic Gospels* has encouraged us to prepare this work.

Once again our book is outfitted with maps, photographs, charts, and helpful appended descriptions. These have been put together, as previously, by our colleague, Thomas A. Hoffman, S.J., of Creighton University. It is our pleasure to thank him for his contributions in making this volume more useful.

Readers will find a wealth of resources related to this project—including the full texts of some of our articles and links to other pertinent sites at

http://www.lclark.edu/~rbaugh/john.html

We likewise wish to express appreciation of our colleagues in the Context Group as well as to the many people in foreign lands who befriended us with the favors of their patronage and friendship. Finally, we thank our spouses, who have borne the culture shock of overseas study with us and shared their broad-ranging, perceptive insights into that familiarly strange Mediterranean world that serves as setting for the New Testament documents.

BRUCE J. MALINA
RICHARD L. ROHRBAUGH

INTRODUCTION

Our primary purpose in writing a social-science commentary on the Gospel of John is to enable the reader to interpret the Gospel in a way that would be fair to its original author and audience. That is of first importance. Yet, while we wish to understand the Gospel in the way John's initial audience might have understood it, nonetheless, our focus is not intended to divert attention or interest from important features of the modern world. In fact, both ends of the interpretive chain are of decisive importance.

It is not at all difficult to see why this is so. In the introduction to our volume on the Synoptic Gospels (Malina and Rohrbaugh 1992:1–17), we underscored the fact that the Industrial Revolution has had a significant impact on our ability to read and understand the New Testament. This great watershed (or "Great Transformation," as we called it) that we in the Western tradition have now irrevocably passed threatens our ability to hear what the Bible so clearly said to its earliest readers. After all, the Bible was written in an agrarian, preindustrial world, in which things were very different from what they are now. Neither the biblical authors nor their primary audiences could have anticipated anything like the formation of European nation-states or the formation of an Enlightenment nation-state like the United States. Our new social arrangements, with the separation of religion and economics from kinship and politics, would have been inconceivable to them. In fact, the separation of church and state, and of economics and state, are truly radical and unthinkable departures from what has heretofore been normal on the planet.

U.S. social forms and values, coupled with the technologies deriving from the Industrial Revolution, have resulted in permanent, radical change in vast areas of human experience. With these changes has come a new way of perceiving, a new outlook on the world. It offers a radically different way to interpret human experience and, consequently, a radically different way to construct our interpretations of reality. Moreover, if the outlook of the earlier era was so markedly different

1

from ours today, and our contention is that it was emphatically so, it would hardly be surprising that something fundamental has happened to our capacity to read and understand the Bible.

It has become commonplace, of course, to recognize the time-and-place boundedness of the Bible. We know the New Testament to be the product of a small group of people living in the first century C.E. in the eastern Mediterranean region. It thus stands at a distance from us in the twentieth century. But that distance between the world of the New Testament and our own has usually been calculated in historical terms, in terms of the flow of events or ideas that might account for what biblical documents ostensibly describe. Much scholarly effort has gone into describing the main ideas emerging from that story in some historically sensitive way.

Such approaches are not sufficient, however, in accounting for the viewpoints of the contemporary reader of the Bible. We must also recognize, as indeed recent social-scientific studies of the New Testament have begun to do, that the distance between ourselves and the Bible is as much *social* as it is temporal and conceptual. Such social distance includes radical differences in social structures, social roles, values, and general cultural features. It involves being socialized into a different understanding of the self, of others, of nature and time and space, and perhaps even of God. In fact, it may be that such social distance is the most fundamental distance of all. It may have had a greater impact on our ability to read and understand the Bible than much of what has preoccupied scholarly attention to date.

The World of the New Testament
and the World of John's Gospel

As we have noted, the New Testament writings derive from the preindustrial period of human experience. More specifically, they are rooted in the advanced agrarian societies that characterized the first-century Mediterranean region. Yet, while this advanced agrarian setting is common to all the New Testament writings, the situation of the Gospel of John stands apart from the rest. It is different. Nearly everyone who has closely studied the Gospel of John insists that this Gospel is different from the rest of the documents in the Christian canon. It has been quite appropriately labeled the "maverick Gospel" (Kysar 1976).

What specific qualities set John apart from the rest? It is well known that beginners interested in learning the Greek language of the New Testament period, for example, often begin with the document called "John." This of course points only to the "wording" level of language. The wording level refers to the patterns of sounding and spelling that we usually call "vocabulary, grammar, and syntax." Language learning is often identified with learning the distinctive patterns of native language speakers: their words, sentence structure, word order, and paragraph construction. It is easy to learn Greek wording by analyzing and memorizing the patterns that emerge in the Gospel of John. Yet wording is not meaning. Sociolinguists tell us that wording is the linguistic way humans express meaning (see Halliday 1978). The meanings that languages express are not in the wording level. Rather, meanings themselves always derive from some social system. Native speakers inevitably realize meanings from their local social system. Unless aware of this, foreign speakers often express meanings from their own social system while using the wordings of the local languages. So U.S. college students often learn to speak English in Spanish, German, and French, while students of the Bible speak English in Greek and Hebrew. Those readers of John who have no knowledge of the social system of the author of the Gospel and his original audience invariably find John expressing meanings that are quite relevant to the United States and the modern, individualist American reader. Consider the sheets with John 3:16 on them at so many U.S. football games! Words such as *love, world, believe,* and the like are presumed to have the same meanings as those U.S. persons ascribe to them. But perhaps those words express social realities quite different from those of contemporary Americans. The modern student of New Testament Greek therefore has the option of using meanings derived from our U.S. social system (the usual choice) or of learning the first-century Mediterranean social system that endowed John with its original meanings.

If it is true that the meanings communicated by means of written or spoken language derive ultimately from a social system, then what sort of social system might account for the distinctive features of the document called John's Gospel? After all, this document we label "John," like all written documents, is a meaningful configuration of language intended to communicate. A text is a unit of communication larger than a sentence and expressing some complete meaning. In this sense, John's Gospel is a "text." People write texts in order to have some social effect. In fact, it could be said that language is essentially a form of social interaction. People direct language at each other in order to mean something and thereby to create some effect in a social context. Who spoke "John" to whom, in what social context, and for what purpose? Can social context be inferred from the language people use?

It is here that persons who study language as a form of social interaction offer some very useful insights. They tell us, for example, that what persons talk about is meaningful to their conversation partners, not so much because these partners do not know what a speaker (or writer) is going to say, but because the partners *do* know. Any listener or reader has abundant evidence of what some speaker or writer is going to say, both from his or her knowledge of how the language works and from a practiced sensibility to what one in fact can say in specific situations. What persons can and do say in specific situations is part of the set of scenarios that all of us learn in the process of socialization into the social system we call our own. For example, in the United States, any person at the site of an auto accident and witnessing a physician speaking with an injured person can be fairly certain they are not discussing Italian cooking, the price of eggs, the problems of adolescence, farming in Somalia, or the crime rate in New York City. The situation rules out literally hundreds of thousands of conversation topics. Similarly, an American churchgoer is generally rather certain that the Sunday sermon will not be about atomic physics, the details of Third World import quotas, or the proper chemical formulas for describing the structure of crystals. Players talking in a huddle during a football game will not be conversing about permanent life insurance, Zen Buddhism, or the stock market. As a rule, members of various societies can predict the types of meanings that might be exchanged from the situations in which speaking takes place.

It was this insight that led a number of German biblical scholars early in the twentieth century to describe the social situation of early Jesus-Messiah groups on the basis of the patterns of speech or literary forms found in the New Testament. Yet, while these scholars came up with some fine insights, most often their assessment of the social situations available to early Jesus Messianists mirrored the situation of the modern church and its concerns rather than situations and concerns of the first-century Mediterranean society. Consequently, if we seek to understand what John's Gospel meant to its original audiences, our question should be: What sort of situation and what set of concerns might adequately explain the scenes presented in the document called the Gospel of John?

Features of the Language of John

Several years ago at a meeting of biblical scholars, well-known Bible translator Eugene Nida mentioned that in his vast experience among various peoples of the world, the one New Testament document that caused the most trouble to translators was the Gospel of John. For even though John's vocabulary and syntax are simpler than other New Testament writings, professional translators have difficulty in articulating in the various languages of the world exactly what John meant. Perhaps this holds for our current English translations as well. Why this state of affairs? Does the Gospel of John derive from a social system atypical even in the first-century eastern Mediterranean?

Consider some of the peculiar features of this document. Perhaps the most direct way to approach John is to note its author's distinctive development of and penchant for new phrases in place of old ones, for many words for the same activity. For example, Paul speaks of "faith in Christ Jesus" when he wants to speak of faith in Christ Jesus. But John speaks of "believing *into* Jesus." And to express this reality, he has recourse to terms such as: *following* him, *abiding in* him, *loving* him, *keeping his word, receiving* him, *having* him, or *seeing* him. While for us all these verbs express different facets of behavior, not so in John. All these words describe "believing into Jesus." The same is true for John's selection of words to refer to the realm of God: *spirit, above, life, light, not of the/this world, freedom, truth, love.* This feature bespeaks *language partially relexicalized.* Relexicalization refers to the practice of using new words for some reality that is not ordinarily referred to with those words. To call money "bread" or to call a pistol a "piece" are instances of relexicalization. The implicit principle behind relex-icalization seems to be: same grammar but different vocabulary, though only in certain key areas.

Relexicalization points to items and objects affecting areas of central concern to the group. John's relexicalizations derive from the interests and activities of John's group. In John this concern is articulated as follows: "that you may con-tinue to believe that Jesus is the Messiah, the Son of God, and that through believ-ing you may have life in his name" (John 20:31). In other words, the author of John is concerned with spelling out the meaning of Jesus of Nazareth as "the Mes-siah, the Son of God," and in developing emotional anchorage "in Jesus" for his collectivity. It is to this end that the author develops his very different vocabulary.

Furthermore, John does not simply relexicalize in his area of concern, he *over-lexicalizes*. To overlexicalize is to have many words for the central area of con-cern. In John's Gospel the author employs a broad range of words and phrases to cover a single area, as we have noted. First, there is his contrast between *spirit, above, life, light, not of the/this world, freedom, truth, love*, and their opposites, *flesh, below, death, darkness, the/this world, slavery, lie, hate*. These two sets of words are variants used to describe contrasting spheres of existence, opposing modes of living and being. Similarly, and with very little appreciable difference in meaning, John speaks of *believing into Jesus, following* him, *abiding in* him, *loving* him, *keeping his word, receiving* him, *having* him, or *seeing* him. This kind of redundancy is what we mean by overlexicalization.

Sociolinguists in the neo-Firthian tradition tell us that languages entail three linguistic modes of meaning: the *ideational*, the *interpersonal*, and the *textual*. The *ideational* refers to what is being said or described; the *interpersonal* looks to the personal qualities of the communicating partners; and the *textual* pertains to the qualities of language to form units of meaning at a level higher than the sentence, for example, by means of cohesion of paragraphs into some whole. Again, *what* one says is ideational, *with whom* one speaks is interpersonal, and *how* one speaks is textual (Halliday 1978:8–36; also the model on 69 and its explanation on 125–26). We single out these components here because John typ-ically de-emphasizes the ideational (what he has to say) and focuses rather heavily on the interpersonal (with whom the conversation occurs) and textual (how one speaks).

For example, a comparison of the text of John (the whole Gospel as written document) with the Synoptic Gospels will readily indicate that John downplays the ideational feature of language. Narrative critics to the contrary, in John there really is no progressive description of who Jesus is, no progressively mounting opposition from enemies, no progressive presentation of Jesus' ministry and teaching. All John really has to say is said in the prologue: "He came to his own people and they did not receive him. But to all who received him he gave the power to become children of God, born . . . of God, for God's Utterance has been enfleshed and has taken up residence in our midst" (1:11-14). The vignettes in the Gospel are variations on this theme.

By contrast, John indeed highlights the interpersonal and textual functions of language. The linguistic dimensions of how Jesus speaks (textual component) and with whom he speaks (interpersonal component) come through in a way not found in the Synoptic narratives. For example, overlexicalization based on the textual function of language (how Jesus speaks, how others speak to Jesus) is revealed in forms of verbal display, such as punning and wordplay. This feature is quite apparent in John's well-known pattern of ambiguity, misunderstanding, and clarification (John 2:19ff.; 3:3ff.; 4:10ff.; 4:32ff.; 6:33ff.; 8:31ff.; 8:38ff.; 11:11ff.; 11:23ff.; 13:8ff.; 14:4ff.; 14:7ff.; 14:21ff.; 16:16ff. These passages, or text segments, reveal verbal display or wordplays relative to the following: the destruction of the temple, being born again, water, food, bread, freedom, father, sleep, resurrection, washing, way, seeing, manifestation, a little while respectively). This feature is likewise manifested in John's penchant for irony (John 2:9-10; 4:12; 7:27, 42, 52; 11:16, 36; 12:19; 13:37; 18:31, 38; 19:5, 14, 19ff.). Halliday notes that it is these two dimensions (interpersonal and textual) that account for the overlexicalization we spoke of earlier.

The interpersonal dimension of language is especially important in John. The overlexicalization deriving from this function (who is involved, of whom and to whom Jesus speaks) is indicated by the set of words that has the same denotation but has quite a different connotation based on the attitude and commitment the set of words entails in an interpersonal context. This includes, for example, all of the "I am . . ." statements of Jesus. "Bread" (John 6:35), "light" (8:12), "door" (10:9), "life" (11:25-26), "way" (14:6), and "vine" (15:5) have the same denotation in the contexts in which they are employed; they refer to various real-world objects. However, when identified with Jesus in an "I am . . ." proposition, each takes on some interpersonal dimension. For example, Jesus is not bread, but he is like bread for those who stay attached to him; he is not a door, but he is like a door to God for those who believe in him. The synonyms for the activities of discipleship (to *believe, come, abide, follow, love, keep words, receive, have, see*) and those for the two contrasting realms (*above, spirit*, etc., and *below, flesh*, etc., listed previously) point in the same direction—that is, to the interpersonal component of language.

This orientation toward the interpersonal and textual modes of the linguistic system accounts for the way *social values* are foregrounded, highlighted, and underscored in John. It also indicates that John and his group seek the implementation of new values, not new structures, in place of old ones. The Synoptics and Paul, by contrast, emphasize new structures to replace old ones. Their new structures are called "the kingdom of God," "the kingdom of heaven" (i.e., the sky), "church," "body of Christ," those "in Christ," and the like. This emphasis on new structures underscores and features the ideational mode of the linguistic system; who is involved and how things are said are of lesser concern. In the Gospel of John, however, who is involved and how things are said are everything.

John's Language as Antilanguage

This consistent relexicalization and overlexicalization, along with focus on the interpersonal and modal aspect of language, point to what Halliday has labeled as "antilanguage" (Halliday 1978:164–82). "Antilanguage" is the language of an "antisociety," that is "a society that is set up within another society as a conscious alternative to it. It is a mode of resistance, resistance which may take the form either of passive symbiosis or of active hostility and even destruction" (Halliday 1978:171). The instances of antilanguage that Halliday studied include the language of individuals put into prison or reform schools in Poland, members of the underworld in India, and of vagabonds in Elizabethan England. All these individuals formed groups that were in fact antisocieties set up within a larger, broader society, and in this setting their language came to express their social experience. In other words, antilanguage and antisociety go hand in hand. Or as Giblett notes, "There can be no society without language, and no antisociety without an antilanguage" (1991:1).

Consider the relexicalization and overlexicalization typical of persons in the so-called U.S. drug culture. For example, the Washington-based Drugs and Crime Data Center and Clearinghouse (1-800-666-3332 or via the Internet: http://www.askncjrs@ncjrs.aspensys.com) lists over fifteen hundred terms used for drugs and the drug trade. Here the key area of relexicalization and overlexicalization are features typical of the drug culture. We find similar relexicalization among prison populations, the underworld, and street gangs. The words and phrases in question are well known among the general U.S. population, thanks to TV shows and movies. For example, even the most casual TV watcher knows ten or more words for *pistol* (*piece, gun, gat, heater, rod, Magnum, Mauser, Smith-and-Wesson, Beretta, .45*).

The following sample of antilanguage is taken from the Omaha Police Department *Gang Slang Dictionary* (as printed in the *Omaha World Herald,* August 22, 1996, p. 14).

Are you claiming? = Do you belong to a gang?
Bent = To get drunk.
Boned out = Quit. Chickened out, left, backed down.
Brown plant = Heroin.
Cheese out = Snitch. Give up.
Chicken = Homosexual prostitute.
Clucker = Crack cocaine addict.
Dissin' = Being disrespectful.
Don = Second-highest-ranking gang member.
Dropping the flag = Leaving the gang.
Everything is everything = It's all right.

Five O = Police. Police are coming.

Frog = Girl with low moral standards; she jumps in anybody's car.

General = Third-highest-ranking gang member.

Hood = Neighborhood.

Hangin' = Not directly involved.

Hustler = Not into gangs, strictly out to make money or impress girls.

Ice cream truck = Vehicle used to sell drugs.

I'd rather be judged by 12 than carried by 6 = I'll kill you before you kill me.

Jackin' = Robbing others.

King = Highest-ranking gang member.

Kite in the wind = Letter in the mail.

Knockin' boots = Having sex.

K Swiss = Kill slobs when I see slobs.

Love = Rock cocaine.

Married = Joined a gang, group.

Nut up = Fake ignorance or stupidity.

OG = Original gangster. Old gangster or organized gangster.

Old bird = Mother.

Old jude = Father.

One time = Police officers are near.

Pancake = Person who becomes a homosexual due to his experience in jail.

Poor box = Container for the items collected by gang members as dues or
    payment for protection.

Put in some work = Doing a shooting.

Queen = Female gang member.

Rig = Combination of hypodermic needle, bottle cap, and string to tie off
    arm before injecting drugs.

Road dog = Close friend.

Rock star = Crack-addicted woman who trades sex for drugs.

Safe house = Place where large amounts of drugs and money are stored.

Sell out = To sell out your race.

Snatch a birth date = Kill someone.

Snow bunny = White female.

Strapped = To carry a weapon.

TWA = Teenie weenie afro.

Triple OG = Third generation gangster.

Undercover = Plain gang car.

Violations = To break gang rules and receive punishment.

Word = OK, all right

Even in this brief sampling, notice the overlexicalized items: terms for gang boundaries and boundary violations, drugs, women. Similarly, notice the old terms for new realities: king, general, don; police terms given new and opposite meanings: safe house, undercover, violations, etc.

It is curious to note that recent antisocieties, as a rule, have a negative relation to the law. They are either on the margins of the law or have broken the law. They are not outside society, but an outside hollowed within society. They are both objects of the power of the law and subjects of their own counterlanguage, which resists and undermines the power of the law (Giblett 1991:2). Just as society is not opposed to antisociety, so too language is not opposed to antilanguage. Rather, it is antisociety that is opposed to society, antilanguage to language. Halliday notes that "anti-language arises when the alternative reality is a counter-reality, set up in opposition to some established norm" (Halliday 1978:171).

What this means for the Gospel of John is that the individuals comprising John's group were not rejected by their opponents because of anything reported in John's Gospel. This is a significant point for those attempting a history of John's group. For the Gospel does not present the beliefs and attitudes of group members that led to their expulsion by others. Rather, John's Gospel reflects the alternate reality John's group set up in opposition to its opponents, notably "this world" and "the Judeans." In the eyes of these opponents, John's group was either on the margins of prevailing norms or laws or transgressed these. On the margins, they are not illegal but are in a space that custom or law does not (or cannot) cover because they are not really subject to the law. Or, as lawbreakers, they subsist in an "outside" hollowed within society. They are objects of the power of the law and subjects of their own antilanguage, which resists and undermines the power of the law. Like all antilanguage, John's is "consciously used for strategic purposes, defensively to maintain a particular social reality or offensively for resistance and protest" (Halliday 1978:178–79). In other words, an antilanguage is a language deriving from and generated by an antisocietal group. And an antisocietal group is a social collectivity that is set up within a larger society as a conscious alternative to it.

John's Antisociety

The reasons why persons come up with a conscious alternative to the society in which they are embedded are many and varied. Consider prison inmates and members of street gangs, the drug culture, the underworld, new religious cults, and underground political groups. Some of these persons might have been labeled as deviant and treated with active hostility by members of society at large. Or a given category of persons might experience total lack of social concern, resulting in their living in the greater society in a state of passive social symbiosis. Outside the United States, persons might be exiled or rejected due to negative outcomes of an uprising or revolt and thus have to fend for themselves. Finally, persons might be confined to concentration camps, maximum security prisons, restricted wards in mental hospitals, and the like.

All such persons are variously labeled by the dominant society as deviants: whether criminals, sinners, unbelievers, apostates, prisoners, inmates, or mental

9

patients. As deviants, they often undergo daily and progressive public disconfirmation of their ability to act as adult persons. Their movements and choices are restricted. In extreme cases, officials of the broader society publicly evaluate them in terms of a moral system that socially denies that they are capable of being genuine agents on their own behalf. To use contemporary terms, they are declared to be nonpersons. Their movements and utterances are denied the status of significant human actions. Since what they say and do is defined as mere behavior, as going through meaningless motions, they must be, so it is pronounced, without capacities to act in human fashion. Antilanguage and its generating alternate society derive from individuals who have experienced such socially sanctioned depersonalization (Harris 1989:606).

In John's case, the document does indeed point to an audience composed of individuals who emerged from and stand opposed to society and its competing groups. In concrete terms, the larger groups, which John's collectivity opposes, include "the (this) world" (79 times in John; 9 times in Matthew, and 3 each in Mark and Luke), and "the Judeans" (71 times in John; 5 times in Matthew and Luke; 7 times in Mark). These groups adamantly refuse to believe in Jesus as Israel's Messiah, and therefore the Johannine group stands over against them. In addition, Raymond Brown (1979:168–69) has singled out four other competing groups: the adherents of John the Baptist who do not as yet believe in Jesus, and three groups that claim to believe in Jesus—"crypto-Christians," "Christians from the house of Israel," and "Christians of the apostolic churches." This last group comprises perhaps "the sheep that do not belong to this fold" (John 10:16), with which John's group has some relationship through the "shepherd." John's antilanguage is a form of resistance to this range of competing groups and develops for positive and negative reasons to be considered shortly.

The Meanings of John's Antilanguage

It is important to realize that antilanguage is not simply a specialized or technical variety of ordinary language used in a special way or in particular, technical contexts (for example, technical jargons, argots, and the like). Rather, an antilanguage arises among persons in groups espousing and held by alternative perceptions of reality—reality as experienced and set up in opposition to some established mode of conception and perception. Consequently, an antilanguage is nobody's "mother tongue." Nor is it a predictable mother-tongue derivative. In other words, no other New Testament author assesses and describes Jesus as John does. John's Gospel points to people being resocialized, for antilanguage exists solely in a social context of resocialization. Like any other language, it is a means of realizing meanings from the social system of the society in question. It is a means of expressing perceptions of reality as interpreted by persons socialized in that social system. Socially, the use of language actively creates and maintains the prevailing interpretations of reality. But unlike ordinary language, antilanguage creates and expresses an interpretation of reality that is inherently an alternative reality, one that emerges precisely in order to function as an alternative to society at large.

In John's antilanguage we find the expression of an alternative to the society of first-century Mediterranean Hellenism in general and of its Israelite version in particular. Thus, what is significant in John's antilanguage is not its distance from the language of Hellenistic Judea, but the tension between the two. Both Judean society and the Johannine group share the same overarching system of meaning, just as both are part and parcel of the same overarching social system. Yet they stand in opposition to and in tension with each other. The reason for underscoring this point is that to appreciate the new values and perceptions generated by an antisocietal collectivity such as John's group, one must understand the larger society to which it stands opposed. Antisociety makes no sense without the society over against which it stands. This is important, for John's group and the story that held it together make sense only in the Judean society in which it originated. Thus, when removed from the society in which it directly and immediately made sense, the Gospel of John quickly loses its original meanings.

What uses do antilanguages serve? Halliday observes that antilanguages are generally replications of social forms based on highly distinctive values. These values are clearly set apart from those of the society from which antisocietal members derive. Like language itself, antilanguage is the bearer of social reality, but of an alternative social reality that runs counter to the social reality of society at large. Thus, antilanguage serves to maintain inner solidarity in the face of pressure from the wider society (from which group members stem, and in which they are to a large extent still embedded). Furthermore, for individuals to maintain solidarity with their fellow antisocietal members and not fall back into the margins of the groups they left or from which they were ejected, some sort of alternative ideology and emotional anchorage in the new collectivity is necessary.

This necessity is best served by demonstrations of mutual care and concern on the part of those in the antisocietal group. The result is that strong affective identification is established on the part of newcomers into the group as well as those on its fringes ready to swing out. This describes a process of resocialization (Mol 1976:50–54; 142–201). Just as language is crucial to the social interpretation of reality and to the socialization of new members into that social interpretation, so too antilanguage is crucial to the social reinterpretation of the alternate reality and to the resocialization of newcomers into that social interpretation. John is an instance of such antilanguage in the Jesus-Messiah tradition.

John's Gospel as a Resocializing Story

From the viewpoint of linguistics, the process of resocialization and the maintenance of group solidarity make special demands on an antilanguage. It is especially important that the antilanguage facilitate the process of establishing strongly affective ties with both the reputed legitimate authority, who is the central influence in the collectivity, and also with significant others in the group. Moreover, this process has to be geared to the individual group member, just as was the original socialization process.

Obviously, the linguistic genre most appropriate to this end is conversation and its implicit modes of reciprocity. Thus, in John's Gospel there is ample evidence of distinctive conversations with Jesus that serve a resocialization function (John 3:1—4:42; 5:10ff.; 6:22ff.; 9:13—10:42; 11:1-4; 11:45—12:36a; 13-17). How these conversations unfold is well known. Jesus begins to converse with an individual, moves on to address that person in monologue fashion, and finally the monologue turns into an address to the reader/hearer. Throughout these passages there is heavy foregrounding of interpersonal meanings directed to individuals. It is therefore not surprising that these conversations are the feature of John that hold constant and perennial appeal for individualistically oriented persons (for example, U.S. persons). In John's Gospel Jesus speaks to his conversation partners as individuals, not as participants in some larger group, as is the case in the Synoptics or for the addressees of the remaining New Testament writings.

John's characteristic antilanguage is what accounts for this feature of the Gospel. In this regard, we must also note the use of the personal pronoun. Unlike English, Greek verb forms can be inflected in such a way that one need not use pronouns (as with Latin and Spanish, for example). When one uses the second person personal pronoun with verbs, the resulting nuance is one of emphasis on the person(s) addressed. Therefore, in John the use of the pronoun *you,* singular in Greek, is distinctive: 60 times in John, 10 in Mark, 18 in Matthew, and 26 in Luke. The same is true of the use of the personal pronoun *you,* plural in Greek: 68 times in John, 11 in Mark, 30 in Matthew, and 28 in Luke. Such emphatic use of the pronoun in Greek simply underscores the interpersonal dimension.

The alternative reality generated by groups such as the Johannine group has several important implications. First, it implies an emphasis on new core values and an attempt to create standards and structures to implement those values. Similarly, it implies a preoccupation with social boundaries, social definition and the defense of identity, usually by means of repeated and varied articulation of the new reality now so clearly perceived. Both of these points are realized in John's strong contrast between *above, spirit,* etc., and *below, flesh,* etc., and the forms of behavior proper to each. Furthermore, the counterreality in question implies a special conception of information and knowledge—a feature amply highlighted in John, where Jesus is eminently a revealer. And finally, such counterreality implies that social meanings will be seen as oppositions and values defined in terms of what they are *not* (for example, "not . . . but," 1:13; 3:17; 6:27, 28, 32; 7:16; 8:55; 10:18; 11:4; "no one . . . except," 1:18; 3:2, 13; 6:46; "I have not come . . . ," 7:28; 12:47; 15:22; "I have not done . . . ," 15:24). Further, in John it is quite clear that Jesus' prodigies are not simply about what is going on—that is, healing or rescue—but about something more and something other than one can ostensibly witness. They are in fact "signs" that disclose and elucidate Jesus himself to those who affectionately accept his offer of light and life.

In addition to such interpersonal dimensions of antilanguage, Halliday has pointed out that the overlexicalization of antilanguages is a form of variant in linguistics. In general, a variant is an alternative realization of a linguistic element on the next, or some higher level of abstraction in the linguistic system. A higher-level realization always has the same meaning in some respect as the items falling beneath it. For example, the lexical items or words *fruit, vegetables, meat,* and *bread* have *food* as their variant. *Food* is an alternative realization of a linguistic element such as *bread* or *meat* on a higher level in the linguistic system. This higher-level realization, food, always has the same meaning in some respect as the items falling beneath it—in this case, fruit, vegetables, meat, and bread. Thus, the words *fruit, vegetables, meat,* and *bread* each can mean "food." Moreover, the lexical item *food* can be used to mean any of the foregoing; they are technically variants of the word *food.*

Similarly, in John, *spirit, above, life, light, not of the/this world, freedom, truth,* and *love* are all variants of the "new reality" John identifies with and in Jesus of Nazareth. By contrast, *flesh, below, death, darkness, this/the world, slavery, lie,* and *hate* are all variants of what John and the collectivity addressed in the work oppose: the "old reality" of the society from which they came.

As Halliday notes, however, the significant thing about the lexical items (words and sentences) proper to an antilanguage is that many of them have no equivalent meanings at all in the standard language of the broader society. Sentences such as "I and the Father [God] are one" (John 10:30) and "Truly, truly I say to you, before Abraham was, I am" (8:58), and the identification of Jesus of Nazareth with the preexisting Word of God become flesh (1:1ff.), would be socially meaningless in the language of the broader society. Similarly, among contemporary antisocieties, treasured gang titles (king, don, general) are valueless in society at large. This does not mean that such titles and statements could not be understood and judged to be meaningless, or that they could not be translated (after all, our English versions of John do them adequate justice). Rather, it means that such propositions did not function as language with verifiable social meaning in the semantic system of regular language, even the regular "religious" language of contemporary Israel in general or early Jesus-Messianism in particular. It is quite significant to note that there are no such sentences in Paul's writings or the other Gospels and non-Johannine New Testament documents.

The foregoing considerations point to the fact that an antilanguage is a metaphor for the regular language of society at large. Metaphorization takes place when some common, often implicit, quality proper to one entity is predicated of another; for example, "My brother is a lion." Here the implicit property is strength or ferocity; thus, the explicit sentence would read: "My brother is as strong as/as ferocious as a lion." In antilanguage such a metaphorical quality appears all the way through the system. Halliday tells us that it is this fundamental metaphorical quality that defines an antilanguage.

In John this metaphorical quality can be seen in the "I am . . . " statements, in which Jesus says that he is bread, light, a door, life, way, vine, and the like. The metaphorical quality inherent in the list of ambiguity-misunderstanding-clarification sequences noted previously provides another example. Of course, the metaphor that constitutes antilanguage is present in all language to some extent. Much of everyday language is in fact metaphorical; for example, horsepower in an automobile, a cell in biology, the conception of ideas, and the like. Yet the metaphorical quality of everyday language is frequently lost. For instance, people forget that a cell originally referred to the monastery room of a monk. Today the word is commonly used in biology and popular science and is identified with a dimension of reality itself. By contrast, what distinguishes an antilanguage is that when it is compared with the existing language system of the culture in which it emerges (and the society against which it stands), it is clearly seen to be a metaphorical entity. Hence, in antilanguage, metaphorical modes of expression are the norm. They are an antilanguage's regular pattern of realization.

As we noted above, the main form of discourse used in socialization and reality maintenance is conversation. The reality-generating and -maintaining power of language lies in conversation. The impact of conversation is cumulative and depends for its effectiveness on continuous reinforcement in social interaction. It is important to note, then, that John's Gospel is the only New Testament writing presenting extended conversations. Furthermore, all of the great Johannine metaphors emerge in conversations. That is where the metaphorical points are made.

In sum, the resocialization quality of John's Gospel is maintained as the reader/hearer is addressed by Jesus in conversations where dialogue eventually becomes monologue. In supporting the resocialization process, these Johannine conversations rely heavily on foregrounding and highlighting interpersonal meanings. For their power to generate reality, such conversations depend on their being casual, as Jesus' conversations in John so often are. And most important, they are often with individuals with whom the reader/hearer can empathize. This allows the reader to take on the role of conversation partner with Jesus as dialogue moves on to monologue in the second part of the conversation.

How John Makes His Point

Before leaving the subject of antilanguage, we must note one final point. Within the ideational mode of meaning (*what* is being talked about), an antilanguage may adopt linguistic structures and lexical collocations that are self-consciously opposed to the norms of established language. This is especially typical of the more intellectual antilanguages. There is evidence of this feature in John, although such items are often "translated out" in English versions. For example, in John the verb "to believe" most often is followed by the preposition "into"; "to follow" Jesus is "to be born again"; Jesus refers to his death as "being lifted up";

and for John "seeing" is believing. Thus, in antilanguage the modes of linguistic expression, especially when seen from the standpoint of the established language, appear diffuse, roundabout, and metaphorical—and so they are from that angle.

But seen on their own terms, they appear direct and forceful. They are powerful manifestations of the linguistic system doing service in the construction of a new interpretation of reality. From this point of view, it is the new interpretation being constructed and maintained (rather than the language) that is oblique, since it can only be seen as a metaphorical transformation of the "true" reality of the greater society. But the function of a document expressed in some antilanguage is to reinforce the new interpretation of reality. Hence, it can be seen as all the more direct because the new interpretation of reality is one that needs much reinforcement. It expresses the new experience and perceptions of the group.

John is indeed different from the other Gospels. Our sociolinguistic considerations point up precisely why this is the case. John writes for persons actually living in an alternate society embedded in a larger society—the society of "this world" and of "Judeans." While John's social situation does not determine his personal genius or the exact form that his work has taken, it does determine and define the limits within which he can select features that would make sense to his audience. It also determines the general shape of the patterns of perception available to persons in his group. These perceptions of the author of John are realized and articulated in language, and John's language is antilanguage.

The Value of Social Analysis

The sociolinguistic level of analysis proposed here is simply a first step toward understanding the Johannine group by means of its shared story. Yet it is an important first step. It furnishes an explanation for the distinctive Johannine ways of describing God, Jesus, and human relations with both. This explanation, of course, is rooted in the social behavior of John's group, which is used as an analogy for explaining the God revealed in Jesus. Moreover, this perspective helps the modern student to discover the sort of persons to be found in that difficult yet exhilarating social situation. It enables us to know and appreciate the personages who embodied faith in Jesus in first-century Mediterranean contexts typical of alternate societies. We can appreciate their willingness to identify Jesus with the divinity of Israelite tradition, their self-distancing from their original mooring in temple-based Israelite Yahwism, and especially their emphatic stance relative to interpersonal commitment within their group. They are persons who made sense of the overarching meaning of human existence "in Jesus" in highly creative and significant ways.

Finally, such analysis highlights the special problem of the individuals and their groups who lived in alternate societies. Alternate societies are impermanent arrangements within a broader society. They do not continue unchanged. Thus, persons who form alternate societies must eventually face the need to return to the more stable, surrounding society and, in the case of John's group of Jesus Messianists, the need to articulate their experience of Jesus in a way befitting that larger society. Perhaps the three Johannine letters found later in the New Testament evidence some stages in this return to ordinary society. Perhaps they recount the beginnings of the dissolution of John's antisocietal group.

Reading John

Ethnocentric and anachronistic readings of the New Testament are quite common in our society. Such readings result from the fact that readers most often use scenarios rooted in their contemporary social experience to envision what they read in the New Testament. That the ensuing misreadings of ancient documents raise few mental eyebrows simply underscores our recognition that reading is a social act. Yet how can contemporary American Bible readers participate in a historically sensitive reading if we have been socialized and shaped by the experience of living in twentieth-century America rather than an alternate society of first-century Palestine? Will we not continue to conjure up reading scenarios that the first readers of John could never have imagined? If we do, of course, the inevitable result is misunderstanding. Too often we simply do not bother to acquire some of the reservoir of experience on which the author of John naturally expected his reader to draw. For better or worse, we read ourselves and our world back into the document in ways we do not suspect.

The important point we are making here, indeed the one that gives reason for the commentary that follows, can be made another way. The New Testament was written in what anthropologists call a "high-context" society. People in high-context societies presume a broadly shared, well-understood, or "high," knowledge of the context of anything referred to in conversation or in writing. For example, everyone in ancient Mediterranean villages would have had concrete knowledge of what sowing entailed, largely because the skills involved were shared by most male members of that society. No writer would need to explain it. Thus, writers in high-context societies usually produce sketchy and impressionistic documents, leaving much to the reader's or hearer's imagination. Often they encode information in widely known symbolic or stereotypical statements. In this way they require the reader to fill in large gaps in the "unwritten" portion of the document—what is between the lines. They expect all readers to know the social context and therefore to understand the references in question.

In this way biblical authors, like most authors writing in the high-context ancient Mediterranean world, presume that readers have a broad and concrete knowledge of their common social context. That is a given. Moreover, a document like John makes the additional assumption that its original readers/hearers were members of an alternate society. It expects them to have a high knowledge of that peculiar context and thus offers little by way of extended explanation. In a sense, John's alternate society was even higher context than the surrounding society. When John writes of Jesus meeting a Samaritan woman at a well at noon, for example, he feels no necessity to explain for the reader the gender-based meaning of time and place associated with a well. Jesus was clearly out of place, as the disciples intimate, but John does not explain the socially loaded situation. He assumes his readers already know that. Nor does John explain the critical significance of a community's water supply in determining the strength and potency of the populace. His readers know all about that too. These features are crucial to understanding Jesus' ensuing conversation with the woman, though little of this information is known to modern readers of his story.

By contrast, "low-context" societies are those that assume "low" knowledge of the context of any communication. They produce highly specific and detailed documents that leave little for the reader to fill in or supply. Since the United States and northern Europe are typical low-context societies, readers from these societies expect writers to give the necessary background when referring to something not shared by all in the society. A computer operator, for example, learns a certain jargon and certain types of logic (for example, Boolean) that are not widely understood outside the circle of computer initiates. Within that circle these concepts can be used without explanation because they are easily understood by any competent reader of technical computer manuals. They can remain a part of the unwritten document the writer expects a reader to supply. But since computer jargon and technical information are not yet part of the experience of the general public, when writing for a nontechnical audience, a writer who wishes to be understood must explain the jargon and technical information at some length.

A moment's reflection will make clear why modern industrial societies are low context whereas ancient agrarian ones were high context. The computer scenario alluded to above is an all too common experience in modern life. Life today has complexified into a thousand spheres of experience the general public does not share in common. There are small worlds of experience in every corner of our society that the rest of us know nothing about. Granted, there is much in our writing that needs no explanation because it relates to experience all Americans can understand; nonetheless, the worlds of the engineer, the plumber, the insurance salesperson, and the farmer nowadays are in large measure self-contained. Should any one of these people write for the layperson who is not an engineer, plumber, insurance salesperson, or farmer, he or she would have much to explain. This is sharply different from antiquity, where change was slow and where the vast majority of the population had the common experience of farming the land and dealing with family, landlords, traders, merchants, and tax collectors. People had more in common, and experience was far less discrepant. Thus, ancient writers counted on their specific circle of readers to fill in the gaps from the behaviors into which all were socialized in a rather unspecialized world.

The obvious problem this creates for reading the biblical writings today is that low-context readers in the United States frequently mistake the biblical writings for low-context documents. They erroneously assume that the author has provided all of the contextual information needed to understand it. Consider, for example, how many U.S. and northern European people believe the Bible is a perfectly adequate and thorough statement of Christian life and behavior! Such people assume they are free to fill in between the lines of the New Testament from their own experience, because if that were not the case, the writers, like any considerate low-context authors, would have provided the unfamiliar background a reader requires. Unfortunately, this is rarely the case, because expectations of what an author should provide (or has provided) are markedly different in American and ancient Mediterranean societies.

Recontextualization

The mention of American readers reading ancient Mediterranean documents requires us to clarify the situation one step further. We have already suggested that each time a document is read by a new reader, the fields of reference tend to shift and multiply because of the reader's different cultural location. Among some literary theorists, this latter phenomenon is called "recontextualization." This term refers to the multiple ways different readers may "complete" a document as a result of reading it over against their different social contexts. (Documents may also be "decontextualized" when read ahistorically for their aesthetic or formal characteristics.)

Awareness of such recontextualization is critically important for students of the Gospel of John. As we noted above, John is an even higher-context document than other New Testament writings because it derives from an antisociety, not an ordinary ancient Mediterranean one. Therefore, while the Gospel's author writes for members of an alternative society in their common antilanguage, his statements have traditionally been taken to mean what they meant in normal Mediterranean society and its ordinary language. Thus, "I and the Father are one" is usually taken as a straightforward description of Jesus' self-understanding even though it surely is not. The problem was created as soon as the Johannine alternate society disappeared and the Gospel began to be read among ordinary Mediterraneans of antiquity. John became "the Theologian," with all sorts of information about the nature of Jesus simply unknown to any other New Testament writings.

Reading John as though it were of the same social and linguistic quality as the Synoptics was a significant but inappropriate form of recontextualization. In whatever measure this recontextualization "completed" the document differently than an original hearer of John might have done, an interpretive step of significant proportions had been taken. For the understanding of John and his group, this was unfortunate. The same is true for recontextualizations of John into the world of the modern reader. Indeed, the concern of our entire commentary is to raise awareness of this phenomenon among readers of John who usually move the document in stages, first from the antisociety of John to the ordinary Mediterranean culture of the first century, and then again into the new setting in the Western, industrialized society where it is now read. The outcome of such a process is a recontextualization of John twice removed.

What makes this problem especially complicated with the Gospel of John is the fact that an antisociety lives in relationship with and over against a dominant society. This means that for all the uniqueness of John's alternate society, it remains a hollowed out space within the context of the larger eastern Mediterranean world. In this light both the alternate society and the dominant society it opposes are significant elements in the social context of John's Gospel. The last recontextualization, the one into our modern world, has problems we will be dealing with throughout the commentary. Our thesis is that this particular recontextualization, this modernization of the document, is profoundly social in character, and that readers socialized in the industrial world are unlikely to complete the Gospel of the John in ways ancient recontextualizers did, and much less in ways the original audience could have imagined.

In sum, we insist that meanings realized through reading documents inevitably derive from a social system. Reading is always a social act. If both reader and writer share the same social system, the same experience, it is highly probable that reading will provide adequate communication. But if either reader or writer comes from mutually alien social systems, then as a rule, nonunderstanding, or at best misunderstanding, will be the rule. Because this is so, understanding the range of meanings that were plausible to a first-century Mediterranean in-group reader of John requires the contemporary reader to seek access to the social system(s) available to the author's original audience. One of these is the dominant social system of the eastern Mediterranean in antiquity; the other is the antisociety of John. Moreover, in order to recover these social systems, in whatever measure that is possible, we believe it essential to employ adequate explicit, social-scientific models of society and human behavior that have been drawn especially from circum-Mediterranean studies. Only in this way can we fill out the written documents as considerate readers who, for better or worse, have imported them into an alien world.

The Perspective Adopted in This Book

In its entirety this book is an attempt to provide the reader with fresh insight into the social system shared by the unknown author of the Gospel of John and his original, first-century Mediterranean audience. Hence, its purpose is to facilitate a reading that is consonant with the initial cultural contexts of that writing. Throughout the commentary we present models and scenarios of Mediterranean norms and values over against which the work might appropriately be read. We suggest that these scenarios or conceptual schemes are not too different from what a first-century reader would have conjured up from the social system he or she shared with the author. Whether we are talking about honor and shame, or the perception of basic divisions in human society, or about how people behave in conflict, or about any of the ceremonies and rituals or major institutions of the time, we are talking about the ancient Mediterranean taken-for-granted understanding of social life, equivalent to the things that are commonplace for us in our society. None of these things needed to be explained to a first-century audience; they understood. The fundamental point, then, is a simple one. If we wish to learn John's meanings, we must learn the social system his language encodes, even if it is an antilanguage.

Our commentary attempts to assist a reader's interpretation of the Gospel document. It is important to say, however, that our approach does not include everything one might want to know about the document. It is intended to be *supplemental* to much traditional Johannine scholarship in which the authors of this book have been duly trained (for an overview and full bibliography, see Ashton 1991). For example, it prescinds from concerns about the historical origin and development of the Johannine tradition. These are important issues, but they are beyond the scope of our commentary. Similarly, traditional historical studies provide basic information about events in the story that we often presuppose in the comments we make. We usually do not recount historical events, provide linguistic information, explain literary allusions, or trace the history of the cultural concepts to which the document often refers. Nor do we include the type of literary analysis that seeks to portray plot structure, narrative logic, the various rhetorical features, or even the literary forms contained in the Gospel stories. That, too, is supplemental to our work. What we do seek to provide is what these more traditional approaches do not: insight into the social system in which John's language is embedded.

It is also important to say that we are fully aware of the fact that the anonymous final author of John, with his own distinctive purposes and in his own editorial way, tells us of the significance for his group of what others said Jesus said and did. Thus we are cognizant of the many layers one must probe to do a history of the Johannine tradition or to find data for a historically acceptable life of Jesus. We do not make the precritical assumption that John simply reports the words or actions of Jesus. But we do insist that John is a document that emerged in and for a first-century Mediterranean, alternate society, written in antilanguage. And we do intend to facilitate a reading of the document as its stands in order to find out what the final author said and meant to say to his audience.

We believe we can do this with a social-scientific approach for two reasons. First, meanings derive from social systems. To present the social system available to John's audience is to help modern readers gain access to meanings then available. Second, models operate at a level of abstraction somewhat above that of historical inquiry. Whatever level of the Johannine tradition one might look to and whichever person one might wish to focus on—Jesus, his hearers, later collectors of tradition, or the Gospel writer himself—all of these assume the social system of the advanced agrarian, Mediterranean world. They are presented in John in a way that befits an alternate eastern Mediterranean society. All such persons, even those in alternate societies, live in an honor-shame culture. All presume collectivist personality; all understand patrons, brokers, and clientage. All are aware of Mediterranean male and female roles. All have experienced kings, temples, priests, and sacrifices. All have faced the power of rulers in the frequent presence of soldiers. All know of the behavior proper to elites and nonelites. No stage in the developing Johannine tradition stands outside these social realities.

Since our intention is to facilitate a reading of the Gospel in its final form and in terms of John's first-century Mediterranean audience, we can bypass concern about the stages leading to the final versions of the Gospel we now possess. For the same reason we have chosen not to distinguish between the so-called story world internal to the work and the external world from which the Gospel writer draws his scenarios. Doing so might be an important aspect of narrative criticism, but it is unnecessary for our task since both worlds depend on language embedded in a common social system and the antilanguage spawned from that system. That is true even when the narrative world seeks to contravene the social system.

Occasionally, of course, it is necessary to move to a lower level of abstraction to help modern readers understand the changing conditions in early Jesus-Messianism that account for certain references in the narrative. Here we will feel free to distinguish between the period of Jesus and that of the Gospel document, or between the broader Greco-Roman world and the narrower Jesus-Messiah group envisioned in the work. Sometimes differences in the social systems of Hellenism in general and of eastern Mediterranean Semites (Phoenicians, Syrians, Arabians, and Israelites) are important as well, just as important perhaps as the differences in the social settings of small urban elites and a large rural peasantry. Where appropriate, we have made such distinctions.

What all this means is that ours is not a complete literary and historical commentary on the Gospel of John. It is rather a simplified social-scientific commentary. For other types of information, the reader will want to consult other scholarly resources that provide what is needed (see Ashton 1991). But no matter what other information is acquired from more traditional sources, without the type of social and cultural information offered here, it is highly doubtful one would find out what the author of the Gospel of John was so concerned to say to his initial audiences.

How to Use This Book

Two types of material are provided in the commentary. Of first importance are the **"Reading Scenarios"** drawn from anthropological studies of the Mediterranean social system. This is the social system that has been encoded in the language of John in ways that are not always obvious to modern readers. We have tried to locate these **Reading Scenarios** adjacent to passages in which their language or dynamics are amply illustrated and therefore easily understood. They are indicated in the body of our work by the symbol "⇨." A list of **Reading Scenarios** is also provided at the beginning of the commentary, and they are indexed at the end of the volume.

A second type of entry consists of short **"Notes"** commenting on specific passages of the Gospel. These draw the reader's attention to the encoding of the social system in the actual language of the Gospel. The **Notes** provide a kind of social-science commentary that can supplement the traditional studies available on John's work. Together with the **Reading Scenarios,** the **Notes** offer clues for filling in the unwritten elements of the passage as a Mediterranean reader might have done and thereby help the modern reader develop a considerate posture toward the ancient author.

In an appendix, we offer "gospel notations" that account for our division of various segments of this document. Finally, the illustrations, maps, and diagrams included are intended to serve as a reminder that in reading the New Testament we are indeed entering a different world. The scenarios these illustrations and our comments invoke, and which we ask the reader to understand, come from a time and place that for all of us remains on the far side of the "Great Transformation." It is unlike anything we are inclined to imagine from our experience in the modern West and thus requires a conscious effort on our part if we are to understand it. It is a world we invite our readers to enter as thoughtful and considerate persons.

THE GOSPEL OF JOHN

OUTLINE OF THE GOSPEL
AND READING SCENARIOS

◆ *Secrecy*
◆ *Lying*

7:10-14a   Around the Feast of Sukkoth in Jerusalem:
           Divided Public Judgment about Jesus

Opening Marker I: Jesus went up into the temple and taught 7:14b

7:14b-18   At Sukkoth in Jerusalem: Initial Challenge
           to Jesus about His Authority to Teach and Interpret Scripture
           ◆ *Challenge and Riposte*
7:19-28   Jesus' Riposte: Moses Gives the Law, but You
           Do Not Observe It
           ◆ *Deviance Labeling*

Marker II: Jesus proclaimed as he taught in the temple 7:28

7:29-36   Second Challenge in Jerusalem: Attempts to Arrest Jesus
           ◆ *Encomium (In Praise of . . .)*

*Central Marker III: Jesus proclaimed in the temple: If anyone thirst, let him come
to me and drink! 7:37-39*

7:37-52   On the Last Day of the Feast: Jesus' Proclamation
           and Ensuing Controversy over Jesus' Status and Role

*Central Marker IV: Jesus again spoke to them saying, "I am the light of the
World" 8:12*

8:12-20   Jesus' Revelation as Israel's Light: Controversy
           over Jesus' Testimony

Marker V: He spoke in the treasury, as he taught in the temple 8:20

8:21-30   Jesus Uses a Riddle as a Counterchallenge
8:21-24a   First Gambit
8:24b-30   Second Gambit
8:31-59   Controversy over Kinship with Abraham
8:33-37a   Abraham's Free Descendants
8:37b-40a Abraham Your Father?
8:40b-42   Abraham's Deeds
8:43-47   Your Father the Devil
8:48-50   Slurs on Jesus' Lineage and Status
8:51-58   Before Abraham, I Am
           ◆ *Collectivist Personality*

Later Insertion: Jesus Rescues a Woman Caught in Adultery (7:53—8:1-11)

CHAPTER I
JOHN 1:1-18
PROLOGUE: PRESENTING JESUS,
ISRAEL'S MESSIAH—THE SOURCE OF LIGHT
AND LIFE THAT MAKES US CHILDREN OF GOD

A Poem about the Messiah's
Cosmic Status and Mission to Israel, 1:1-18

1:1 In the beginning was the Word, and the Word was with God, and the Word was God. [2]He was in the beginning with God. [3]All things came into being through him, and without him not one thing came into being. What has come into being [4]in him was life, and the life was the light of all people. [5]The light shines in the darkness, and the darkness did not overcome it.

6 There was a man sent from God, whose name was John. [7]He came as a witness to testify to the light, so that all might believe through him. [8]He himself was not the light, but he came to testify to the light. [9]The true light, which enlightens everyone, was coming into the world.

10 He was in the world, and the world came into being through him; yet the world did not know him. [11]He came to what was his own, and his own people did not accept him. [12]But to all who received him, who believed in his name, he gave power to become children of God, [13]who were born, not of blood or of the will of the flesh or of the will of man, but of God.

14 And the Word became flesh and lived among us, and we have seen his glory, the glory as of a father's only son, full of grace and truth. [15](John testified to him and cried out, "This was he of whom I said, 'He who comes after me ranks ahead of me because he was before me.'") [16]From his fullness we have all received, grace upon grace. [17]The law indeed was given through Moses; grace and truth came through Jesus Christ. [18]No one has ever seen God. It is God the only Son, who is close to the Father's heart, who has made him known.

✦ *Notes:* John 1:1-18

The group's storyteller marks off the opening to this prologue, or preface, to the Gospel of John with a high-context reference to the Word. This well-known Word was with God (who was generally located on the other side of the vault or firmament of the sky). And he closes the introductory segment with reference to Jesus as Son of Man (v. 51), who offers access to the other side of the vault of the sky, the proper realm of God. Given the themes in this prologue, a good name for John's antisociety would be "The Children of God" (v. 12).

1:1-18 These verses have caused both wonder and controversy throughout Christian history. Most modern scholars consider this passage to be a poem. ▻ **Poetry,** 1:1-18. When read as ordinary language, they are majestic and profound yet bristling with interpretive and theological difficulties. Was this poem part of the original Gospel or a later addition? Does an early messianic hymn lie behind it, or was it composed later as a summary of the Gospel? These and many other important questions lie beyond the scope of a social-science commentary (ample discussion of these matters can be found in the usual commentaries, which the reader should consult; for bibliography, see Ashton 1991).

Instead, our interest is in the way these verses introduce the cosmic Messiah and describe his mission on behalf of those who "believe into him." We consider the Gospel to be a document written in antilanguage for an antisociety. Focus is always on the interpersonal. Hence, the general purpose of the Gospel is to support interpersonal bonding of the members of John's group with one another, with Jesus, and with God. The "us" in our headings refers to members of John's group. What we learn from this opening piece is that, thanks to the coming of the Word of God, "enfleshed" in Israel in the person of Jesus of Nazareth, members of John's group have become "children of God." John's is a Gospel for a close-knit, loyal in-group that stands over against "this world" and the "Judeans." Its members form an antisociety, a group in opposition to the dominant society. ➪ **Antisociety,** 1:35-51. This poem introduces the reader to the cosmic status of Israel's Messiah, who has brought the group into being.

In these verses we also get the first glimpse of the bewildering variety of terms John uses (and piles up) to articulate the polar oppositions between his antigroup and the "world." They are thus a first look at the peculiar antilanguage of John's Gospel, which is so important for the understanding of the way the Gospel functioned for its community. In proceeding, therefore, it will be especially important for the reader to understand the relationship between antisociety and antilanguage. ➪ **Antilanguage,** 1:19-28.

Among the things scholars do agree upon is the fact that this opening poem contains many of the themes that will recur (and be explained) throughout the Gospel. The list is impressive: preexistence of the Word, 1:1 = 17:5; light of the world, 1:4, 9 = 8:12; 9:5; 12:35-36, 46; opposition of light and dark, 1:5 = 3:19; 11:9-10; witness/testimony, 1:7 = 1:19; 3:11, 32-33; 4:39; 5:31-36; 8:13-17; 19:35; 21:24; life, 1:4 = 3:15-16, 36; 4:14, 36; 5:21-29, 39-40; 6:27-68; 8:12; 10:10-28; 11:25; 12:25, 50; 13:37-38; 14:6; 15:13; 17:2-3; 20:31; world, 1:10 = 1:29; 3:16-19; 4:42; 6:14, 33, 51; 7:4, 7; 8:12, 23, 26; 9:5, 39; 10:36; 11:9, 27; 12:19, 25, 31, 46-47; 13:1; 14:17-31; 15:18-19; 16:8-33; 17:5-25; 18:36-37; glory, 1:14—2:11; 5:41, 44; 7:18; 8:50, 54; 11:4, 40; 12:41, 43; 17:5, 22, 24; the only Son, 1:14, 18 = 3:16; no one save the Son has seen God, 1:18 = 6:46. Some of these themes are unique to John, while others receive special emphasis not seen elsewhere in the New Testament. They are thus part of John's special vocabulary—that is, part of the antilanguage of his antisocietal group.

One term that appears prominently in this opening poem, yet seems to disappear throughout the rest of the Gospel, is "Word." To think of it disappearing, however, would be misleading. In v. 14 we are told that this Word becomes "enfleshed" in Jesus of Nazareth. Hence, it is as the story of Jesus that the "Word" appears in the rest of John. ➪ **Word,** 1:1-18.

The latter part of this opening poem also introduces us to Jesus as God's only

Son. While the term *son* is primarily a kinship designation, it is also an honor claim. Being the son of a village artisan family would give Jesus no public status whatsoever. Yet if he is God's Son, the honor status that implies would legitimate any tasks he undertakes. ➪ **Son of God,** 1:29-34. That would be further enhanced by the special association of Jesus with God's self-revelation ("Word"), which gives cosmic significance to all that he will do.

Finally, it is necessary to reiterate the point that interpersonal bonding is what this Gospel is all about. Becoming children of God (1:12-13) means developing kinship-like loyalties to God, Jesus, and other group members. One of the key functions of antilanguage is to create and sustain such bonds. ➪ **Antilanguage,** 1:19-28. This opening poem is the first step in drawing the reader into that process.

1:1-5 The opening line of this poem unmistakably evokes the opening line of Genesis: "In the beginning . . . " (Gen. 1:1). It is often said that this points to "time before time"—that is, before the temporal sequence of history. Such chronological designations, however, derive from the modern sense of history. To ancient peasants the "present" included everything in living memory plus everything in visible prospect. All else, whether past or future, was imaginary time, God's time. That is where "the beginning" appropriately lies.

"Word" is one of John's terms for God's self-revelation. In the sensibilities of the Mediterranean world, "word" has to do with the mouth-ears, hence with that part of the human being especially associated with communication, self-disclosure, self-expression. ➪ **Word,** 1:1-18. The Word is God's utterance, hence a creature from God's point of view. But given the fact that this Word produces all created reality, it is surely divine from a creature's point of view. God's word, unlike human words, is always creative and powerful (Gen. 1). It is found throughout creation, which is itself a part of God's self-revelation. In v. 14 John will announce to his readers that this creative and powerful Word was to be found in Jesus of Nazareth, Israel's Messiah. Note that in the Old Testament God's word is associated with two functions: God's creation (Gen. 1; Ps. 33:6) and his self-revelation to the prophets (Jer. 1:4; Ezek. 1:3; Amos 3:1).

Throughout John's Gospel light and life are closely associated. ➪ **Light,** 1:1-18; **Life,** 1:1-18. So also are darkness and death. Such strong oppositions reveal the way John and his antisociety look at the world: For them everything is good or bad, black or white. Moreover, such strong oppositions in language imply strong distinctions in social groupings. John's in-group is sharply set off from its surrounding out-group. Thus, as the story unfolds, we will learn to draw equally strong distinctions between those related to Jesus and those outside, those loyal to Jesus and those in opposition.

In the conflicting relation between light and dark, we are already assured that light will win. Note that the contention between light and dark, here (vv. 3-4) said to have been initiated at the cosmic level, will be played out in Jesus among his fellow Israelites (vv. 6-8, 10-14). The conflict will move from the imaginary time of God to the "present" time of Jesus and his opposition.

1:6-8 Here is the first explicit notice that the cosmic conflict will move from the imaginary time of God to the "present"—what is known in living memory. While John the Baptist is acknowledged as God's intermediary, or broker (v. 6), the author quickly makes it clear that John himself was not the light coming into the world. That is a way of saying that his mission was not the messianic one (v. 8). On the coming of light as a messianic event, see the **Notes** below.

This is the first of five occasions when John the Baptist will be ranked below Jesus on the scale of honor (1:8, 15; 3:30; 5:36; 10:41). See the **Notes** at these other verses for additional comments.

As we noted earlier, many of the themes sounded in this poem are present throughout the Gospel. The constant repetition of such terms is a key feature of antilanguage. These terms are being singled out for special meaning in the anti-society.

One of these repeated terms is "witness" or "testimony." To testify for another is to vouch for the honor of the other. Since honor is a public matter, it always requires such public affirmation. Here John the Baptist's special testimony is acknowledged, though he (1:7, 15, 32, 34; 3:36; 5:33) is only the first in a long line of public witnesses: the Samaritan woman (4:39), the works of Jesus (5:36; 10:25), the Scriptures (5:39), the crowd (12:17), the Advocate (15:26), the followers of Jesus (15:27), the Father (5:32, 37; 8:18).

1:9-13 Light coming to Israel is a messianic event. As Isaiah says of Israel, "The people who walked in darkness have seen a great light; those who lived in a land of great darkness—on them light has shined" (9:2; also 52:6; 60:1-2; Matt. 4:16). This is exactly what the Gospel will argue throughout. For John, the people in darkness, like their land, is Israel. ⇨ **Light,** 1:1-18.

Yet the coming of the light also occasions a divide in Israel (cf. 3:19-21). The "world," the "Judeans," even Jesus' "own" (here "his own" may refer either to his family or to Israel or to both) will not receive the light (Jesus) (1:10-11; 3:19). ⇨ **World/Cosmos = Israelite Society,** 17:1-26. In John's pointed phrase, the world did not "know" Jesus. In the Old Testament to "know" someone is to experience and maintain a close personal relationship (Jer. 31:34). That is also true of antisocieties, since close interpersonal relations are a key feature of such groups. ⇨ **Antisocieties,** 1:19-28. Note that the Greek term here translated "received" *(lambano)* in a social context refers to showing hospitality to those with whom one is in solidarity (2 John 10). The refusal to receive or accept Jesus is confirmed later in the Gospel (3:11; 4:44; 5:43).

Those who believe "into" (are embedded in, remain loyal to) Jesus' name will be made God's kinfolk. It cannot be overemphasized that in the Mediterranean world "name" is much more than a simple personal label. ⇨ **Name,** 17:1-26. First, it is the closest term for what we mean by "person." Since first-century Mediterranean persons were collectivistic persons, their "name" represents the entire family, along with the family's honor in the community. Here in the opening poem John lets us know what will be explained and emphasized throughout the Gospel: this new fictive kin status of believers will not be the result of birth (blood) or flesh (like begets like) or human choice (a man seeking an heir). In Israel's traditional Middle Eastern biology, blood is the seat of life, transmitted through procreation; the will of the flesh (the sexual drive) is in the fat (and kidneys); and the will of man, human choice, is in the heart. These human dimensions surrounding the birth of offspring are not what characterize those who are interpersonally related to Jesus. Rather, believers will be born "of God" and designated "children of God," thus acquiring a new mode of existence along with lofty honor status of their own. ⇨ **Lineage and Stereotypes,** 8:31-59. See also the discussion of birth "from above" in the **Notes** at 3:1-21.

1:14 This verse has been the foundation of incarnational theology and may have been intended in opposition to those who saw Jesus as an angel or spirit rather than a fully human being. The Greek term the NRSV translates "lived" literally means to "pitch a tent," and may have been intended to draw associations with Israel's exodus story, in which the tent (or tabernacle) symbolizes the presence of God in the midst of Israel (see Exodus 26).

"Glory" is another of the special words in the lexicon of John's antilanguage. ⇨ **Antilanguage,** 1:19-28. It is a common Hellenistic word for opinion, honor, or reputation, and is one of the terms used by John to indicate Jesus' honorific status. Every Mediterranean person would understand the special honor that attaches to an only son of a father.

Honor, of course, must be publicly acknowledged. Thus, John insists that Jesus' glory was visible in his own lifetime (1:14; 2:11). Whereas most people seek public recognition, Jesus does not (5:41, 44; 12:43). He seeks God's glory instead (8:50; 11:4, 40; 17:1), and in turn it is God who glorifies him (8:54; 13:32; 16:14; 17:1). God will be glorified in the actions of Jesus' followers (15:8). He had this honorific status with God from the very beginning and asks that his followers will be able to see that it is from God (17:5, 24). It is a glory Jesus passes along to his followers (17:22). This same honor also attaches to Jesus' death (7:39; 12:16, 23; 13:31; 21:19; see also Mark 10:35ff., where glory is attained through suffering and death).

1:15 This is the second of five occasions in which the author explicitly places John below Jesus in an honor ranking (1:8, 15; 3:30; 5:36; 10:41). See the **Notes** at these other verses. The implied defensiveness on this topic may be an indication of rivalry between disciples of Jesus and John.

1:16-18 The Greek word *charis* (Latin *gratia*) may be translated "grace" or "favor." The language of grace or favor is the language of patronage. ⇨ **Patronage,** 5:21-30. Patrons are higher-status persons who provide favors to clients in return for respect, honor, and generalized obedience. Patrons owed nothing whatsoever to clients. When they gave something to a client, they bestowed favors, and they were understood to be "gracious." The contrast between what came through Moses and what comes through Jesus is thus the contrast between what was required and what was gracious.

The poem moves from the celestial realm of the God of Israel to the people of Israel among whom the Word is enfleshed and then back to the celestial realm. In first-century Mediterranean terms, the realm of God in the sky is located directly over Jerusalem, the "center" of Israel—there is nothing "universal" here in our sense of the term. Thus, the poem ends where it began ("The Word was *with* God . . ."): the close interpersonal relationship between Father and Son is what makes it possible for the Son to reveal the Father. As the Gospel proceeds, it will also be the bond that creates and enables bonding among group members to Jesus and to each other.

✧ *Reading Scenarios:* John 1:1-18
Poetry, 1:1-18

According to many commentators, the opening of John's Gospel is a poem. It is the only poem in John, and it sets the cognitive and emotional tone for the interpersonal dimensions of the story that follows. The literate, print-oriented societies of the West are relentlessly prose-oriented. Poetry is offered on occasion but is not a regular part of everyday speech. In oral societies, in which the vast majority cannot read or write, poetic verse is a principal form in which the tradition is recalled. It is an especially honorific way of speaking and is a common feature of everyday speech for both men and women.

The poetry of men and women differs. The public world, the male world, is the world in which the Great Tradition is preserved and recounted. ⇨ **Public/Private,** 4:1-42. Male poetry, therefore, is frequently in the form of recitation of the tradition and is a common phenomenon in public, especially at ceremonial occasions. To be able to quote the group's tradition from memory, and to apply it in creative or appropriate ways to the situations of daily living, not only brings honor to the speaker but also lends authority to his words. Note that John makes just this use of Israel's tradition as he cites the Scriptures (1:23; 2:17; 6:31, 45; 10:34; 12:13, 15, 38, 40; 13:18; 15:25; 19:24, 36, 37).

The private world, the world of women, is the world of a different kind of poetry. Women's poetry is more likely to be informal and spontaneous than the public poetry of men. For example, Mary's song in Luke (1:47-55) is especially interesting because it displays a characteristic that apparently has remained present across time (it is true of women's poetry in the Middle East today): women's poetry is frequently about subjects forbidden in public discussion (in Mary's case, conception), expressing deeply felt sentiments and concerns that one normally does not talk about in public. Doing so in poetry is not only acceptable, however, it is honorable. Such public, poetic expressions of the forbidden were taken to show a woman's deep caring and sensitivity and usually elicited strong feelings of sympathy from all who heard.

The ability to use the Great Tradition creatively implied extensive, detailed knowledge of it and brought great honor to the speaker able to pull it off. Often the phrases drawn from the tradition are given in cryptic bits and pieces that do not need to be filled out by the speaker because the audience knows how to finish each fragment cited. A good example can be seen in John 10:34, where John presumes that the audience knows the circumstance of the quotation from Psalm 82:6 (see the **Notes** at 10:22-39). Unless the audience could fill in the quotation, the argument by Jesus would make no sense.

While the presence of such poems as John 1:1-18 strikes us today as unusual speech, in Mediterranean cultures it is not. It is an especially honorable way to begin the story of Jesus.

Word, 1:1-18

We may presume that for the author of the Gospel of John, as for us, statements about entities other than human beings are often based on analogies with the human. This holds notoriously true for theological statements about God; all such statements are anthropomorphic analogies. Thus, the "Word" that was with God in the beginning must be something like a human word.

The Greek term for "Word" is *logos.* However, it does not mean what most schooled people mean by the term *word:* the smallest recognizable lexical item, the smallest unit of wording (whether spoken or written), that can stand on its own as a label for something and be listed in a dictionary. A better understanding can be found in the way nonliterate persons use the term *word.* For nonliterate people, a word is a statement, an utterance, the whole thing a person says. To ask a nonliterate individual (who does not think in terms of words, sentences, and paragraphs) to repeat a word often results in having that person repeat everything he or she just said. This is what is involved with the term *logos* here. The Word that was with God in the beginning refers to God's total utterance that has resulted in everything created, visible and invisible.

What sense does it make to ascribe such a Word to God? Whereas some philosophically oriented persons in the Greco-Roman world thought of the human person in terms of body and soul, the Mediterranean world traditionally thought in terms of what anthropologists call "zones of interaction" with the world around. Three such zones make up the human person and all appear repeatedly in the Gospels:

1. *The zone of emotion-fused thought* includes will, intellect, judgment, personality, and feeling all rolled together. It is the activity of the eyes and heart (sight, insight, understanding, choosing, loving, thinking, valuing, etc.).

2. *The zone of self-expressive speech* includes communication, particularly that which is self-revealing. It is listening and responding. It is the activity of the mouth, ears, tongue, lips, throat, and teeth (speaking, hearing, singing, swearing, cursing, listening, eloquence, silence, crying, etc.).

3. *The zone of purposeful action* is the zone of external behavior, or interaction with the environment. It is the activity of the hands, feet, fingers, and legs (walking, sitting, standing, touching, accomplishing, etc.).

Dimensions of human activity will be described in terms of any appropriate zone(s), or even all three.

For example, to explain opposition to Jesus, John cites Isaiah to the effect that

God "has blinded their eyes and hardened their heart, lest they should see with their eyes and perceive with their heart, and turn for me to heal them" (12:40). Here the zone of emotion-fused thought is involved. "Hardened hearts" refers to an inability to think, perceive, and assess properly. Hard hearts are hearts that malfunction, largely due to ill will.

When a writer refers to all three zones, we can assume comment is being made about complete human experience. Thus, we read in 1 John 1:1: "What was from the beginning, what we have heard, what we have seen with our eyes, what we have looked at and touched with our hands, concerning the word of life. . . ." This is a popular expression of total involvement, "body and soul" as we would say. All three zones are likewise given special attention in the latter part of the Sermon on the Mount: eyes-heart (Matt. 6:19—7:6), mouth-ears (7:7-11), and hands-feet (7:13-27). The same is true of the interpretation of the parable of the sower in Luke 8:11-15. For additional examples, see Exod. 21:24; 2 Kings 4:34; Prov. 6:16-10; Dan. 10:6.

In this way of thinking, then, the "word" has to do with a person's mouth-ears. It comes from the zone of self-expressive speech and thus stands for self-revelation and self-communication. The Word that was with God in the beginning was God's self-revelation, God's self-communication. John's poem about God's making the world by means of the Word is a first-century updated retelling of the "Law" (Torah) given by Moses (v. 17). For a similar updated presentation of the Law, consider the opening of Genesis as found in the Aramaic version of the Torah, the Targum. (In the following we cite the Palestinian Targum [Neofiti]; *Word* renders the Aramaic *Memra*.)

> Gen 1:1: From the beginning with wisdom the Word of the Lord created and perfected the skies and the earth.
>
> 2 And the earth was waste and unformed, desolate of man and beast, empty of plant cultivation and of trees, and darkness was spread over the face of the abyss, and a spirit of mercy from before the Lord was blowing over the surface of the waters.
>
> 3 And the Word of the Lord said: Let there be light, and there was light according to the decree of his Word.
>
> 4 And it was manifest before the Lord that the light was good and the Word of the Lord separated the light from the darkness.
>
> 5 And the Word of the Lord called the light daytime and the darkness he called night. And there was evening and there was morning in the order of the work of creation: the first day.
>
> 6 And the Word of the Lord said: Let there be the firmament in the midst of the waters and let it separate the lower waters from the upper waters.
>
> 7 And the Lord created the firmament and separated the waters that were under the firmament from the waters that were above the firmament, and it was so according to his Word.
>
> 8 And the Word of the Lord called the firmament the sky. And there was evening and there was morning in the order of the work of creation: the second day.

9 And the Word of the Lord said: Let the waters under the skies be gathered together into one place and let the dry land appear. And it was so according to his Word.

10 And the Word of the Lord called the dry (land) the earth and the gathering-place of the waters he called the Seas. And it was manifest before the Lord that it was beautiful and proper.

11 And the Word of the Lord said: Let the earth put forth the herbage of grass which produces seed, a fruit tree which yields fruit according to its kind, whose shoots are from it and in it upon the earth. And it was so according to his Word.

12 And the earth put forth herbage of grass which produces seed according to its kind, a fruit tree which produces fruit, whose shoots are from it and in it according to its kind. And it was manifest before the Lord that it was beautiful and proper.

13 And there was evening and there was morning in the order of the work of creation, the third day.

14 And the Lord said: Let there be lights in the firmament of the skies to separate daytime from the night; and let them act as signs of (sacred) seasons and so that the intercalation of moons (and) months may be consecrated by them.

15 And let them shine in the firmament of the skies to shine upon the earth. And it was so according to his Word.

16 And the Word of the Lord created the two great lights; the greater light to rule in the daytime and the lesser light to rule in the night, and the arrangement of the stars.

17 And the Glory of the Lord set them in the firmament of the skies to shine upon the earth,

18 and to rule in the daytime and in the night and to separate the light from the darkness. And it was manifest before the Lord that it was beautiful and proper.

19 And there was evening and there was morning: in the order of the work of creation, fourth day.

20 And the Word of the Lord said: Let the waters swarm forth a swarm of living creatures and let the birds fly above the earth, over the face of the air of the firmament of the skies.

21 And the Lord created the two great monsters and every living creature that moves, which the waters swarmed forth, according to their species, and every bird that flies according to its species. And it was manifest before the Lord that it was beautiful and good.

22 And the Word of the Lord blessed them saying: Become strong and multiply and fill the waters of the seas and let birds multiply upon the earth.

23 And there was evening and there was morning; the order of the work of creation: the fifth day.

24 And the Word of the Lord said: Let the earth bring forth living creatures according to their species: cattle and creeping things and beasts of the earth according to their species. And it was so according to his Word.

25 And the Word of the Lord created the beasts of the earth according to their species and the cattle according to their species, and everything that

creeps upon the earth according to their species. And it was manifest before the Lord that it was beautiful and good.

26 And the Word of the Lord said: Let us create man in our image, similar to ourselves, and let him have dominion over the fishes of the sea and over the birds of the skies, and over the cattle and over all the earth, and over every creeping thing that creeps upon the earth.

27 And the Word of the Lord created the son of man in his (own) image, in a resemblance from before the Lord he created him, male and his partner he created them.

28 And the Word of the Lord blessed them and the Word of the Lord said to them: Be strong and multiply and fill the earth and subdue it and have dominion over the fishes of the sea and over the birds of the skies, and over every living thing that creeps upon the earth.

29 And the Word of the Lord said: Behold I have given you all the herbs that produce seed that are on the face of all the earth and every tree that has fruit on it—the fruit-bearing tree—to you I have given them as food.

30 And to every beast of the earth and to all the birds of the skies and to everything that creeps upon the earth, that has in it the breath of life, (I have given) every herb as food. And it was so according to his word.

31 And there was manifest before the Lord everything that he had made and it was very beautiful and good. And there was evening and there was morning; the order of the work of creation: the sixth day.

2:1 And they completed the creatures of the skies and earth and all the hosts of them.

2 And the Word of the Lord completed on the seventh day his work which he had created because there was rest and repose before him on the seventh day from all his work which he had created.

3 And the Word of the Lord blessed the seventh day and declared it holy because on it there was a great rest and repose before him from all his work which the Glory of the Lord had created to do.

The Palestinian Targum continues mentioning God's Word *(Memra)* each time God intervenes in the stories that the Torah unfolds. Why did ancient Israel's translators feel compelled to have all of God's dealing with creation and creatures mediated by God's Word? It seems that thinkers of the house of Israel adopted the Hellenistic truism of the existence of God's Word (the Greek for Word, *Logos,* also means "Reason") and applied it to the speaking activity of God in the Torah. Perhaps the clearest explanation comes from the learned Philo, a person of the house of Israel who lived in Alexandria during the first century of our era. Note Philo's explanation:

> To His Word (Greek *Logos*), His chief messenger (Greek *archangelos*), highest in age and honor, the Father of all has given the special prerogative, to stand on the border and separate the creature from the Creator. This same Word both pleads with the immortal as suppliant for afflicted mortality and acts as ambassador of the ruler to the subject. He glories in this prerogative

and proudly describes it in these words "and I stood between the Lord and you" (Deut. 5:5), that is neither uncreated as God, nor created as you, but midway between the two extremes, a surety to both sides; to the parent, pledging the creature that it should never altogether rebel against the rein and choose disorder rather that order; to the child, warranting his hopes that the merciful God will never forget His own work. "For I am the harbinger of peace to creation from that God whose will is to bring wars to an end, who is ever the guardian of peace." (*Who Is the Heir?* 205–14)

The Word of God is thus personified; God's commanding and ordering speech is a person, a "chief messenger." It exists from the beginning ("the highest in age and honor"); from the viewpoint of human beings, the Word is uncreated, but from the viewpoint of God, the Word is created. The Word thus mediates, standing as it does between God and creatures.

Hellenistic philosophers of the eastern Mediterranean deduced the existence of such a divine Word or Reason present in the created world. They based their thinking on the fact that human beings could know with certainty, absolutely, without doubt. For example, how is it possible for humans to know that $1 + 1 = 2$ with absolute certainty; or that if $A = B$ and if $B = C$, then $A = C$? If humans are created beings, there is nothing about them that warrants their knowing anything with absolute certainty. The quality of absoluteness (that is, unrelated to anything or anyone) belongs to God alone; and absolute certainty is an attribute of God alone. If finite, limited, and relative humans share in such absolute certainty, then there must be someone in the created world who mediates the divine absolute. This mediating entity is the Word (*Logos,* Reason).

In the Israelite tradition, since *Logos* equally means Word, the Word with God "in the beginning" is God's creative and powerful Word. This Word was not abstract Reason, but God's self-revelation and self-communication. ⇨ **Feet,** 13:1-17. This Word is to be found in all creation, which is God's communication and revelation. Hence, the existence of the Word with God from the beginning was the commonly shared perception of various Hellenistic thinkers in the first-century Mediterranean. However, what is distinctive of John's group is the identification of this Created/Uncreated Word with the Israelite personage, Jesus of Nazareth. For after its experience of Jesus, the group that celebrated God's mediating, creative Word with this poem at the opening of John's Gospel makes the claim that this creative and powerful Word had to be identified with Jesus of Nazareth.

This prologue to John's story of Jesus clearly uses Israel's sacred story of creation as its template. That revelation was believed to have come through the prophet Moses, directed to Israel, for Israel. Since John's antisociety is specifically anti-Israel, its antilanguage will be quite ethnocentric, fully focused on Israel. John tells an ethnocentric story in which God, concerned exclusively with Israel, sends his "grace and truth" to his own people, who largely reject them. Moreover, this ethnocentric perspective is maintained throughout John's Gospel. It is a thoroughly Israelite account of Jesus, Israel's Messiah. This explains why it is that God's creative and powerful Word "became flesh and lived among us" Israelites, "his own people" (1:11, 14). The antisociety for which John writes is totally unconcerned with non-Israelites.

Light, 1:1-18

For the ancient Mediterranean, light was the presence of light, and darkness was the presence of darkness. That is, both light and darkness were positive entities having no relationship to any source of light or darkness other than themselves. Thus, the sun did not "cause" daylight nor did the moon or stars "cause" light at night. Day and night were simply the structured framework in which the sun and moon operated.

Likewise, while the sun and moon marked the changing of the seasons, they had no influence on the seasons any more than they influenced day or night. The relative darkness of winter was due to the cloudy sky, not to the low path of the sun. In fact, the sun was noted for its warmth rather than its light. Light was present due to the presence of light itself, not to the presence of the sun. This meant that the onset of celestial light over the land was the dawn, and the coming of celestial darkness over the land was dusk (not sunrise and sunset).

In the story of creation, the creation of light set light itself apart from preexisting darkness, just as the creation of land (earth) set it apart from ever-present water (Gen. 1). Note that light (day) was created before the sun and night before the moon. Dawn (morning) and dusk (evening) occur independently of the sun as well. The presence of light and land (earth) allowed for the coming of earthlings. Earthlings, human and otherwise, are created from earth, animated with the breath of life (Gen. 2:7), and endowed with the light of life (Job 33:30; Ps. 56:14), or "living light" as opposed to the light of the sky. Thanks to their living light, animate beings can see.

Sight consists of light emanating from the eyes of living beings. Just as the main humanly controlled source of light is fire, so too it is because the eyes are made of fire that humans see. As Jesus says, "The eye is the lamp of the body" (Matt. 6: 22). Aristotle observed: "Is it because in shame the eyes are chilled (for shame resides in the eyes), so that they cannot face one?" (*Problems* 31, 957b).

"Sight (is made) from fire and hearing from air" (960a). "[V]ision is fire" (959b).

Similarly, the Israelite tradition believed God's sky-servants (angels) were made of fire. Hence, when they appear to humans, they look like brilliant light. The fact that celestial bodies, such as stars or comets, emanate light means that they are alive. Stars, whether constellated or not, are living animate entities, as all ancients knew. That is why they move while the earth stands still at the center of creation.

Since all living beings have light, light and life go hand in hand (1:4). In this perspective, all light and life have their origin in the creative work of God alone; they can be handed on by human beings but not created by them.

Life, 1:1-18

Like light, all life derives from God alone. Life is in the blood of humans and animals, just as life is in the produce of a field (bounded land). Animate beings that are dead are just like fields that are fallow. Humans are born of the blood of woman and a male's seed, just as produce comes from the life force of a field and a seed.

In John, Jesus comes to bring life. God has life in himself (5:26) and so also does the Son (5:26). Jesus is the bread of life (6:48), the living resurrection (11:25), and the words he speaks are life as well (6:63). He has come that his followers might "have life, and have it abundantly" (10:10). The term *life* appears 47 times in John's Gospel (6 in Matthew; 3 in Mark; 5 in Luke).

Every incident in John's Gospel is about life:
- Jesus changes water, which is inert, to wine (living liquid; look at its effects!)
- Jesus speaks to Nicodemus about being born and being born again
- Jesus uses water in a well to tell a woman about living water (from the realm of God and angels, rain)
- Jesus tells an official whose son is on the point of death that he will live
- Jesus speaks of bread, bread from the sky, and living bread (life-giving)
- Jesus restores a blind (death) man's eyesight (animated light, a synonym for life)
- Jesus raises dead Lazarus to life
- Jesus dies to give life

Note by contrast that the opponents of Jesus are trying to take life, to "kill" him (5:18; 7:1, 19, 25; 8:37, 40).

The presence of life is marked by animation, by Spirit (Latin *anima,* and its Greek equivalent, *pneuma,* mean "wind," "breeze," "spirit").
- wine has spirit
- born again is reanimation
- living water has spirit
- bread of life has spirit
- animate light ("light of life") is full of spirit
- resurrection occurs thanks to spirit.

It is on the cross that Jesus bows his head and gives the Spirit, thus giving life to "the world." The purpose of the Gospel is to support those who believe in Jesus so that they "might have life in his name" (20:31).

41

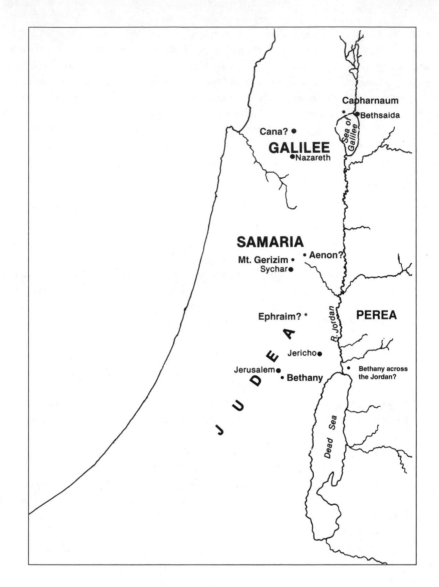

1:28 The Palestine of John's Gospel. ("This happened in Bethany, across the Jordan, where John was baptizing.") Bethany across the Jordan is mentioned nowhere else in ancient literature. Its exact location is in considerable doubt. Many geographers think the most likely place is two or three miles east of the Jordan opposite Jericho in a spot where there are some springs. Strangely, our author does not mention any activity of the Baptist clearly connected with the Jordan River, nor does he mention Jesus' Baptism. Other places mentioned only in John's Gospel and about which there is doubt (indicated on the map with a question mark) are Cana (2:1; 4:46; 21:2), Aenon near Salim (3:23), and Ephraim (11:54).

CHAPTER II
JOHN 1:19-51
PRESENTING JESUS OF NAZARETH,
ISRAEL'S MESSIAH

The Witness of John the Prophet about Himself, 1:19-28

19 This is the testimony given by John when the Jews sent priests and Levites from Jerusalem to ask him, "Who are you?" [20]He confessed and did not deny it, but confessed, "I am not the Messiah." [21]And they asked him, "What then? Are you Elijah?" He said, "I am not." "Are you the prophet?" He answered, "No." [22]Then they said to him, "Who are you? Let us have an answer for those who sent us. What do you say about yourself?" [23]He said,

"I am the voice of one crying out in the wilderness,
'Make straight the way of the Lord,'"

as the prophet Isaiah said.

24 Now they had been sent from the Pharisees. [25]They asked him, "Why then are you baptizing if you are neither the Messiah, nor Elijah, nor the prophet?" [26]John answered them, "I baptize with water. Among you stands one whom you do not know, [27]the one who is coming after me; I am not worthy to untie the thong of his sandal." [28]This took place in Bethany across the Jordan where John was baptizing.

✦ *Notes:* John 1:19-28

After the opening poem, the first item the author deals with is the personage of John, an ostensibly well-known prophetic type of person who practiced a symbolic dipping of Israelites in the "living" or running water of the Jordan River (v. 28). This first segment presents John's testimony or witness concerning himself.

1:19-23 In contemporary American society the question "Who are you?" is a question about what uniquely characterizes an individual. It is a question that only the individual can really answer. In collectivist societies, however, identity normally derives from and traces back to the group in which one is embedded. ⇨ **Collectivist Personality,** 8:31-59. One is "of Nazareth," or "of Cyrene," identifying the place/community in which identity resides. At a more specific level, one is "son of Joseph," or "son of Abraham." Thus, identity is family identity. When persons did not behave in accord with the expectations of the group in which they were embedded, confusion reigned. Here John's behavior is rather unusual. Symbolic river-dipping is a prophetic act in Israel. Such behavior would be out of keeping with John's (or anyone else's) birth status, thereby raising questions about his identity. The inquirers, Judeans from Jerusalem, have the first word in the story. Their concern is whether some special status other than birth status is implied in John's behavior.

1:24-28 What could be (the Greek is ambiguous) a second delegation now asks a question that clearly associates behavior and status: "Why do you baptize if you are neither the Messiah, Elijah, nor the prophet?" John justifies his actions, not in terms of his own birth status, but as a prelude to the coming of one greater than he. Though John's actions had suggested to onlookers a status higher than his own birth status, he himself offers a different assessment. He suggests that his interlocutors have misread the situation rather sharply. Since untying sandals for another was an action proper to a slave (again, behavior and status go together) and was considered beneath even the pupil of a teacher, the implication is that John's status is low indeed. Note that this is the third of the five occasions in which the author asserts that John is beneath Jesus on the scale of honor (1:8; 1:15; 3:30; 5:36; 10:41).

✧ *Reading Scenarios:* **John 1:19-28**
Jews/Judeans, 1:19-28

In the NRSV and a number of other English translations, verse 19 is translated: " . . . when the *Jews* sent priests and Levites" (our emphasis). That is unfortunate since meanings derive from the social system of the reader/speaker, and modern readers will think John makes reference to those persons whom readers today know from their experience to be Jews. The fact is, from a religious point of view, all modern Jews belong to traditions developed largely after the time of Jesus and compiled in the Babylonian Talmud (sixth century C.E.). As for ethnic origin, Central European Jews (called Ashkenazi Jews) largely trace their origin to Turkic and Iranian ancestors who comprised the Khazar empire and converted to Judaism in the eighth century C.E. (*Encyclopaedia Britannica*, 15th ed. Micropaedia, 5:788; on the Internet: www.khazaria.com). Thus, given the sixth-century C.E. origin of all forms of contemporary Jewish religion, and given the U.S. experience of Jews based largely on Central European Jews, themselves originating from eighth-century C.E. converts, it would be quite anachronistic to identify any modern Jews with the "Judeans" mentioned in John's Gospel or the rest of the New Testament.

Both here and in all of the sixty-nine other instances in John where the term *Judeans* (Greek *Ioudaioi*) appears, there is nothing of the modern connotations of "Jew" or "Jewishness." Hence, it is simply inappropriate to project those modern meanings backward into the period when John was written. Rather, Judean meant a person belonging to a group called Judeans, situated geographically and forming a territory taking its name from its inhabitants, Judea. Judea is precisely a group of people, Judeans, organically related to and rooted in a place, with its distinctive environs, air, and water. Judean thus designates a person from one segment of a larger related group, Israel (John 1:47, 49), who comes from the place after which the segment is named, Judea (*Ioudaia*). The correlatives of *Judean* in John are "Galilean" and "Perean," and together they make up Israel. The customary ethnocentric opposite of Israel is non-Israel, the nations other than Israel, or simply "the nations" or "Gentiles."

(Note that in Josephus, *Life,* the word *Ioudaios* likewise always means Judean and refers to the people living in that territory to which it gives its name.)

Given the prominent role of the Judeans in John's Gospel, usually as opponents of Jesus, this is an important translation correction. The term *Ioudaios* (Judean), used either as a substantive or an adjective, appears 70 times in John's Gospel. It is used only 5 times in Matthew, 6 times in Mark, and 5 times in Luke. This striking contrast between John and the Synoptics makes understanding the term critically important.

The territorial designation of Judea connoted different territories at different times in Israel's history, and the use of it can be confusing. During the period of Persian rule it designated only the small area around Jerusalem since that is where all Judeans were to be found. Other members of the house of Israel were designated otherwise. Under the Maccabees, the term *Judea* was used to refer to the larger population the Maccabees controlled. This population dwelled both in Jerusalem and in its environs, as well as in Samaria, Galilee, Idumea, the coastal plain (except Ashkelon), and much of Transjordan. Thus, under the Maccabees, the number of Judeans grew appreciably.

In the Roman period, the Roman province of Syria-Palestine included Galilee, Samaria, and Judea, which, along with Perea (the name Josephus gives to Transjordan), included the population controlled by Herod the Great under the title "King of Judea." After the death of Herod, his son Archelaus became ethnarch of a Judea that included only the Jerusalem area, Idumea, and Samaria. It excluded Galilee and Perea. When Archelaus was removed in 6 C.E., subsequent procurators governed only this same smaller area. Thus, in Jesus' time, Judea, Galilee, and Perea constituted three population areas that together made up the "house of Israel." On the other hand, other peoples of the Mediterranean called all members of the house of Israel Judeans, after the region in which the central place was located—Jerusalem in Judea.

In sum, when the terms *Judea* or *Judean* are used in the Gospel of John, they should be understood as referring to the persons living in a territory located in the southern and western part of the Roman province of Syria-Palestine. Thus, John notes correctly that the Judeans send priests and Levites from Jerusalem (1:19). The Passover of the Judeans was near, so Jesus goes up to Jerusalem (2:13; 5:13; 6:4; 7:11; 11:55). A discussion arises between the disciples of John and a Judean (3:25). Judeans do not share things in common with Samaritans (4:9). Jesus goes about in Galilee where he is safe but does not go about in Judea because the Judeans were trying to kill him (7:1). In 8:31 there are Judeans who initially believe in Jesus, but after the conversation deteriorates, they decide Jesus is not really one of them. Hence, he must be a Samaritan (8:48). In 10:31 and 11:8 we again learn that Judea is dangerous territory for Jesus, and in 20:19, following the crucifixion/resurrection, it will be a dangerous place for Jesus' followers as well. Judeans console Mary and Martha after the death of Lazarus (11:31), but after raising Lazarus, Jesus can no longer go around openly among Judeans, so he retreats to the region near the wilderness of Judea (11:54). At the supper with his disciples, where he washes the disciples' feet, Jesus distinguishes between Judeans and his inner group (13:31). Jesus is arrested by the Judean police (18:12), and in his trial, Pilate asks Jesus if he is king over the people and area governed by Pilate, namely, Judea (18:33). Jesus then makes it very clear to Pilate that his kingdom has nothing to do with Judean society (18:36), even though his tormentors taunt him with the mock title "King of the Judeans" (19:3). The inscription over the cross (19:19) has in it a wonderful irony that would have rankled Jesus' Judean opponents: It spells out Jesus' identification as "Jesus of Nazareth"—that is, Jesus, a Galilean, is being designated "King of the Judeans."

The fact that the author uses the term *Judean* to designate "others" suggests to some that the author himself was a Galilean. That may be true. In Syria-Palestine, the common in-group name for members of the house of Israel was "Israel." When members of this in-group sought to distance their own group from others in Israel, the distinction between Judea, Galilee, and Perea came into play. However, the common out-group name for the house of Israel was Judeans, perhaps largely due to the presence of the temple of the God of Israel in Judea, along with the priesthood and traditional kingship. Since "Judean" was not normally the way inhabitants of that geographical area referred to themselves (they were "Israelites"), but rather the way outsiders referred to them, the most we can say for certain is that by using this term for his opponents, John strongly asserts their outsider status in relation to his antisociety. He and his group are not Judeans, but those who are in opposition to them are.

Antilanguage, 1:19-28

As we have noted at length in our introduction, antisocieties (⇨ **Antisociety,** 1:35-51) are especially inclined to develop in-group languages all their own. They use ordinary terms from the ordinary language of the larger society but give them special in-group meanings that are understood only by insiders. Given the conflictual and antisocietal character of John's community, we are not surprised to find in the Gospel extremely high-context communication in an antisocietal key. This in-group language, or antilanguage, derives its peculiar meaning from the social context of John's antisociety.

It is important to understand exactly what antilanguage is. Antilanguage derives from an antisociety that is set up within another society as a conscious alternative to it. A genuine antilanguage, as opposed to simple slang or idiom, is the product of a disaffected group. It is not mere affectation or literary flair. It lives only among the genuinely estranged who are in conflict with the values of the society in which they live. An antisociety, along with its antilanguage, is an alternate society rooted in a form of social conflict carried on by dissociated persons living in a hollowed-out social sphere within the dominant social order. The Gospel has the main characteristics of antilanguage: heavy overlexicalization (many words for the same reality of concern to the group), new oppositional terminology for the in-group and its concerns (usual words filled with unusual, new meanings), emphasis on the interpersonal (interpersonal relationships between author and group members and Jesus and group members), and social contrast with the out-group (society).

An antisociety is a social structure based on interpersonal relationships, on persons and their significance, on mutual trust and group loyalty. It is not a society based on truths; it is little concerned with ideological propositions or statements of doctrine. Hence, the main question involved in Johannine antilanguage is, how do its vocabulary and its referents facilitate interpersonal bonding? Consider the Johannine contrasts:

In-group Dimensions	Out-group Dimensions
light	darkness 1:5
born of water/spirit	born of blood/flesh/humans 1:13
above	below 8:23
spirit	flesh 3:6
life	death 3:36
truth	lie 8:44-45
sky	land (earth) 3:31
God	Satan 13:27
Israel	Judeans 1:19, 47
not of this world	(this) world = Israelite society 17:1

As antilanguage vocabulary, all of these words take on in-group or out-group specific, interpersonal qualities. Each of them refers to persons in their in-group or out-group dimensions.

Thus, in-group members have hearts full of light. They have been born of God's power, and are Spirit-filled, really alive, truthful, and open to God. They are also experiencing the sky dimensions of Jesus (alternate states of consciousness). They are Israelites but not of Israelite society.

Members of the topside out-group, on the other hand, have hearts full of darkness. They have been born of human desire, and they are simply human. For all practical purposes, they are already dead. They speak only falsehoods, are tied to earthly experiences, and are deceived by Satan and succumb to his loyalty tests. They are Judeans, devoted to the social symbols located in Judea (Jerusalem and the temple), forming Israelite society at large.

In John's Gospel, Jesus' behavior and that of his in-group always manifest the dimensions that derive from the attitudes and behavior of those not of this world, not of Israelite society as it is constituted. On the other hand, all opponents of Jesus and his in-group have all the features of Israelite society in general, of Judeans in particular.

As expressed in antilanguage, these in-group/out-group dimensions underscore horizontal boundaries, societal boundaries. ⇨ **In-group and Out-group,** 15:18—16:4a. Those in the know, however, can flip these boundaries on their vertical side, with in-group on top, and get to realize where this in-group really has its moorings—in the above, with God and the One he sent, Jesus, the true Son of God (⇨ **Son of God** 1:29-34) and Son of Man (⇨ **Son of Man** 1:35-51).

In sum, the social function of antilanguage and its in-group and out-group labels is to support and cement relationships within the in-group. Such group attachment in the anti-introspective ancient Mediterranean is called "love," the basic requirement of Jesus in this Gospel. The author thus express-es the in-group dimensions of social interrelationship in terms of reciprocal love. Group attachment enables members to experience the abiding presence of Jesus, notably through the Spirit or power of God. ⇨ **Seeing Jesus: Alternate States of Consciousness,** 20:1-29.

Teacher (Rabbi) and Disciple, 1:19-28

The distinctive feature of John's story of Jesus is that Jesus does not proclaim a forthcoming theocracy for Israel. There is no talk of "the kingdom of God" (or of heaven—that is, of the sky). In the Synoptics we read of Jesus recruiting a faction of apostles to help him out with his political-religious task of proclaiming theoc-racy. In John, Jesus has persons seeking him out to become his disciples. Apos-tles are persons sent with a commission; in the Synoptic story that commission is to help Jesus in his own task of revitalizing Israel by informing Israelites of the forthcoming theocracy and preparing people for it with healing and exorcisms. There is no mention of "apostles" in John, only of disciples. Disciples are fol-lowers of a teacher; they join up with a teacher in order to learn a way of living. This was the task of the various philosophers of the Hellenistic world who sought to teach human beings how to live a meaningful human existence. Israel's scribes were rather similar, basing their instruction on distinctive appropriations of Israel's Torah. Jesus as teacher would be perceived as such a scribe or philoso-pher, depending on who was assessing him.

It is a distinctive feature of John that we are told nothing of Jesus' concern about a forthcoming theocracy. Instead, after introducing John's witness about himself and about Jesus, we are told that John himself has "disciples" (1:35), who then seek out Jesus to know where he is staying (1:37-39). The only disciple of John's that Jesus seeks out is Philip (1:43), who in turn invites Nathanael to come to Jesus (1:47). Similarly, Nicodemus, "a teacher in Israel" (3:10), seeks Jesus to find out more about him. Next the Samaritans come to him at the Samaritan woman's invitation (4:29-30). In this cycle of events beginning with Jesus and his disciples in Cana (2:1) and his return to Cana (4:46), people seek out Jesus as "Teacher," representing a way of life that essentially consists in attachment to Jesus because of who he is and whom he reveals. In 4:47 and 11:9 Jesus is sought as healer, yet in 12:18-19 Greek-speaking Israelites seek him as teacher as well.

Jesus and his disciples do not form a political faction in this Gospel; we are not told whether Jesus was ever bent on the revitalization of Israel as we are told he was in the Synoptic narratives. Rather, Jesus sets forth a way of living focused on attachment to himself—a fictive kinship group much like the group for whom John wrote this Gospel.

48

The Witness of John the Prophet about Jesus, 1:29-34

29 The next day he saw Jesus coming toward him and declared, "Here is the Lamb of God who takes away the sin of the world! [30]This is he of whom I said, 'After me comes a man who ranks ahead of me because he was before me.' [31]I myself did not know him; but I came baptizing with water for this reason, that he might be revealed to Israel." [32]And John testified, "I saw the Spirit descending from heaven like a dove, and it remained on him. [33]I myself did not know him, but the one who sent me to baptize with water said to me, 'He on whom you see the Spirit descend and remain is the one who baptizes with the Holy Spirit.' [34]And I myself have seen and have testified that this is the Son of God."

✦ *Notes:* John 1:29-34

John the prophet now sets forth his testimony concerning Jesus, who here steps forward onto the scene.

1:29-30 It was a truism in antiquity that physique or form determined character. Thus, a lion has a powerful physique and a disposition to match. Using animal analogies for people therefore offered comment on their character. In the astral lore of antiquity the Lamb (called Aries by the Latins) was the first of the celestial bodies created by God, hence the head or leader of the periodic changes in the universe. ⇨ **Lamb of God,** 1:29-34. Celestial bodies were believed to be living servants of God (⇨ **Light,** 1:1-18). To call Jesus the "Lamb" of God was thus to designate him as both divine servant and cosmic leader. Note how in 1:35-37, when John the Baptist announces that Jesus is the Lamb of God, two disciples immediately follow him. One of them interprets John's witness as a direct reference to Israel's Messiah (Andrew is first to do so, 1:41; it is Andrew who informs Simon of this fact).

Hierarchical ranking is extremely important in honor-shame societies. It not only provides the social compass for interactions between people, it legitimates leaders and lends authority to teaching. As we have noted, the author's frequent stress on the superiority of Jesus over John (five times in John: 1:8, 15; 3:30; 5:36; 10:41) is probably indicative of a polemic against a group comprised of followers of John the Baptist.

The rationale for the superiority of Jesus presented here is important. To the out-group, all members of a family are generally accorded the group's honor rating; in this sense they have the same honor rating. But not so within the family. A firstborn male is ascribed greater honor among siblings; he opens the womb and thus allows the others to be born. (Firstborn females are accorded respect but not the honor of a firstborn son.) Josephus reports a comment of Herod the Great that his sons should not be accorded equal honor, but greater honor should be given to the firstborn (*War* 1.459). If John knew Luke's tradition, then on the principle of birth order in Israel, Jesus would stand second to John, having been born later.

But John says nothing about Jesus' or John's birth. Rather, for the author of this Gospel, John the Baptist precedes Jesus in having been called by God to take up the prophetic role in Israel. Since Jesus appears later, John here appeals to Jesus' preexistence as justification for hierarchical (honor) precedence.

1:31-34 John's admission that he did not recognize Jesus is emphasized twice (vv. 31, 33; also Matt. 11:2; Luke 7:19). This perhaps indicates that Jesus' low station in life (low birth, hence his low honor rating) would not normally have led anyone to look for or expect the public role he undertook. It certainly provided him no justification for a public hearing. The divine legitimation for Jesus' activity in the public sphere is here rooted in the testimony of John concerning his vision of God's power alighting on and abiding in Jesus. John's message from the sky, like sky messages in general, had extraordinary authority. It thus supplied John with more than adequate reason to acknowledge Jesus' preeminence in spite of his low birth. If Jesus is really Son of God rather than son of an obscure villager (6:42), he would have all the status necessary for the public career he was about to begin. ⇨ **Son of God,** 1:29-34. His status also would have justified his central place among the members of the antisociety he recruits in the following verses.

✧ *Reading Scenarios:* John 1:29-34

Lamb of God, 1:29-34

There is but a single lamb in all creation that merits the title "Lamb of God," and that is the constellation labeled Aries by the Latins. In the book of Revelation, this constellation is directly identified as "the Lion of the tribe of Judah, the Root of David" (Rev 5:5), that is, the Messiah of Israel. The same is true here in John's Gospel, where John the prophet identifies Jesus as Lamb of God (1:29, 36), and his disciples conclude he is Israel's Messiah (1:40).

In spite of its later Roman name, the constellation called Aries the Ram was originally considered to be a male lamb. The ancient Phoenician name for Aries, evidenced in Tyre about 1200 B.C.E., was *Teleh,* "male lamb, young ram." The Latin and Greek names of this constellation (Latin *Aries,* from Greek *Ares,* lamb, and Greek *krion,* both used to mean "ram") are rather recent. The traditional name of this zodiacal being (Phoenician *Teleh;* Hebrew *Tale',* Arabic *Al-Hamal*) was "Male Lamb." In the most ancient representations of the sky, Aries was always pictured as a male lamb with a "reverted" head—that is, as facing directly over its back to Taurus. Thus Manilius describes Aries in his poem: "Resplendent in his golden fleece, first place holder Aries looks backward admiringly at Taurus rising" (Manilius, *Astronomica* 1.263–64, LCL). Only a being with a broken neck could have its head turned directly backward as the celestial Aries does; and yet it remains standing in spite of the broken neck. Clearly, Aries was an obvious choice to be perceived in terms of the Messiah-Jesus group's story according to which God's Lamb was slaughtered yet continues to stand (as in Rev. 5).

This label for the constellation was adopted by Second Temple Israel. It was used by Pharisees for this constellation according to Epiphanius (*Panarion* 16.2.1). In later Talmudic zodiacs the constellation in question was always called *Tale'*, meaning "male lamb, young ram, young man." Arab astronomers maintained this Semitic designation, naming the constellation *Al-Hamal*, "the young ram." Given this tradition, it is no surprise that the cosmic Lamb behaves like a young ram. The Greeks had little difficulty in identifying Aries with a young ram. Lucian has one of a pair of contending brothers behave as follows: "Thyestes then indicated and explained *(semenamenos)* to them the Ram *(krion)* in the sky, because of which they mythologize that Thyestes had a golden Lamb *(arna)* (*On Astrology* 12; Loeb 5:356).

It is important to note that Aries is the first created cosmic being, the first constellation in the zodiac, the center and head of the cosmos, as the astronomers say. Nigidius Figulus, first century C.E., calls Aries "the leader and prince of the constellations"; the *Scholia in Aratum* (545) relates that "the Egyptians [Nechepso-Petosiris] say Aries is the head"; Nonnos says that Aries "is the center of the whole cosmos, the central navel of Olympus"; Vettius Valens, Rhetorios and Firmicus Maternus are quite similar.

Thus, Aries is the leader of the stars of the ecliptic: "The Wool-Bearer leads the signs for his conquest of the sea" (Manilius, *Astronomica* 2.34, LCL). According to astronomical lore that focused on the zodiac and its ecliptic belt, at the beginning of the universe, Aries stood in mid-sky (Greek *mesouranema* is an astronomic technical term)—that is, at the "head" of the cosmos, at the summit of it all. For example, Firmicus Maternus writes:

> We must now explain why they began the twelve signs with Aries. . . . In the chart of the universe which we have said was invented by very learned men, the mid-sky is found to be in Aries. This is because frequently—or rather, always—in all charts, the mid-sky holds the principal place, and from this we deduce the basis of the whole chart, especially since most of the planets and the luminaries—the Sun and the Moon—send their influence toward this sign. (*Mathesis* III, 1, 17-18, trans. Rhys Bram 75)

Ancient Israel likewise recognized the prominence of Aries in its original New Year celebration connected with its foundational event, the Exodus (Exod. 12:2; the Exodus occurs in the first month of the year). And the ritual marking the Exodus involved a male lamb, replicating springtime Aries itself. ✧ **Passover Lamb,** 19:16b-37. The point is that the Lamb of God is a celestial entity. The new feature in John's Gospel is that John the Baptist identifies Jesus of Nazareth as this celestial entity, the Lamb of God.

A final point: this Lamb of God takes away the sin of the world (v. 29). How is this done? Once more, it was common ancient lore that when the vault of the sky returns to the position it had at the very time of creation, it will be with the Lamb at the point of preeminence, the head of the cosmos. And such a return to beginnings was expected (below we quote Cicero as but a single example; the book of Revelation is well known). By ushering in a new created order, with a new sky and a new land, the cosmic Lamb of God does away with everything that preceded. All previous accounts are set aside; it is a new beginning. The sin of the world, ways of living that disgrace or dishonor God, ceases to be. The Lamb of God thus takes away the sin of the world just as light does away with darkness, just as life does away with death.

> For people commonly measure the year by the circuit of the sun, that is, of a single star alone; but when all the stars return to the place from which they at first set forth, and, at long intervals, restore the original configuration of the whole sky, then that can truly be called a revolving year. . . . I hardly dare to say how many generations of men are contained within such a year; for as once the sun appeared to men to be eclipsed and blotted out, at the time when the soul of Romulus entered these regions, so when the sun shall again be eclipsed at the same point and in the same season, you may believe that all the planets and stars have returned to their original positions, and that a year has actually elapsed. (Cicero, *The Republic VI*, 22.24, trans. C. W. Keyes, Loeb 277–79)

Son of God, 1:29-34

Throughout the Gospel, the title Son of God serves as the basis for John's claim for Jesus' exalted ranking. Right from the outset, we find John the Baptist (v. 34) and Nathanael (v. 49) using it. Martha believes that Jesus is the Son of God (note there it is the equivalent of Messiah), but those who do not believe are condemned (3:18). In 5:25 Jesus says the dead will hear the voice of the Son of God, which is exactly what happens in the raising of Lazarus. In 19:7 the Judeans assert that in making the claim to be the Son of God, Jesus has violated the law. In 20:31 the purpose of the Gospel is said to be that readers might continue to believe that Jesus is the Son of God (note here also the association with the title Messiah).

In the present context, "Son of God" points to Jesus as a divine personage from the realm of God, the sky. Along with the other titles in this opening segment (Word, Light, Life, Lamb of God, Son of Man, King of Israel, even Messiah), this seems to be another title of an entity who is uncreated relative to humans but created relative to God, like the Word as explained by Philo. What is the formal difference here?

First, it is important to note that the title "son of God" during Jesus' time was common and publicly applied to Roman emperors. Some inscriptions read, "Tiberius Caesar, the August God, the son of the God Augustus, emperor, most great high priest, etc." (Dittenberger, OGI 583) and "Tiberius Caesar, the son of the God Augustus, the grandson of the God Julius, August personage, most great high priest, etc." (Dittenberger, OGI 471). This made perfect sense since, as the dictum had it, "The king is the last of the gods as a whole, but the first of human beings" (*Corpus Hermeticum,* vol. 3, fragment 24, 3d ed., Nock-Festugière, 53). Then, too, non-kings might also be recognized as gods. Consider Acts 14:11-12: "When the crowds saw what Paul had done, they shouted in the Lycaonian language, 'The gods have come down to us in human form!' Barnabas they called Zeus, and Paul they called Hermes, because he was the chief speaker."

To determine the meaning of the title Son of God, it seems best to begin with a linguistic observation fitting the Semitic cultures of the time. A phrase such as "son of X" means "having the qualities of X." Thus "son of man" would mean having the qualities of man, hence human (the NRSV translates the Greek phrase "Man," which is confusing in John; ➪ **Son of Man,** 1:35-51). Thus, "son of the day" means having the quality of the day—hence, full of light, morally upright. And "son of hair" means hairy or hoary.

In this vein, "Son of God" would mean "having the quality of God," hence divine, divine-like. In an Israelite context, it is important to note that Son of God could hardly mean "having the essence of the Most High God." Note that in the Sermon on the Mount, Jesus says that God considers peacemakers as "sons of God" (Matt. 5:9). What attributes might a human have that would qualify as those of a "son of God"?

Among Israelite elites of the Greco-Roman period, God's power is of two chief kinds: creativity and control. Philo calls God's creative power *dynamis poietike* (power to make/do) and his controlling power *dynamis basilike* (power to rule as king). God's creative power includes goodness, beneficence, kindness, and creativity itself. It is through this power that God "creates and operates the universe" (Philo, *Quest. Gen.* 4.2). God's controlling power includes sovereignty, authority, jurisdiction, retribution and ruling. By this power "God rules what has come into being" (Philo, *Quest. Gen.* 4.2). These two powers, therefore, represent the complete and fundamental aspects of the Deity. Thus, any person, invisible (such as angels in Gen. 6:1-4; Job 1) or visible (such as kings), who evidences creativity and control over other beings to a significant degree will be considered "divine," hence a "son of God." Like Philo's "Word," such persons are like the uncreated God from the human point of view, but creatures from God's point of view.

The designation Son of God is also important to the legitimation of Jesus' career. In honor-shame societies, it is always assumed that one will act in accord with his publicly recognized honor rating. Highborn persons are expected to lead in public, and their birth status provides legitimacy for doing so. A lowborn person is not expected to lead in public, and when that happens, some explanation must be found. His (only males act in public) "power" might be explained by some extraordinary event or circumstance, but if nothing like that could be found, his abilities would be attributed to evil forces (8:48). Being the son of a village artisan family, Jesus' legitimacy as a public figure was nil. If he was the Son of God, however, his legitimacy would be beyond question (8:49).

The Origins of Jesus' (Our) Antisociety, 1:35-51

35 The next day John again was standing with two of his disciples, [36]and as he watched Jesus walk by, he exclaimed, "Look, here is the Lamb of God!" [37]The two disciples heard him say this, and they followed Jesus. [38]When Jesus turned and saw them following, he said to them, "What are you looking for?" They said to him, "Rabbi" (which translated means Teacher), "where are you staying?" [39]He said to them, "Come and see." They came and saw where he was staying, and they remained with him that day. It was about four o'clock in the afternoon. [40]One of the two who heard John speak and followed him was Andrew, Simon Peter's brother. [41]He first found his brother Simon and said to him, "We have found the Messiah" (which is translated Anointed). [42]He brought Simon to Jesus, who looked at him and said, "You are Simon son of John. You are to be called Cephas" (which is translated Peter).

43 The next day Jesus decided to go to Galilee. He found Philip and said to him, "Follow me." [44]Now Philip was from Bethsaida, the city of Andrew and Peter. [45]Philip found Nathanael and said to him, "We have found him about whom Moses in the law and also the prophets wrote, Jesus son of Joseph from Nazareth." [46]Nathanael said to him, "Can anything good come out of Nazareth?" Philip said to him, "Come and see." [47]When Jesus saw Nathanael coming toward him, he said of him, "Here is truly an Israelite in whom there is no deceit!" [48]Nathanael asked him, "Where did you get to know me?" Jesus answered, "I saw you under the fig tree before Philip called you." [49]Nathanael replied, "Rabbi, you are the Son of God! You are the King of Israel!" [50]Jesus answered, "Do you believe because I told you that I saw you under the fig tree? You will see greater things than these." [51]And he said to him, "Very truly, I tell you, you will see heaven opened and the angels of God ascending and descending upon the Son of Man."

✦ *Notes:* John 1:35-51

The start of the group that "believes into" Jesus is marked by Jesus' invitation to two sets of persons who come to know about Jesus by a process of networking. ⇨ **Networking,** 1:35-51. The passage describes two invitations given by Jesus: vv. 35-42 and vv. 43-51.

1:35-37 When John identifies Jesus as the Lamb of God, two of John's disciples immediately become followers of Jesus. Since peripheral members of antisocieties are often loosely committed to a leader or even divide their loyalty with other groups or leaders, the rapid switch here may indicate that Andrew and the other disciple were peripheral members of John's group. No doubt there were others like them who also made the switch. Note the rivalry between the members of John's group and those of Jesus' group in 4:1. Andrew and an unnamed disciple are thus the first adherents in Jesus' new antisociety. The title Lamb of God clearly carries authority for Jesus as a group leader. ⇨ **Lamb of God,** 1:29-34;

also the **Notes** at 1:29-34. Here the two disciples address Jesus as "Rabbi," which the author says means "teacher"; they thus recognize Jesus' authority. Later (1:41) they will identify him as the Messiah. Both identifications make clear that a group is forming around a new leader.

1:38-39 The Greek verb for *remain (meno)* is used 40 times in John's Gospel but only 12 times in the Synoptics. It is used three times in these verses and is another part of John's antilanguage. John uses the word to indicate loyalty or deep attachment, suggesting here that while the loyalty of these two disciples to John the Baptist (see 1:35-37 above) and his group may have been marginal, their new attachment to Jesus and his antisocietal group is not. A similar connotation exists in John's use of the Greek verb for "follow" *(akoloutheo)* in 1:37, 38, 40, 43. Since antisociety membership implied a sharp break with the dominant social order, loyalty was always a matter of concern.

1:40-42 Simon Peter's recruitment into the Jesus group comes at the hand of his brother Andrew, who is the first to recognize Jesus as Israel's Messiah. Note the emphasis on "following"; see the **Note** on 1:38-39 above. Giving Simon a name is an indication that he will become a core member of Jesus' group. ⇨ **Name,** 17:1-26. Among core antisociety members, loyalty is usually very high and membership often permanent. While Peter's denial of Jesus (18:25-27) breaks the loyalty bond and removes Peter from the position established here, his position as a core member and leader in the Jesus group will be reconstituted in chapter 21.

1:43-46 This is the second invitation described in the passage. Two more members of Jesus' group are recruited here. See the **Notes** on 1:35-42 above and especially the comments on "following" at 1:38-39. The identification of the hometown of Philip, Andrew, and Peter encodes much social information about them. ⇨ **Kinship,** 8:31-59.

Philip's identification of Jesus as the one about whom Moses and the prophets had written would have created the further expectation that someone had appeared who was of high or even royal birth. When Philip adds that Jesus is the son of Joseph from Nazareth, Nathanael is rightly incredulous. Since people in antiquity were expected unfailingly to act in accord with their birth status, Jesus' messianic credentials were nonexistent. As a tiny, obscure village, Nazareth would hardly be expected to produce anyone of messianic stature. ⇨ **Lineage and Stereotypes,** 8:31-59.

1:43-46 In Jesus' day Nazareth was a tiny village, clustered around a small spring. Built atop the steep ridge that forms the north side of the Esdraelon Valley, it was concealed in a saucer-like depression as if to emphasize its insignificance. (It is not mentioned in the Old Testament or any other literature before Christ.) Photo by Avraham Hay.

1:47-49 The NRSV translation here, "Where did you get to know me?" is completely anachronistic. It implies a modern type of social interaction in which people get personally acquainted. A better translation of the Greek would read, "From where do you know me to come?" That is, Nathanael assumes Jesus would know him if he knows where he is from. If Jesus can identify the place of Nathanael's origin, he would know all there is to know about him. ⇨ **Lineage and Stereotypes** and **Kinship,** 8:31-59. Note that in 21:2 we are told that Nathanael is from Cana, a small Galilean village near Nazareth.

Jesus' reply to Nathanael, that he saw him under the fig tree, refers to an Old Testament metaphor, in which fig tree stands for one's home; see Isa. 36:16, Mic. 4:4, Zech. 3:10. If Jesus is saying that he had seen Nathanael at home (Cana is near Nazareth), he would be saying he knows all there is to know about him.

Nathanael's surprise that Jesus knows him leads to a clear statement that Nathanael knows Jesus. Aside from the respectful address ("Rabbi"), the titles used here have more than messianic significance in John's Gospel. In 20:31 we are told that the purpose of this Gospel is to enable people to recognize Jesus as Israel's Messiah and Son of God. ⇨ **Son of God,** 1:29-34.

1:50-51 Twice earlier in 1:35-51 new recruits to Jesus' group are told to "come and see" (vv. 39, 46). "Seeing" is, of course, a frequent Johannine antilanguage term for believing into, knowing, and the like; it is prominent throughout the Gospel (the term is used 107 times). ⇨ **Antilanguage,** 1:19-28. While 2:1-11 presents the first of the "signs" that reveal the glory of Jesus, this verse may be preparation for that story. The full glory of Jesus will be seen, however, only after his death and resurrection.

The phrase "Amen, Amen, I say to you" (NRSV: "Very truly, I tell you") is extremely frequent in this Gospel, appearing 25 times. The Synoptics always use a single "Amen" for this expression (Matthew 30 times; Mark 13 times; Luke 7 times). The formula means something like, "I give you my word of honor." In effect it is an oath, explicitly and publicly giving one's word of honor concerning the veracity of what one is saying. It is not unlike swearing on the Bible in U.S. court. In Mediterranean societies putting one's honor on the line in public is a very serious matter. The prevalence of secrecy, deception, and lying in the first-century Mediterranean made life very exasperating. These negative values are the high-context presuppositions of the discussion in 8:43-48. Jesus' frequent word of honor assures his audience that he intends to speak the truth. ⇨ **Secrecy,** 7:1-9. ⇨ **Lying,** 7:1-9.

Verse 51 is the first time in John's Gospel that Jesus is identified as the "Son of Man." It may evoke the imagery of the Jacob story in Gen. 28:10ff. Whatever its origin, it suggests that Jesus is the point of contact between sky and earth. Standing in this intermediary position, Jesus acts as God's mediator, or broker. ⇨ **Patronage,** 5:21-30. In light of this imagery, a better translation would be "Sky Man." ⇨ **Son of Man,** 1:35.

✧ *Reading Scenarios:* **John 1:35-51**

Networking, 1:35-51

Networking refers to the way people interact on the basis of established pathways of social relationships. People have social positions and relate to others on the basis of those positions. For example, here John the Baptist points out Jesus to his disciples (v. 35); the relationship of John to his disciples (one unnamed, the other Andrew) forms a pathway of social relationships allowing for the interaction depicted in this Gospel segment. Further, communication between brothers (v. 40) or friends (v. 45) points to a similar pathway of social relationships permitting the interaction between Andrew and Simon Peter (brothers) and between Philip and Nathanael (friends).

Social organization consists of structures of relations and processes of interaction. People relate to one another in patterned ways (structures) and interact with one another along pathways set out by those patterned ways (structures). The patterned ways people relate to one another form social networks. When people transact with one another along network pathways, such behavior is called social exchange. In this segment of John, the social exchange consists of the communication of new information from the Baptist to his disciples, from brother to brother, from friend to friend. Such social exchange is a process that changes the distribution of resources, and the outcome is a change in social structure. The resource here is information, and the outcome is the formation of a new group with Jesus at its center.

Further dimensions of Jesus' network are revealed in the next chapter when Jesus and his disciples join his mother at a wedding party in Cana. Through Jesus and his mother, Jesus' disciples are introduced into a new network of relations with residents of Cana present at the wedding, although Nathanael of Cana had strong ties there.

Networks, then, consist of social interactions between and among persons tied to one another with varying degrees of intensity. Brothers and friends have strong ties; Jesus' disciples and Cana villagers have weak ties (apart from Nathanael). Strong ties are relations with close relatives and friends, while weak ties derive from occasional contact with persons. As a rule, in face-to-face societies such as those of the first-century Mediterranean, weak ties are minimal since people are geographically and socially stable for the most part. A lack of a range of weak-tie relations reveals the following characteristics:

- the social system is fragmented and incoherent
- new ideas spread slowly; technological endeavors are handicapped
- subgroups are separated by ethnicity, race, and geography; hence they have difficulty reaching a modus vivendi
- strong-tie groups are usually never aware of specifically who controls their lives, but they do know that control lies outside their group; their lives do not actually depend on what happens within their group
- strong-tie group members think stereotypically, hence everyone knows why people act as they do; there is no need to gauge the inward intention of others
- speech is high context (speakers assume everyone shares and knows the same social context)
- strong ties point to similarity among persons in many dimensions.

Strong ties thus produce stable, relatively closed groups. Significantly new information, however, generally derives from weak ties that bridge strong-tie groups (for example, occasionally meeting people on pilgrimage; interacting with a wandering healer; meeting others on the occasion of a prophet's baptizing). Weak-tie interactions that bridge strong-tie groups carry innovations and information across the boundaries of social groups (between villages, between statuses in a polis). Strong ties affect the credibility and influence of innovations, making such cross-group interactions suspect. Such networking considerations offer a very important way to envision the rationale behind the expansion of a social organization (usually described in terms of mission and conversion).

Here John the Baptist is the bridging weak tie to the Bethsaida brothers, Andrew and Simon Peter, and to Philip and the unnamed disciple. Nathanael of

Cana would have strong ties in Cana, while both he and Jesus connected the disciples with the villagers of Cana (2:2). ✿ **Gossip Network,** 4:1-42.

Antisociety, 1:35-51

In the introduction to this book, we used sociolinguistics to suggest that John's Gospel is an instance of antilanguage. ✿ **Antilanguage,** 1:19-28. We also made clear that antilanguage goes hand in hand with antisociety. Our thesis is therefore that the so-called community of the Beloved Disciple was in fact an antisociety. It was a hollowed-out social space within the larger society over against which it stood in opposition (in structure, not unlike modern big-city gangs).

Such an antisociety should not be confused with a liminal group, that is, a group in transition to some new social status (from unmarried to married, unordained to ordained, free citizen to prison inmate, innocent to guilty, and so on). Especially in preliterate societies, people ritually separated from the larger society find themselves between roles or even between statuses. In such transition situations, they often begin to treat each other without regard to previous social rank, privileges, entitlement, and the like. They ignore the usual social trappings. Even today this attitude can be found among those who find themselves stripped of previous indicators of rank and role; these persons can be "anything they want to be"—for example, people thrown together in boot camp when drafted into the army, people put together in holding cells and introduced into prisons or concentration camps, people on vacation with others who leave social indicators behind, people sharing a hospital ward (all clothed in hospital gowns), novices in religious orders. In the midst of such transitions, people are basically in an antistructural situation, in the sense that they are in conflict with and against prevailing social structures (*not* countercultural). Their relationship with one another on the basis of common humanity has been called *communitas*. They do not form antisocieties, although they may be on their way to becoming members of an antisociety.

Antisocieties, by contrast, are antisocietal structures. Members remain in the society but are opposed to and in conflict with it (in John's terms, they are in the world but not of it). Antisocieties are usually made up of people who have been socially displaced in one way or another, even by those considered socially deviant. As we said in the introduction, members of an antisociety have frequently experienced a socially sanctioned depersonalization that makes them outsiders to the rest of society. As a result, they begin to find interpersonal relationships within their antisocietal group of more value than relationships with those in the broader society. They develop intense in-group loyalty (John's word for this is "love") that is centered on the key figure in the group. The group comes to share the qualities of a kin group with close interpersonal relationships.

Much language in John suggests this kind of antisocietal thinking. The Johannine group is deeply antagonistic to the "world," which in John is the larger Israelite, and especially Judean, society. In John, Jesus speaks often of his own social alienation. He tells his brothers that the world hates him because he publicly condemns its evil works (7:7). He reminds the Pharisees that they are part of the larger society but he is not (8:23). Moreover, he is conscious of his own alienation (15:18) and knows that his solidarity with his followers has emerged from this mutual experience of alienation (17:14, 16). In 15:18-19 Jesus says, "If the world hates you, be aware that it hated me before it hated you." Thus, while both Jesus and his followers have been marginalized, Jesus' alienation has a longer history. When he says, "If you belonged to the world, the world would love you as its own" (15:19), he speaks a truth all socially alienated people immediately understand.

Jesus is also aware that there is no going back. Solace cannot be found in a return to the larger society but only by staying with the group—that is, with Jesus. He reminds his followers, "My peace I give to you. I do not give to you as the world gives" (14:27); hence, they can get from him the opposite of what they got from society. Since they will only find conflict in the world (16:33), it is "in Jesus" alone that they can expect comfort. Only if they "hate their life in this world" (12:25) will they find eternal life.

Here is where we should see the significance of the peculiar Johannine phrase "believing *into*" Jesus (1:12; 2:23; 6:35; et al.; 34 times in John). It suggests the close interpersonal relationships in antisocietal groups. So also does the concern that one "remain" or "abide" (these translate the same Greek verb, 53 times in John; see the **Notes** at 1:38-39) in Jesus. With this language as well he articulates the close interpersonal ties that bind members of antisocieties together.

As we noted in the introduction, an antisociety is hollowed out from the larger society with which it stands in conflict. Its members are indeed in the world even if their loyalties are not with it. Thus, Jesus does not pray that his followers be taken out of the world (17:15); instead, he sends them into the world (17:18). While he has been with them he has protected them (17:12), but he asks God to protect them when he leaves (17:15). Such language recognizes the precarious position of all antisocieties. The hostility toward them is genuine.

Here in 1:35-51 we see the formative beginnings of Jesus' antisociety. Significantly, the first two disciples had already been in John the Baptist's antisociety group and switch to following Jesus only when he is identified by John as the divinely appointed leader. ⇨ **Lamb of God,** 1:29-34. Then several significant things happen. First, they want to know where Jesus is "staying" (1:38) so they can "remain" with him. Next, when Andrew recruits his brother Peter, Jesus knows immediately that Peter is one of them. He gives Peter a nickname, a common feature of antisocietal practice (compare the nicknaming practices of socially alienated motorcycle gangs in the United States). Philip, being from the same city as Andrew and Peter, suggests a network of marginalized acquaintances through which the group begins to grow. Nathanael is from Cana (21:2), not Bethsaida, but Philip finds him quickly. Jesus already knows he is one of them (see the **Notes** at 1:47-49), and he too becomes part of the group. It is thus by close, face-to-face (interpersonal) interaction that antisocieties are created.

The group or community of John was an antisociety characterized by antisocietal structure. It was not a liminal community characterized by *communitas* and its liminal antistructure. The following table presents a comparison among liminal, societal, and antisocietal structures.

Liminality	Society	Antisociety
transition	stable state	precarious condition
totality	partiality	selectivity
homogeneity	heterogeneity	multigeneity
communitas	structure	antistructure
equality	inequality	parallelism
anonymity	systems of titles/roles	systems of nicknames
absence of property	property	shared property
absence of status	status	placement
nakedness or uniform clothing	distinctions of clothing	unconcern for clothing indicators
sexual continence	sexuality	antisexuality
minimization of sex distinctions	maximization of sex distinctions	reversal of sexual roles
absence of rank	distinctions of rank	antidistinction of rank
humility	just pride of position	just pride in antiposition
disregard for personal appearance	care for personal appearance	care not to shame in-group
no distinctions of wealth	distinctions of wealth	distinctions of antiwealth
unselfishness	selfishness	other-centered
total obedience	obedience only to superior rank	obedience to one another
sacredness	secularity	antisecular
sacred instruction	technical knowledge	revealed knowledge
silence	speech	antilanguage
suspension of kinship rights and obligations	kinship rights and obligations	fictive kinship rights and obligations
continuous reference to mystical power	intermittent reference to mystical power	mystical power is ordinary
foolishness	sagacity	insightfulness
simplicity	complexity	interpersonal intricacy
acceptance of pain and suffering	avoidance of pain and suffering	ignoring of pain and suffering
heteronomy	degrees of autonomy	antiautonomy

Son of Man, 1:35-51

In John the Son of Man is a sky being, hence a "Sky Man." We learn this when we are told that as the sky opens, God's angels can use this Son of Man as a cosmic ladder, to ascend into the realm of God and descend from it (v. 51). In this role, he stands midway between the vault of the sky and the land. Furthermore, this Son of Man has himself descended from the sky and therefore can ascend into the sky (John 3:13). In fact, the Son of Man will ascend to where he was before (John 6:62). Similarly, in the Synoptic tradition, when Jesus refers to the Son of Man as an entity other than himself (e.g., Mark 8:38; Luke 9:26; 12:8), this Son of Man is a sky being who will descend from the sky with great power and glory (Mark 13:26; cf. 14:62; Matt. 26:64). While sharing Mark's tradition concerning the Son of Man, Matthew refers to the coming of the Son of Man as a generic point in time. Thus:

> "When they persecute you in one town, flee to the next; for truly I tell you, you will not have gone through all the towns of Israel before the Son of Man comes." (Matt. 10:23)
>
> "Truly I tell you, there are some standing here who will not taste death before they see the Son of Man coming in his kingdom." (Matt. 16:28)
>
> Jesus said to them, "Truly I tell you, at the renewal of all things, when the Son of Man is seated on the throne of his glory, you who have followed me will also sit on twelve thrones, judging the twelve tribes of Israel." (Matt.19:28)

Similarly Luke 18:8:

> "I tell you, he will quickly grant justice to them. And yet, when the Son of Man comes, will he find faith on earth?"

In the Synoptics, the coming of the Son of Man is a time of final judgment:

> "The Son of Man will send his angels, and they will collect out of his kingdom all causes of sin and all evildoers." (Matt. 13:41)
>
> "For the Son of Man is to come with his angels in the glory of his Father, and then he will repay everyone for what has been done." (Matt. 16:27).
>
> "When the Son of Man comes in his glory, and all the angels with him, then he will sit on the throne of his glory." (Matt. 25:31; the context is judgment)

Thus, in a number of passages in the Synoptics, as generally in John, the Son of Man is a sky being. If we take into account Israel's astronomic tradition, we also find reference to this Son of Man in the book of Revelation and in that major astronomic work, 1 Enoch. First consider the origins of this Son of Man in Rev. 12:1-5:

And a great sign was seen in the sky, a Woman clothed with the Sun, and the Moon under her feet and on her head a wreath of Twelve Stars. And having in the womb, and she cries out having childbirth pains and tormented to give birth. And another sign was seen in the sky, and behold a great fire-colored Dragon, having seven heads and ten horns and on its heads seven diadems. And its tail sweeps away the third of the stars of the sky, and it threw them onto the earth, and the Dragon stands before the Woman about to give birth, in order when she gives birth to eat up her Child. And she gave birth to a son, a male, who is going to shepherd all the nations with an iron rod. And her Child was taken up to God and to his throne.

In this context, the author of Revelation is more deeply involved with cosmic sky searching and prehistoric scenarios than with concern about a historic personage. Yet he does record the tradition that there is such a prehistoric celestial human-like "son" enthroned with God from prehistoric times. For this Dragon-Serpent fell from the sky and was already in the garden when humans were created (Gen 3:1).

Consider now the Israelite traditions reported in 1 Enoch, where the antediluvian sage, Enoch, notes in one of his visions:

> At that place I saw the One to whom belongs the time before time. And his head was white like wool, and there was with him another individual, whose face was like that of a human being. His countenance was full of grace like that of one among the holy angels. And I asked the one—from among the angels—who was going with me and who had revealed to me all the secrets regarding the One who was born of human beings, "Who is this and from whence is he who is going as the prototype of the Before-Time?" And he answered me and said to me, "This is the Son of Man, to whom belongs righteousness, and with whom righteousness dwells." (1 Enoch 46:1-3, trans. E. Isaac, OTP 1:34)

Thus, in his sky visions, Enoch reports seeing a "Son of Man" with God. He then states:

> [The] Son of Man was given a name, in the presence of the Lord of the Spirits, the Before Time; even before the creation of the Sun and the moon, before the creation of the stars, he was given a name in the presence of the Lord of Spirits. He will become a staff for the righteous ones in order that they may lean on him and not fall. He is the light of the Gentiles and he will become the hope of those who are sick in their hearts. All those who dwell upon the earth shall fall and worship before him; they shall glorify, bless, and sing the name of the Lord of the Spirits. For this purpose he became the Chosen One; he was concealed in the presence of (the Lord of the Spirits) prior to the creation of the world and for eternity. And he has revealed the wisdom of the Lord of the Spirits to the righteous and the holy ones, for he has preserved the portion of the righteous because they have hated and despised this world of oppression (together with) all its ways of life and its habits in the name of the Lord of

Spirits; and because they will be saved in his name and it is his good pleasure
that they have life. (1 Enoch 48:2-7, trans. E. Isaac, OTP 1:35)

Enoch further sees God, the Lord of the Spirits, commanding the elites of this
world (kings, governors, high officials, and landlords) to recognize this Chosen
One, "how he sits on his throne of glory," a point repeatedly underscored (1 Enoch
62:2, 3, 6). Enoch notes how this "Son of Man sitting on the throne of his glory . . .
was concealed from the beginning, and the Most High One preserved him in the
presence of his power; then he revealed him to the holy and elect ones" (1 Enoch
62:7, trans. E. Isaac, OTP 1:43). We are then told that this Son of Man:

shall never pass away or perish from before the face of the earth. But those
who have led the world astray shall be bound with chains; and their ruinous
congregation shall be imprisoned; all their deeds shall vanish from before the
face of the earth. Thenceforth nothing that is corruptible shall be found; for
that Son of Man has appeared and has seated himself upon the throne of his
glory; and all evil shall disappear from before his face; he shall go and tell to
that Son of Man, and he shall be strong before the Lord of the Spirits. (1
Enoch 69:27-29, trans. E. Isaac, OTP 1:49)

While these sections of the book of Enoch date from the end of the first century C.E., there can be little doubt that the descriptions in Revelation and Enoch point
to a common tradition. With the author of Revelation, who observes the prehistoric
birth of the sky woman's Son and sees him enthroned with God early on in the history of the cosmos, we are viewing the origins of Enoch's Son of Man. And there
is equally little doubt that this Enochian Son of Man is the Messiah of Israelite
expectation. "The Lord of Spirits and his Messiah" are mentioned in one breath at
the end of the passage where this Son of Man is described (1 Enoch 48:10, trans.
E. Isaac, OTP 1:36). And later on we are told, "All these things which you have
seen happened by the authority of his Messiah so that he may give orders and be
praised upon the earth" (1 Enoch 52:4, trans. E. Isaac, OTP 1:37).

This seems to be the only celestial Son of Man known in Israel's tradition.
Hence, if Jesus is the Son of Man in John's Gospel, there can be little doubt that
Jesus is this Son of Man who has descended from the realm of God through the
opened sky. Since this is the missing context for John's high-context perspective,
it is better to translate "Son of Man" as "Sky Man" or even "Star Man."

God sets his seal on this Sky Man (6:27), who will give life-sustaining food to
his own (6:53). In typical Johannine irony, Jesus, the Sky Man, who comes down
and goes up as he likes, will be lifted up by human beings (3:14; 8:28; 12:34) and
thus be glorified (12:23) and draw all Israel to himself (12:32). "Being lifted up"
shows "by what death he was to die" (12:33). Furthermore, since this cosmic Son
born of the sky woman has no stated father, his father must be God himself (as in
the case of Adam, begotten "of God" in Luke's genealogy, Luke 3:38). This Sky
Son, the Star Man born of the pregnant sky woman before the foundation of the
world, must necessarily be God's Son, the Son who came down from God, the
Son sent by God.

CHAPTER III
JOHN 2:1–4:54
JESUS BEGAN BRINGING LIFE TO ISRAEL: FROM GALILEE TO JERUSALEM AND BACK

In John's Gospel, Jesus' so-called public ministry is the story of how he brought life and light to Israel through his self-disclosure. The major events of this story take place at celebrations and/or feasts that were full of feeling for first-century Israelites. The author notes how Jesus initiates his self-disclosure at a wedding in Galilee. The series of self-disclosures, called "signs," comes to a close with a funeral in Judea. In between there is a series of Israelite feasts that punctuate Jesus' revelation to Israel. Events such as weddings, funerals, and feasts are special times that mark off the high points of human living. Everyday living, on the other hand, follows "clock time." In Hellenistic Greek, special time, qualitatively significant time, is called *kairos,* while regular clock time is called *chronos.* Jesus calls his own special, qualitatively significant time his "hour." The author of the Gospel of John places the special times of Jesus' self-presentation and revelatory activity within the framework of the special times of Israel. These latter times include both domestic special times, such as weddings and funerals, and political special times, such as pilgrimages and temple feasts. To appreciate what the author is doing, it helps if a reader can understand the emotions Israelites felt during those special times—emotions such as those modern U.S. readers feel for birthdays, anniversaries, or Christmas. As a high-context document written in antilanguage for an antisociety, such feelings evoked by domestic and political festive times are presumed by the author. This feature further underscores the interpersonal dimensions of the Gospel.

A Wedding in Galilee:
Jesus' Initial Self-Disclosure, 2:1-12

2:1 On the third day there was a wedding in Cana of Galilee, and the mother of Jesus was there. [2]Jesus and his disciples had also been invited to the wedding. [3]When the wine gave out, the mother of Jesus said to him, "They have no wine." [4]And Jesus said to her, "Woman, what concern is that to you and to me? My hour has not yet come." [5]His mother said to the servants, "Do whatever he tells you." [6]Now standing there were six stone water jars for the Jewish rites of purification, each holding twenty or thirty gallons. [7]Jesus said to them, "Fill the jars with water." And they filled them up to the brim. [8]He said to them, "Now draw some out, and take it to the chief steward." So they took it. [9]When the steward tasted the water that had become wine, and did not know where it came from (though the servants who had drawn the water knew), the steward called the bridegroom [10]and said to him, "Everyone serves the good wine first, and then the inferior wine after the guests have become drunk. But you have kept the good wine until now." [11]Jesus did this, the first of his signs, in Cana of Galilee, and revealed his glory; and his disciples believed in him.

12 After this he went down to Capernaum with his mother, his brothers, and his disciples; and they remained there a few days.

✦ *Notes:* John 2:1-12

The story opens "on the third day." Note the enumeration of days: the first day covers 1:1-28; "the next day," 1:29-34; "the next day," 1:35-39; and a presumed next day: 1:40-42; with a final "the next day" in 1:43-51. With these five days over, " the third day" here (2:1-11) would be the eighth day. And this eighth day marks the first day after the close of the first (creation) week since the beginning (1:1). That first week is John's creation week. After this eighth day, there is no more counting of days (so in v. 12 we read "a few days"). "On the third day" also reflects the day of Jesus' being raised, the eighth day of the week (see vss. 19-20: "after three days").

2:1-2 The location of Cana is not known for certain; it is probably the small village of Khirbet Qânâ about nine miles north of Nazareth. Since it was the home of Nathanael (21:2), that may account for the presence of Jesus, his mother, his brothers (v. 12), and the disciples. An invitation to a wedding implies at least a neighborly relationship and results in a social obligation in return.

Jesus' mother is not named in John's Gospel but instead is given the customary honorific title "mother of Jesus" (2:2, 3), the respectful way of referring to a woman who has borne a son; the birth of a son defines the woman as a complete, adult person. ➪ **Mother/Son,** 19:17-37.

In the gender-divided societies of the Mediterranean world, a house is normally considered private space. As such, it is the domain of women. On certain occasions, such as funerals and weddings, however, this private space could become public and thus allow for at least some mixing of the sexes. Some parts of a wedding celebration still took place in gender-divided space where men and women celebrated separately, but other parts were open to all for the duration of the wedding. ➪ **Wedding Celebrations,** 2:1-11.

2:3-5 "There is no rejoicing save with wine" (*b. Pes.* 109a). The fact that the family hosting the wedding has run out of wine threatens a serious loss of honor. Friends, especially those from the inner group of wedding celebrants, usually sent gifts such as wine ahead of time to be available for the wedding celebration. Lack of wine thus implies lack of friends. If Jesus was among the "members of a wedding association" (Hebrew *shushbinim*) of this bridegroom (➪ **Wedding Celebrations,** 2:1-11), he was among those obligated to provide such gifts.

It is not surprising that Jesus' mother knows the wine is short, because she, along with most of the other women, would have been involved in the food preparation for the celebration. Working discreetly behind the scenes as Jesus' Mother does would avoid social humiliation of the family. If she is a kinswoman

2:1-2 Cana. This is a view of the present site of the ruin that is currently known as Khirbet Qânâ, the most likely site of the ancient village of Cana. Photo by Avraham Hay.

of the groom (as some traditions hold), she would view the matter with some urgency, since the shame would also fall on both Jesus and herself. Even if not a family member, she is acting as a loyal friend. In relaying the concern about wine to Jesus, his mother plays the role of broker on behalf of the bridegroom and his family.

The (implied) request to Jesus (which may have come from a discreet member of the family) would be a challenge to his honor if his mother's request had come in public. By informing Jesus about the shortage of wine, his mother appears to be asking him to play the role of a "wedding associate" in providing for the host family being threatened with humiliation.

The address Jesus uses here, "Woman," sounds harsh to modern ears. Its use in 19:26, however, makes clear that it is not. It may have been characteristic of Jesus (see also 4:21; 8:11; 19:25; 20:13; Luke 13:10). The bond between mother and son is the closest interpersonal relation known in the Middle East. It is generally much closer than that of husband and wife. Hence, the mother of Jesus is able to presume upon Jesus to act as patron on behalf of this family.

In this Gospel, Jesus takes the initiative to help those whom he believes need his help (in the Synoptics, by contrast, he normally does nothing unless he is asked to do so). He is rarely approached by others for help in John. Yet, in those few instances when people do in fact make requests, as here, Jesus' response is always one of delaying reluctance, followed by compliance, and then a return to the conflict with the hostile Judeans. We find such a pattern in 2:1-11; 4:46-54; 7:2-14; and 11:1-16.

It is interesting to note that all of these requests come from in-group persons whose in-group status derives from birth or natural position: mother, town-mate, brothers, closest of friends. Yet it is only after a display of reluctance that Jesus eventually complies with their requests and immediately afterward engages Judeans in further conflict. In "straight" society, as opposed to antisociety, these in-group persons all deserve and receive immediate compliance. These in-group persons define one's collective self and are really alter egos. Perhaps John uses this pattern to inform members of his group about how to deal with their relatives and other natural in-group persons. Here are the four examples of this pattern in John (after Giblin 1980):

2:1-14	4:46—5:1, 18	7:2-10	11:1-8
Request	**Request**	**Request**	**Request**
. . . When the wine failed, the mother of Jesus said to him, "They have no wine."	And at Capernaum there was an official whose son was ill. . . . he went and begged him to come down and heal his son, for he was at the point of death.	So his brothers said to him, "Leave here and go to Judea, that your disciples may see the works you are doing."	Now a certain man was ill, Lazarus of Bethany. . . . So the sisters sent to him, saying, "Lord, he whom you love is ill."
Stalling Reluctance	**Stalling Reluctance**	**Stalling Reluctance**	**Stalling Reluctance**
And Jesus said to her, "O woman, what have you to do with me? My hour has not yet come."	Jesus therefore said to him, "Unless you see signs and wonders you will not believe."	Jesus said to them, "My time has not yet come, but your time is always here. . . . Go to the feast yourselves; I am not going up to this feast, for my time has not yet fully come."	But when Jesus heard it he said, "This illness is not unto death. . . . So when he heard that he was ill, he stayed two days longer in the place where he was.
Compliance	**Compliance**	**Compliance**	**Compliance**
Jesus said to them, "Fill the jars with water." And they filled them up to the brim.	Jesus said to him, "Go; your son will live."	But after his brothers had gone up to the feast, then he also went up, not publicly but in private.	Then after this he said to the disciples, "Let us go into Judea again."
Conflict with the Judeans	**Conflict with the Judeans**	**Conflict with the Judeans**	**Conflict with the Judeans**
The Passover of the Judeans was at hand, and Jesus went up to Jerusalem. In the Temple he found people selling cattle, sheep and doves, and the money changers seated at their tables. Making a whip of cords he drove all of them out of the Temple.	After this there was a feast of the Judeans, and Jesus went up to Jerusalem. [healing at Bethzatha] . . . For this reason the Judeans were seeking all the more to kill him.	The Judeans were looking for him at the feast, and saying, "Where is he?" And there was considerable complaining about him among the crowds.	The disciples said to him, "Rabbi, the Judeans were just now trying to stone you, and are you going there again?"

2:6 Stone water jars. Since each held twenty to thirty gallons, they would have reached to waist height, and it would have taken the servants some time to carry enough water to fill them all "to the brim." Photo by Eugene Selk.

2:6 Stone water jars were preferable for holding water for purification since clay pots had to be destroyed if they were contaminated by contact with the carcass of an unclean animal (Lev. 11:33). ⇨ **Purity/Pollution: Purification Rites,** 3:22-36. Most village families would have had no more than one such jar (which held about twenty gallons), hence the presence of six stone jars may indicate that others have been borrowed from neighbors for the occasion.

2:7-11 By providing wine for the wedding celebration, Jesus rescues the honor of the bridegroom. Traditional Western theological comment that Jesus here usurps the role of host (thus turning this into a sacramental story) misses a key point in the story. By providing wine for this threatened family, Jesus honors the bridegroom and saves *his own* prestige.

In 1:50 Jesus had told Nathanael that he would see "greater things" than had yet appeared. Here we see the first of these things. Jesus has been challenged to act as one of the wedding associates for the beleaguered family of the groom, and he responds by turning the water into wine. He proves to be a good friend (and dutiful son). By fulfilling the role of "wedding associate" for a village family, Jesus acted in a way that enhanced or pointed to his own honor ("glory"). It is as a friend willing to save the honor of those in need that Jesus here elicits belief from the disciples. For members of John's antisociety, the incident clearly underscores what group members might expect from Jesus. They would expect that he would deal with them in the same way.

In this Gospel, a sign is something that reveals who Jesus really is. Jesus' signs are self-disclosures that provoke interpersonal affectionate adherence.

2:12 This verse has occasioned much consternation through the centuries among those uneasy at the idea that Jesus' mother had other children. Jesus' biological and fictive families are here portrayed as traveling together. The notice is strange in light of 7:5.

✧ *Reading Scenarios:* John 2:1-12
Wedding Celebrations, 2:1-12

In antiquity a wedding did not celebrate the marriage of two individuals, but of two families. Wedding celebrations were of immense significance as public demonstrations of family honor. Families often went deeply in debt trying to outdo each other in the honorific competition to provide the best wedding the village had ever seen. Because a wedding celebration would often include a whole village, arrangements were usually quite elaborate and could take many days to complete. A family often required heavy assistance from neighbors and friends in the preparation of food and drink. Since a family would normally have only one stone water jar, the presence of six such jars here (v. 6) may be an indication of neighborly cooperation.

To run out of food or wine at a wedding involved a serious loss of family honor. It signaled not only a lack of financial resources, but even more a lack of friends. In order to avoid such embarrassment and ensure a wedding that brought a family public honor, associations (Hebrew *shushbinim*) were formed among village men for the purpose of mutual assistance (probably the ones referred to as the "sons of the bridal-chamber" in Mark 2:19). Those designated by this term usually included close relatives and friends, especially age-mates of the groom, who formed an in-group of celebrants at a wedding feast. The closest of them were sometimes involved in negotiations for a betrothal, and among all of them it was common to send gifts ahead of the wedding that could be used as provisions for the feast.

Each time another member of this in-group got married, reciprocal obligations came into play. It is possible that these obligations had a role in Jesus' mother's request to her son. In scribal Pharisaism, as we learn from the Talmud, there were astonishingly strict rules for insuring the precise equivalence of this reciprocal obligation (*b. Baba Batra* 145b). In fact, a wedding gift was considered a loan (unless the gift was wine!) and was recoverable in a court of law (*m. Baba Batra* 9.4).

Obviously, then, a wedding celebration was not a private family affair. It culminated in festivities at the home of the groom, and everyone in the village participated. The wedding day began with the village women washing the bride in her own home. It was a joyful ritual of preparation that included perfuming, anointing, and dressing the bride. Elaborate clothing and adornment were provided. Then came the "home-taking," a torchlight procession in which the bride was accompanied to the groom's house. There was much singing and dancing as she walked, or even rode in a decorated carriage. If a virgin, she wore her hair loose and a wreath upon her head. Both men and women participated in the procession. The well-known Pharisaic scribes of Jesus' day (Hillel and Shammai) argued over whether it was permissible to exaggerate a bride's beauty during the singing. Roasted ears of grain, wine, and oil were strewn in the path of the procession.

After arriving at the groom's house, the bride was introduced into her husband's family and then the celebration began in the home of the groom. Such wedding celebrations traditionally began on a Wednesday and lasted seven days if the bride was a virgin and if the family and its village had enough resources; they would begin on a Thursday and last three days if the bride was a widow (Judg. 14:12; Tob. 11:19; *m. Ket.* 1.1). Though the house was normally private space, for a wedding celebration it was opened to all and thereby open to public scrutiny. Since such scrutiny could be dangerous (leading to rumor and gossip), it would be a matter of great concern to the host family that everything be in order.

Feasts, 2:1-12

The word *feast* refers to a type of time and a type of meal. As a type of time, a feast refers to the day(s) when significant past events are commemorated or when significant present events take place. As a type of meal, a feast is a formal, elaborate meal, often called a banquet, consumed because of the significance of the time. Here the time is a wedding, the joining of the honor and interests of two families with a view to new life.

The festive meal points to the fact that people all over the world use food and drink not only as nourishment, but also as an important method of communication. A meal to which others are invited sends important social messages exchanged between the person(s) issuing invitations and those actually invited, those who should/might have been invited but were not, and those who decline the invitation. Just as the material used for communication in speech is language, so the material used for communication in a meal is food, drink, and their setting.

Therefore, the type of food and drink chosen for a feast, its mode of preparation and presentation, and the seating or reclining arrangements all say something about the host's assessment of those invited. A festive meal differs from simply sharing a meal with another person or persons, much like a formal speech differs from casual conversation. A festive meal is formal rather than informal communication and usually implies messages of great significance.

From the point of view of the kinds of messages involved, there are two general types of banquets: ceremonial and ritual. A ceremonial feast is a banquet in which the host and the guests celebrate their mutual solidarity, their belonging to one another, their oneness. The festive meals of Israel's appointed feasts (see Lev. 23:2-44), much like the national and personal celebrations in the story of Esther (banquet for Persian elites, nonelites, and women: Est. 1:3-9; in honor of Esther: Est. 2:18; and of the king and, by ruse, of Mordecai, Est. 5:1-7:10), were such ceremonial festive meals. The same is true of the gathering of Jesus Messianists described by Paul in 1 Cor. 11:17-33. The problem noted by Paul of each one going ahead with his own meal, and one going hungry while another got drunk (v. 21), points to wrong meanings being communicated. Instead of mutual solidarity and oneness, the behavior communicated "factions" (v. 19).

A ritual festive meal is one that marks some individual's or group's transition or transformation. It is held to give honor to those undergoing some important social change. As a ritual feature of hospitality, festive meals indicate the transformation of a stranger into a guest (Gen. 19:3-14; Luke 5:29), of an enemy into a covenant partner (Gen. 26:26-31; 2 Sam. 3:20). Feasts mark important transitional points in a person's life—for example, Isaac's weaning day (Gen. 21:8), Jacob's weddings (Gen. 29:22), Pharaoh's birthday (Gen. 40:20), Samson's wedding (Judg. 14:10), the wedding banquet in the parable of Matt. 22:2-10; Herod's birthday (Mark 6:21), the victory banquet hosted by God in Rev. 19:17, and the Lamb's marriage (Rev. 19:9).

In the Synoptic Gospels, at his final meal with his disciples, Jesus changes the ceremonial banquet of the Israelite Passover into a ritual banquet effectively symbolizing the meaning of his impending death (Mark 14:12-25). But in John, Jesus' final meal is a ritual at which disciples become friends, and Jesus reveals what he knows of the future. ⇨ **Final Words,** 13:1-17.

First Passover: Jesus' Opposition to the Temple System Elicits Belief, 2:13-25

13 The Passover of the Jews was near, and Jesus went up to Jerusalem. [14]In the temple he found people selling cattle, sheep, and doves, and the money changers seated at their tables. [15]Making a whip of cords, he drove all of them out of the temple, both the sheep and the cattle. He also poured out the coins of the money changers and overturned their tables. [16]He told those who were selling the doves, "Take these things out of here! Stop making my Father's house a marketplace!" [17]His disciples remembered that it was written, "Zeal for your house will consume me." [18]The Jews then said to him, "What sign can you show us for doing this?" [19]Jesus answered them, "Destroy this temple, and in three days I will raise it up." [20]The Jews then said, "This temple has been under construction for forty-six years, and will you raise it up in three days?" [21]But he was speaking of the temple of his body. [22]After he was raised from the dead, his disciples remembered that he had said this; and they believed the scripture and the word that Jesus had spoken.

23 When he was in Jerusalem during the Passover festival, many believed in his name because they saw the signs that he was doing. [24]But Jesus on his part would not entrust himself to them, because he knew all people [25]and needed no one to testify about anyone; for he himself knew what was in everyone.

✦ *Notes:* John 2:13-25

The three main pilgrimage feasts of Israel were Passover in spring, Pentecost in summer, and Sukkoth in the fall. ⇨ **Pilgrimage,** 2:13-25.

2:13 As throughout John's Gospel, the term here translated "Jews" by the NRSV should instead be translated "Judeans." ⇨ **Jews/Judeans,** 1:19-28. Note that the wording of this verse, as often in John, implies a certain distance between Jesus, a Galilean, and the Judeans from the south.

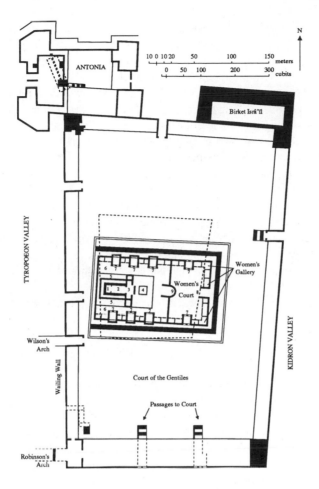

2:14 Diagram of the Temple of Herod the Great. The temple consisted of an immense, flat, somewhat irregular quadrangle, roughly 1,000 feet wide and 1,500 feet long. In the smaller area in the middle were the interior courts. There were the temple building (#1-3), the altar of sacrifice (#4), and the areas where the actual worship of the Judean people took place (#7-9). The large outer area, called the Court of the Gentiles, was enclosed on three sides by columned porches, and on the south by a large covered structure (sometimes referred to as a basilica) that was open to the court. It was undoubtedly in this place, which provided shelter from sun and rain, where the sellers and buyers gathered and where the incident described in John 2:14 took place. Diagram by Parrot Graphics.

2:14-16 Scholars have been unable to decide whether this incident represents an attempt at reforming the temple (often called the "cleansing") or a prophetic action symbolizing the temple's destruction. It is one of the few incidents recorded in all four Gospels, though the accounts are quite divergent in both content and chronology. John alone places it early in Jesus' public career.

73

While the temple was obviously a religious center in ancient Israel, it was also the central economic and political reality in the society. ⇨ **Temple,** 2:13-25. It was the center of a redistributive economy in which the economic surplus was effectively drained from the rural areas. Both John and Mark (the source of the accounts in Matthew and Luke) agree that Jesus attacked both money changers and others buying and selling in the temple. The sacrificial animals for sale would have been bought by those who either could not or preferred not to bring suitable animals from distant homes. Money changers provided the Tyrian coinage in which the temple tax had to be paid in place of the Roman coins in general use (*m. Bekh.* 8.7). In Mark's Gospel Jesus accuses the buyers of making what should be a house of prayer into a den of social bandits (Greek *lestai,* usually translated "robbers"). In John, however, Jesus claims that the temple has been made a house of trade (Greek *emporion*). Whether temple trade was dishonest or not has often been debated by modern scholars, but the different terms used in Mark and John would have been synonymous and unambiguous in the minds of ancient peasants. For many peasants, *all* traders or merchants were dishonorable extortioners and presumed to be dishonest.

The words of Jesus here may be a reference to Zech. 14:21, which looked forward to the day when there will be no traders in the house of the Lord of hosts. An action of the sort described in vv. 14-16 would have been a serious public challenge to persons in charge of the temple that could hardly be overlooked.

2:17-22 The notice that Jesus made a whip of cords suggests genuine anger to Westerners. However, the quotation from Ps. 69:9 remembered by the disciples suggests that more is involved. Drawing upon the tradition to interpret contemporary events was an honorable (male) thing to do. Such quotations were often given in truncated form, however, because audiences could be depended on to fill in the missing sections. ⇨ **Poetry,** 1:1-18. One value of this device is that by forcing the audience to supply the missing element, it forced their attention upon it and thereby highlighted its significance. The missing part of the quotation in Ps. 69:9 says this: ". . . the insults of those who insult you have fallen on me." The implication is that Jesus has taken upon himself the shame that has been directed at God. Since shame must always be avenged (⇨ **Honor and Shame,** 5:31-47), Jesus takes upon himself the task of restoring the honor of God.

At some points in John considerable hostility between Jesus and temple personnel is implied (8:59; 11:56), although at other points he teaches openly in the temple courts (18:20). In 8:48 Jesus is called a "Samaritan," an epithet that would have had antitemple overtones. The notices in both v. 17 and v. 22 that the disciples "remembered" also indicate that retrospective reflection is being used to interpret actions and sayings of Jesus. Such ability to understand retrospectively what Jesus was about was shared by members of John's antisociety, it seems. It was attributed to the presence of the "other advocate" (Greek *parakletos*) now present in the group; see **Notes** at 14:16.

The response from the Judeans demanding a sign is clearly a public challenge put to Jesus. His response, in the form of a cryptic riddle, is a riposte designed to make his challengers look foolish. ⇨ **Challenge and Riposte,** 7:14-24. That the riposte has been successful, at least in the minds of the (retrospectively percep-tive) disciples, is indicated by the author's notice that it elicited belief.

2:23-25 The signs spoken of here are not specified, though the power of signs to elicit belief is what prompts John's stories about them (20:30-31). Nonetheless, the following story will suggest that signs must be supplemented by teaching and explanation. That may account for the curious comment here about Jesus not fully entrusting himself to others. The claim that he knew what was in everyone is a claim to divine power since only God truly knows the secrets of the heart (Ps. 44:21; Rom. 2:16).

✧ *Reading Scenarios:* John 2:13-25
Pilgrimage, 2:13-25

A pilgrimage is a religious journey to some hallowed shrine. It normally entails consecrated persons traveling to sacred places in order to experience the divinely sacred, most often at sacred times. (Note: what is "sacred" is what is exclusive to a human or to God, what is set apart for a person or for God.) What makes a pil-grimage different from a vacation trip is that the whole pilgrimage process derives from religious responsibility, whether by divine command, divine revela-tion, or reverence for ancestors and ancestral heroes. In Israel there were shrines rooted in Israelite kinship religion (for example, the tombs of the patriarchs in Hebron, of David in Jerusalem, of Joseph in Samaria, of Rachel near Bethlehem, and the like). And there was the central shrine of political religion in Jerusalem.

Israelite males were obliged by Mosaic command to go on pilgrimage to Jerusalem three times annually: "at the festival of unleavened bread, at the festi-val of weeks, and at the festival of booths"—that is, Passover, Pentecost, and Sukkoth (Deut. 16:16). This meant traveling to the central city of Judea, Jerusalem, in the spring, summer, and fall. During the time of the Maccabees in the second century B.C.E. a winter pilgrimage festival was added to the previous three, the commemoration of the rededication of the temple (Hanukkah). Accord-ing to the Hellenist Israelite Philo of Alexandria, the reason Moses commanded pilgrimages was the following:

> . . . he [Moses] does not permit those who desire to perform sacrifices in their
> own houses to do so, but he orders all men to rise up, even from the furthest
> boundaries of the earth, and to come to this Temple, by which command he
> is at the same time testing their dispositions most severely; for he who was
> not about to offer sacrifice in a pure and holy spirit would never endure to
> quit his country, and his friends, and relations, and emigrate into a distant
> land, but would be likely, being under the influence of a more powerful
> attraction than that towards piety, to continue attached to the society of his

most intimate friends and relations as portions of himself, to which he was most closely attached. And the most evident proof of this may be found in the events which actually took place. For innumerable companies of men from a countless variety of cities, some by land and some by sea, from east and from west, from the north and from the south, came to the Temple at every festival. (*Special Laws* 1.12.68–69)

What benefits do they find in such pilgrimage? Again Philo reports they come

as if to some common refuge and safe asylum from the troubles of this most busy and painful life, seeking to find tranquillity, and to procure a remission of and respite from those cares by which from their earliest infancy they had been hampered and weighed down, and so, by getting breath as it were, to pass a brief time in cheerful festivities, being filled with good hopes and enjoying the leisure of that most important and necessary vocation which consists in forming a friendship with those hitherto unknown, but now initiated by boldness and a desire to honor God, and forming a combination of actions and a union of dispositions so as to join in sacrifices and libations to the most complete confirmation of mutual good will. (*Special Laws* 1.12.69–70)

. . . because in such assemblies and in a cheerful course of life there are thus established seasons of delight unconnected with any sorrow or depression supporting both body and soul; the one by pleasure and the other by the opportunities for philosophical study which they afford. (*Special Laws* 2.33.214)

Josephus describes the pilgrimage obligation and its outcomes as follows:

Let those that live as remote as the bounds of the land which the Hebrews shall possess, come to that city where the Temple shall be, and this three times in a year that they may give thanks to God for his former benefits, and may entreat him for those they shall want hereafter; and let them, by this means, maintain a friendly correspondence with one another by such meetings and feastings together—for it is a good thing for those that are of the same stock, and under the same institution of laws, not to be unacquainted with each other; which acquaintance will be maintained by thus conversing together, and by seeing and talking with one another, and so renewing the memorials of this union; for if they do not thus converse together continually, they will appear like mere strangers to one another. (*Ant.* 4.8.7, 203–4)

The point being made by both of these witnesses (who themselves participated in pilgrimages to Jerusalem around the time of Jesus) was that such sacred journeys were exhilarating experiences. Pilgrims typically leave the demands of conventional social structure far behind and enter another world. Everyday norms of social status, hierarchy, and interaction are abandoned in favor of the development of spontaneous association and shared experiences. A temporary state of what is termed *communitas* can be reached, as the pilgrim enters a special time, set apart from the everyday, which is kept in abeyance. (For a comparison of the *communitas* experience and life in an antisociety ⇨ **Antisociety,** 1:35-51.) Pilgrims frequently avoid the overt display of status differences by the wearing of standard clothes and converging on a sacred site for the common purpose of festive worship.

Thus, pilgrimages are precisely those occasions when people can temporarily escape the constraints of everyday social concerns and structures. The experience of travel in a society that insists on immobility, the constant possibility of encountering the new in a society that values the old, elements of implicit comparison between one's customary home values and behavior and those of the magnificent shrine center and its visitors, all produce an interactive process of response to what is encountered on the journey and at the goal. ⇨ **Networking,** 1:43-51. Returning home, the pilgrim can only feel excitement and exhilaration. This would hold even for Israel and its localized political religion.

It is such feelings of excitement and exhilaration that John evokes in his ancient Mediterranean audience by mention of Israel's pilgrimages and feasts.

Temple, 2:13-25

In the ancient Middle East, a temple was a building complex constructed according to a divinely revealed plan to serve as a worthy residence for a visiting divinity who dwelled in the sky over the temple on the other side of the firmament. The building of a temple generally served as the founding event for the development of a Middle Eastern city. In such temple cities, there were no citizens. Instead, residents of the city, from the king down, were all servants of the God(s) who was (were) accessible in the temple. Jerusalem, along with a number of other eastern Mediterranean cities, was a Middle Eastern temple city of this sort, even during the time of Herod the Great. The social institution represented by the temple was political religion in the form of a theocracy.

To understand how the temple functioned, we might begin with how the palace worked, for the temple is a replication of the palace. What this means is that temple personnel, temple interactions, and temple activities follow the pattern of palace personnel, interactions, and activities. For the God(s) accessible in the temple stood in the same relationship to their subjects (all the residents of the temple city and temple region) as the king did to the populace he governed. Thus, if the palace houses a king with a large body of servants, from prime minister to royal slaves running royal farms to feed the palace household and army alike, then the temple houses a God who is a divine monarch with a large body of servants ranging hierarchically from primary majordomo (high priest), subsidiary servants (priests, Levites), an army with officers and soldiers, to temple slaves working temple lands to feed the God (sacrificial animals), the temple household, and staff alike. The Hellenistic, Greco-Roman polis was not a temple city founded at the behest of a deity. Rather, the ancient polis was usually founded by some heroic figure(s), while more recent ones were founded by benevolent kings. In either case, such cities were not founded by a deity. Further, the range of Greco-Roman temples and their gods were usually the concern of local elite families and not of a distinctive priesthood serving a palace-like temple. The important thing to note is that, in the ancient Mediterranean, in no case were temples directly for the benefit of worshipers, just as palaces are not directly for the benefit of loyal subjects. Temples were for God(s), palaces were for kings. It was at the direction of God and king that the populace had access to these pre-eminent persons in their buildings.

Moreover, the eastern Mediterranean temple provided a locus of divine presence, a cosmic center often understood to be the navel of the world. Since the deity was to be found above the firmament directly above the temple, it was the place where sky and earth converged, hence the control center for the deity's dealings with the world. As such, it legitimated both the monarch chosen to serve God and the people chosen by God for divine service.

The Jerusalem temple followed the design of Middle Eastern temples that traced back to Mesopotamia. The temple thus replicated in physical space what was understood to be the holy order of creation. Reaching outward in concentric circles from the Holy of Holies to the Court of the Gentiles (that is, outsiders; an inscription warned foreigners not to go beyond this latter area on pain of death), the temple precincts replicated an ethnocentric view of the cosmos:

> There are ten degrees of holiness: The Land of Israel is holier than any other land. . . . The walled cities (of the land of Israel) are still more holy. . . . Within the walls (of Jerusalem) is still more holy. . . . The Temple Mount is still more holy. . . . The rampart is still more holy. . . . The Court of the Women is still more holy. . . . The court of the Israelites is still more holy. . . . The Court of the Priests is still more holy. . . . Between the Porch and the Altar is still more holy. . . . The Sanctuary is still more holy. . . . The holy of holies is still more holy. . . . (*m. Kelim* 1.6-9)

What this makes clear is that the temple itself functioned not only as a religious central place for all of Israel, but also as the map for social relations between various groups of Israelites and between Israelites and all others. It articulated the structured social relations that were the correlative of Israel's ethnocentric view of creation.

Equally important was the political and economic significance of the temple in Jerusalem. Just as the king collected taxes for the maintenance of the elites and their institutions, so did the deity. Jerusalem was the center of Israel's political economy. This meant that the roles, goals, and values of the polity serve to articulate and express economics. The chief beneficiaries of the economy were the central political personages, whether in palace or temple. The system of taxation and tribute looks to the well-being of elites. It would be hard to overestimate the import of the temple as the center of a redistributive political economy. With large treasuries and storehouses for material of all sorts, the temple functioned somewhat like a national bank and storage depot. It became the repository of large quantities of money and goods extracted from the surplus product of the peasant economy. Because most of the temple precincts were inaccessible to all but a handful of priests and were closely guarded against intrusion, they offered a high level of security for the economic resources of the political and religious elite.

It is important to note, then, that in the first-century Mediterranean world, corporate entities such as "the temple" and "the palace" were more than simply structures or locales for certain kinds of activities. They were heavily invested with social significance. In fact, they were personified and viewed as moral persons. They had ascribed honor just as did any family or individual and could be insulted, cursed, hated, and dishonored. By dishonoring the temple, one also dishonored all of its personnel, from high priest down, including the One who commanded its construction and occasionally dwelled there—God.

Jesus' Conversation with Nicodemus Signals the Coming Opposition between Believers Who Have New Life and Unbelievers Who Do Not, 3:1-21

3:1 Now there was a Pharisee named Nicodemus, a leader of the Jews. ²He came to Jesus by night and said to him, "Rabbi, we know that you are a teacher who has come from God; for no one can do these signs that you do apart from the presence of God." ³Jesus answered him, "Very truly, I tell you, no one can see the kingdom of God without being born from above." ⁴Nicodemus said to him, "How can anyone be born after having grown old? Can one enter a second time into the mother's womb and be born?" ⁵Jesus answered, "Very truly, I tell you, no one can enter the kingdom of God without being born of water and Spirit. ⁶What is born of the flesh is flesh, and what is born of the Spirit is spirit. ⁷Do not be astonished that I said to you, 'You must be born from above.' ⁸The wind blows where it chooses, and you hear the sound of it, but you do not know where it comes from or where it goes. So it is with everyone who is born of the Spirit." ⁹Nicodemus said to him, "How can these things be?" ¹⁰Jesus answered him, "Are you a teacher of Israel, and yet you do not understand these things?

11 "Very truly, I tell you, we speak of what we know and testify to what we have seen; yet you do not receive our testimony. ¹²If I have told you about earthly things and you do not believe, how can you believe if I tell you about heavenly things? ¹³No one has ascended into heaven except the one who descended from heaven, the Son of Man. ¹⁴And just as Moses lifted up the serpent in the wilderness, so must the Son of Man be lifted up, ¹⁵that whoever believes in him may have eternal life.

16 "For God so loved the world that he gave his only Son, so that everyone who believes in him may not perish but may have eternal life.

17 "Indeed, God did not send the Son into the world to condemn the world, but in order that the world might be saved through him. ¹⁸Those who believe in him are not condemned; but those who do not believe are condemned already, because they have not believed in the name of the only Son of God. ¹⁹And this is the judgment, that the light has come into the world, and people loved darkness rather than light because their deeds were evil. ²⁰For all who do evil hate the light and do not come to the light, so that their deeds may not be exposed. ²¹But those who do what is true come to the light, so that it may be clearly seen that their deeds have been done in God."

✦ *Notes:* John 3

At the close of our **Notes** about the social dimensions in this entire chapter, (p. 93) we offer indications as to how the whole chapter was composed as a diptych—that is, two scenes standing side by side in parallel fashion. The first scene describes Jesus' conversation at night with Nicodemus, a Pharisee "ruler," about becoming a child of God (born anew/from above) and receiving new life thanks to God's sending his Son, the Son of Man from the sky (vv. 1-21). The second scene describes John the prophet witnessing to the prominence of the Son sent by God from above with new life exclusively for those who believe in the Son (vv. 22-36). This time John witnesses before a Judean and his own disciples.

✦ *Notes:* John 3:1-21

3:1-2 Nicodemus is called a "ruler" *(archon)* of the Judeans (✿ **Jews/Judeans,** 1:19-28). While the word may mean that he was a member of the Sanhedrin, the label surely identifies him as a member of the urban elite. His coming at night (note how this is emphasized in 19:39) indicates that John wishes to contrast the light that Jesus provides Nicodemus with the darkness in which he arrives (3:19-21; John later mentions his fear of his fellow Judean Pharisees, 7:13; 12:42). Some believe night was the typical time for scribal discussion. In context, it was the proper time to learn about the sky as opposed to the earth (see v. 10). Like a number of other characters in this Gospel, Nicodemus functions as a kind of foil who offers Jesus the opportunity for an explanatory monologue.

The title Nicodemus gives to Jesus, "Rabbi," is an honorific one (used of disciples for their "teacher," as specified in 1:38; see 1:49; 4:31; 9:2; 11:8; John's disciples address him in this way, 2:26). It would be somewhat startling, if not highly improbable, for a member of the Jerusalem elite to address a Galilean villager in this way. Nathanael's comment (1:46, "Can anything good come out of Nazareth?") is more appropriate. Note that in 7:15 Jesus is said to be uneducated.

The reference to "signs" points to Nicodemus as representative of those Judeans mentioned in 2:23-24, who believe on the basis of signs, but to whom Jesus would not entrust himself; see 8:30-59. Nicodemus correctly asserts that it is God's presence that makes the signs possible (5:19). The term *from God* is in the emphatic position in Greek, which underscores the point. As is typical of John's ironic style of storytelling, little does Nicodemus realize what is really involved in his noting that Jesus is "a teacher who has come from God"—the underlying premise of the whole discussion that follows.

3:3 The entire conversation with Nicodemus is punctuated by Jesus giving his word of honor before making a statement: "Very truly, I tell you . . ." (vv. 3, 5, 11); see **Notes** at 1:50-51. Here it underscores Jesus' comment involving a well-known play on the ambiguous Greek word *anothen.* Like the English phrase "from the top," the Greek means both "again" (as when a conductor says: "Take it from the top") and "from above" (as when a furniture mover tells his crew: "Take it from the top"). Antilanguage regales in puns, and this Greek word is an important one for John's argument.

It is critical to recognize that the topic here is *birth.* Birth status was the single, all-important factor in determining a person's honor rating. Ascribed honor, the honor derived from one's status at birth, was simply a given. It usually stayed with a person for life. ✿ **Honor and Shame,** 5:31-47. Small gains and losses occurred throughout life, but one's basic ascribed honor status usually was not substantially altered. This meant that aside from extraordinary circumstances, a nonelite peasant remained a nonelite peasant until death, and a member of the elite remained a member of the elite until death. To be born *over again,* born for a second time (one meaning of *anothen*), however unthinkable that event might be, would alter one's ascribed honor status in a very fundamental way. A new ascribed honor status would derive from a new birth.

Thus, a second birth, especially if it differed substantially in honor level from the first birth, would be a life-changing event of staggering proportions. Something like this occurred when elite Romans adopted slaves or other nonelite persons, made them legal heirs, gave them the family name, and hence reestablished their honor status. While Israelites did not practice adoption, later scribal Pharisee sources tell us that for all legal purposes a circumcised proselyte is to be considered a newborn child (*b. Yeb.* 22a, 48b, 62a, 97b, *b. Bekh.* 47a). Such proselytes were usually males forced by circumstances to marry into an Israelite family. While their new status might entail legally noted honor consequences within the new group, such was not the case in daily life. The fact that separate legal directives *(halakoth)* existed for proselytes demonstrates that they were not seen as ingroup members in every respect.

However, a child born into the kin group always has the honor status of the family into which he or she has been born (see 5:23). In talking about being born again, therefore, Jesus is talking about a new level of honor. The quality of the honor is underscored by the second meaning of the pun.

To be born "from above"—that is, to be born of the sky, of the realm of God— is to belong to that realm, to become a veritable child of God. This, of course, is to acquire an honor status of the very highest sort. As John previously noted of Jesus, "to all who received him, who believed in his *name,* he gave power to become children of God" (1:12; Matt. 5:9 notes a tradition according to which God makes peacemakers his children). Thus, whatever honor status a person might have in Israelite society, being born "from above" would re-create that person at a whole new level. In addition, since all children of the same father share that father's honor status, differences in status among "the children of God" obviously disappear, except for the firstborn. (Note a similar equalizing idea in Paul, where baptism gives one the legal status of heir and thus levels the honor distinctions among all God's children, Gal 3:26-29. By using the Greco-Roman metaphor of adoption, Paul notes this same change in honor status for those who become God's kin, Gal. 4:5.)

3:4-5 While Nicodemus obviously has not fully comprehended the possibilities in the term *anothen,* he does recognize that something very radical is being proposed. Once again his comment becomes the occasion for Jesus to clarify his earlier remark. And once more Jesus gives his word of honor: "Very truly, I tell you." In his explanation, Jesus says one must be born of water and Spirit to enter the kingdom of God. To understand what is involved here, one must read the whole passage. First, Jesus notes that he is really speaking of "celestial" or "sky" things (v. 12). Neither here nor anyplace else in John does the "kingdom of God" refer to a forthcoming theocracy. John offers no indication of Jesus recruiting apostles to proclaim some forthcoming rule of God. Rather, as Jesus explains in vv. 13-15, the sky things about which he speaks refer to experiencing new life through the Son of Man, who came down from the sky, and, after being lifted up, ascends to the Father only to descend repeatedly to his disciples and friends (chaps. 20-21). The group for whom this Gospel was written consists of an anti-society of those disciples and friends of the resurrected Jesus who continue to experience his "descents."

On the other hand, as promised in 1:51, the Son of Man on whom persons can ascend and descend to God is Jesus, who now offers access to the sky in his post-death appearances. This access is attributed to birth of "water and Spirit." The significant bestowal both of water and Spirit by Jesus occurs when he is "lifted up," John's pun for Jesus' crucifixion. On the cross, Jesus is not said to "die," but rather to bow his head and give over his spirit (19:30). Similarly, while still "lifted up," his side was pierced and out came blood and water (19:34), not just blood. The focus here is on the water, since reference to the availability of his flesh and blood will be noted elsewhere (chap. 6). Furthermore, note that both the water and the Spirit in chapter 19 come "from above," from Jesus on the cross! Hence, in John's Gospel, it will be the lifting up of the Son of Man that provides the water and Spirit that give new life to those who believe in the "lifted up" Son of Man (vv. 14-15). To be born of water and the Spirit and thus enter the kingdom now means to believe "into," hence, experience, Jesus as God's Son, who descends from the sky. Thanks to the experience of Jesus in alternate states of consciousness in John's group, one can enjoy the new life of the children of God. ⇨ **Seeing Jesus: Alternate States of Consciousness,** 20:1-29.

It is a matter of scholarly controversy whether "water and Spirit" here equally allude to the baptismal rite that marked entrance into the groups succeeding the Jesus movement group. For example, the association of Spirit and baptism appears in 1 Cor. 12:13. And baptism and new birth are associated in Titus 3:5, where the new birth is said to be effected by the Holy Spirit. While in the following parallel scene of this chapter, John and Jesus are explicitly reported to be baptizing (see **Notes** on 3:22-23), there is no mention of that behavior here. Rather, the important point here is that through a new birth effected by "water and the Spirit," those attached to Jesus gain a whole new honor status as kinfolk of God.

3:6-8 The idea that what is born of flesh is flesh and what is born of Spirit is spirit accords well with ancient physiognomics. The ancients believed that like begets like. The Old Latin and Old Syriac versions of this passage thus add an explanatory note: "What is born of flesh is flesh *because* it is born of flesh." Note that there is a subtle difference between being born "of Spirit" and the common modern notion of a "spiritual" birth. To be born "of" Spirit is like being born "of" Joseph—that is, it is the result of seed and therefore creates a like kind. The seed determines one's characteristics and makes one related to the donor. It thus establishes kinship. Note 1 John 3:9, where one begotten of God is said to have God's seed inside of him or her. Such persons cannot sin because they have been born "of God." In 1 Peter 1:23 the new birth is said to be the result of imperishable seed, unlike the perishable seed that produced the first birth. The notion of being "born of God" is prominent in 1 John: 2:29; 3:9; 4:7; 5:1, 4, 18. See the **Notes** below at 8:15 and 8:19-20.

Given this belief in like begetting like, the new birth from above should not be surprising; it cannot be from the flesh, because that would not result in kinship with God. How the new Spirit-birth happens is not specified. It is simply said to be as mysterious as the wind was to ancient people. Note the play on words here using the Greek word *pneuma,* which means "spirit" and "wind" as well as "breath."

3:9-13 Nicodemus's puzzlement leads to a further explanatory speech by Jesus. It begins with what would be a serious insult if spoken in public. Here in private the put-down points to Nicodemus as the presumably higher-status, learned person really unqualified to assess the matter at hand. In antiquity this sort of put-down was directed at those interested in things of the sky yet unable to properly understand life on earth. Consider the following well-known instances of the contrast. Thales fell into a pit while studying the stars, and was then addressed by the philosopher Diogenes: "For you, O Thales, cannot see the things at your feet but seek to know what is in the sky above" (Diogenes Laertius 1.34). Again, when Nectanebus sought to teach Alexander the Great astrology, Alexander told him, "Not knowing the things of the earth, you seek out the things of the sky" (Ps. Callisthenes, *Life of Alexander* 1.14; see 2.41). Cicero notes: "The famous words of Achilles in the Iphigenia: The astral signs that are observed above, When Goat or Scorpion of Jove arise, Or other beasts; all gaze intent thereon, Nor ever see what lies before their feet!" (Cicero, *De Republica* 1.30; for a similar contrast, note Wis. 9:16: "We can hardly guess at what is on earth . . . but who has traced out what is in the sky?" or 4 Ezra 4:2: [The angel Uriel] "said to me: 'Your understanding has utterly failed regarding this world, and do you think you can comprehend the way of the Most High?'"; and finally, Seneca, *Apocolocyntosis* 8.3: one of the gods says to Hercules: "He [Claudius] does not know what he does in his own room, and yet he 'gazes intently on the traces of the sky'"). Thus, given the cliché quality of the statement, the contrast is not between earthly and celestial information, but between the questioner and the one who possesses the information.

For "Very truly, I tell you . . . " (v. 11), see the **Note** at 3:3. Jesus once more emphatically puts his honor on the line. In vv. 5-8 Jesus explained to Nicodemus the import of being born "from above" by stating that it is comparable to birth "from flesh." Jesus' comment on the latter, the birth that is earthly, did not make much of an impact on Nicodemus. Hence, Jesus sees little chance that the former, birth "from above," will make any impact either. But John makes clear that "above" (celestial) and "below" (earthly) are to be contrasted in the same way that "of flesh" and "of God" were contrasted earlier. Being born "from above" and being born "of God" are two ways of saying the same thing. Being born "from below" and being born "of the flesh" are likewise the same thing.

Throughout this discussion it is important to recognize that where a person was from determined both character and status. See the **Notes** at 1:47-48 and 8:12-20; ✧ **Lineage and Stereotypes,** 8:31-59. One could not aspire to ascend to the sky (assume divine honor status) unless one was originally from that region. Attempting to do so was the sin of the King of Babylon (Isa. 14:12-14), whose arrogance was severely punished. The constant refrain in John's Gospel that Jesus had come "from" or was sent "from" God thus makes sense in this context. He will return, and can return, because that is where he is from. For him, returning implies no reaching for honor beyond the level of his origin.

For John, then, " to enter the kingdom of God" does not refer to experiencing political theocracy, with Jesus as Messiah. Rather, to enter the kingdom of God is to see the open sky and the angels on high; this is the alternate state-of-consciousness experience described at the close of the Gospel with Jesus' appearances to his friends. Thanks to the Son of Man, this is the experience reserved exclusively for those born "from above," "of God," hence of those who have become "children of God."

3:14-16 Moses' lifting up of a bronze serpent for all Israelites to see served as a healing remedy for the snake bites of Israel's wilderness generation (Num. 21:8-9); so, too, the lifting up of the Son of Man. John constantly refers to Jesus' being "lifted up," where the Synoptic authors speak of "dying." What is important in the antilanguage imagery is the spatial dimension. Spatial separation from what is below is significant here; see the **Notes** for vv. 12-13 above. John's love of irony is thus evident in seeing Jesus' humiliation and death as an exaltation, lifting Jesus above what is of the earth.

Throughout John's Gospel there is a concern for "life." ✧ **Life,** 1:1-18. Johannine scholarship commonly points out that while the duration of life (endless) is no doubt involved here, it is the *quality* of life, life of a new and better sort, that is central to John's antilanguage. It is the life that God lives and that the Son has from the Father (5:26; 6:57). The Gospel was written to maintain this life in John's antisociety (20:31). This life emerges as Jesus bows his head and breathes out "his spirit" (19:30). Jesus' final breath is in fact the new breath of life, surpassing in quality the original "breath of life" with which God animated humankind (Gen. 2:7). In an interpersonal setting, Jesus' friends receive this Spirit when Jesus "breathes" on them (20:22; see the **Notes** at 3:6-8 on the meaning of *pneuma* as wind, breath, and spirit).

This is the new life that energizes members of the Johannine group and animates the antisociety. Talk of life is thus "antilanguage"—language about a social alternative to the "world" (Israelite or Judean society) that members of the Johannine group have abandoned. ✧ **World/Cosmos = Israelite Society,** 17:1-26. ✧ **Antilanguage,** 1:19-28; see also the **Introduction** on antilanguage and antisociety.

85

3:17-21 John repeatedly reports that Jesus said that he was "sent" into the world. In the Synoptic Gospels, Jesus is "sent" to Israel (Matt. 15:24; Luke 4:43). The language about being sent is patronage language. Patrons "send" clients or brokers to carry out their business. ⇨ **Patronage,** 5:21-30. To be "saved" is an equivalent term for enjoying "eternal life" in John. See the **Note** immediately above.

In much of the Gospel of John, particularly in the first half, there is a positive concern for the "world" (1:29; 3:17; 4:42; 6:14, 33, 51; 8:12; 9:5; 10:36; 11:27; 12:47). But at other points, and particularly in the second half of the Gospel, the "world" is to be judged and often is hostile (7:7; 9:39; 12:31, 35-36; 14:17; 15:19; 16:8-11, 20, 33; 17:14, 16; 18:36). In 17:18 Jesus sends his followers out into the world, but they do not belong to the world (17:16) and indeed are hated by the world (17:14). In 16:33 Jesus says that he has conquered the world. Note that the term *world* in John usually refers to the surrounding Israelite or Judean society from which he and his community are alienated. ⇨ **World/Cosmos = Israelite Society,** 17:1-26.

This kind of antilanguage draws boundaries between an antisociety and the larger society from which it is alienated. So also does contrastive language about some people being exposed to the light in order to reveal their evil deeds while others love light, obviously because they do the truth. Boundary language drawn in such stark contrasts (light-dark, good-evil) suggests sharp division and strong social conflict. We see insiders and outsiders here with sharp boundaries in between. ⇨ **Love/Hate,** 3:1-21. ⇨ **In-group** and **Out-group,** 15:18—16:4a.

Secrecy and lying are common social strategies in honor-shame societies where damaging information must be kept from others in order to avoid public shame. Doors and windows of houses are kept open during the daytime to show neighbors that nothing unseemly is being hidden. Of course, exaggerated displays of openness often raise suspicion to the contrary. God is the only real knower of all that is hidden, but since hidden things can contain serious danger for everyone, any evil exposed to the public eye brings great relief to the neighborhood. Light, which distinguishes good from evil, would thus offer comfort to all. ⇨ **Secrecy,** 7:1-9.

In the Synoptic Gospels good acts make one "like" God. In John, however, good acts derive from kinship with God. Since birth determined character, those born well act well, and doing good deeds was prima facie evidence of birth from above.

✧ *Reading Scenarios:* John 3:1-21

Love/Hate, 3:1-21

First-century Mediterranean persons were strongly group-oriented. They quickly learned that a meaningful human existence required total reliance on the groups in which they found themselves embedded. Most important were the kin group, the village group, the neighborhood, and/or the factions one might join.

In various ways these groups provided a person with a sense of self, with a con-science (always external to the individual in honor-shame societies), and with a sense of identity. Such first-century Mediterranean persons always needed others to know who they were and to support or restrain their choices of behavior. The group, in other words, was an *external* conscience. Because of this, "truc" or enlightened behavior would always match what the group valued.

An important result of such group orientation was an anti-introspective way of being. Persons had little concern for things psychological. What we would call psychological states were usually ascribed to spirits, good and bad. It follows that in such cultural arrangements words referring to internal states always connote a corresponding external expression as well. For example, the verb "to know" always involved some experience of the object known. "To covet" always involved the attempt to take what one desired (hence it is best translated "to steal").

Two words nearly always assigned to *internal* states in our society are *love* and *hate*. To understand what they meant in the first-century Mediterranean world, however, it is necessary to recognize both their group orientation and their corre-sponding *external* expression. The term *love,* for example, is best translated "group attachment," or "attachment to some person." To *love* the light is to be attached to the enlightened group. There may or may not be affection, but it is the inward feeling of attachment, along with the outward behavior bound up with such attachment, that love entails. So naturally those who love or are attached to the group do what the group values.

Correspondingly, *hate* would mean "disattachment," "nonattachment," or "indifference." Indifference is perhaps the strongest negative attitude that one can entertain in Mediterranean interpersonal relations (see, e.g., Rev. 3:16). Once again, there may or may not be feelings of repulsion. But it is the inward feeling of nonattachment, along with the outward behavior bound up with not being attached to a group (and the persons that are part of that group), that hate entails. To hate the light would thus be to be disattached from the enlightened group or to be attached to an outside group and to behave accordingly. Those who "hate the light" (3:20) thus do what the enlightened group considers evil.

Since "to hate" is the same as "to disattach oneself from a group," one can describe departure from one's family "for the sake of Jesus and the Gospel" as either "hating" one's father, mother, wife, and children (Luke 14:26), loving "father or mother more than me" (Matt. 10:37), "leaving everything" (Matt. 19:27; Mark 10:28), or more precisely "leaving one's house" (Luke 18:28). Paul's famous triad in 1 Cor. 13:13 (faith, hope, love) might be best translated: "personal loyalty, enduring trust in another, group attachment," and, of course, the greatest of these is group attachment.

From a historical and social point of view, it is important to note that in the ancient world, love extended only to other members of the in-group, not to those outside the group. This holds for the Golden Rule (Lev. 19:18: "You shall love your neighbor as yourself," borrowed from Mesopotamian tradition), where one's "neighbor" is a fellow Israelite, an in-group person. In Israel's traditions from the time of Jesus, for example, we read about Isaac's final words to Esau and Jacob as follows: "Be loving of your brothers as a man loves himself, with each man seeking for his brother what is good for him . . . loving each other as themselves" (Jub. 36:4-5). This sentiment is also apparent in Jesus-Messiah groups: Mark 12:31; Rom. 13:9; Gal. 5:14; 1 Thess. 4:9. The well-known parable of the Good Samaritan in Luke 10:29-37 simply extends Israel's in-group to include Samaritans; see **Notes** at 4:5-6.

In sum, when John speaks of the world hating believers, or hating light and loving darkness, he is using the same language of attachment and disattachment, loyalty and disloyalty to his enlightened group. He is drawing the strongest possible contrast between his own group and all outsiders. This topic will be highlighted later when John describes what Jesus said and did at his last meal with his friends (13:1—17:26).

Fictive Kinship/Ascribed Honor/New Birth, 3:1-21

Kinship norms regulate human relationships within and among family groups. At each stage of life, from birth to death, these norms determine the roles we play and the ways we interact with each other. Moreover, what it meant to be a father, mother, husband, wife, sister, or brother was vastly different in ancient agrarian societies from what we know in the modern industrial world.

Note, for example, the lists in Lev. 18:6-18 and 20:11-21. By New Testament times these had become lists of prohibited marriage partners. They include a variety of in-laws for whom we do not prohibit marriage today (e.g., see Mark 6:18). Moreover, for us marriage is generally neolocal (a new residence is established by the bride and groom) and exogamous (outside the kin group). In antiquity marriage was patrilocal (the bride moved in with her husband's family) and endogamous (marrying as close to the conjugal family as incest laws permitted). Cross-cousin marriages on the paternal side of the family were the ideal, and genealogies always followed the paternal line of descent.

Since marriages were fundamentally the fusion of two extended families, the honor of each family played a key role. Marriage contracts negotiated the fine points and ensured balanced reciprocity. Defensive strategies were used to prevent loss of males (and females as well whenever possible) to another family. Unlike U.S. families, which are essentially consuming units, the family was the producing unit of antiquity. Therefore, the loss of a member through marriage required compensation in the form of a bride-price. By far the strongest unit of loyalty was the descent group of brothers and sisters. It was here that the strongest emotional ties existed, rather than between husband and wife.

Socially and psychologically, all family members were embedded in the family unit. Preserving family integrity, physically, socially, and morally, was the paramount value. Individualism simply did not exist. Males acted toward the outside on behalf of the whole unit, while females focused on the inside, often involved with the management of the family purse as well. Females not embedded in a male (widows without sons, divorcees) were women without honor and often viewed as more male than female by the society (note the attitude toward widows in 1 Tim. 5:3–16).

Religion in the first century was embedded in either politics or kinship—political religion or domestic religion. Domestic religion took its social cues from the household or family system then in vogue. Thus, extant household or family forms and norms provided the early Jesus-Messiah movement with one of its basic images of social identity and cohesion.

In antiquity, the extended family meant everything. It was not only the source of one's honor status in the community, but also functioned as the primary economic, religious, educational, and social network. Loss of connection to the family meant the loss of these vital networks as well as loss of connection to the land. But a surrogate family, what anthropologists call a fictive kin group, could serve many of the same functions as a biological family. The Johannine antisociety functioned as a surrogate family. It transcended the normal categories of birth, class, race, sex, education, wealth, and power; hence, it was inclusive in a startling new way. For those already detached from their biological families (for example, noninheriting sons who went to the city), the surrogate family became a place of refuge. For the well-connected, however, particularly the city elite, giving up one's biological family for the surrogate family focused on Jesus as Messiah to come or as living Lord was a decision that could cost one dearly. It meant an irrevocable break with the networks on which the elite lifestyle depended.

John's Affirmation of Jesus' Superiority Signals Coming Opposition between Believers Who Have New Life and Unbelievers Who Do Not, 3:22-36

22 After this Jesus and his disciples went into the Judean countryside, and he spent some time there with them and baptized. [23]John also was baptizing at Aenon near Salim because water was abundant there; and people kept coming and were being baptized [24]—John, of course, had not yet been thrown into prison.

25 Now a discussion about purification arose between John's disciples and a Jew. [26]They came to John and said to him, "Rabbi, the one who was with you across the Jordan, to whom you testified, here he is baptizing, and all are going to him." [27]John answered, "No one can receive anything except what has been given from heaven. [28]You yourselves are my witnesses that I said, 'I am not the Messiah, but I have been sent ahead of him.' [29]He who has the bride is the bridegroom. The friend of the bridegroom, who stands and hears him, rejoices greatly at the bridegroom's voice. For this reason my joy has been fulfilled. [30]He must increase, but I must decrease."

31 The one who comes from above is above all; the one who is of the earth belongs to the earth and speaks about earthly things. The one who comes from heaven is above all. [32]He testifies to what he has seen and heard, yet no one accepts his testimony. [33]Whoever has accepted his testimony has

certified this, that God is true. [34]He whom God has sent speaks the words of God, for he gives the Spirit without measure. [35]The Father loves the Son and has placed all things in his hands. [36]Whoever believes in the Son has eternal life; whoever disobeys the Son will not see life, but must endure God's wrath.

✦ *Notes:* John 3:22-36

Since many commentators do not treat this section as a parallel scene forming a diptych with the first (3:1-21), they find notorious difficulties of a chronological, historical sort for understanding the development of relationships between Jesus and John the Baptist. They argue that it may be a section misplaced from the Gospel's original opening scenes. Yet in John's Gospel this passage serves as a parallel scene to the previous segment. Nicodemus, the eminent Pharisee teacher, is thus contrasted with John, the prophet who baptized.

3:23 Aenon. Another uncertain site. Some scholars have recently identified it with this place of several springs ("abundant" water) between Sychar (see Jacob's Well, 4:5) and the Jordan River. See the map at 1:28. Photo by Avraham Hay.

3:22-24 The segment opens with information about Jesus and his disciples baptizing in the Judean countryside. However, it is only in 4:2 that the author refocuses the scene by noting that Jesus himself did not baptize anyone; his disciples did the baptizing. The next verse tells of John baptizing. In this Gospel John himself testifies that he was sent by God to baptize with water so that the one greater than he, the Son of God, "might be revealed to Israel" (1:31-34). While readers are not explicitly told why Jesus and his disciples baptized, in the framework of John's prophetic witness, it would seem that Jesus' disciples baptized for the same reason: to reveal Jesus to Israel. Baptism was a revelatory experience for the Johannine community. While baptism in the New Testament usually derives its significance from Jesus' death and resurrection, in John it is a revelatory experience (light) that eventually leads to new birth through the experience of Jesus (see **Notes** on 3:1-21 above; by mid-second century [Justin Martyr, Roman catacomb art] John 3:1-21 was read as having baptismal implications, undoubtedly because of the explicit mention of baptism in 3:22-23).

Baptism as New Birth

The idea that baptism is a "new birth" was symbolized in the Israelite practice of proselyte baptism. Converts were baptized naked, just as a baby is born naked, to symbolize the fact that everything old was being left behind and a new start was being made. In the second century Hippolytus reports that Jesus Messianists followed a similar practice. To preserve decency, men and women were baptized separately:

> And at the hour when the cock crows they shall first pray over the water. When they come to the water, let the water be pure and flowing. And they shall put off their clothes. And they shall baptize the little children first. . . . And next they shall baptize the grown men; and last the women, who shall have loosed their hair and laid aside their gold ornaments. Let no one go down into the water having any alien object with them. (*Apostolic Tradition* 21.1–5)

What is being reenacted here is birth into a new family: the fictive kin group of the Jesus movement. ⇨ **Fictive Kinship/Ascribed Honor/New Birth**, 3:1-21.

3:25-30 Though disputes over purification are really disputes over group boundaries and identity, we are not told specifically what the dispute is about here. ⇨ **Purity/Pollution: Purification Rites,** 3:22-36. Instead, the focus of attention turns directly to Jesus and his group's incursion into John's field of activity. The report to John here indicates that Jesus is a subject of gossip—that is, talk between two parties about an absent third party. Gossip talk is always (implicitly or explicitly) evaluative talk. It discusses people in relation to group values and expectations and in relation to each other. ⇨ **Gossip Network,** 4:1-42.

The larger aim of this passage, then, is to present an evaluation of Jesus. In reporting that Jesus is the subject of evaluative talk, the author introduces his own evaluation, in which he places John in a subordinate position to Jesus. See **Notes** at 1:29-30. John defends Jesus and testifies to the divine origin of his mission. Later calendar makers placed the birth of John the Baptist at June 24 (three days after the summer solstice), on the day light noticeably begins to decrease, and the birth of Jesus at December 25 (three days after the winter solstice), the day light noticeably begins to increase. The notion is also suggested by the fact that the Greek verbs here for "to increase" and "to decrease" are those used for the waxing and waning of light from celestial bodies. For comment on weddings and the "friend of the bridegroom," see **Notes** at 2:1-11.

3:31-36 As in a number of places in John's Gospel, it is difficult to tell who is speaking here. Since the passage parallels the themes of the previous scene (3:1-21), it may well be the author's summary of what has gone before. For the contrast on what is from above and what is from the earth, see the various **Notes** at 3:9-16. The issue here is origin. In antiquity people were always expected to act and speak in accord with their birth status. Thus, the one who is from the earth speaks about the earth. The one from above can testify to what would be known only by one from there. In v. 34 the metaphor changes to one of patrons (who send) and brokers (who do what they are sent to do with the resources they are given). For **Notes** on being "sent," see 3:17-21. God, the patron, gives to the Son, the broker, all things—which he can then distribute in the name of the patron. ⇨ **Patronage,** 5:21-30. Since love means "attachment," hate and wrath mean the opposite: "disattachment." See the **Notes** at 3:17-21. If one rejects the broker, the Son, one naturally loses any attachment with the patron, God.

As indicated at the beginning of this chapter, we now offer a description of the parallel patterns in which the author develops his scenes (after Neyrey 1980). The parallel scenes develop rather identically both as regards contents in general and as regards interest in the person of Jesus in particular. First the parallel contents:

3:1-21	**3:22-36**

1. Occasion
  a) a Pharisee
  b) born of water/spirit
  c) with Jesus
	1. Occasion
	  a) a Judean
	  b) over purification
	  c) with John's disciples

2. Address: "Rabbi . . ."	2. Address: "Rabbi . . ."
3. Christology: "A teacher from God"	3. Christology: "He who was with you . . . to whom you bore testimony, here he is baptizing, and all are going to him"

4. Reply of Jesus
  a) unless you are born *anothen*
  (from above/again)
  b) metaphor of wind (spirit) (v. 8)
	4. Reply of John the Baptist
	  a) unless it is given him from the
	  sky
	  b) metaphor of bridegroom (v. 29)

5. Nicodemus and his eminence: "You a teacher of Israel do not know this?" (v. 10)	5. John the Baptist and Jesus' eminence: "He must increase and I must decrease" (v. 30)

As for parallel themes, largely focused on the person of Jesus:

3:1-21	**3:22-36**
1. Born *anothen* (from above) (3:3, 7)	1. the one coming *anothen* (from above) is above all (3:31)
2. Jesus: the one who came down from sky (3:13)	2. Jesus who comes down from sky (3:31b)
3. opposing types of people—flesh and spirit (3:6); earthly and celestial (3:12)	3. opposing types of people—earthly and celestial (3:31)
4. "We speak of what we know and testify to what we have seen, yet you do not accept our testimony" (3:11)	4. "He testifies to what he has seen and heard, yet no one accepts his testimony" (3:32)
5. God sent the Son (3:17)	5. the one whom God has sent (3:34)
6. "that whoever believes in the Son may have eternal life" (3:15, 16)	6. "Whoever believes in the Son has eternal life" (3:36)
7. Judgment (3:19-21)	7. Judgment (3:36)

✧ *Reading Scenario:* John 3:22-36

Purity/Pollution: Purification Rites, 3:22-36

All enduring human societies provide their members with ways of making sense out of human living. Such ways of making sense out of life are systems of meaning. When something is out of place as determined by the prevailing system of meaning, that something is considered wrong, deviant, senseless. Dirt is matter out of place. When people clean their houses or cars, they simply rearrange matter, returning it to its proper place. The point is, the perception of dirt and the behavior called cleaning both point to the existence of some system according to which there is a proper place for everything. This system of place is one indication of the existence of a larger system for making sense out of human living.

One traditional way of talking about such an overall system of meaning is in terms of a purity system, a system of pure (in place) and impure (out of place) or a system of clean (in place) and unclean (out of place). Pure and impure, clean and unclean, can be predicated of persons, groups, things, times, and places. Such purity distinctions embody the core values of a society and thereby provide clarity of meaning, direction of activity, and consistency for social behavior. What accords with these values and their structural expression in a purity system is considered "pure" and what does not is viewed as "polluted."

Hence pollution, like dirt, refers to what qualifies something or someone as out of place, what does not belong. Purity systems thus provide "maps" designating social definitions or bounded categories in which everything and everybody either fits and is considered clean or does not and is regarded as defiled. As such, these socially contrived maps provide boundaries that fit over individuals, over groups, over the environment, over time, and over space. These boundaries are known to everyone enculturated in the society, so that one knows when one's behavior is "out of bounds." Cleaning, or purification, refers to the process of returning matter (or persons) to its proper place.

Pollution is a way of speaking of something or someone out of place. Purity systems provide "maps" designating social space and time in which everything and everybody either fits and is considered clean or does not and is regarded as defiled. As such, they provide boundaries marking off the places and times where things and people belong. The Israelite Yahwism of Jesus' day provided such maps of: (1) *time,* which specified rules for the Sabbath, when to say the Shema, and when circumcision should be performed; (2) *places,* which spelled out what could be done in the various precincts of the temple or where the scapegoat was to be sent on the Day of Atonement; (3) *persons,* which designated whom one could marry, touch, or eat with, who could divorce, who could enter the various spaces in the temple and temple courtyards, and who could hold certain offices or perform certain actions; (4) *things,* which designated what was considered clean or unclean and could be offered in sacrifice or allowed contact with the body; (5) *food rules,* which determined what could be eaten, how it was to be grown, prepared, or slaughtered, in what vessels it could be served, when and where it could be eaten, and with whom it could be shared; and (6) *uncleanness,* which offered guidelines for avoiding polluting contact. Consider the following maps taken from third-century C.E. Pharisaic documents. First a map of times:

Map of Times

m. Moed

1. Shabbat and Erubim	(Sabbath)
2. Pesachim	(Feast of Passover)
3. Yoma	(Day of Atonement)
4. Sukkoth	(Feast of Tabernacles)
5. Yom Tov	(Festival Days)
6. Rosh Hashanah	(Feast of New Year's)
7. Taanit h	(Days of Fasting)
8. Megillah	(Feast of Purim)
9. Moed Katan	(Mid-festival Days)

Now a map of uncleanness:

Map of Uncleanness

m. Kelim 1, 3

1. There are things which convey uncleanness by contact
   (e.g., a dead creeping thing, male semen).
2. They are exceeded by carrion . . .
3. They are exceeded by him that has a connection with a menstruant.
4. They are exceeded by the issue of him that has a flux,
   by his spittle, his semen, and his urine . . .
5. They are exceeded by the uncleanness of what is ridden
   upon by him that has a flux . . .
6. The uncleanness of what is ridden upon by him that
   has a flux is exceeded by what he lies upon . . .
7. The uncleanness of what he lies upon is exceeded
   by the uncleanness of him that has a flux . . .

On the Way Back to Galilee:
Jesus Encounters a Samaritan Woman, 4:1-42

4:1 Now when Jesus learned that the Pharisees had heard, "Jesus is making and baptizing more disciples than John" [2]—although it was not Jesus himself but his disciples who baptized—[3]he left Judea and started back to Galilee. [4]But he had to go through Samaria. [5]So he came to a Samaritan city called Sychar, near the plot of ground that Jacob had given to his son Joseph. [6]Jacob's well was there, and Jesus, tired out by his journey, was sitting by the well. It was about noon.

7 A Samaritan woman came to draw water, and Jesus said to her, "Give me a drink." [8](His disciples had gone to the city to buy food.) [9]The Samaritan woman said to him, "How is it that you, a Jew, ask a drink of me, a woman of Samaria?" (Jews do not share things in common with Samaritans.) [10]Jesus answered her, "If you knew the gift of God, and who it is that is saying to you, 'Give me a drink,' you would have asked him, and he would have given you living water." [11]The woman said to him, "Sir, you have no bucket, and the well is deep. Where do you get that living water? [12]Are you greater than our ancestor Jacob, who gave us the well, and with his sons and his flocks drank from it?" [13]Jesus said to her, "Everyone who drinks of this water will be thirsty again, [14]but those who drink of the water that I will give them will never be thirsty. The water that I will give will become in them a spring of water gushing up to eternal life." [15]The woman said to him, "Sir, give me this water, so that I may never be thirsty or have to keep coming here to draw water."

16 Jesus said to her, "Go, call your husband, and come back." [17]The woman answered him, "I have no husband." Jesus said to her, "You are right in saying, 'I have no husband'; [18]for you have had five husbands, and the one you have now is not your husband. What you have said is true!" [19]The woman said to him, "Sir, I see that you are a prophet. [20]Our ancestors worshiped on this mountain, but you say that the place where people must worship is in Jerusalem." [21]Jesus said to her, "Woman, believe me, the hour is coming when you will worship the Father neither on this mountain nor in Jerusalem. [22]You worship what you do not know; we worship what we know, for salvation is from the Jews. [23]But the hour is coming, and is now here, when the true worshipers will worship the Father in spirit and truth, for the Father seeks such as these to worship him. [24]God is spirit, and those who worship him must worship in spirit and truth." [25]The woman said to him, "I know that Messiah is coming" (who is called Christ). "When he comes, he will proclaim all things to us." [26]Jesus said to her, "I am he, the one who is speaking to you."

27 Just then his disciples came. They were astonished that he was speaking with a woman, but no one said, "What do you want?" or, "Why are you speaking with her?" [28]Then the woman left her water jar and went back to the city. She said to the people, [29]"Come and see a man who told me everything I have ever done! He cannot be the Messiah, can he?" [30]They left the city and were on their way to him.

31 Meanwhile the disciples were urging him, "Rabbi, eat something." [32]But he said to them, "I have food to eat that you do not know about." [33]So the disciples said to one another, "Surely no one has brought him something to eat?" [34]Jesus said to them, "My food is to do the will of him who sent me and to complete his work. [35]Do you not say, 'Four months more, then comes the harvest'? But I tell you, look around you, and see how the fields are ripe for harvesting. [36]The reaper is already receiving wages and is gathering fruit for eternal life, so that sower and reaper may rejoice together. [37]For here the saying holds true, 'One sows and another reaps.' [38]I sent you to reap that for which you did not labor. Others have labored, and you have entered into their labor."

39 Many Samaritans from that city believed in him because of the woman's testimony, "He told me everything I have ever done." [40]So when the Samaritans came to him, they asked him to stay with them; and he stayed there two days. [41]And many more believed because of his word. [42]They said to the woman, "It is no longer because of what you said that we believe, for we have heard for ourselves, and we know that this is truly the Savior of the world."

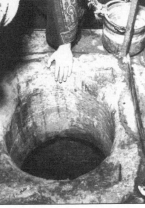

4:6 Jacob's well in the crypt of a shrine commemorating Jesus' encounter with the woman. There is no reference to a well of Jacob in the Old Testament, but since he bought land here (Gen. 33:18-20), he would have needed to dig a well. Most scholars today identify Sychar with the Old Testament city of Shechem. Photos by Richard Rohrbaugh.

✦ *Notes:* John 4:1-42

4:1-4 In this Gospel, the symbolic dipping of a person in water, baptism, was performed initially by John and his disciples so that God might thereby reveal Jesus to Israel (1:31); and Jesus' disciples seem to be doing the same. This activity is effective since Pharisees in Judea are quite aware of Jesus' growing reputation.

The reason why the author explicitly notes in v. 2 (contrary to his general statement in 3:22) that Jesus himself did not baptize is that Jesus' personal baptism is with the Spirit of God, not with water (1:33). The fact that Jesus learns of the Pharisees' awareness of him suggests a very active gossip network. Not only is information being passed along by means of gossip, but the process of gossiping is evaluative in nature. The evaluation involved serves to underscore and identify leadership roles. Jesus' reputation was growing while John's was waning. ⇨ **Gossip Network,** 4:1-42.

4:5-6 John is careful to note the general (Samaritan city of Sychar) and specific (Jacob's well) location and time (noon) of the interaction that is to follow. Samaritans traced their origin to the ancient kingdom of Israel; however, Judeans considered the Samaritans' Israelite pedigree to have been bastardized due to intermarriage with Assyrian colonists before Judean elites were exiled by Babylonian conquerors (586 B.C.E.). Since in antiquity people and their land were organically connected, it followed that both Samaritans and their land were unclean or impure in Judean eyes.

4:7-15 This opening scene is very concerned with water. There is much in it that would have caught the attention of ancient Mediterranean people. For lower-class women at least, whose daily task was to fetch water for the household, wells would have been a place of frequent gathering. Normally, however, women went to draw water in the cool of the morning or the evening (Gen. 24:11). They also did so in the company of other women (1 Sam. 9:11), effectively making the well women's "private" space during the time that they were there. ⇨ **Public/Private,** 4:1-42.

The fact that the woman at the well is alone and that she comes at midday when the other village women are not there suggests that she has been shunned by the other women. She is perhaps seen as socially deviant (4:16-18). That Jesus would be there in the heat of the day is perhaps not surprising, but that he would talk to the woman in what is now "public" space is astonishing indeed (4:29). Men were expected not to talk to strange women in public. The narrator, however, emphasizes that they are alone (4:8) and that the woman herself is surprised that Jesus would speak to her. Her reply to Jesus emphasizes that she is both female and a native (a Samaritan), while Jesus is both male and an outsider. Such awareness of gender and origin was quite typical of social interaction in antiquity.

The narrator's gloss in 4:9 makes the point even more strongly. The Greek term the NRSV translates "share in common" *(synkraomai)* literally means to share dishes or eating utensils and thus points to a concern for ritual purity. An early

Pharisaic regulation asserted the perpetual impurity of Samaritan women for Judeans: ". . . the daughters of the Samaritans are [deemed unclean as] menstruants from the cradle" (*m. Nid.* 4.1). According to Lev. 15:19ff., not only is everything a menstruating woman lies or sits upon unclean, so also is anyone who touches these items. In addition, if the woman is living with a man not her husband, she is impure on that ground as well. From the point of view of Judean values, then, this whole scene appears socially deviant.

A curiosity in this passage is that the woman, a Samaritan, calls Jesus a "Judean." In 8:48 the Judeans call him a "Samaritan." Such name-calling is a way of designating someone an outsider. ⇨ **In-group and Out-group,** 15:18—16:4a. Jesus, a Galilean, is literally an outsider to both groups. For either group, the labels they normally use for each other will suffice to suggest the social distance being expressed between themselves and Jesus.

These verses represent yet another example of the Johannine literary technique in which Jesus (1) makes a statement, (2) which is misunderstood, and (3) is followed by an explanation (see 3:3ff.; 4:31ff.; 6:41ff.; 8:21ff.; 11:11ff.; 12:27ff.; 14:4ff.). There are a series of such conversation cycles in this story of Jesus encountering the Samaritan woman, as we outline at the close of the comments on this chapter. (p. 102) In the course of these, the woman is being progressively led from outsider who misunderstands to enlightened insider. That process will be complete at the end of Jesus' self-revelation in 4:26. ⇨ **In-group and Out-group,** 15:18—16:4a. At the beginning of the conversation, Jesus says, "If you knew . . . ," but she does not. If she did, she would be the one to ask for a drink, not Jesus. By v. 15 she is asking for the water. Jesus offers "living" water (double meaning: both an ancient way of referring to naturally flowing water and John's antilanguage for "life"), but again she misunderstands and queries him about a bucket. Jesus again explains, this time pointing out that the water he offers brings eternal life. ⇨ **Life,** 1:1-18. She wants the water but still does not fully understand. She imagines avoiding the daily drudgery of carrying water from the well (five gallons of water weigh about sixty-five pounds).

Note that Jesus is willing to share a drinking vessel with the woman, a seriously polluting act by Pharisee standards, given the fact that he is a stranger sharing a utensil with a Samaritan woman. Yet she is willing to share with him. He, in turn, treats her like family, and now she begins to reciprocate. The point is important because it signals that the space Jesus and the woman occupy is being transformed from "public" space, where their actions would have been considered deviant, to "private" space, where they are not. Interpersonally, the woman is becoming part of the group of disciples forming around Jesus, hence, no longer a woman with whom he should not speak.

4:16-19 The theme here turns to the woman's husbands. The command Jesus gives the woman is not misunderstood but cannot be followed. She responds truthfully, and twice Jesus praises her (vv. 17, 18). The candor of dialogue between Jesus and the woman here indicates that they now understand this as a "private" conversation. The matters they speak of would never be talked about in

4:20-26 "Our ancestors worshiped on this mountain." "This mountain" is Mount Gerizim pictured above, taken from Mount Ebal. The Samaritans restricted their sacrificial worship to this mountain, just as the Judeans confined all sacrificial worship to the Temple in Jerusalem. With Mount Ebal, which rises immediately to its north, Mount Gerizim creates a narrow pass through which the main road to Galilee must make its way. The two mountains, and the ancient city of Shechem that lies between them, are very prominent in the books of Genesis and Joshua. A tiny community of Samaritans still worships on Mount Gerizim today. Photo by Avraham Hay.

public. This is further evidence that the social space has been transformed. See the **Note** immediately above.

It is important to recognize that Jesus shares "insider" knowledge with the woman. His address to her, "Woman," is the same he uses with his own mother (2:4; 19:26) and with other women who are part of his fictive family (8:10; 20:13). Moreover, as her incorporation into the Jesus group continues, the woman is able to identify Jesus as a prophet (v. 19).

4:20-26 The theme turns to worship. Jesus' explanation that worship will no longer be centered at the public shrines, which are primarily the space of privileged males, provides the basis for the woman's full incorporation into the group. She in turn acknowledges that she expects the Messiah and expects to be fully enlightened by him. This occurs when Jesus finally reveals himself to her fully.

4:27-31 The Pharisaic scribes warned against speaking too much to women in public (*m. Aboth* 1.5). The narrator's notice that the disciples were astonished and that they should have asked Jesus questions about his behavior deliberately draws attention to its inappropriate character. The narrator thus underscores the transformation we have been describing. The disciples do not know that this transformation has occurred and therefore assume this is still public space. Questions (always a challenge) could have been asked. While there is no indication that others were present, which would have made a challenge to Jesus public and therefore embarrassing, nonetheless the disciples refrain.

As with the conversation between Jesus and the woman at the well, this scene is full of cultural anomalies. Leaving the water jar indicates that the woman is not going home. Instead she goes to the city. If she has gone to the place in town where people are normally gathered, that is, to the public square, she is in decidedly public, male space. She had been told to go back to private space (her husband), but she goes straight to the most public space available.

With no hesitation whatsoever, the woman tells the men about her conversation with Jesus. ▷ **Gossip Network,** 4:1-42. As a new insider in the Jesus group, she shares insider information. That she decides to report a conversation about her own questionable sexual behavior, however, is strange indeed. It suggests she feels no obligation to defend or protect her sexual exclusivity. She appears to be either an adulteress or a "mistress," a fact that the author presumes to have been known to her audience. Her positive shame, her honor status, was thus beyond retrieval. In any case, such talk in public between unrelated men and women about sexual matters goes far beyond cultural expectations. Not only this, but in her report she indicates that she had been doing the same thing (talking about sexual matters) with a total stranger to their neighborhood (Jesus)! The outcome of the episode, however, indicates that yet another transformation is in process; the men to whom she spreads the news are also becoming fictive kin of Jesus.

4:32-38 As the theme turns to "harvest," the intervening conversation between Jesus and the disciples plays again on the contrast of misunderstanding followed by explanation. It describes what is in fact going on back in the city where the woman is spreading her story about herself and Jesus.

4:32-38 Fields ripe for harvesting. Photo by Avraham Hay.

4:39-42 The notice that many Samaritans believed because of the woman's testimony suggests that the circle of fictive kinship into which the woman had been drawn is expanding. Just as the public space (the well) in which Jesus and the woman had their conversation was transformed into the private space of a fictive kin group (see the **Notes** above), so also the public square is now being transformed as those occupying it join the Jesus kin group. The notice in v. 40 that these new believers wished Jesus to "stay" with them and that he did indeed stay with them for two days confirms their newly acquired in-group status. See the **Notes** at 1:38-39. What we see unfold in the course of 4:1-42 is thus a pattern of the social transformation experienced by members of the Johannine group.

The final sentence of this passage contains the only use of the term *Savior* in John. The only other use of the word in the Gospel tradition is in the Lukan birth narrative. The term is more widely used of the resurrected Jesus in other New Testament documents. It was a common term in the Greco-Roman world for gods, heroes, and even emperors who provided their devotees or adherents with rescue from some difficult situation. The full phrase here, "Savior of the world," is used in a Roman context in inscriptions referring to Emperor Hadrian early in the second century. Here in John the title reveals Jesus as rescuer of all Israel, including that branch of Israel considered a bastard offshoot by Judeans.

Note the pattern of statement-misunderstanding-explanation as it runs through this chapter:

4:5-6:	Time and Place
4:7-15:	Theme: Water
4:7	Statement leading to a
4:9	Misunderstanding requiring a
4:10	Clarification which is a Statement leading to a
4:11-12	Misunderstanding requiring a
4:13-14	Clarification which is a Statement evoking
4:15	Misunderstanding
4:16-19:	Theme: Husbands: Command-Clarification-Fulfillment
4:16	Command
4:17-19	First Clarification
4:20-26:	Theme: Worship
	Second Clarification
4:27-31a:	Theme: The Christ?
	Fulfillment of Command
4:31b-38:	Theme: Harvest
4:31b	Invitation to eat leads to

4:32	Statement leading to
4:33	Misunderstanding requiring a
4:34	Clarification
4:35-38	Further clarification

4:39-42:   Epilogue. Theme: outcome of the incident: Samaritans know that Jesus is the Savior of the world

✧ *Reading Scenarios:* **John 4:1-42**

Gossip Network, 4:1-42

While gossip no doubt plays an important role in all societies, it does so with special force where a majority of the population is nonliterate. It is used for a variety of purposes, including simple information sharing, but in general it functions as a sort of informal means of social control in which the behavior of a person is held up to evaluation by others when he or she is not present.

Most ancient elite comment about gossip is negative. Plutarch offers a first-century example: "Just as cooks pray for a good crop of young animals and fishermen for a good haul of fish, in the same way busybodies pray for a good crop of calamities, a good haul of difficulties, or novelties and changes, that they, like cooks and fishermen, may always have something to fish out or butcher" (*On Being a Busybody* 518E). He complains that gossips pass up nearly anything beautiful or worthwhile so they can "spend their time digging into other men's trifling correspondence, gluing their ears to their neighbor's walls, whispering with slaves and women of the streets, and often incurring danger, and always infamy" (*On Being a Busybody* 519F). Such gossipers were stereotypically presumed to be women, though complaints about men engaging in gossip are also common.

Gossip, however, is not always negative. It frequently serves to clarify, maintain, and enforce social values. It socializes the young into a community's way of thinking. In providing an assessment of individuals, it suggests who can be trusted and who cannot, who might make a reliable business deal and who would cheat. Among the more important social functions of gossip is group formation and boundary maintenance. Those who are let in on a group's gossip are insiders. Those excluded from the gossip networks of a group are obviously outsiders to the group. Moreover, the values of a group are powerfully reinforced and enforced by the fear of being shamed by public gossip. In this way the compliant and the deviant are sorted out and become known to everyone in the community. A very important function of gossip is to identify leaders. As evaluative talk occurs, some people begin to emerge in a positive way. As stories about them circulate, reputation grows. It is tested again and again and gradually becomes standard wisdom. Note how the story about Jesus that the woman brings back to the city in 4:29 convinces many in the city to believe in Jesus (4:39). When their own experience confirms the woman's gossip, their belief in him as Savior of the world is corroborated (4:42).

Gossip is an interpersonal channel of communication. Some of the more important distinguishing characteristics of interpersonal communication when compared with mass-media channels (all types of print and electronic channels) include:

Communication Characteristics	Interpersonal Channels	Mass-Media Channels
1. Direction of message flow	Two-way	One-way
2. Speed to a large audience	Slow	Rapid
3. Message accuracy to a large audience	Low	High
4. Ability to select receiver	High	Low
5. Ability to overcome selectivity processes	High	Low
6. Amount of feedback	High	Low
7. Possible effect	Attitude Change	Increase Knowledge

Much like peasants today, Mediterraneans of antiquity were interpersonally and locally oriented. The low message accuracy sometimes encountered with interpersonal communication channels is illustrated by the fact that oral exchange is usually regarded as an identifying characteristic of gossip and rumors. The latter are often defined by communication specialists as false or at least unverified messages. Gossip and rumors are particularly common when innovations are introduced among peasants, as John illustrates. The frequency of gossip and rumor mongering under conditions of innovation diffusion might be accounted for by the fact that gossip and rumors occur most often:

(1) when there is great anxiety but inadequate knowledge about an idea (as usually occurs in the case of innovations), and

(2) when mass media fail to carry the message load (a common happening among peasants where media exposure is low or nonexistent).

Consider the actual case of a rumor among Peruvian Indians reported by Rogers and Svenning. The rumor blamed American change agents, who were introducing improved potatoes, of intending to fatten the local residents so that they could be boiled down for oil for American machinery. Now think of the gossip resulting from a group experiencing Jesus as Israel's prophet and savior!

(Everett M. Rogers with Lynne Svenning. *Modernization among Peasants: The Impact of Communication* [New York: Holt, Rinehart and Winston, 1969]).

Public/Private, 4:1-42

In the world of eastern Mediterranean antiquity, at least among the elite, space was carefully divided according to gender. Males belonged in public space, females in private space. Males performed tasks appropriate to males, either out of doors or in public spaces beyond the home. Females performed tasks appropriate to females, usually indoors and inside the circle of the family. As Philo of Alexandria put it:

> Market-places and council-halls and law-courts and gatherings and meetings where a large number of people are assembled, and open-air life with full scope for discussion and action—all these are suitable to men both in war and peace. The women are best suited to the indoor life which never strays from the house, within which the middle door is taken by the maidens as their boundary, and the outer door by those who have reached full womanhood. (*Special Laws* 3.169ff.)

The architecture of Greek and Middle Eastern elite houses reflected this division, with special sections for males *(andrionitis)* and for females *(gynaikonitis)*.

Interactions between men and women outside the family circle were carefully controlled and subject to a variety of norms. In some areas, there was even an elected official called a *gynaikonomos* charged with regulating this interaction. In some regions during the first century, women were still veiled in public places (1 Cor. 11:5-6; Dio Chrysostom, *Orat.* 33:48-51), thus maintaining their "private" space while out of the house. Women did not talk to males outside the family when in public. Here in John 4 the disciples are astonished when they discover Jesus talking with a woman in a public place (4:27).

Similarly, women were to behave in such a way as to provoke no public comment. As Plutarch put it, "The best woman is she about whom there is least talk among persons outside." This included *either* censure or commendation. Says Plutarch, "The name of the good woman, like her person, ought to be shut up indoors and never go out" (*In Praise of Women* 242E).

While there could be a great deal of local variation in specifics, gender segregation was a constant throughout the eastern Mediterranean world of antiquity, at least among elites. Elites were the trendsetters. While nonelites sought to imitate their social betters, in most peasant societies of that region the lines of gender division among nonelites would have been much more difficult to maintain since they were subject to a variety of different pressures. Among nonelites, women were more likely to interact with men in work or marketing situations and less likely to have separate quarters of their own.

Jesus' Honor in Galilee, 4:43-45

43 When the two days were over, he went from that place to Galilee ⁴⁴(for Jesus himself had testified that a prophet has no honor in the prophet's own country). ⁴⁵When he came to Galilee, the Galileans welcomed him, since they had seen all that he had done in Jerusalem at the festival; for they too had gone to the festival.

✦ *Notes:* **John 4:43-54**

4:43-45 This short transitional statement puzzled even the earliest interpreters of John's Gospel. The journey back to Galilee, interrupted at 4:5, is resumed. The saying in v. 44 explains Jesus' rejection in Galilee in the Synoptics (for example, Mark 6:4), but here in John it is juxtaposed to a report in v. 45 that Jesus is in fact welcomed in Galilee. The proverb then refers to why Jesus leaves Samaria after two days. To begin with, it is in Samaria that Jesus is recognized as a prophet: "Sir, I see that you are a prophet" (4:19). The reason prophets have no honor in their own country has to do with the general perception of limited good in ancient Mediterranean society. When all goods are seen to be limited, for example, like land, there is no way to get ahead except at the expense of another person or group. When a prophet arises in a community, group members perceive that one of their own is rising above all others in the group. The prophet clearly "gets ahead" of others in the group and thus is seen as depriving others in the group of whatever it is that makes the prophet prominent. The result is social imbalance that must be rectified. It is because he causes such community imbalance that a prophet is without honor in his own closed society, his own in-group. Hence the saying that "a prophet is not without honor, except in his own country, and among his own kin, and in his own house" (Mark 6:4). The closed community has ready arguments for rejecting an achiever (see Matt. 11:19; Luke 7:34).

In trying to explain this passage, some commentators assume the "inadequacy" of the Galileans' faith (cf. 4:48), while others resort to theories of clumsy editing. While all such explanations are little concerned with social plausibility, it can at least be noted that John's concern for Jesus' public reputation is being carried forward.

A Healing in Galilee:
Jesus' Second Self-Disclosure, 4:46-54

46 Then he came again to Cana in Galilee where he had changed the water into wine. Now there was a royal official whose son lay ill in Capernaum. ⁴⁷When he heard that Jesus had come from Judea to Galilee, he went and begged him to come down and heal his son, for he was at the point of death. ⁴⁸Then Jesus said to him, "Unless you see signs and wonders you will not believe." ⁴⁹The official said to him, "Sir, come down before my little boy dies." ⁵⁰Jesus said to him, "Go; your son will live." The man believed the word that Jesus spoke to him and started on his way. ⁵¹As he was going down, his slaves met him and told him that his child was alive. ⁵²So he asked them the hour when he began to recover, and they said to him, "Yesterday at one in the afternoon the fever left him." ⁵³The father realized that this was the hour when Jesus had said to him, "Your son will live." So he himself believed, along with his whole household. ⁵⁴Now this was the second sign that Jesus did after coming from Judea to Galilee.

4:47, 51 Three times the story describes the trip from Cana to Capernaum as a "coming down" or "going down." (See vv. 47. 49, 51; also 2:12.) Cana was about 1,000 feet above sea level, but only about 14 miles from the Sea of Galilee, which is 680 feet below sea level. The final descent was by way of the ancient road through the Arbel Pass, pictured here from below. Photo by Thomas Hoffman.

✦ *Notes:* John 4:46-54

4:46-54 This account may be another variant of the healing story in Matt. 8:5-13 and Luke 7:1-10. It takes place in Cana, the location of the "first sign," which Jesus did in Galilee. Both signs elicit belief (2:11; 4:53). The Greek term *basilikos* is usually assumed to refer to a royal official, as the NRSV translates it. However, the word is simply the adjective *royal* and could refer equally well to a royal personage, such as a member of the Herodian family. The latter seems more likely in view of the reference to his whole household in 4:53 and to slaves in 4:51. In any case, whether a royal retainer or a royal aristocrat, the man whose son is near death would be very high on the social scale in a town like Capernaum. He is certainly not the type who would normally seek the patronage of a villager from Nazareth. ⇨ **Patronage,** 5:21-30.

It is clear that the gossip network (⇨ **Gossip Network,** 4:1-42) is at work spreading the reputation of Jesus. That someone of royal status would "beg" (the term used when seeking a favor from a patron; note also the use of the polite term, "Sir") for help from him is perhaps an indicator of Jesus' emerging status in the public mind. Since word of the aristocrat's begging would spread quickly in a small town, he risks serious public dishonor by doing so unless his behavior was warranted by Jesus' reputation.

In 3:16, 36 Jesus says that whoever believes will have new life. That too is the indicated purpose of the Gospel in 20:31. That is what happens here; note the stress on it in vv. 50, 51, and 53. For additional comment on healing, ⇨ **Healing/ Health Care,** 5:1-18.

CHAPTER IV
JOHN 5:1–6:71
JESUS' BRINGING LIFE
TO ISRAEL PROVOKED CONTROVERSY
IN JERUSALEM AND GALILEE

A Feast in Jerusalem:
Controversy over Jesus' Rescue of a Lame Man, 5:1-20

5:1 After this there was a festival of the Jews, and Jesus went up to Jerusalem.

2 Now in Jerusalem by the Sheep Gate there is a pool, called in Hebrew Beth-zatha, which has five porticoes. [3]In these lay many invalids—blind, lame, and paralyzed. [5]One man was there who had been ill for thirty-eight years. [6]When Jesus saw him lying there and knew that he had been there a long time, he said to him, "Do you want to be made well?" [7]The sick man answered him, "Sir, I have no one to put me into the pool when the water is stirred up; and while I am making my way, someone else steps down ahead of me." [8]Jesus said to him, "Stand up, take your mat and walk." [9]At once the man was made well, and he took up his mat and began to walk.

Now that day was a sabbath. [10]So the Jews said to the man who had been cured, "It is the sabbath; it is not lawful for you to carry your mat." [11]But he answered them, "The man who made me well said to me, 'Take up your mat and walk.'" [12]They asked him, "Who is the man who said to you, 'Take it up and walk'?" [13]Now the man who had been healed did not know who it was, for Jesus had disappeared in the crowd that was there. [14]Later Jesus found him in the temple and said to him, "See, you have been made well! Do not sin any more, so that nothing worse happens to you." [15]The man went away and told the Jews that it was Jesus who had made him well. [16]Therefore the Jews started persecuting Jesus, because he was doing such things on the sabbath. [17]But Jesus answered them, "My Father is still working, and I also am working." [18]For this reason the Jews were seeking all the more to kill him, because he was not only breaking the sabbath, but was also calling God his own Father, thereby making himself equal to God.

19 Jesus said to them, "Very truly, I tell you, the Son can do nothing on his own, but only what he sees the Father doing; for whatever the Father does, the Son does likewise. [20]The Father loves the Son and shows him all that he himself is doing; and he will show him greater works than these, so that you will be astonished.

✦ *Notes:* John 5:1-47

From the viewpoint of content, it might be useful to note how the author of John tells his stories of Jesus' Sabbath healings here in chapter 5 and in chapter 9. These passages have a number of parallel features.

Chapter 5	**Chapter 9**
1. Jerusalem feast (5:1)	1. Jerusalem feast: Tabernacles
2. Sabbath healing (5:10)	2. Sabbath healing (9:14)
3. old, proven infirmity (5:5)	3. old, proven infirmity (9:1)
4. illness and sin (5:14 "sin no more . . .")	4. illness and sin (9:2 "who sinned . . .")
5. site: a pool—Beth-zatha (5:2)	5. site: a pool—Siloam (9:7)
6. command ("rise, take . . . ," 5:7) obedience/cure (5:9)	6. command ("go, wash," 9:7a) obedience/cure (9:7b)
7. court of inquiry (5:9b-16) • healed man • court of inquiry • charge: Sabbath violation • defense (5:31-47)	7. court of inquiry (9:13-34) • healed man • court of inquiry • charge: Sabbath violation • defense (9:30-34)
8. form: healing/controversy	8. form: healing/controversy
9. ideological issue: belief • Question: who is he? (5:12-13) he did not know	9. ideological issue: belief • Question: where is he? I do not know (9:12) • Question: What do you say about him? a prophet! (9:17)
10. subsequent meeting • Jesus *found* him (5:14) • no Christophany • report to Judeans about Jesus (5:14)	10. subsequent meeting • Jesus *found* him (9:35) • Christophany (9:35-38) • Do you believe? Lord, I believe (9:35-38)
11. judgment: tables turned • they judge Jesus (5:9-16) • Jesus judges them (5:38-47)	11. judgment: tables turned • they judge Jesus (9:13-34) • Jesus judges them (9:39-41)

5:2 The pool of Bethzatha was located to the northeast of the city just outside the walls (see the map at 9:7). The first picture is a section of a model of Jerusalem as it is thought to have looked in the time of Herod Agrippa I, king of Palestine, 41–44 C.E., thus about ten years after the death of Jesus. The pool of Bethzatha is the low building in the foreground of the picture. The five porches are on the four sides and the one through the middle. Note the Antonia fortress just behind and the temple structures in the background. The pool was originally built to supply water for the temple, but by Jesus' time this function seems to have been superseded with newer water sources, and it seems to have acquired a reputation for healing qualities. After the second Judean revolt in 135 C.E., the emperor Hadrian turned it into a healing sanctuary dedicated to the god Serapis. The second picture shows the ruins revealed by archaeological excavations in the nineteenth century as they look today. They include parts of the ancient cistern and the remains of a crusader church from the twelfth century. Photos by Thomas Hoffman.

✦ *Notes:* John 5:1-20

5:1-20 This story marks the beginning of what will be a major motif in the remainder of John's Gospel: conflict between Jesus and the Judeans. Here (vv. 1, 10, 15), as elsewhere in John, it is important to correct the anachronistic translation "Jews." ➪ **Jews/Judeans,** 1:19-28. It is unclear which festival it is that brings Jesus to Jerusalem this time (he had been there earlier for Passover; 2:23). The Sabbath healing in this story will remain a matter of controversy when he returns to Jerusalem again for the Feast of Sukkoth (7:23).

5:1-3 Sick persons lying beside the pool would have been there, not only to seek healing, but also to beg. Such beggars were among the socially expendables, the unclean "throwaway" people who frequented every preindustrial city. In this same category were prostitutes, the poorest day laborers, tanners (forced to live outside the cities because they smelled), peddlers, bandits, sailors, hustlers (for example, gamblers, usurers), ass drivers, dung collectors, and even some merchants. Such persons were usually forced out of cities at night when gates were locked but frequented the cities during the daytime to beg or find work. These people without social standing (we would see them as the "poorest") lived just outside the city walls or along the hedgerows of adjacent fields. While these people were not a large portion of the total population (perhaps 10 percent), their living conditions were appalling by our standards. Verse 4, which provides an explanation for the healing power that came with the stirring of the waters (v. 7), is almost certainly a later addition and not part of the original text. The NRSV has put in it a footnote.

5:5-9a The sick person described here is totally unable to maintain even a minimally honorable social position. This would imply that he was "poor" from a Mediterranean point of view. The bare details of the Johannine story do not tell us how the man who had been sick for thirty-eight years survived (there is no implication in v. 6 or elsewhere that he had been at the pool for the whole thirty-eight years). He could get around, however slowly (v. 7), but it is not explained how he was fed or how he got to the pool on a daily basis. The man's acknowledgment that he had "no one" to put him in the pool is a direct admission that he was without family or friends. It is difficult to imagine a beggar in that position surviving for any length of time.

How Jesus knew the man had been at the pool for a long time is not explained. The sick man's reply to Jesus makes clear his friendless, and therefore hopeless, situation. It could also imply that he is wondering whether Jesus is making an offer to be the needed friend to put him into the pool. Since the sick man does not know who is talking to him, he obviously does not anticipate being healed by Jesus. Instead, his focus remains on the curative powers of the stirred water. Form critics have suggested that Jesus' command to the man to stand, take up his mat, and walk away probably ended the original miracle story in John's source. ➪ **Healing/Health Care,** 5:1-20.

5:9b-13 Jesus' command to the healed man to walk away with his mat directs him to break one of Israel's Sabbath regulations mediated by Moses and emphasized by Jeremiah: "Thus says the LORD: For the sake of your lives, take care that you do not bear a burden on the sabbath day or bring it in by the gates of Jerusalem. And do not carry a burden out of your houses on the sabbath or do any work, but keep the sabbath day holy, as I commanded your ancestors" (Jer. 17:21-22). ⇨ **Purity/Pollution: Purification Rites,** 3:22-36. In an Israelite literalist reading of the Torah, the final action of God after creation was to rest: "So God blessed the seventh day and hallowed it, because on it God rested from all the work that he had done in creation" (Gen. 2:3). The present age of creation is precisely this seventh day. For scribal Pharisees, what God is doing at present is resting, just as Moses said. This is the point at issue with Jesus' claim that God is working even now (5:17). What Jeremiah's explanation of the Sabbath command sets forth is the prohibition of "servile work," work done by slaves in elite households. The Sabbath was a weekly replication of the annual Passover that celebrated Israel's status as free persons, now devoted to the service of their liberator God. On the Sabbath Israelites were to be free elites, free for the service of their God alone. Here the man, presumably an Israelite, carries his mat around so publicly that his actions come to the attention of the Judeans who accuse him of breaking God's law. This controversy between Jesus and the Judeans over lawbreaking (and later, over Jesus' claims of kinship with God) will eventually lead to Jesus' death.

5:14 Scholars often puzzle over the fact that while Jesus rejects the idea that suffering is payment for sin in 9:2, here he seems to accept it. If we assume that Jesus' reference to something "worse" happening to the man is a reference to his illness, the puzzle is indeed present. Jesus seems to be threatening another disease if the man should sin again. But if we recognize that in Mediterranean societies "sin" is a breach of interpersonal relations, there ceases to be a problem. For if sin is whatever destroys one's relationship with the group, and if we note that this man was devoid of friends to put him in the pool, Jesus' comment makes perfect sense. As a friendless outcast, the man was indeed a "sinner," an outsider unattached to a group. He may have been sick, but he was also ill. ⇨ **Healing/Health Care,** 5:1-20. Given his age and the short life expectancies in antiquity, should the man repeat whatever disrupted his relationship with the group, he would indeed risk the worst of all fates: having no one to bury and remember him.

5:15-16 Commentators have often suggested that the healed man proves to be an ingrate, running to tell the Judeans of Jesus' identity as soon as he learns it. Perhaps that is the case, but having been accused of lawbreaking himself, perhaps the healed man seeks that crucial item he has not had for the last thirty-eight years: attachment to the dominant social group. His breach with them could not be reestablished if he did not act decisively to repair it; therefore, he attends to the matter quickly.

5:17-18 Jesus argues that the conflict over Sabbath activity exists at all because his Judean opponents are unaware that God himself continues to work, even on the Sabbath. How can human beings confine God's activity to six days? Mention of God's activity connects with the topic of life in the face of death along with Jesus' claims to kinship with God. These items fuel the ongoing controversy between Jesus and the Judeans until his death. It is important to recognize that honor derives from one's family, and thus kinship claims are always honor claims (genealogies are a good example). When Jesus claims kinship with God, he is claiming God's honor for himself. The reaction of his Judean opponents is therefore not surprising; they would have been truly astounded by such a claim. But not members of John's antisociety!

5:19-20 Jesus' word of honor here once more underscores his intent to speak the truth; see **Note** at 1:50-51. These verses represent an important kinship statement in which the ancient dictum "Like father, like son" is reaffirmed. Kinship is not only a matter of biology; it is also a matter of loyalty and solidarity. As Jesus says in 10:30, "The Father and I are one" (also 14:10). The language about doing what he sees the Father doing evokes the picture of a workshop apprentice in which the son learns directly from his father. The first of the works of the Father that the Son now does (v. 21) is the giving of life.

For Westerners the statement in v. 20 that the Father loves the Son (see also 3:35) conjures up images of family affection. We imagine it to be a description of an inner, psychological state. Whole Christologies have been built around such notions. But in the group-oriented Mediterranean society, the term *love* describes attachment or loyalty (especially *group* attachment) and the behavior that goes along with it rather than the emotion of affection. To "love one's neighbor as oneself" (Matt. 19:19) is to be attached to the people in one's neighborhood or even one's ethnic group as to one's own family. ▷ **Love/Hate,** 3:1-21. The Greek tense used here implies continuous action—that is, ongoing loyalty.

✧ *Reading Scenario:* **John 5:1-20**

Healing/Health Care, 5:1-20

In the Synoptic Gospels much of Jesus' public reputation derives from healing the sick. Terms for healing appear 25 times in Luke, 17 times in Matthew, and 8 times in Mark. By contrast, there are only three healing stories in the entire Gospel of John (4:46-54; 5:1-20; 9:1-41). However, both here and in the parallel story in chapter 9, the focus of the interaction falls upon controversy over "work" on the Sabbath. In other words, in John's story, Jesus' healings are not a flash point for anyone's reaction; rather, the controversy centers on the "work" entailed in the healings, whether done by the one healed or by Jesus. Nonetheless, these healings are three of the seven "signs" that are central to John's story. The term *well* appears four times in the story of the man at the pool (vv. 6, 9, 11, 14), emphasizing Jesus' healing power.

In non-Western medicine, the main problem with sickness is the experience of the sick person being dislodged from his/her social moorings and social standing.

Social interaction with family members, friends, neighbors, and village mates comes to a halt. To be healed is to be restored to one's social network. In contemporary Western medicine, we view disease as a malfunction of some organism that can be remedied, assuming cause and cure are known, by proper biomedical treatment. We focus on restoring a sick person's ability to function, to do. Yet, often overlooked is the fact that health and sickness are always culturally defined and that in many societies the ability to function is not the heart of the matter. In the ancient Mediterranean world, one's state of being was more important than one's ability to act or function. Thus, the healers of that world focused on restoring a person to a valued state of being rather than to an ability to function.

Anthropologists therefore distinguish between *disease* (a biomedical malfunction afflicting an organism), and *illness* (a disvalued state of being in which a person's social networks have been disrupted and social significance lost). Illness is not so much a biomedical matter as it is a social one. It is a matter of deviance from cultural norms and values and is therefore attributed to social, not physical, causes. Moreover, because sin is a breach of interpersonal relationships, it is clear why sin and sickness often go together (note, however, that in 5:14 Jesus seems to accept that connection, while in 9:3 he does not).

Ancient leprosy provides a good illustration of the distinction between disease and illness. First of all, leprosy in the world of Jesus and earlier was not Hansen's disease; it was not what we today call "leprosy." Greeks encountered this affliction in India, later in Egypt, and called it *elephantiasis*. On the other hand, the Greek word *lepra* (translated "leprosy" in the Bible) referred to outbreaks on the skin: rashes, psoriasis, acne, and the like. In our society, a person with an acute rash or psoriasis has a skin disease and may be unable to function. But in ancient Palestine, a leper had an illness. She or he was unclean, socially out of place, because whatever it was that emerged on the skin was out of place. Lepers were to be excluded from the community. Similarly, the blind, lame, malformed, and those with itching scabs, crushed testicles, or injured limbs were not permitted to draw near the altar (Lev. 21:16-14). What is described in the Bible, therefore, is not so much disease as illness—a range of anomalous social and cultural human afflictions, some of which had a basis in a physical condition (crippled limbs) and others of which did not (the inability or refusal to see or understand a teaching).

Since people in antiquity paid little attention to impersonal cause-effect relationships, they paid little attention to the biomedical aspects of disease. Hence, healers focused on the social relationships in which a person was enmeshed rather than on malfunctioning organs in the biomedical sense. What bothered people derived from socially rooted symptoms involving the person rather than organic and impersonal causes. As for professional healers or physicians, these persons seldom, if ever, touched the ones they treated. Any physical handling of the sick would be done by a slave. The professional healer preferred to talk about illnesses like a philosopher rather than treat them as the nonprofessional, traditional healer did. Failed treatment could mean death for a healer who actually touched the sick. Such professional physicians are referred to infrequently in the New Testament (Mark 2:17; 5:26; Luke 4:23; 8:43; Col. 4:14), mostly in proverbial sayings common in contemporary Mediterranean literature. ⇨ **Folk Healers,** 9:1-41.

In contrast to professional healers, traditional healers who were willing to use their hands and risk a failed treatment were more commonly available to peasants. Jesus appears as such in the Synoptic Gospels—he is a Spirit-filled prophet who vanquishes unclean spirits and a variety of illnesses and thus restores people to their place in the community. He deals not so much with disease as with illness. Such healers accept all symptoms, especially social ones, as important (see Luke 8:26-33 for a detailed description of symptoms). The healing process is considered directly related to a person's solidarity with and loyalty to the overall belief system typical of the culture in general. (Note that this perspective remains implicit in our modern health-care delivery system.) In John this connection between belief and healing is especially strong (4:50, 53; 8:24; 9:18, 35-36; 10:37-38; 11:42). Unlike the Synoptic picture of Jesus, the Johannine Jesus heals because of his interpersonal relationship with the Father. Jesus is full of life and volunteers to share that life with those whom the Father sends to him. Undoubtedly, members of John's antisociety knew this from experience.

To have one's illness healed, a sick person is often required to have his/her interpersonal relations in order. Here Jesus seeks out the healed man to remind him that further breaches in interpersonal relations might cause even greater harm (5:14; see the **Notes** above). Community acceptance of a traditional healer's actions is also essential, though here when the healed man seeks such acceptance from the Judean community, the Sabbath controversy dominates the community's reaction (5:16).

Jesus as God's Honored Broker, 5:21-30

21 Indeed, just as the Father raises the dead and gives them life, so also the Son gives life to whomever he wishes. [22]The Father judges no one but has given all judgment to the Son, [23]so that all may honor the Son just as they honor the Father. Anyone who does not honor the Son does not honor the Father who sent him. [24]Very truly, I tell you, anyone who hears my word and believes him who sent me has eternal life, and does not come under judgment, but has passed from death to life.

25 "Very truly, I tell you, the hour is coming, and is now here, when the dead will hear the voice of the Son of God, and those who hear will live. [26]For just as the Father has life in himself, so he has granted the Son also to have life in himself; [27]and he has given him authority to execute judgment, because he is the Son of Man. [28]Do not be astonished at this; for the hour is coming when all who are in their graves will hear his voice [29]and will come out—those who have done good, to the resurrection of life, and those who have done evil, to the resurrection of condemnation.

30 I can do nothing on my own. As I hear, I judge; and my judgment is just, because I seek to do not my own will but the will of him who sent me.

✦ *Notes:* **John 5:21-30**

5:21 This is a classic statement of Jesus' brokerage. The broker does not have the resources; the patron does. It is God the patron who raises the dead and gives them life. But the broker acts as a surrogate patron and does nothing on his own (reiterated in 5:30). Trusting a broker is a matter of trusting that this surrogate relationship is in place. ⇨ **Patronage,** 5:21-30.

5:22-25 The second work of the Father (patron), which he has given to the Son (broker) to do, is judging. The verb "to judge" usually means "to condemn," hence "to shame in a public forum." The purpose of legal trials in the ancient Mediterranean was not so much to determine the truth as to dishonor one's opponent in public. While the statement that the Father does not judge would surprise Jesus' hearers, the claim that the patron has delegated judgment to the broker does not mean the judgment is no longer God's. Brokers offer a *patron's* resources. The faithfulness with which the brokerage is performed brings honor to both Son and Father. Honor claimed but not acknowledged by the public has no validity; here John says that Jesus' brokerage will bring honor from "all." ⇨ **Honor and Shame,** 5:16-30. Since kin group members are embedded in each other and share a common honor status, to refuse honor to one is to refuse honor to all. Note once again the use of the word-of-honor formula, "Very truly I tell you." See the **Note** at 1:50-51.

It should be remembered that in this context Jesus is responding to the charge that he has made himself equal to God. But his claims to be a loyal broker suggest otherwise, because brokers are never the equal of the patrons they serve. As a loyal broker, Jesus claims to do nothing other than what the patron does (5:19). Claims of kinship come much closer to being claims of equality, yet in 14:28 Jesus says, "The Father is greater than I." Kin group members always share a roughly equal honor status, though a father always has greater honor than a son. By acknowledging this, Jesus shows himself to be loyal to his Father. Verse 25 again repeats the formula, "Very truly I tell you." See the **Note** at 1:50-51. The importance of what is being said could not be underscored more clearly.

5:26-30 Some scholars see vv. 26-30 as a second version of the speech in vv. 21-25. Since the middle of the nineteenth century, the word *eschatology* has been used to refer to the final condition of humankind. Some scholars have held that John speaks of this final condition of humankind as occurring already. They call this feature in John "realized eschatology," and they find it in vv. 21-25; on the other hand, they see a "final" eschatology in vv. 26-30 that is quite different. There is much dispute, however, about which section is older. Verse 27 uses the title Son of Man in a fashion not unlike the Synoptics. ⇨ **Son of Man,** 1:35-51. However, it seems that eschatology is not at issue in this Gospel. Rather, John simply expresses his usual antisocietal perspective: Jesus gives new life already now, new life enjoyed by members of John's group in their continuing interpersonal experiences of the Son of Man. For life in the antisociety, all time collapses into the present—a broad, enduring present.

✧ *Reading Scenario:* John 5:21-30

Patronage, 5:21-30

Patronage is a system of generalized reciprocity between social unequals in which a lower-status person in need (called a client) is granted favors by a higher-status, well-situated person (called a patron). A favor is something either not available to a client or not available when needed. By being granted a favor, the client implicitly promises to pay back the patron whenever and however the patron determines. By granting the favor, the patron, in turn, implicitly promises to be open to further requests at unspecified later times. Such open-ended relations of generalized reciprocity are typical of the relationship between the head of a family and his dependents: wife, children, and slaves. By entering a patron-client arrangement, the client relates to his patron as to a superior and more powerful kinsman, while the patron sees to his clients as to his dependents.

Patronage existed throughout the Mediterranean world in the first century; the Roman version of the system looked as follows. From the earliest years of the Roman Republic, the people who settled on the hills along the Tiber had, as a part of their families, freeborn retainers called "clients." These clients tended flocks, produced a variety of needed goods, and helped farm the land. In return they were afforded the protection and largesse of their patrician patrons. Such clients had no political rights and were considered inferior to citizens, though they did share in the increase of herds or goods they helped to produce. The mutual obligations between patron and client were considered sacred and often became hereditary. Virgil tells of special punishments in the underworld for patrons who defrauded clients (*Aeneid* 6.609). Great houses boasted of the number of their clients and sought to increase them from generation to generation.

By the late years of the Republic, the flood of conquered peoples had overwhelmed the formal institution of patronage among Romans. A large population torn from previous patronage relations now sought similar ties with the great Roman patrician families. Consequently, patronage spread rapidly into the outer reaches of the Roman world, even if in a much less structured form. By the early years of the empire, especially in the provinces, we hear of the newly rich competing for the honor/status considered to derive from a long train of client dependents. These latter were mostly the urban poor or village peasants who sought favors from those who controlled the economic and political resources of the society.

Many of the details of a Roman client's life are given to us by Martial in his *Epigrams.* In the more formalized institution in Rome itself, the first duty of a client was the *salutatio*—the early morning call at the patron's house. Proper (and clean) dress was important. At this meeting one could be called upon to serve the patron's needs and thereby take up much of the day. Menial duties were expected, though public praise of the patron was considered most fundamental. In return, clients were due one meal a day and might receive a variety of other petty favors. Humiliation of clients was frequent and little recourse was available. Patrons who provided more were considered gracious.

As the Roman style of patronage behavior spread to provinces such as Syria (Palestine), its formal and hereditary character changed. The newly rich, seeking to aggrandize family position in a community, competed to add dependents. Formal, mutual obligations degenerated into petty favor-seeking and manipulation. Clients competed for patrons just as patrons competed for clients in an often desperate struggle to gain economic or political advantage.

Patronage language is astonishingly common in the Gospel of John. Forty-three times in John we are told that Jesus was "sent" by God, language that appears only twice in Matthew (10:40; 15:24), once in Mark (9:37), four times in Luke (4:18, 43; 9:48; 10:16), and once in Paul (Rom. 8:3). While this may be a feature of Johannine antilanguage and its double meaning, the fact is "send" belongs to the vocabulary of patronage. Moreover, there is frequently a defensive tone about "being sent" in John, as when Jesus declares: "The Father who has sent me has himself testified on my behalf. You have never heard his voice or seen his form, and you do not have his word abiding in you, because you do not believe him whom he has sent" (5:37-38). Later Jesus prays that "the world may know that you have sent me" (17:23).

The "sent" messenger is one beholden to a patron. He acts as an intermediary between the patron and those for whom the message is intended—that is, he acts as a broker. This is a role Jesus plays throughout John's Gospel. Note also that eight times we are reminded that Jesus will return to his patron (7:33; 13:1; 14:12, 28; 16:5, 10, 17, 28), suggesting that the broker has ready access to and from the patron who sent him. Eventually, Jesus will turn over the broker role to his own favored clients (disciples), who will take up the role on behalf of Jesus: "As you have sent me into the world, so I have sent them into the world" (17:18). Sorting out the players in the patronage system will help make all this clear.

Patrons are powerful individuals who control resources and are expected to use their positions to hand out favors to inferiors based on "friendship," personal knowledge and favoritism. Benefactor-patrons were expected to generously support city, village, or client. The Roman emperor related to major public officials this way, and they in turn related to those beneath them in similar fashion. Cities related to towns and towns to villages in the same way. A pervasive social network of patron-client relations thus arose in which connections meant everything. Having few connections was shameful. Throughout the New Testament, God is seen as the ultimate patron.

Brokers mediate between patrons above and clients below. First-order resources—land, jobs, goods, funds, power—are all controlled by patrons. Second-order resources—strategic contact with or access to patrons—are controlled by brokers who mediate the goods and services a patron has to offer. City officials serve as brokers of imperial resources. Holy men or prophets could also act as brokers. This is clearly a role in which John casts Jesus. Jesus says, "You are from below, I am from above" (8:23). He also makes clear that the Patron (God, Father) has given his resources to the Son to distribute as he will: "The Father loves the Son and has placed all things in his hands" (3:35).

Clients are those dependent on the largesse of patrons or brokers to survive well in their society. They owe loyalty and public acknowledgment of honor in return. Patronage was voluntary but ideally lifelong. Having only one patron to whom one owed total loyalty had been the pattern in Rome from the earliest times. But in the more chaotic competition for clients/patrons in the outlying provinces, playing patrons off against one another became commonplace. Note that, according to Luke, one cannot be client of both God and the wealth/greed system (Luke 16:13).

Friends play a role in the patronage system as well. While clients sometimes boasted of being "friends" of their patrons (for example, Pilate as a "friend of Caesar," John 19:12), friends were normally social equals. Having few of them was shameful. ⇨ **Friends,** 15:12-17. Note that the difficulty of the lame man in 5:1-20 is that he was friendless. Bound by reciprocal relations, friends felt obligated to help each other on an ongoing basis. Patrons (or brokers) did not. Patrons had to be cultivated because they owed nothing.

In the New Testament the language of "grace" is the language of patronage. God is seen as the ultimate patron whose resources are graciously given and often mediated through Jesus as broker (note John's comment that Jesus spoke or acted with the authority of his patron; 5:27; 17:2).

Legitimation of Jesus' Brokerage, 5:31-47

31 "If I testify about myself, my testimony is not true. ³²There is another who testifies on my behalf, and I know that his testimony to me is true. ³³You sent messengers to John, and he testified to the truth. ³⁴Not that I accept such human testimony, but I say these things so that you may be saved. ³⁵He was a burning and shining lamp, and you were willing to rejoice for a while in his light. ³⁶But I have a testimony greater than John's. The works that the Father has given me to complete, the very works that I am doing, testify on my behalf that the Father has sent me. ³⁷And the Father who sent me has himself testified on my behalf. You have never heard his voice or seen his form, ³⁸and you do not have his word abiding in you, because you do not believe him whom he has sent.

39"You search the scriptures because you think that in them you have eternal life; and it is they that testify on my behalf. ⁴⁰Yet you refuse to come to me to have life. ⁴¹I do not accept glory from human beings. ⁴²But I know that you do not have the love of God in you. ⁴³I have come in my Father's name, and you do not accept me; if another comes in his own name, you will accept him. ⁴⁴How can you believe when you accept glory from one another and do not seek the glory that comes from the one who alone is God? ⁴⁵Do not think that I will accuse you before the Father; your accuser is Moses, on whom you have set your hope. ⁴⁶If you believed Moses, you would believe me, for he wrote about me. ⁴⁷But if you do not believe what he wrote, how will you believe what I say?"

✦ *Notes:* **John 5:31-47**

5:31-47 The reader should note the defensive character of these verses. Jesus' claim to kinship with God (5:17) brought an immediate and angry response from his hearers. His consequent claim that honoring God means honoring him (5:23) was a claim that required a serious defense. To claim honor for oneself is to play the fool. Honor is *always* a matter of public recognition from others. ⇨ **Honor and Shame,** 5:31-47. Jesus himself acknowledges that fact in 5:31 (though note the contradiction in 8:14, which has led some commentators to posit different redactors). In the first part of this passage (vv. 31-40), Jesus is described as claiming there are four witnesses other than himself who vouch for his honored status: his Father (vv. 32, 37), John the Baptist (v. 33), his works (v. 36), and Israel's Scriptures (v. 39). The list is impressive and no doubt occasioned by controversy over Jesus' status, which the Gospel addresses repeatedly. In the second part (vv. 41-47), Jesus says that he does not look for honor recognition from human beings (v. 41). He accuses his opponents of solely valuing honor derived from human acknowledgment (v. 44a) and rejecting honor based on God's recognition of worth (v. 44b). For choosing their own criteria rather than God's, even their prophet Moses will condemn them (v. 46). By not believing Jesus, they demonstrate that they do not believe their prophet Moses either.

5:31-40 These verses speak of witnesses to the Son. The "other" spoken of here is almost certainly God the Father. There is precedent for this. Wisdom 1:6 says of the blasphemer, "God is witness of his inmost feelings, and a true observer of his heart." Since ancient Mediterranean people were not introspective, the comment in 1 Sam. 16:7 is virtually a truism: "For the LORD does not see as mortals see; they look on the outward appearance, but the LORD looks on the heart (see also Ps. 44:21; Rom. 2:16; 1 Cor. 14:25). Honor claims can mistakenly elicit acquiescence from humans because they can be fooled by surface appearances. God cannot be so deceived.

The testimony of John the Baptist is invoked here even though Jesus says he does not accept honor validation from humans (also 5:41). The other claim in this section is that Jesus' works validate his honor status. The notion that actions speak louder than words was a truism of the ancient world as well as the modern one. What is at issue here, however, is whether the works of Jesus are the works of God. If they are, it would be difficult for his opponents to reject his status claims.

5:39-40 The final witness of the four (see the **Notes** above) to Jesus' honor claim is the Scriptures. In v. 41 Jesus asserts that he does not accept human affirmations of honor, but, as the word of God, the Scriptures are more than "human" testimony; they are also the source of life. "He who has acquired the words of the Law has acquired for himself the life of the world to come" (*m. Aboth* 2.8). If the Scriptures testify to Jesus, then he has life to give.

5:41-47 This final segment of the chapter shows Jesus accusing his opponents of choosing their own value criteria over those of God. The Judeans, professed followers of Moses, reject the honor "that comes from the one who alone is God" in favor of honor that they give one another (v. 44). Jesus, on the other hand, rejects honor from human beings, and thus goes contrary to a central concern of the Mediterranean world. ⇨ **Honor and Shame,** 5:31-47. When Jesus claims the love of God is not in (or, among) his opponents, he is challenging their loyalty to God. ⇨ **Love/Hate,** 3:1-21. Note that in John the term *believe,* often expressed as "belief *into*" Jesus, has these same connotations of loyalty or attachment. Earlier (v. 41) Jesus rejected honor affirmations from human beings, but here (v. 43) he not only recognizes the prevailing wisdom that such affirmations were essential, he also turns it into an accusation of disloyalty to God. Lack of loyalty to God, in turn, causes the opponents to reject Jesus.

5:45-47 Elsewhere in John (9:28-29) the opponents of Jesus assert with some pride that they are followers of Moses and indeed know that God has spoken to Moses. That view is the conviction of those opposing Jesus here. But Jesus accuses them of lack of loyalty to Moses (see the **Note** above on the term *belief*), hence he is not surprised that they have no loyalty to him.

✧ *Reading Scenario:* **John 5:31-47**

Honor and Shame, 5:31-47

All human groups enculturate their members into internalized sanctions that keep those members from disrupting the group. The sanctions available to humans run from anxiety to shame to guilt. Every society, it seems, emphasizes one of these, while the other two step into the background. Traditionally, Enlightenment Western society has been a guilt-oriented society. On the contrary, the primary social sanction of first-century Mediterranean society was shame. The positive side of anxiety is a sense of security, of shame is honor, of guilt is a sense having done nothing wrong.

Honor and shame were the core, the heart, the soul of social life in Mediterranean antiquity. Concern for honor permeated every aspect of public life. Philo speaks of "wealth, fame, official posts, honors and everything of that sort with which the majority of mankind are busy" (*Det.* 122). He complains that "fame and honor are a most precarious possession, tossed about on the reckless tempers and flighty words of careless men" (*Abr.* 264).

Simply stated, honor is public reputation. It is symbolized in good name or eminent family of origin. It is one's status or standing in the village together with the public recognition of it. Public recognition is all-important. In John 5:23 God has acted so that "all" will honor the Son. To claim honor that is not publicly recognized is to play the fool. To grasp more honor than the public will allow is to be a greedy thief. To try to claim honor for oneself is shameful: Jesus speaks a truism when he says, "If I glorify myself, my glory is nothing" (John 8:54; also 7:18; 8:50). Thus, when Jesus says in 5:41 (also 12:43) that he does not accept glory from human beings, he is rejecting a core value of Mediterranean societies. When he claims in 5:44 that one should seek only the honor that comes from God, he is saying that only God has the wisdom to legitimate an honor gain. This, of course, makes perfect sense for members of John's antisociety, given their experience in "straight" society.

Honor is likewise a relative matter in which one claims to excel over others, to be superior. It thus implies a claim to rights on the basis of social precedence. As a result, honor and shame are forms of social evaluation in which both men and women are constantly compelled to assess their own conduct and that of their fellows in relation to one another. In this way the vocabulary of praise *(kalos)* and blame *(aiskros)* can function as a social sanction on moral behavior. It is perpetuated by a network of evaluation, the gossip network, which creates an informal but effective mechanism of social control.

Honor is considered a limited good, quite like those other scarce resources that include land, crops, livestock, political clout, and female sexuality. Being limited, honor gained by one is always honor lost by and taken from another. Envy is thus institutionalized and subjects those seeking to outdo their neighbors to hostile gossip and the pressure to share. Legitimate honor that is publicly recognized opens doors to patrons; honor withheld cuts off access to the resources patrons can bestow.

In a very pervasive way, then, honor determines dress, mannerisms, gestures, vocation, and posture, as well as who can eat with whom, who sits at what places at a meal, who can open a conversation, who has the right to speak, and who is accorded an audience. It serves as the prime indicator of social place (precedence) and provides the essential map for persons to interact with superiors, inferiors, and equals in socially prescribed or appropriate ways.

Given all this, we are not surprised to find that the vocabulary of honor/shame is pervasive in the literature of antiquity. Josephus speaks of honors bestowed by Caesar, Vespasian, David, Saul, Jonathan, Augustus, Claudius, and the city of Athens (*War* 1.194, 199, 358, 396, 607; 3.408; *Life* 423; *Ant.* 6.168, 251; 7.117; 13.102; 14.152; 19.292). He tells of the honor that belongs to consuls, governors, priests, village judges, and prophets (*War* 4.149; 7.82; *Ant.* 4.215; 10.92; 11.309; 15.217). Philo speaks often of honor, glory, fame, high reputations, being adorned with honors and public offices, noble birth, the desire for glory, and honor in the present and a good name for the future (*Migr.* 172; *Leg. All.* 3.87; *Det.* 33, 157; *Post.* 112; *Abr.* 185, 263). Plutarch, in his *Roman Questions* 13, par. 267A, tells us that the Latin word *honor* is *glory* or *respect* in Greek. These Greek terms for honor are the words used to translate the Hebrew word for glory in the third-century B.C.E. Greek translation of the Hebrew Bible. English versions of the Bible often translate these words with "glory." The point is that "honor" and "glory" refer to the same reality—the public acknowledgment of one's worth or social value. Note Romans

12:10, where Paul admonishes those "in Christ" to outdo one another in show-ing honor.

It is important here to note how honor is obtained. The usual way is by birth. An honor status is *ascribed* the day one is born and is derived from the social standing that one's family has —and has always had—in the village or city quar-ter (honor as status or precedence). Because it is derived from birth, all members of the family, both male and female, have the same general honor rating, though significant differences could also occur within families (birth order is an obvious example). As Herod (according to Josephus) reminds the people of Jerusalem, they must take care how they honor his three sons: "Do not pay undue or equal respects to them, but to every one according to the prerogative of their births; for he that pays such respects unduly, will thereby not make him that is honored beyond what his age requires so joyful, as he will make him that is dishonored sorrowful" (*War* 1.459).

Honor could be gained or lost. ⇨ **Challenge and Riposte,** 7:14-24. Thus, acquired honor (honor as virtue) might be bestowed as the result of favors done for a beneficent patron. It could be won in the pursuit of virtue, or could be grant-ed to those with skill in the never-ending game of challenge and response. Sig-nificant gain might result from great exploits of one family member, and all would benefit. Major loss could occur from some public shame, and every mem-ber of the family would suffer grief.

As in all honor-shame societies, so too in the ancient Mediterranean, family loyalty— doing whatever is necessary to uphold the honor of the family in pub-lic—is the quintessential virtue. Since family integrity is valued above all, fam-ily honor determines everything. Since the honor of one's family determines potential marriage partners as well as with whom one can do business, what functions one can attend, where one can live, and even what religious role one can play, family honor must be defended at all costs. The smallest slight or injury must be avenged or honor is permanently lost. Moreover, because the family is the basic unit in traditional societies rather than the individual, having a "flushed face" (*wajh* in Arabic, meaning a "face blushing due to being shamed"), as Middle Eastern villagers call it, can destroy the well-being of an entire kin group. We can see, therefore, why aspersions cast on lineage—that is, on family honor—are the most serious insults the Middle East has to offer. They are considered vulgar in the extreme. In Luke 3:7 when John the Baptist (also Jesus in Matt. 12:34; 23:33) calls the crowd the "offspring of female snakes," literally snake bastards, we have the Mediterranean equivalent of an extremely insulting and "dirty" mouth.

Finally, it also is important not to misunderstand the notion of shame. One can "be shamed." This refers to the state of public loss of honor—negative shame. But to "have shame" means to have concern about one's honor—posi-tive shame. It can be understood as sensitivity for one's own reputation (honor) or the reputation of one's family. Because it is sensitivity to the opinions of oth-ers, it is a positive quality. To lack this positive shame is to be *shameless.*

Women were the special bearers of this positive shame role in agrarian societies; they were expected to have this sensitivity in a notable way and to teach it to their children. People without shame, without sensitivity to the opinions of significant outsiders, make fools of themselves in public. Note the lament in Job 14:21 that a family's "children come to honor, and they do not know it; they are brought low, and it goes unnoticed."

Appearances are very important. The way others perceive a person is equivalent to a person's (or family's) actual social worth. Certain people, such as prostitutes, innkeepers, and actors, among others, were considered shameless, or without honor, in antiquity. This was because their occupations loudly announced that they did not possess this sensitivity for honor. They did not respect the boundaries or norms of the social system and thus threatened social chaos.

Of special importance is the sexual honor of a woman. While male honor is flexible and can sometimes be regained, female honor is absolute and once lost is gone forever. This is the emotional-conceptual counterpart of virginity and marital fidelity. Any sexual offense on a woman's part, however slight, would destroy not only her own honor, but that of all males in her paternal kin group as well. Interestingly, the order of those expected to defend (to the death) the honor of younger women, even married ones, ranks as follows: brother(s), husband, father. For older married women, the son(s) is the primary defender of her honor.

6:1 Sea of Galilee, taken from a boat, looking west toward toward Capernaum. Photo by Richard Ziegler.

Second Passover, in Galilee:
An Outdoor Meal of Bread and Fish, 6:1-15

6:1 After this Jesus went to the other side of the Sea of Galilee, also called the Sea of Tiberias. ²A large crowd kept following him, because they saw the signs that he was doing for the sick. ³Jesus went up the mountain and sat down there with his disciples. ⁴Now the Passover, the festival of the Jews, was near. ⁵When he looked up and saw a large crowd coming toward him, Jesus said to Philip, "Where are we to buy bread for these people to eat?" ⁶He said this to test him, for he himself knew what he was going to do. ⁷Philip answered him, "Six months' wages would not buy enough bread for each of them to get a little." ⁸One of his disciples, Andrew, Simon Peter's brother, said to him, ⁹"There is a boy here who has five barley loaves and two fish. But what are they among so many people?" ¹⁰Jesus said, "Make the people sit down." Now there was a great deal of grass in the place; so they sat down, about five thousand in all. ¹¹Then Jesus took the loaves, and when he had given thanks, he distributed them to those who were seated; so also the fish, as much as they wanted. ¹²When they were satisfied, he told his disciples, "Gather up the fragments left over, so that nothing may be lost." ¹³So they gathered them up, and from the fragments of the five barley loaves, left by those who had eaten, they filled twelve baskets. ¹⁴When the people saw the sign that he had done, they began to say, "This is indeed the prophet who is to come into the world."

15 When Jesus realized that they were about to come and take him by force to make him king, he withdrew again to the mountain by himself.

✦ *Notes:* John 6:1-15

6:1-15 A number of scholarly controversies attend this story since it is the only account of an extraordinary feeding reported in all four of the Gospels. It has become the focus of debate over whether John knew any of the Synoptics. Some have seen the story as full of allusions to the account in 2 Kings 4:42-44, where Elisha multiplies barley loaves and feeds a throng. More common are scholarly views that the story in John as well as in the Synoptics is heavily influenced by the ritual meal practices of Jesus groups. While it is the disciples who serve the crowd in Mark's account, here Jesus himself distributes the food in a manner reminiscent of Synoptic accounts of Jesus' Last Supper. Yet it is also true that in this Gospel Jesus typically takes the initiative (v. 5) and is described as being in control. For a consideration of such scholarly controversies concerning this chapter of John, consult the standard commentaries.

6:1-4 John typically introduces significant interactions of Jesus with an accurate designation of the time and place of the event. Here the time is when the Judean Feast of Passover was near; the place is the other side of the Sea of Galilee (also known as the Sea of Tiberias). Specifically, the location was "the" mountain. The mountain in Mediterranean culture was a height outside inhabited and cultivated space, that is, outside the city, the village, or the town. A mountaintop was a well-attested place for communing with God (like Sinai in the Exodus). Since the areas outside towns and villages were considered chaotic and uncontrolled by humans, however, they were believed to be inhabited by various spirits or demons. Meals did not normally take place there. People did not picnic (or do recreational swimming or go mountain climbing) in the first-century Mediterranean world. In the "wild," proper care could not be taken in the preparation of food or in meeting the other necessities of ritual purity. The fact that purchasing food is discussed in the story is an indication that the people in the crowd are some distance from kin from whom they would normally seek food when away from home for a time.

6:9 Barley was used for making bread among lower-status people because it was much cheaper than wheat (and less nutritious). ⇨ **Bread,** 6:1-15. Philo comments that barley "is of somewhat doubtful merit, suited for irrational animals and men in unhappy circumstances" (*De Spec. Leg.* 3.57).

6:10 A crowd of five thousand men (plus women and children) would have been larger than the population of all but a handful of the largest urban settlements and is undoubtedly an example of hyperbole in the tradition.

6:14-15 The people see the sign and conclude that Jesus is "the prophet" who is to come to Israel (see Deut. 18:15-22). But even more than this, they would forcibly make him king of Israel. Kings are not simply a political equivalent of a "president" with rights of hereditary succession. Rather, kings have total control of and responsibility for their subjects; they are expected to provide them with fertility, peace, and abundance. ⇨ **King of the Judeans,** 18:28—19:16a. Kingship is a significant motif in the Johannine passion narrative. In 18:36 Jesus declares that his kingdom is not of this world (not over Israel). Obviously, then, the kingship the crowd seeks to force upon him here is misplaced. ⇨ **World/Cosmos = Israelite Society,** 17:1-26.

At the conclusion of this story, Jesus goes off "to the mountain" by himself; see **Note** above. This is very strange behavior. In antiquity persons remaining alone in the wild for any length of time were considered a dangerous anomaly. Moreover, here Jesus goes into the region of powers beyond human control. The fact that he can do so unharmed is evidence of his place in the hierarchy of cosmic powers. ⇨ **Demons/Demon Possession,** 10:19-24.

6:9 "Five barley loaves and two fish." See Reading Scenario, **Bread** at 6:1-15. Photo by Avraham Hay.

✧ *Reading Scenario:* John 6:1-15

Bread, 6:1-15

The diet of nonelite, first-century Mediterranean peoples consisted of a few basic staples, with other items depending on availability and cost. For Roman Palestine we have only one food list that offers any specifics. According to a third-century Pharisaic document (*m. Ket.* 5.8-9), a husband must provide an estranged wife with bread, legumes, oil, and fruit. The amounts specified presume an intake of about eighteen hundred calories per day.

Of the three staple commodities—grain, oil, and wine—by far the most important was grain and the products made from it. The word *bread* meant both bread and food in general. Bread constituted one-half of the caloric intake in much of the ancient Mediterranean region (just as it does today). Wheat was considered much superior to barley; hence, barley (and sorghum) bread was the staple for the poor and slaves. Barley's lower gluten content, low extraction rate, less desirable taste, and indigestibility left it the staple of the poor in Roman times. Both the Old Testament (2 Kings 6:1, 16, 18) and the Mishnah authors (*m. Ket.* 5.8) assume wheat meal to be twice the value of barley meal. Growing barley requires less water than wheat, and it is less sensitive to soil salinity. Therefore, it became the major crop in arid parts of the Mediterranean world. The husband who provided an estranged wife with barley bread was required to provide her twice the ration of wheat. Sorghum was less common than either wheat or barley and likewise considered an inferior product.

While most peasants ate "black" bread, the rich could afford the sifted flours that made "clean" bread (*m. Mak.* 2.8). Milling was done at night and would require three hours of work to provide 3 kilograms (assuming a 0.5 kilogram daily ration) for a family of five or six. Bread dough would be taken to the village baker in the morning. In the towns and cities, bread could be purchased, so those who could afford it avoided the difficult labor of daily milling. The authors of the Mishnah imply that milling and baking would have been the first chores handed over by any wife with an available bondswoman or daughter-in-law (*m. Ket.* 5.5).

127

Jesus' Power over the Sea, 6:16-23

16 When evening came, his disciples went down to the sea, [17]got into a boat, and started across the sea to Capernaum. It was now dark, and Jesus had not yet come to them. [18]The sea became rough because a strong wind was blowing. [19]When they had rowed about three or four miles, they saw Jesus walking on the sea and coming near the boat, and they were terrified. [20]But he said to them, "It is I; do not be afraid." [21]Then they wanted to take him into the boat, and immediately the boat reached the land toward which they were going.

22 The next day the crowd that had stayed on the other side of the sea saw that there had been only one boat there. They also saw that Jesus had not got into the boat with his disciples, but that his disciples had gone away alone. [23]Then some boats from Tiberias came near the place where they had eaten the bread after the Lord had given thanks.

✦ *Notes:* John 6:16-23

6:16-21 The fact that the story of Jesus' walking on the sea intervenes between the feeding of the five thousand and the discourse on the bread of life leads many scholars to think John has slavishly followed a source in which the two "miracle stories" were together. They also appear in this sequence in Mark. The scenario covers "evening," "dark," and "the next day"—that is, a whole night. Jesus thus comes to his disciples on a stormy night.

6:18 Heavy windstorms are a common occurrence on the Sea of Galilee at certain times of the year, and the suddenness with which they can arise is truly astonishing. In antiquity, winds and seasons of the year were personified or attributed to certain invisible cosmic forces or powers.

6:19 It is important to note that "they saw Jesus walking on the sea." The sea is an essentially different entity from water. To walk on the sea is to trample on a being that can engulf people with its waves, swallow them in its deep, and support all sorts of living beings. Given the structure of boats in the period, people who traveled over or worked on the sea literally put their lives in the hands of the spirit(s) or deity that revealed its moods in the varying movements of the sea, from stormy, to rough, to calm, and the like. The Greco-Romans identified the "living" sea with the important deity Poseidon/Neptune (Semites called this deity Tiamat or Tehom), a deity noted for violent power. Jesus' ability to walk on the sea is evidence of his place in the hierarchy of cosmic powers. ➪ **Demons/Demon Possession,** 10:19-24. Early Jesus Messianists took this story as evidence of Jesus' power to save his people in the midst of fearsome trouble. It surely had this sort of resonance for John's antisociety.

Seeking Jesus:
A Challenge to Jesus at Capernaum
on the Other Side of the Sea, 6:24-31a

24 So when the crowd saw that neither Jesus nor his disciples were there, they themselves got into the boats and went to Capernaum looking for Jesus.

25 When they found him on the other side of the sea, they said to him, "Rabbi, when did you come here?" 26Jesus answered them, "Very truly, I tell you, you are looking for me, not because you saw signs, but because you ate your fill of the loaves. 27Do not work for the food that perishes, but for the food that endures for eternal life, which the Son of Man will give you. For it is on him that God the Father has set his seal." 28Then they said to him, "What must we do to perform the works of God?" 29Jesus answered them, "This is the work of God, that you believe in him whom he has sent." 30So they said to him, "What sign are you going to give us then, so that we may see it and believe you? What work are you performing? 31Our ancestors ate the manna in the wilderness; as it is written, 'He gave them bread from heaven to eat.'"

✦ *Notes:* John 6:24-31a

6:24 The sequence of events in this small narrative is not altogether clear. The main point, however, is simply that the crowd went looking for Jesus. Verse 23 suggests that some of the same crowd had eaten the loaves and fishes the day before. This serves to connect the feeding story to the discourse that will follow.

6:25-27 The title "Rabbi" points to Jesus as teacher (see 1:38). The question put to Jesus in v. 25 is a typical double-meaning question characteristic of John's anti-language. Culturally, it was very important to know where Jesus is from so that he might be situated in the status ranking order in terms of geography and genealogy. This was the way to obtain proper stereotypical knowledge of him. For Nicodemus, for example, Jesus' origin is like the wind/spirit: you do not know where it comes from and where it goes (3:8). We later learn of the Jerusalemites' burning concern to know where Jesus was from in the discussion in chapter 7 (vv. 27-29, 37-52). Judeans know that God spoke to Moses, but this man "we do not know where he is from" (9:29). Finally, even Pilate seeks to know: "Where are you from?" (19:9).

As usual, questions of Jesus' origins lead to a dialogue in which questions put to him are not directly answered (see the **Notes** on chaps. 3, 4), his comments are misunderstood, and he responds with an explanatory monologue. The dialogue here closely parallels the one in chapter 4. While in chapter 4 the issue was water that either temporarily or permanently relieves thirst, here the issue is food that perishes or that endures to eternal life. Such contrasts are further instances of the antilanguage that typifies groups embedded in some larger society, that feel compelled to draw strong and consistent either/or, inside/outside boundaries. ➪ **Antilanguage, 1:19-28.**

Jesus begins by putting his honor on the line ("Very truly, I tell you"); see the **Notes** at 1:50-51. Food as a metaphor for the divine gift of life was widespread in antiquity; such a metaphor would perhaps occur readily in situations where the vast majority of people lived at the bare subsistence level, a condition that lasted in nearly all the world until the Industrial Revolution (nineteenth century). Having bread literally meant having life. ⇨ **Bread,** 6:1-15. Working to provide that subsistence was a difficult daily struggle for all but the elite (recall that it was barley bread, the food of the majority, nonelites, that Jesus multiplied; see the **Notes** at 6:1-15). Having been fed bread by Jesus the day before, the crowd apparently hoped for more of the same. What he offers them is life-sustaining bread of a different sort.

6:28-29 Since they are used to working for bread, the response of the crowd is to inquire (presumably) what kind of work is necessary to receive this bread. If this bread Jesus offers is of a different kind, perhaps the work will be as well. They are told to work for the food that remains for eternal life, which the Son of Man gives (vv. 27, 58). And this work means to believe "into" the one whom God has sent (v. 29; cf. vv. 36-40, 45-47).

Believing "into" is a characteristic Johannine idiom. Many commentators have pointed out that this construction implies trust rather than simple intellectual assent. Given the collectivist character of relationships in ancient Mediterranean societies, however, even more is implied. ⇨ **Collectivist Personality,** 8:31-59. Collectivist persons become embedded in one another. A unity and loyalty is involved that is extremely deep. Since personal identity in collectivist cultures is always the result of the groups in which one is embedded, that too is involved. John's peculiar idiom (the Greek tense used connotes ongoing or continuous action) suggests exactly this kind of long-term solidarity with Jesus. Note that the language about being "sent" is brokerage language; see the **Notes** at 5:19-30.

6:30-31a The response of the crowd, in which they ask for a sign that they might believe, involves a striking change in the Greek tense used. Jesus had asked continuous and long-term belief from them (see above). The Greek tense they use in their response avoids the long-term (hence collectivist) implications of Jesus' demand that they "believe."

The demand for a sign is understandable, of course, since Jesus has just asked for solidarity with and loyalty to himself. But ironically the sign demanded here had just been given the day before when Jesus multiplied the loaves and fed the crowd! The day before, the crowd saw Jesus' sign and believed him to be a prophet, ready to make him king. In this encounter, he is simply a teacher expected to produce a further visible sign so that the crowd might believe Jesus to be the Son of Man providing "everlasting bread"—that is, bread from the realm of God.

It is also important to recognize that a question put to Jesus in public is a serious honor challenge. Jesus had put his honor on the line (v. 26), and it is now challenged directly with a reference to Israel's exodus experience and a scriptural quotation from Exod. 16:15.

The crowd would be familiar with the idea of bread from the sky from the story of the manna in Exodus 16. The implication is that their ancestors' loyalty to Moses had its basis in the fact that he was able to broker for them God's gift of life-giving bread in the wilderness. Thus, by withdrawing their honor assessment of the day before and by citing this story, they have sharpened the challenge to Jesus significantly: why should they switch their loyalty from the prophet Moses to Jesus? Moses, like a king, provided them with security and sustenance. What will Jesus do? The stakes in the public challenge are now extremely high.

6:30-31a Manna, as it is described in the Old Testament (see esp. Exodus 16), is clearly miraculous. The source of the word is the Hebrew *mān-hû'*, which means, "What is that?" (Exod. 16:15). Still, scientists look for a natural phenomenon that might be the origin of the idea. One of the most frequently mentioned possibilities is the sweet exudation on the branches of white hammada (*Hammada salicornica*), a relatively common shrub in the southern Sinai, where these pictures were taken. Photos by Thomas Hoffman.

131

Jesus Explains the Passage Cited
from Exodus 16 by His Challengers, 6:31b-59

31b: "as it is written: 'HE GAVE THEM BREAD FROM HEAVEN TO EAT.'"

32 Jesus then said to them, "Truly, truly, I say to you, it was not Moses who *gave* you the *bread* from *heaven*; my *FATHER gives* you the true *bread* from *heaven.*

33 For the *bread* of God is that which comes down from *heaven,* and *gives life* to the world."

34 They said to him, "Lord, give us this *bread* always."

35 Jesus said to them, "I am the *bread* of *life;* he who comes to me shall not hunger, and he who believes in me shall never thirst.

36 But I said to you that you have seen me and yet do not believe.

37 All that the *FATHER gives* me will come to me; and him who comes to me I will not cast out.

38 For I have come down from *heaven*, not to do my own will, but the will of him who sent me;

39 and this is the will of him who sent me, that I should lose nothing of all that he has given me, but raise it up at the last day.

40 For this is the will of my FATHER, that every one who sees the Son and believes in him should have eternal *life;* and I will raise him up at the last day."

41 The Jews then murmured at him, because he said, "I am the *bread* which came down from *heaven.*"

42 They said, "Is not this Jesus, the son of Joseph, whose father and mother we know? How does he now say, 'I have come down from *heaven*'?"

43 Jesus answered them, "Do not murmur among yourselves.

44 No one can come to me unless the FATHER who sent me draws him; and I will raise him up at the last day.

45 It is written in the prophets, 'And they shall all be taught by God.' Every one who has heard and learned from the FATHER comes to me.

46 Not that any one has seen the FATHER except him who is from God; he has seen the FATHER.

47 Truly, truly, I say to you, he who believes has eternal *life.*

48 I am the *bread* of *life.*

49 **Your fathers ate the manna in the wilderness,** and they died.

50 This is the *bread* which comes down from *heaven*, that a man may *eat* of it and not die.

51 I am the living *bread* which came down from *heaven;* if any one *eats* of this *bread*, he will *live* for ever; and the *bread* which I shall *give* for the l*ife* of the world is my *flesh.*"

52 The Jews then disputed among themselves, saying, "How can this man *give* us his *flesh* to *eat?*"

53 So Jesus said to them, "Truly, truly, I say to you, unless you *eat* the *flesh* of the Son of man and drink his *blood,* you have no *life* in you;

54 he who *eats* my *flesh* and drinks my *blood* has eternal *life*, and I will raise him up at the last day.

55 For my *flesh* is food indeed, and my *blood* is drink indeed.

56 He who *eats* my *flesh* and drinks my *blood* abides in me, and I in him.

57 As the living FATHER sent me, and I *live* because of the FATHER, so he who *eats* me will *live* because of me.

58 This is the *bread* which came down from *heaven,* not such as the **fathers** ate and died; he who *eats* this *bread* will *live* forever."

59 This he said in the synagogue, as he taught at Capernaum.

✦ *Notes:* **John 6:31b-59**

6:31b-59 Jesus' response to the crowd's challenge takes the form of a modulating and repetitive consideration of the passage cited from Exodus 16. We have noted this dimension of Jesus' answer in the way we have punctuated the passage printed above. He points out that Moses was not the patron providing food to the Israelites; God was. Moses was simply God's broker. By identifying God as his own Father and God as the one who gives the bread, Jesus is asserting his own claim as the new broker of God's life-giving bread. ➪ **Patronage,** 5:21-30.

6:35-40 This is the first of the seven "I am" statements in John. In antiquity bread really was a matter of life. Since bread provided 50 percent of the calories available to most nonelite people, the metaphor suggests something very fundamental indeed (➪ **Bread,** 6:1-15). Jesus is the sustenance of life at its most basic level.

6:59 "This he said in the synagogue . . . in Capernaum." These are the remains of the fourth century C.E. synagogue of the village of Capernaum. It is most likely that the synagogue of Jesus' day occupied the same spot. Photo by Richard Rohrbaugh.

The statement that Jesus will not turn away those who come to him is important group information. As the parallelism in v. 35 (also 7:37-38) makes clear, the phrase "come to me" is the equivalent of "believing into" Jesus. A dyadic relationship is envisioned that is the basis of being part of Jesus' antisociety (see the **Notes** above at 6:28-29). Verses 38-40 are a near summary of the Gospel itself. They make clear that the life-sustaining and redeeming "bread" (and drink) Jesus offers are being brokered by him on behalf of God.

6:41-42 Once more, the issue here is where Jesus is from (see **Note** on vv. 6:25-27 above). Since the honor ascribed to persons depended on family lineage, where they were from determined who they were and what honor standing they had in the eyes of the community. ⇨ **Collectivist Personality,** 8:31-59. ⇨ **Lineage and Stereotypes,** 8:31-59. If Jesus is "from" Joseph and his mother, two people known to be members of the village nonelite, he cannot be "from" the sky with all of the honor status that would imply. Note that a similar argument about where Jesus is "from" occurs in 8:31-59 (cf. Luke 4:22). See the **Notes** there.

6:43-46 Jesus' reply is very carefully crafted. If he were to claim that people are drawn to him because of what he is in himself, he would be making honor claims that could not be sustained by one of his lineage. But when he asserts that the drawing power is God's, and that he is merely the broker (⇨ **Patronage,** 5:21-30) sent to convey it, the objection raised in vv. 41-42 falls to the ground. This deference to God is restated in the idea that those who come to Jesus have learned from and been taught by God, a quotation from Isa. 54:13.

6:47-51 Jesus asserts his word of honor for the third time in this dialogue (see the **Notes** at 6:26, 47, 52). John uses the term *believe* to indicate loyalty to Jesus and his faction (see the **Notes** at 6:28-29). The reward for such loyalty is new life that is endless.

"Your ancestors" (in Greek "your fathers") suggests considerable social distance between Jesus and his opponents. The bread the ancestors ate in the wilderness did not produce the same kind of life that is available to those who form a dyadic bond with Jesus. The introduction of the term *flesh* will occasion the controversy that follows.

6:52-59 This is yet another example of the frequent literary technique in John's Gospel in which questions put to Jesus offer the occasion for lengthy explanations. The Greek here suggests a violent disagreement. Jesus' response is an excellent instance of antilanguage. To those outside the antisociety, Jesus urges cannibalism. Yet in terms of antilanguage, to eat Jesus' flesh and drink his blood is synonymous with the words *to welcome, accept, receive, believe into,* and the like. In Israel's tradition, the question of eating flesh and blood is raised in passages dealing with sacrifice. In this perspective the nuance here is accepting Jesus even in spite of his being "lifted up" and "glorified" on the cross. ⇨ **Flesh and Blood,**

6:41-59. Significantly, the failure of Jesus' opponents to perceive the new definition of the term *flesh* (v. 55) is an indication that they are not insiders who can comprehend the insider language (antilanguage) of the Johannine group.

Jesus' reply begins with his typical (in John) way of placing his own honor on the line. This is the fourth time he has done so in this discourse (vv. 26, 32, 47, 53). See the **Notes** at 5:19-30. When Jesus raises the repulsive prospect of drinking blood, he demands something expressly forbidden in the Torah (Gen. 9:4; Lev. 3:17; Deut. 12:23; Acts 15:20). The metaphorical meanings offered in v. 55, however, redefine these terms for Johannine insiders: they become part of the antilanguage of this special community (see the **Notes** below at 6:60-71). As v. 56 then suggests, eating and drinking the flesh and blood of Jesus creates the kind of dyadic, collectivist relationship with him that brings eternal life. ⇨ **Collectivist Personality,** 8:31-59.

✧ *Reading Scenario:* John 6:41-59

Flesh and Blood, 6:41-59

Jesus' insistence in John's Gospel that Israelites eat his flesh and blood in order to have the life that befits children of God is antilanguage at its most obvious. The context is entirely different from that of the Synoptic Last Supper, at which Jesus offers bread and wine as his body and blood (Matt. 26:26-29; Mark 14:22-25; Luke 22:15-20; see also 1 Cor. 10:16; 11:23-27). John has no prophetic symbolic action with bread and wine as in the Synoptics (and Paul), just straightforward antilanguage, which made good sense to the members of John's antisociety.

The use of the phrase "flesh and blood" derives from two different social contexts. One context refers the phrase to human beings as created, while the other refers to animals, especially those used in sacrifice.

Relative to human beings, "flesh and blood" pertains to the human being in general (Gal. 1:16; Heb. 2:14), specifically as a created, hence perishable, entity: "What I am saying, brothers and sisters, is this: flesh and blood cannot inherit the kingdom of God, nor does the perishable inherit the imperishable" (1 Cor. 15:50). Human opponents are "flesh and blood," but sky beings such as "principalities, powers, world rulers, and other wicked spirit warriors" are not (Eph. 6:12).

Relative to animals, the phrase is used to make proper distinctions concerning what is edible by humans. To begin with, in Israelite priestly lore, edible meat derives only from temple sacrifice, and two parts of all sacrificed animals belong to God alone, the blood and the fat around the kidneys. In the first place, blood is always prohibited. In Israel's tradition, all human beings, regardless of ethnic origin, are prohibited by God from eating flesh with blood; the prohibition is stated early in Genesis: "Only, you shall not eat flesh with its life, that is, its blood" (Gen. 9:4). For Israel, the legal prohibition reflecting the Genesis directive is found in Deuteronomy: "Only be sure that you do not eat the blood; for the blood is the life, and you shall not eat the life with the meat"

(Deut. 12:23; it is found also in Lev. 17:11: "For the life of the flesh is in the blood; and I have given it to you for making atonement for your lives on the altar; for, as life, it is the blood that makes atonement"; and Lev. 17:14: "For the life of every creature—its blood is its life; therefore I have said to the people of Israel: You shall not eat the blood of any creature, for the life of every creature is its blood; whoever eats it shall be cut off"). Eating flesh with the blood in it is redolent of witchcraft: "You shall not eat anything with its blood. You shall not practice augury or witchcraft" (Lev. 19:26).

Second, the other organic ingestible prohibited in Israel is fat, equally a life source. "All the fat is the LORD's" (Lev. 3:16). In sacrifice, blood was to be thrown against the altar, while the fat was to go up in smoke. The fat in question is the fat surrounding the kidneys. The kidneys with the fat surrounding them were considered the "seat of life" because of the connection with the sexual organs (see Ps. 139:13). It is true that later legislation loses the connection of fat and kidneys to sexual organs and life (see Lev. 4:19-20, 26, 31, 35, et al.), yet in Israel's tradition fat and blood emerge as independent vehicles of life. Thus, the prohibitions of fat and blood single out those organs, human or animal, that serve as the seat of life. Life is from God alone and belongs to God alone. To ingest fat or blood is to strive to be like God.

Interestingly, apart from the regulations governing sacrifice, there is no reference to fat as the vehicle of life. Since the fat is Yahweh's, the portions to be burned are all included in the term *fat* (Lev. 4:18-35; 7:3, 30-33; 9:18-20; Num. 18:17; et al.), even when the kidneys are explicitly mentioned. In fact, the word *fat* can become a term for the sacrifice itself (Lev. 9:24; 1 Sam. 15:22; Isa. 1:11; cf. 1 Kings 8:64). The priestly authors even formulated the law so that all fat, even that of animals not suitable for sacrifice, was the property of Yahweh (Lev. 3:16-17). Ezekiel refers to fat and blood as God's food (Ezek. 44:7). Fat and blood even stand for sacrificed life. Yahweh's sword drips with his enemy's blood and fat, which fill the whole land (Isa. 34:6-7). God can even give the blood and fat of the enemy to animals as food (Ezek. 39:19).

The reference to Jesus' flesh and blood as the source of eternal life is best explained in terms of Israel's tradition of fat and blood as the source of life. In quite antisocietal fashion, Jesus urges upon his followers what has been prohibited as food to humans from the time of Noah, and even, a fortiori, what is truly cannibalistic. In terms of antilanguage, to ingest Jesus' flesh and blood is synonymous with welcoming, accepting, receiving, believing in, and the like. Given the sacrificial context of fat/flesh and blood, the nuance here is accepting Jesus even in spite of his being "lifted up" and "glorified" on the cross. Thus, to all who welcomed Jesus, "to all who received him, who believed in his name, he gave power to become children of God, who were born, not of blood or of the will of the flesh or of the will of man, but of God" (1:12-13). Blood is the seat of life. The will of the flesh is in the fat (and kidneys), while the will of man is in the heart. It is through ingesting Jesus' flesh and blood, through accepting and welcoming Jesus as the Word become Israelite human, crucified as "king of the Judeans," that those who believe in Jesus have their life as children of God.

Insider Talk Unmasks Antisociety Disloyalty, 6:60-66

60 When many of his disciples heard it, they said, "This teaching is difficult; who can accept it?" [61]But Jesus, being aware that his disciples were complaining about it, said to them, "Does this offend you? [62]Then what if you were to see the Son of Man ascending to where he was before? [63]It is the spirit that gives life; the flesh is useless. The words that I have spoken to you are spirit and life. [64]But among you there are some who do not believe." For Jesus knew from the first who were the ones that did not believe, and who was the one that would betray him. [65]And he said, "For this reason I have told you that no one can come to me unless it is granted by the Father."

66 Because of this many of his disciples turned back and no longer went about with him.

✦ *Notes:* John 6:60-66

6:60-66 The term *disciples* here includes more than the Twelve, who are singled out in v. 67. All antisociety groups include both core members, who maintain strong loyalty to the leader, and peripheral members whose relationships with the leader (and group) are more fluid. ➪ **Antisociety,** 1:35-51. Jesus seems to be aware that peripheral members are troubled by what he has said.

The Greek in v. 60 is ambiguous. It could mean, as the NRSV has it, that the teaching was hard to accept. It could also mean that because of the hard teaching, Jesus was difficult to accept. The latter makes more sense in terms of the demands of group loyalty.

As noted above (see the **Notes** at 6:28-29), in John to "believe" means to have complete trust in and absolute loyalty to Jesus as central personage in the antisociety. One of the major interests in John has been to defend the brokerage of Jesus as genuinely one from God (see the many **Notes** where language is used about Jesus being "sent" from God, the patron). Faced with the disloyalty of peripheral group members, Jesus asks how they would react if they were to see him returning to the patron from whom he came. While we do not hear their response, Jesus goes on to make clear that it is really God, the patron, who determines who does and does not become part of the group.

Reaction of the Twelve, 6:67-71

67 So Jesus asked the twelve, "Do you also wish to go away?" [68]Simon Peter answered him, "Lord, to whom can we go? You have the words of eternal life. [69]We have come to believe and know that you are the Holy One of God." [70]Jesus answered them, "Did I not choose you, the twelve? Yet one of you is a devil." [71]He was speaking of Judas son of Simon Iscariot, for he, though one of the twelve, was going to betray him.

✦ *Notes:* John 6:67-71

6:67-71 These verses comprise the only passage in John's Gospel apart from Jesus' final words (13:1—17:26) where he talks alone to the Twelve, the core insiders of his group. They do not play a major role in John's Gospel as they do in the Synoptics; in fact, the Twelve are explicitly mentioned only here and in 20:17. No antisociety can survive without loyal core members, however, and here they are put to the test. ⇨ **Antisociety,** 1:35-51.

Peter's response is often assumed to be the Johannine equivalent of the confession in Mark 8:27-30. In that passage the issue is Jesus' concern about his proper social role and identity. Here, on the other hand, the issue is one of the central issues in John's Gospel: Is Jesus the genuine broker of God or not? Peter acknowledges that there is no other broker available and that the core group is loyal to Jesus as the Holy One (chosen, special, designated), the broker of God. ⇨ **Patronage,** 5:21-30.

Antisocieties are frequently involved in rivalries with other groups as well as in tension with the surrounding "straight" society in which they are embedded. Peripheral members often divide their loyalties between their own group and outside organizations. They thus undermine an antisocietal group's effectiveness. Tests of loyalty to determine who is in and who is out are common. Here Jesus knows that one of his core group is disloyal and that this will cause trouble (note 17:12 where Judas is called the "son of destruction"). The narrator emphasizes that, though disloyal, Judas was one of the core group.

CHAPTER V
JOHN 7:1–8:59
JESUS BROUGHT LIGHT AND LIFE
TO THE JERUSALEM TEMPLE

Around the Feast of Sukkoth in Galilee:
A Challenge from Jesus' Brothers, 7:1-9

7:1 After this Jesus went about in Galilee. He did not wish to go about in Judea because the Jews were looking for an opportunity to kill him. ²Now the Jewish festival of Booths was near. ³So his brothers said to him, "Leave here and go to Judea so that your disciples also may see the works you are doing; ⁴for no one who wants to be widely known acts in secret. If you do these things, show yourself to the world." ⁵(For not even his brothers believed in him.) ⁶Jesus said to them, "My time has not yet come, but your time is always here. ⁷The world cannot hate you, but it hates me because I testify against it that its works are evil. ⁸Go to the festival yourselves. I am not going to this festival, for my time has not yet fully come." ⁹After saying this, he remained in Galilee.

✦ *A Note about* John 7–8

Chapters 7 and 8 of this Gospel form a single unit. This long passage deals with perhaps the most significant event in the first part of the story—Jesus' teaching in the Jerusalem temple. On this occasion, Jesus presents himself at the center of Israel's social life as "the light of the world," as God's revelation for Israel. The passage is well delineated by mention of Jesus' entrance into the temple area to teach (7:14b) and his exit from the temple (8:59), prefaced by an introduction (7:1-14a) noting first of all that the Judeans sought to kill Jesus (7:1), a subject equally noted at the end of the passage (8:59). The whole piece is punctuated by the refrain recording Jesus in the temple and/or teaching there:

I.	7:14	Jesus went up into the temple and taught.
II.	7:28	Jesus proclaimed as he taught in the temple.
III.	7:37	Jesus proclaimed in the temple: "If anyone thirst . . ."
IV.	8:12	Jesus again said to them: "I am the light of the world."
V.	8:20	He spoke in the treasury as he taught in the temple.
VI.	8:5	Jesus went out of the temple.

While we will look at individual segments that constitute this passage, it will be useful to keep the whole in mind.

7:2 A feature of the feast of Sukkoth (see note on 7:2-9) is the small, rather flimsy huts (Heb.: *sukkoth,* Eng.: booths, tabernacles) like the one pictured here from which the feast takes its name. During the week of the feast the people ate and slept in them in memory of the forty years they spent in tents in the desert. Photo by Avraham Hay.

✦ *Notes:* John 7:1-9

7:1 The writer draws a clear distinction here between Galilee and Judea, which unfortunately gets lost with the NRSV's incorrect translation, "Jews." It should read "Judeans" *(Iudaios),* making clear that Jesus was being received differently by Judeans and Galileans. ➪ **Jews/Judeans,** 1:19-28. The hostility against Jesus that is so prevalent in John mounts here and results in this long section (John 7–8) in which charges against Jesus by outsiders are made, examined, and refuted.

7:2-9 John rather consistently localizes the events he describes in terms of locale and time. Just as hearers of the Gospel were told, "Now the Passover, the festival of the Judeans, was near" (6:4), as the time setting for the previous set of incidents, now the author notes that the Feast of Sukkoth (Booths, Tabernacles, Huts, etc.) was near. While the Passover incident in the previous chapter put us in the spring of year, the Feast of Sukkoth was in the fall. It marked the festivities attending the grape and olive harvests (September–October), and was soon followed by the rainy season (October–March) when travel was impossible. Since the time of Babylonian ascendancy (ca. 600 B.C.E.), the fall festival also marked the beginning of the new year (changed from the spring, in spite of the divine directive noted explicitly in Exod. 12:2). Along with Passover and Pentecost, Sukkoth was one of the three great festivals of the Israelite year. The festival included a prayer for winter rains (water) and for the renewal of sunlight (light). A large golden flagon was filled at the pool of Siloam and brought to the temple for libations (*m. Suk.* 4.9). A huge golden candelabrum with lamps outfitted with wicks made from discarded priestly clothing was also lit during the festival (*m. Suk.* 5.1). For the significance of these in relation to Jesus' actions, see the **Notes** below at 7:37 and 8:12.

7:2-5 Jesus' brothers are portrayed here as outsiders who are not part of Jesus' group ("For not even his brothers believed in him"). Their demand is the first of three challenges to Jesus in the passage. ▷ **Challenge and Riposte,** 7:15-18. The others will come from the Judeans in the temple (7:14-24) and the people of Jerusalem (7:25-31). As Jesus points out (7:7), the brothers have solidarity with the larger society that Jesus does not have. ▷ **Love/Hate,** 3:1-21. ▷ **World/Cosmos = Israelite Society,** 17:1-26. The fact that they wish to see Jesus' reputation grow suggests their own self-interest: if Jesus gains honor, so will every member of his family.

7:6-9 Jesus' riposte to the challenge issued by his brothers (7:2-5) is simply to reject it for the present moment. Rejecting a challenge out of hand was usually the strategy of someone challenged by an inferior and could suggest cowardice if done inappropriately. By suggesting that his hour has not yet come, however, Jesus implies that it soon will. Thus, he is not portrayed as running from the challenge but rather as the one in control of its timing.

✧ *Reading Scenarios:* **John 7:1-9**

Secrecy, 7:1-9

In the honor-shame world of the Mediterranean, reputation meant everything. Since honor is largely determined by public opinion, it becomes critical that the public know nothing that might damage a person's reputation or alter the public image that a family or group has so assiduously cultivated. Information control thus is a strategy used to maintain one's honor.

Among the devices of information control available to humans, secrecy is rather fundamental. Secrecy is a formal, conscious, deliberate, and calculated concealment of information, activities, or relationships that outsiders can gain only by espionage. It is a selective transmission of information, an attempt to control the information flow across the web of social boundaries. The nature of secrecy is that it rests on a premise of distrust.

This premise is quite clearly stated in John's narrative: "When he was in Jerusalem at the Passover festival, many believed in his name because they saw the signs that he was doing. But Jesus on his part would not entrust himself to them, because he knew all people, and needed no one to testify about anyone; for he himself knew what was in everyone" (2:23-25). Such distrust is rooted in uncertainty about how others might react if secret information were made available. Moreover, secrecy makes it difficult for outsiders to predict the actions of insiders and to take counteraction against them.

The need to conceal information comes from competition for and conflict over valued scarce resources such as power, prestige, honor, and wealth. We can see it in the frequent mention of people seeking Jesus to do him harm. After the Bethzatha healing, for example, the Judeans seek Jesus to persecute and kill him (5:12, 16, 18). In chapter 6 the crowds seek to make him king against his will (6:15, 24). In chapters 7 through 11 this conflict intensifies with the Judeans' attempts to capture and kill Jesus (7:30, 44; 8:20, 59; 10:31, 39; 11:53, 56). The climax of the conflict comes in 18:4-5, when Jesus is finally arrested.

It is especially important to cloak anything that happens in the in-group that might be considered a threat by outsiders. In a limited good world, where anything gained—whether new wealth, position, honor, or something else—was always believed to come at someone else's expense, one could never appear grasping or self-aggrandizing in public without raising immediate suspicion. The much-discussed "messianic secret" motif so prominent in Mark (1:25, 34, 44; 3:12; 5:43; 7:24, 36; 8:30; 9:9, 30) can be seen in this light rather than as a theological ploy. And the same is true of the elusiveness of Jesus in John. Having been born into the low social status of a village artisan (John 6:42), claims by Jesus that he is a celestial personage who has "come down from the sky" would have been viewed as grasping in the extreme. In Israel it is only something an antisociety can appreciate. Writing for members of such an antisociety, John asserts this celestial origin of Jesus right from the beginning of the Gospel (see the **Notes** at 1:1-18). But in the narrative Jesus shows himself to be an honorable person by being elusive and trying to keep such information out of the public arena (4:3; 5:13; 6:15; 7:1; 7:10; 8:59; 10:39; 11:54). The time for him to assert his claim is his "hour," and so long as the hour has not yet come, he avoids challenging others on this score (7:30; 8:21). The Father to whom he looks (5:37; 14:8) and the Spirit whom he gives (3:8) are likewise involved in his reticence.

Further, the frequent misunderstandings in the Gospel story (Nicodemus in chap. 3; the woman in chap. 4; Pilate in chaps. 18–19) show Jesus using deliberate confusion and secrecy to enhance his reputation in the eyes of readers. In the same way, secrecy enhances Jesus' reputation when it comes to both his origin (6:42; 19:9-10) and his destination (6:16; 13:33; 14:19). Note how the disciples express their delight at finally being treated as in-group members when Jesus opts for plain language in 16:29.

Insider/outsider talk in John should be judged in this same light. ⇨ **In-group and Out-group,** 15:18—16:4a. The insider interpretation of Jesus' role and goal in the final discourse (chaps. 13–17) is the prime example. John and his antisociety audience see both the outsider and insider versions of the story of Jesus even though Jesus' public hearers do not really understand what he is up to. This is a clear tip-off that John is telling his story for insiders, a part of his fictive kin group whose members are "children of God," and Jesus' friends.

Lying, 7:1-9

In 7:3-4 the brothers of Jesus urge him to go up to Judea for the Feast of Sukkoth to show off the works he does and thereby gain a reputation. Jesus responds (7:7-9) by telling his brothers that he is not going up to the festival because his hour has not yet come. Yet we learn in 7:10 that he does precisely that; as soon as his brothers had gone to the festival, he too went there in a secretive manner.

This action of Jesus appears to Western readers as outright deception, lying to deflect the attention of his siblings. However, to understand what is going on here, it is necessary to understand the way truth-telling is understood in the collectivist cultures of the Mediterranean world.

Anthropologists commonly distinguish three distinctive selves: the privately defined self, the publicly defined self, and the collectively or in-group defined self.

The *private self* is what I myself say about my own traits, states, or behaviors. Who is it I think I really am in my heart of hearts?

The *public self* consists of what the general group says about me. Who does that range of people with whom I regularly come in contact think I am? What do neighbors, merchants, teachers, and the like say about me? Do I live up to their expectations when I interact with them? And what do I think of all that these people think of me?

The *collective* or *in-group self* is what the in-group says about me. Who do my parents say I am? What are their expectations for me? Did my family give me a nickname? What does it say about me? What are the expectations of my grandparents, aunts and uncles, cousins, and brothers and sisters in regard to who I am, how I should behave, what I will be? And what do I think of what these people think of me? What do my friends want me to do over against what my parents want me to do?

To understand the self in terms of social psychology, we need to know the way the defined self emerges in the contrasting collectivist and individualistic cultural types. Consider the following diagram in which the boxed-in defined selves are expected to match to produce "truth."

Collectivist Culture	*Individualist Culture*
Privately defined self **In-group defined self**	**Privately defined self** **Publicly defined self**
Publicly defined self	In-group defined self

The types of self in bold relief form a unity in the respective cultures. What this chart makes clear is that in collectivist cultures there is a general conformity between private self and in-group self. Such people take in-group self-assessments far more seriously than people in individualist cultures. Moreover, individuals are socialized, not to express what they personally think, but to say what their conversation partner or audience needs or wants to hear from the in-group.

When it comes to dealing with in-group others, collectivist societies anticipate that individuals will often think one way and speak another. For the most part, harmony or getting along with in-group neighbors is valued above all sorts of other concerns. Saying the right thing to maintain harmony is thus far more important than telling what seems to be the truth to the private self. In fact, "truth" might be defined here as conformity between what the in-group thinks about some person, event, or thing, and what the private self believes and knows. Collectivist persons are not expected to have personal opinions, much less to voice their own opinions. It is sufficient and required to hold only those opinions that derive from social consensus.

In individualist cultures, by contrast, the in-group self recedes. The public and private selves converge to form a single "objectively" defined private self. Inconsistency between the public and private self is understood to be hypocrisy. One must think and say the same thing. Honesty, frankness, and sincerity are more abstract and less interpersonal for individualists. Everyone is expected to have an opinion on everything, and everyone is supposed to act as though everyone's opinion counted for something.

The way in which the self is defined also determines behavior. The collectivist person represents the in-group and is presumed to always speak in its name. It is shameful to tell the truth if it dishonors one's in-group members or causes them discomfort. It is equally shameful to expect to be told the truth if one is not an in-group member. Out-group persons have no right to in-group truth. Notice how Jesus explains the real meaning of his teaching only to the in-group, in private (chaps. 13–17), or to those in the process of becoming in-group members (for example, Nicodemus, the Samaritan woman).

In nonchallenging situations, out-group persons are almost always told what makes for harmony and what is to be expected. Making a friend feel good by what one has to say is a way of honoring the other, and that is far more important than telling the truth. Thus, in collectivist cultures, the privately defined self and the in-group self tend to coincide. The person speaks in the name of the in-group in public.

By contrast, individualists as a rule fuse the privately and publicly defined selves. The privately defined self and the publicly defined self tend to coincide. The private self is in fact the acting public self. This is called "objectivity," and individualists value being objective in speech. To lie is to say one thing publicly while thinking another privately. Thus, in individualistic cultures a person speaks in his/her own name in public.

In each type of culture, a lie consists of splitting the selves included in the boxes above. Thus, an individualistic lie is to think one thing and say another. That involves splitting what one knows privately from what one says publicly. To a collectivist, however, a lie involves splitting private and in-group "truth." In a collectivist culture, one's private knowledge has nothing to do with truth.

The right to the truth and the right to withhold the truth belong to the "man of honor," and to contest these rights is to place a person's honor in jeopardy, to challenge that person. Lying and deception are or can be honorable and legitimate. To lie in order to deceive an outsider, one who has no right to the truth, is honorable. However, to be called a liar by anyone is a great public dishonor. The reason for this is that truth belongs only to one who has a right to it. To lie really means to deny the truth to one who has a right to it, and the right to the truth only exists where respect is due (in the family, to superiors, and not necessarily to inferiors or to equals with whom we compete). Thus, to deceive by making something ambiguous or to lie to an out-group person is to deprive the other of respect, to refuse to show honor, to humiliate the other.

What Jesus does here would thus be considered right and proper by a collectivist culture. For, as the author notes in v. 5, his brothers had no loyalty toward him; they stood outside his in-group. Jesus withholds the truth from the brothers because they are out-group persons and have no right to it. In so doing, he shows himself to be an honorable person who knows with whom the truth is properly to be shared.

Around the Feast of Sukkoth in Jerusalem: Divided Public Judgment about Jesus, 7:10-14a

> 10 But after his brothers had gone to the festival, then he also went, not publicly but as it were in secret. [11]The Jews were looking for him at the festival and saying, "Where is he?" [12]And there was considerable complaining about him among the crowds. While some were saying, "He is a good man," others were saying, "No, he is deceiving the crowd." [13]Yet no one would speak openly about him for fear of the Jews.
>
> [14] About the middle of the festival, Jesus went up . . .

✦ *Notes:* John 7:10-14a

We have divided several of the passages of the Gospel of John at half-verses. Here the segment runs from v. 10 to v. 14a. (For similar divisions, note John 7:14b—8:59; 15:1—16:4a; 16:4b-33; 18:28—19:16a.) These divisions are based on the verbal notations pointed out in the appendix. Remember that the original documents comprising the Bible had no divisions. The person responsible for dividing the Bible into chapters was the medieval bishop of Canterbury Stephen Langton. The purpose of his making chapters in the so-called Parisian Bible about 1226 was to allow ready reference to portions of the Bible in scholarly study. Robert Estienne, a Renaissance printer, marked off the verses of the Bible for his 1551 edition. Thus, biblical chapter and verse divisions are purely functional.

7:10-14a As a document drawn up for members of an antisociety, one of the pervasive concerns of the Gospel of John is sorting out insiders and outsiders, those with Jesus and those against him. The mention of feasts and places provides

145

the hearer with an appropriate emotional key in which to allow the story its maximum in-group impact. ⇨ **In-group and Out-group,** 15:18—16:4a. Is Jesus a good man or a deceiver? Here the Jerusalemite Sukkoth crowd is divided, though for fear of his opponents (consistently the "Judeans"), they will say nothing positive. The fact that Jesus comes incognito to Jerusalem in the middle of the festival makes clear that he knows of Judean hostility. It also allows him to pick the moment to go public (v. 14). The alternatives posed here by the Jerusalemite crowd (good man or deceiver) are what will be put to the test in the challenges and responses that follow.

At Sukkoth in Jerusalem:
Initial Challenge to Jesus about His Authority
to Teach and Interpret Scripture, 7:14b-18

14 . . . Jesus went up into the temple and began to teach. [15]The Jews were astonished at it, saying, "How does this man have such learning, when he has never been taught?" [16]Then Jesus answered them, "My teaching is not mine but his who sent me. [17]Anyone who resolves to do the will of God will know whether the teaching is from God or whether I am speaking on my own. [18]Those who speak on their own seek their own glory; but the one who seeks the glory of him who sent him is true, and there is nothing false in him.

✦ *Notes:* **John 7:14b-24**

7:14b-15 The passage begins with the opening notice that Jesus went up into the temple and taught (v. 14b). What follows in the ensuing passage (marked by the notice of Jesus' leaving the temple, 8:59), is a description of what Jesus taught in the temple and reactions to his teaching. Having chosen his moment to go public in Jerusalem and in the temple (see the **Notes** at 7:1-9), Jesus is confronted with a second challenge: "How does this man have such learning when he has never been taught?" ⇨ **Encomium (In Praise of . . .),** 7:29-36. Being a public challenge, this hostile question cannot go unanswered.

7:16-18 Jesus' response to the challenge in 7:15 is to assert that his teaching is not his own; therefore, his lack of education is irrelevant. The teaching comes from God, and this feature will be recognized by any who resolve to do what pleases God. It is important to note that "to do the will of God" means to please God. Jesus' response in effect tells his hostile questioners that they have little interest in pleasing God at all. Moreover, he is not seeking his own honor, since if that were the case, he would be parading his own learning. Rather, we are again told, he seeks the honor of the One who sent him. The challenge is thus effectively turned aside with a rather emphatic insult. ⇨ **Challenge and Riposte,** 7:15-18. For comment on the language about being "sent" ⇨ **Patronage,** 5:21-30.

✧ *Reading Scenario:* John 7:14b-18
Challenge and Riposte, 7:14b-18

Ascribed honor (honor as social precedence) is the honor that derives from one's status due to one's birth. But honor can also be gained or lost in daily social interaction. Thus, *acquired* honor (honor as virtue) might be bestowed as the result of public recognition or for favors done for a beneficent patron. It could be won in the pursuit of virtue or granted to those with skill in battle. Significant gain might result from great exploits of one family member, and all would benefit. Major loss could occur from some public shame, and every member of the family would suffer grief.

But most of the gains and losses of honor in ancient village life were small and came on a daily basis. They were the result of the never-ending game of challenge-response that characterized nearly all social interaction. Only equals could challenge each other in any socially significant way. In virtually every public interaction of whatever kind, honor would be subject to challenge. It could be challenged positively by means of a gift or compliment, sometimes so subtly it would be hard for non-Mediterraneans to catch the drift. Or it could be challenged negatively with some small slander or insult, with some gift not given in an appropriate way or time, or even with a hostile question.

Challenges in the form of public, hostile questions put to Jesus are frequent in the Synoptic Gospels (for example, Matt. 16:1; 22:15-17; Mark 2:24; 6:2-4; 8:11; Luke 10:25; 11:16). Such questions also occur in John. When Jesus is in the Portico of Solomon, he is publicly challenged with the question, "How long will you keep us in suspense? If you are the Messiah, tell us plainly" (10:24). Repartee with hearers over whether they are true children of Abraham results in another serious challenge via question: "Are we not right in saying that you are a Samaritan and have a demon?" (8:48). Here in John 7:15ff. the question is raised about how Jesus could have such learning when he had never been schooled. Instead of attending to what he says, his opponents are concerned with his pedigree. Jesus ends his response with a counterquestion: "Why are you looking for an opportunity to kill me?" The crowd responds with a counterchallenge of its own, "You have a demon! Who is trying to kill you?" (7:19).

In every case a public challenge must be met, and that too could be done in a variety of ways. An equal gift or compliment could be returned and a relationship returned to equilibrium. Or a comparable insult could be offered and the playing field once again made level. Sometimes a challenge might be met by a greater challenge, a slightly more expensive gift or deeper insult, and a game of one-upmanship would ensue. Challenges might be answered, brushed aside with the scorn allowed a superior, or responded to in kind, but they should never under any circumstances be run from or ignored. To ignore a challenge is to have no shame. To run from one is a coward's disgrace.

At its best, the game of challenge-riposte was primarily a game of wits. Sometimes things could go too far, however, and result in excessive public damage to the honor of another. Because uncontrolled challenge-response could result in violence (feuding) that would disrupt the stability of the village, a family or group would normally restrain its own belligerent members to keep them from getting into unnecessary feuds. In a sense, then, the overquick resort to violence was frequently an unintended public admission of failure in the game of wits (John 8:59; 10:31-33; 11:8).

Jesus' Riposte:
Moses Gives the Law,
but You Do Not Observe It, 7:19-28

19 "Did not Moses give you the law? Yet none of you keeps the law. Why are you looking for an opportunity to kill me?" [20]The crowd answered, "You have a demon! Who is trying to kill you?" [21]Jesus answered them, "I performed one work, and all of you are astonished. [22]Moses gave you circumcision (it is, of course, not from Moses, but from the patriarchs), and you circumcise a man on the Sabbath. [23]If a man receives circumcision on the Sabbath in order that the law of Moses may not be broken, are you angry with me because I healed a man's whole body on the Sabbath? [24]Do not judge by appearances, but judge with right judgment."

25 Now some of the people of Jerusalem were saying, "Is not this the man whom they are trying to kill? [26]And here he is, speaking openly, but they say nothing to him! Can it be that the authorities really know that this is the Messiah? [27]Yet we know where this man is from; but when the Messiah comes, no one will know where he is from." [28]Then Jesus cried out as he was teaching in the temple, "You know me, and you know where I am from. I have not come on my own. But the one who sent me is true, and you do not know him."

✦ *Notes:* John 7:19-28

7:19-20 The line of riposte begun by Jesus in the previous segment continues here. In fact, this is a classic example of challenge-riposte in which Jesus and his opponents spar with each other. ⇨ **Challenge and Riposte,** 7:15-18. One effective way to deal with a challenger is to offer a counterchallenge. That is what Jesus does here with his accusation. He turns the tables on his challengers, placing them on the defensive with a charge of not keeping the law. And he further counters their challenge by surfacing the motives of Jerusalem's Judean elite: they wish to kill him (already noted in 7:1, provoked by the incident in chap. 5). The Jerusalem crowd's response is an ad hominem argument: they accuse Jesus of being a deviant (⇨ **Deviance Labeling,** 7:19-28). This ups the ante a bit further as the game of challenge-riposte is played out.

7:21-24 The author requires us to recall that implicit in the hostility toward Jesus in Jerusalem is his previous behavior in the city (chap. 5). For Jesus defends himself against the earlier accusation (5:10, 16) of violating the Sabbath by doing "work" as though it were fresh in the minds of all. Jesus now suggests that he addresses a person's needs by "work" on the Sabbath, work required by God, who continues to work for the well-being of people. Even they do the same, not by doing "work" required by God or even by Moses, but to comply with an ancestral custom. Jesus' closing warning to them about judging rightly insultingly implies that they do not.

7:26-28 In an epilogue to Jesus' riposte, we once more are directed to the question of Jesus' origins. Since ascribed honor came from birth, where a person was from was critical information. ⇨ **Honor/Shame,** 5:31-47. ⇨ **Encomium (In Praise of . . .),** 7:29-36.

7:29-36 In antiquity people expected great things from those who were well-born and very little from those who were not. Seeing great deeds come from a lowborn person was sufficiently disconcerting to ancient people that it required speculation about hidden possibilities in the person's origin. ⇨ **Lineage and Stereotypes,** 8:31-59.

The speculation here is triggered by the bold way in which Jesus acts in public and the fact that his opponents can do nothing to him in response. The people of Jerusalem know where Jesus is "from," hence they know that he should not be able to act this way. Peasant artisans from Nazareth simply do nothing of this sort. That Jesus does so raises the possibility that there is more to him than meets the eye. Could he be Israel's Messiah?

Jesus' response to this challenge is typical of his stance throughout John's Gospel: he claims nothing as the result of his own birth status. All comes from God, the patron who sent him. Both he and his opponents know that his birth status would legitimate nothing. Ignorance of the patron on the part of the opponents, however, leads them to misjudge; they assume Jesus speaks on his own and thus mistakenly look to his birth/origins for legitimation of his message. Instead, they should be looking at the status of the One who sent him.

7:28 In this verse we are once more reminded that Jesus taught in the temple.

✧ *Reading Scenario:* **John 7:19-28**
Deviance Labeling, 7:19-28

The dyadic, collectivist orientation (⇨ **Collectivist Personality,** 8:31-59) of Mediterranean societies results in the typical Mediterranean habit of stereotyping. People were not known by their psychologically unique personalities or unique character traits, but rather by general social categories such as place of origin, residence, family, gender, age, and the qualities of other groups to which they might belong. One's identity was always the stereotyped identity of the group. This meant that the social information considered important was encoded in labels such groups acquired. Thus, "Cretans are always liars, vicious brutes, lazy gluttons" (Titus 1:1). "Judeans have no dealings with Samaritans" (John 4:9). Jesus was a disreputable "Samaritan" (8:48) or "Galilean" (7:52). "Can anything good come out of Nazareth?" (John 1:46). ⇨ **Lineage and Stereotypes,** 8:31-59.

Stereotypes, of course, could be either positive (titles such as "lord") or negative (accusations such as demon possession). Negative labeling, what anthropologists call "deviance accusations," could, if made to stick, seriously undermine a person's place and role in the community. In our society, labels such as "extremist," "anti-Semite," "sexist," or "gay" can seriously damage a person's career or place in society (but not "anti-Muslim" or "anti-Arab"). In the Mediterranean world of the first century, labels such as "sinner," "unclean," "demon-possessed," or "barren" could be equally devastating. In a Gospel that has no exorcisms, it is curious to note that the most serious negative labels of all were accusations of sorcery or demon possession. Such labels not only marked one as deviant (outside accepted norms or states), but once acquired could be nearly impossible to shake. In 8:49ff. Jesus seeks to repudiate the charge of demon possession by suggesting that the power behind what he does is God.

In refuting the deviance label in 7:20 (You have a demon!), Jesus makes use of several options available to him:

1. Repudiate the charge (v. 21: "I performed one work, and all of you are astonished").
2. Denial of injury (v. 23: A man has been healed).
3. Denial of a victim (v. 23: A man's whole body is healed).
4. Appeal to higher authority (v. 23: You assume the law of Moses allows similar action).
5. Condemn the condemners (v. 24: "Do not judge by appearances").

In this way Jesus rejects the deviance label his opponents are trying to pin on him, and the crowd (or reader of the story) must judge if the label has been made to stick.

Labels and counterlabels are thus a potent social weapon. Positive labels ("light of the world," "bread of life," "sheep gate," "good shepherd," "vine," etc.) could enhance honor and status if recognized by a community. Unrecognized, they could create dishonor (6:41-42; 8:39). Negative labels—that is, deviance accusations—that could destroy a reputation overnight are typical of Mediterranean social conflict and are frequent in the Gospels ("brood of vipers," "sinners," "hypocrites," "evil generation," "false prophets").

Here in John 7:14-25 Jesus' opponents accuse Jesus of paranoia and demon possession in a game of challenge-riposte; ⇨ **Challenge and Riposte,** 7:14b-18. In sum, as we have seen, an argument over whether Jesus was a good man or a deceiver had taken place before he arrived at the feast. After he arrived and began to teach in the temple, questions were raised about his lack of education. Jesus' response ends in accusations that the crowd has the law of Moses but does not keep it, and a question about why they are trying to kill him. This triggers the deviance accusations about paranoia and demon possession (⇨ **Demons/Demon Possession,** 10:19-21). If the labels could be made to stick, implying as they did that Jesus was an evil deceiver in the guise of good, his credibility with his audience would have been irreparably damaged.

Second Challenge in Jerusalem: Attempts to Arrest Jesus, 7:29-36

29 I know him, because I am from him, and he sent me." [30]Then they tried to arrest him, but no one laid hands on him, because his hour had not yet come. [31]Yet many in the crowd believed in him and were saying, "When the Messiah comes, will he do more signs than this man has done?"

32 The Pharisees heard the crowd muttering such things about him, and the chief priests and Pharisees sent temple police to arrest him. [33]Jesus then said, "I will be with you a little while longer, and then I am going to him who sent me. [34]You will search for me, but you will not find me; and where I am, you cannot come." [35]The Jews said to one another, "Where does this man intend to go that we will not find him? Does he intend to go to the Dispersion among the Greeks and teach the Greeks? [36]What does he mean by saying, 'You will search for me and you will not find me' and 'Where I am, you cannot come'?"

✦ *Notes:* John 7:29-36

7:29 Jesus' continued insistence that God sent him, that he is from God (repeated in v. 33), leads to the violent reaction of those who cannot riposte otherwise.

7:30-31 The crowd reaction here is mixed. Those who try to arrest Jesus tacitly acknowledge that they have lost the series of exchanges. Wits have failed, so the opponents resort to force. ⇨ **Challenge and Riposte,** 7:14b-18. By contrast, those who believe in Jesus do so because of his actions. Great deeds always implied a great person, perhaps, as here, even a Messiah.

7:32-33 The Jerusalem elites (chief priests, Pharisees) pick up on the failed attempt to arrest Jesus (v. 30) by sending their retainers (temple police) to try again. Crowd speculation that Jesus might be the Messiah triggers the attempt. Jesus is apparently still talking to the crowd, perhaps as the temple police are arriving. They will report back what they see in v. 45. Jesus' comment that he will soon return to the One who sent him is frequent in John's Gospel (7:33; 13:1; 14:12, 28; 16:5, 10, 17, 28). In view of the 43 times we are told in John's Gospel that Jesus has been "sent" by the Father, and the 8 times we are told that he will return, it becomes clear that John wishes to portray Jesus the broker as having ready access to and from his divine patron. ⇨ **Patronage,** 5:21-30.

7:34-36 These verses form a concluding comment to the previous interaction. The NRSV translation of the phrase in v. 34 (also v. 36), "search for me," obscures what may be intended as a charge against Jesus' opponents that they are planning to commit murder. It should be "Seek me out; try to find me." The Greek verb used here *(zeteo)* is also used in 7:1, 19, and 25, where it is clear that the intent is to kill Jesus.

7:35-36 The Judean reply indicates that they do not understand the remark of Jesus. They are outsiders. The "Dispersion" (also called "Diaspora") originally referred to Israelites scattered from the kingdoms of Israel and Judea during the time of Isaiah (Isa. 11:12) and later Ezekiel (12:15; 20:23; 22:15; et al.). During the time of Jesus and of John's group, the term referred to Israelites who emigrated or settled as colonists outside Judea, Galilee, and Perea. The original usage implied that the people thus "dispersed" have hopes of returning to the place from which they left. However, over the centuries the Israelite Diaspora became more of a settlement or colonization rather than anything remotely resembling temporary exile. The settlements referred to here are those in the Hellenistic empire of the Romans ("among the Greeks"; see James 1:1; 1 Peter 1:1). It is significant to note that the world of the first-century Mediterranean was politically under Roman control but culturally under the sway of Greek values and cultural forms. This is Mediterranean Hellenism, the world of "the Greeks."

Members of the Judean elite did not care to follow anyone into these Israelite settlements for fear of becoming unclean. However, here they imagine that Jesus will get away among these Israelite émigrés and colonials in the Greek-speaking world. This category of Israelites was labeled "the Greeks" by their Judean fellow ethnics. Jesus, of course, is speaking about returning to his patron. His opponents do not know where he *really* is from (v. 27), hence, they cannot know where he is now going. When they ask what he means by saying, "You will search for me," they appear to be feigning ignorance. Since the verb indicating intent to kill *(zeteo)* appears again (see the **Note** above), the double meaning is hardly lost on John's readers.

✧ *Reading Scenario:* John 7:29-36
Encomium (In Praise of . . .), 7:29-36

In describing how to write an *encomium*—that is, a piece in praise of someone— ancient rhetoricians instructed pupils to pay attention to important items in a subject's background. Two key items were place of origin and education. Ancient instruction manuals called *progymnasmata* provided rules for pupils learning how to write encomium exercises. In them pupils are told that the very first thing to be praised was place of birth, since being born in an honorable city conveyed honorable status:

> If the city has no distinction, you must inquire whether his nation as a whole is considered brave and valiant, or is devoted to literature or the possession of virtues, like the Greek race, or again is distinguished for law, like the Italian, or is courageous, like the Gauls or Paeonians. You must take a few features from the nation arguing that it is inevitable that a man from such a city or nation should have such characteristics, and that he stands out among all his praiseworthy compatriots. (Menander Rhetor, *Treatise II* 369.17–370.10)

Birth in Nazareth would hardly meet this standard. In John 7:26-29 the people of Jerusalem are skeptical that Jesus is the Messiah because they "know where he is from." Great people simply are not born in obscure villages like Nazareth.

The second praiseworthy item on which a fledgling writer is instructed to concentrate in the *progymnasmata* is nurture, or training.

> Next comes "nurture." Was he reared in a palace? Were his swaddling clothes robes of purple? Was he from his first growth brought up in the lap of royalty? Or, instead, was he raised up to be emperor as a young man by some felicitous chance? If he does not have any distinguished nurture (as Achilles had with Chiron), discuss his education, observing here: "In addition to what has been said, I wish to describe the quality of his mind." Then you must speak of his love of learning, his quickness, his enthusiasm for study, his easy grasp of what is taught him. If he excels in literature, philosophy, and knowledge of letters, you must praise this. (*Treatise II* 371.17–372.2)

Education was thus important. This concern is evident in Acts 4:13. There Peter and John astonish the crowd with their boldness when questioned by authorities, something completely unexpected of uneducated peasants: "Now when they saw the boldness of Peter and John and realized that they were uneducated and ordinary men, they were amazed." The public challenge put to Jesus by the Judeans in John 7:15 shows a similar attitude: "How does this man have such learning, when he has never been taught?"

Jesus' birth status and lack of education thus left little room for public praise, and indeed undermined his credibility as Messiah and teacher. The rather defensive responses in John's Gospel to charges about Jesus' birth and education indicate that John is aware of the difficulty.

On the Last Day of the Feast:
Jesus' Proclamation and Ensuing Controversy
over Jesus' Status and Role, 7:37-52

37 On the last day of the festival, the great day, while Jesus was standing there, he cried out, "Let anyone who is thirsty come to me, [38]and let the one who believes in me drink. As the scripture has said, 'Out of the believer's heart shall flow rivers of living water.'" [39]Now he said this about the Spirit, which believers in him were to receive; for as yet there was no Spirit, because Jesus was not yet glorified.

40 When they heard these words, some in the crowd said, "This is really the prophet." [41]Others said, "This is the Messiah." But some asked, "Surely the Messiah does not come from Galilee, does he? [42]Has not the scripture said that the Messiah is descended from David and comes from Bethlehem, the village where David lived?" [43]So there was a division in the crowd because of him. [44]Some of them wanted to arrest him, but no one laid hands on him.

45 Then the temple police went back to the chief priests and Pharisees, who asked them, "Why did you not arrest him?" [46]The police answered, "Never has anyone spoken like this!" [47]Then the Pharisees replied, "Surely you have not been deceived too, have you? [48]Has any one of the authorities or of the Pharisees believed in him? [49]But this crowd, which does not know the law—they are accursed." [50]Nicodemus, who had gone to Jesus before, and who was one of them, asked, [51]"Our law does not judge people without first giving them a hearing to find out what they are doing, does it?" [52]They replied, "Surely you are not also from Galilee, are you? Search and you will see that no prophet is to arise from Galilee."

✦ *Notes:* John 7:37-52

7:37-39 These verses constitute one of the central markers of this passage (the other is 8:12). Coming on the last day of the Feast of Sukkoth and in the temple, this declaration of Jesus suggests that he is the life-nurturing water for which pilgrims prayed (see the **Notes** at 7:2-9).

7:40-44 The declaration of Jesus again divides opinion—as is true of much of the controversy in the Gospel of John. As was the case after the feeding of the crowd in Galilee, Jesus is perceived as "the prophet" (see Deut. 18:15-22). In Galilee he was also judged to be Israel's king and here comparably said to be Israel's Messiah. Insiders are being sorted out from outsiders as questions about Jesus' identity force the issue. ⇨ **In-group and Out-group,** 15:18—16:4a. Note that once again a judgment is being made about the possible stature of Jesus as the Messiah on the basis of where he is from. Galilee is simply not an auspicious enough place to imagine a great person being born there. See the **Notes** at 7:25-27. Once again some wish to resort to force but fail.

7:45-46 The retainers (temple police) report back to the elites who sent them (v. 32) that they have failed to arrest Jesus. What is worse, they come back impressed by what they have heard. Fine speech would be an unlikely basis for withholding an arrest in our modern society, but in antiquity great speaking implied something positive and powerful about the character of a person.

7:47-49 The response of the Pharisees plays heavily upon the common assumption of elite groups in antiquity that they should set the terms for the society. If the elite believe, all should believe. If they do not, none should. They are especially offended that the crowd, who do not keep the Great Tradition of the elders and are therefore accursed, might have had greater influence over their own retainers than they have had themselves.

7:50-52 Nicodemus was a member of the elite group opposing Jesus. He is representative of those Judeans mentioned in 2:23-24, who believe on the basis of signs, but to whom Jesus would not entrust himself (see 8:30-59). As we saw previously (3:19-21), he came to Jesus by night and was given a put-down rooted in star lore. Here he defends Jesus before his fellow elite authorities, but he is quite unlike the man born blind of chapter 9, who is fearless in face of the threat of expulsion (9:22, 34; 12:42) and comprehends the identity of the Son of Man (9:35-36; 3:13ff.). Thus, he acquiesces after he raises an objection on the basis of judicial procedure and is rebuked with what was viewed (especially by the elite) as the proper basis for judgments about people: place of origin. ⇨ **Lineage and Stereotypes,** 8:31-59; also the **Notes** at 7:25-27. Since origin determined both status and character, status and character determined origin. Nicodemus's bad judgment (in the minds of the elite) thus warrants the possibility that he has a matching origin (Galilee).

Jesus' Revelation as Israel's Light: Controversy over Jesus' Testimony, 8:12-20

12 Again Jesus spoke to them, saying, "I am the light of the world. Whoever follows me will never walk in darkness but will have the light of life." [13]Then the Pharisees said to him, "You are testifying on your own behalf; your testimony is not valid." [14]Jesus answered, "Even if I testify on my own behalf, my testimony is valid because I know where I have come from and where I am going, but you do not know where I come from or where I am going. [15]You judge by human standards; I judge no one. [16]Yet even if I do judge, my judgment is valid; for it is not I alone who judge, but I and the Father who sent me. [17]In your law it is written that the testimony of two witnesses is valid. [18]I testify on my own behalf, and the Father who sent me testifies on my behalf." [19]Then they said to him, "Where is your Father?" Jesus answered, "You know neither me nor my Father. If you knew me, you would know my Father also." [20]He spoke these words while he was teaching in the treasury of the temple, but no one arrested him, because his hour had not yet come.

✦ *Notes:* John 8:12-20

Notice the absence of the verses marked 7:53—8:11 that are found in some Bibles. There is a scholarly consensus that these verses are a later addition to the Gospel. We consider them at the end of this commentary as an insertion into the Gospel.

8:12 This verse simply continues the narration from 7:52. Significantly, it marks a second high point in Jesus' teaching in the Temple, presenting another aspect of self-revelation. At 8:12 Jesus is still at the Feast of Sukkoth (7:2) and the controversy previously set under way continues. The statement made by Jesus that he is the light of the world, that is, Israel's everlasting light, triggers a public challenge to the validity of his testimony about himself. ⇨ **Challenge and Riposte,** 7:14-24.

Jesus' (that is, the author's) choice of statement here perhaps makes high-context allusion to considering Jesus as the original behind the large golden candelabrum featured at the Feast of Sukkoth (see the **Notes** at 7:2-9). The statement also functions as a pretext for the following argument. In antiquity light was a substance. It had no source other than itself. Since all living beings were believed to have light, life and light went hand in hand. ⇨ **Light,** 1:1-18. Jesus' temple declaration as Israel's light was thus the equivalent of saying he is the "life of the world," the source of Israel's life and its very substance. ⇨ **Life,** 1:1-18.

8:13-20 At issue here is Jesus' testimony about himself. Concern for false witness was very real in nonliterate societies that depended heavily on the validity of the spoken word. Trial by ordeal (submerging a person in a body of water; for example, a river) to prove the truth or falsity of an accusation was provided for in the Code of Hammurabi (2, 132). In Deuteronomy (19:15) the protection provided is corroboration by a second witness (presumably in addition to the person concerned; see *m. Ket.* 2:9, which proscribes testifying on one's own behalf).

False testimony was of concern in nearly every area of life (business transactions, various kinds of contracts, including marriage contracts, etc.), not simply crime. Indeed, the issue here is not crime but reputation. Reputation (⇨ **Honor and Shame,** 5:31-47) could be made or destroyed by the testimony of others; actually it *consisted of* the testimony of others. False testimony is that of a false prophet (Deut. 18:22) seeking honor from fellow humans rather than from God (5:44). Attempting to create one's own reputation by self-testimony (bragging) was considered shameful behavior.

8:14 The total testimony of Jesus in John is about himself and how he relates to his Father, his disciples, and the world (Israel, "his own"). This testimony is eminently interpersonal. Of course, it bodes well for those who believe "into" Jesus now and later. Here Jesus speaks of the interpersonal *krisis* (judgment, condemnation) of Israel. In the progression of the story, this testimony is identified as Jesus' knowledge of his own origin and destiny, demonstrating his unique relationship with the Father: only Jesus knows where he came from and where he is going (8:14).

"To know" someone in collectivist societies is to know where they come from (Jesus of Nazareth, Saul of Tarsus), especially to know the person's family background (cf. John 6:42). ⇨ **Collectivist Personality,** 8:31-59. ⇨ **Lineage and Stereotypes,** 8:31-59. The question about where Jesus is from is frequent in John's Gospel; see also 3:8; 7:27, 34; 9:29; 13:36; 14:4; 16:5; 19:9. Jesus claims here that he knows these things about himself but that his opponents do not know them. They thus lack the essential social information to make judgments about him. On the comment about coming and going, see the **Note** below at 8:16-18.

8:15 The NRSV translation ("by human standards") here is misleading, implying as it does a contrast with "divine standards." The Greek literally says, "according to the flesh" (Paul is the only other New Testament writer to use this phrase; 2 Cor. 5:16). This correctly reflects the ancient (and collectivist) belief that physique determined character. The study of the way bodily form signaled character was called *physiognomics.* In his treatise on physiognomics, Pseudo-Aristotle explains that "no animal has ever existed such that it has the form of one animal and the disposition of another" (*Physiognomics* 805a, 7–15). A lion, for example, has a fearsome physique and a disposition to match. The ancients believed that by close observation of "a person's movements, postures, colors, facial expressions, hair, skin type, voice, flesh-tone, parts of the body and overall physique," human character could be determined (Pseudo-Aristotle, *Physiognomics* 806a, 22–23). Jesus thus assumes that his opponents have made judgments about him based on his appearance and form.

8:16 Jesus' claim that he does not judge alone is a claim to solidarity with his patron, on whose authority the judgment rests. This accords with a later (late second century) comment of R. Ishmael: "Do not judge alone, for none may judge alone except One" (*m. Aboth* 4.8).

8:17-18 The Greek syntax here places considerable emphasis on the phrase "your law." Speaking as a Galilean, Jesus apparently sees himself at some distance from the elite Judean tradition. ⇨ **Jews/Judeans,** 1:19-28. Thus, all Judean elites, regardless of their specific affiliations, are grouped together.

Jesus here claims the necessary two witnesses: himself and the Father who sent him. As he does frequently throughout the Gospel of John, Jesus claims to have been sent by his patron. ⇨ **Patronage,** 5:21-30. In 8:14 he made a similar claim, to which he adds that he would also return from where he came. By claiming free access to and from his patron, Jesus is asserting a solidarity with the Father that is a significant motif throughout the Gospel and the basis for his claim to be a valid witness.

8:19 The question put to Jesus about the location of his Father/patron confirms that the opponents (1) are outsiders and (2) do not have the necessary social basis for judgment about Jesus because they do not know where he is from. When Jesus adds that if they had known him they would have known his Father, he states a Middle Eastern truism: Like father, like son (see Matt. 11:27; also Deut. 23:2; 2 Kings 9:22; Isa. 57:3; Hos. 1:2; Eccles. 23:25-26; 30:7). Birth, deriving essentially from the father's "seed," was believed to be the basis for character, especially for males. Daughters, on the other hand, were shaped by their mothers: "Like mother, like daughter" (Ezek. 16:44). In the same way, on the basis of an adult's character, one may quite validly deduce his or her genealogy and birth situation. See the **Note** above at 8:15.

8:20 Once again, the author reminds us that Jesus spoke these things in the temple, more specifically, in the treasury. This is the fifth time in the course of Jesus' teaching in the temple that the author notes where he is.

Jesus Uses a Riddle as a Counterchallenge, 8:21-30

21 Again he said to them, "I am going away, and you will search for me, but you will die in your sin. Where I am going, you cannot come." ²²Then the Jews said, "Is he going to kill himself? Is that what he means by saying, 'Where I am going, you cannot come'?" ²³He said to them, "You are from below, I am from above; you are of this world, I am not of this world. ²⁴I told you that you would die in your sins, for you will die in your sins unless you believe that I am he." ²⁵They said to him, "Who are you?" Jesus said to them, "Why do I speak to you at all? ²⁶I have much to say about you and much to condemn; but the one who sent me is true, and I declare to the world what I have heard from him." ²⁷They did not understand that he was speaking to them about the Father. ²⁸So Jesus said, "When you have lifted up the Son of Man, then you will realize that I am he, and that I do nothing on my own, but I speak these things as the Father instructed me. ²⁹And the one who sent me is with me; he has not left me alone, for I always do what is pleasing to him." ³⁰As he was saying these things, many believed in him.

✦ *Notes:* John 8:21-30

8:21-24a This whole passage consists of two sections. The opening gambit consists of vv. 21-24a. It presents yet another example of the Johannine pattern of cryptic statement/misunderstanding/explanation. See the **Notes** on 3:1-21; also 4:10-15, 32-38; 6:41-48; 11:11-15, 23-26; 12:27-30; 13:27-35; 14:4-6; 16:25-33. The misunderstanding on the part of the hearers indicates that they are outsiders who are not privy to the realities of John's antisociety, hence, ignorant of the distinctive Johannine antilanguage.

The contrasting pairs in Jesus' reply draw strong boundaries that separate Jesus (that is, John and his antisociety) from Judean society. ▷ **Antisociety,** 1:31-51. ▷ **World/Cosmos = Israelite Society,** 17:1-26. His statement that his opponents would die in their sins unless they believe in him draws this contrast even more strongly. For comment on the importance of an embedded relationship with Jesus, see the **Notes** at 6:28-29.

8:24b-30 The second gambit in this section looks to the question "Who are you?" This question is not the modern one of personal identity. Identity in the ancient Mediterranean world was always a matter of the groups (especially family) in which one was embedded. In a sense, the hearers are asking to what group(s) Jesus belongs or where he is from (since family origin determined identity).

Jesus' reply in v. 25 is translated by the NRSV, "Why do I speak to you at all?" suggesting impatience on Jesus' part. The Greek literally says, "What have I been telling you from the beginning?" With the latter translation the following verses (26-30) function as a summary of one of the Gospel's major motifs: that Jesus was sent by God, that he does not speak on his own, that his solidarity with God is what validates his words. The allusion in v. 28 to Jesus' being lifted up is in keeping with the Johannine idea that the clarity and validity of everything Jesus does and says will be clear when the hour of his exaltation and glorification (public honor) comes. While the narrator and others speak of Jesus' death and dying, Jesus never uses these words in John's Gospel. This is the outsiders' perspective, the perspective of those not yet privy to where Jesus is really from.

The notice that many believed "into" Jesus is significant. It implies that some of those demarcated as outsiders by Jesus in vv. 23-24 have become insiders. On the idea of believing "into" Jesus, see the **Notes** at 6:28-29.

Controversy over Kinship with Abraham, 8:31-59

31 Then Jesus said to the Jews who had believed in him, "If you continue in my word, you are truly my disciples; [32]and you will know the truth, and the truth will make you free." [33]They answered him, "We are descendants of Abraham and have never been slaves to anyone. What do you mean by saying, 'You will be made free'?"

34 Jesus answered them, "Very truly, I tell you, everyone who commits sin is a slave to sin.

35 The slave does not have a permanent place in the household; the son has a place there forever. [36]So if the Son makes you free, you will be free indeed. [37]I know that you are descendants of Abraham; yet you look for an opportunity to kill me, because there is no place in you for my word. [38]I declare what I have seen in the Father's presence; as for you, you should do what you have heard from the Father."

39 They answered him, "Abraham is our father." Jesus said to them, "If you were Abraham's children, you would be doing what Abraham did, [40]but now you are trying to kill me, a man who has told you the truth that I heard from God. This is not what Abraham did. [41]You are indeed doing what your father does." They said to him, "We are not illegitimate children; we have one father, God himself." [42]Jesus said to them, "If God were your Father, you would love me, for I came from God and now I am here. I did not come on my own, but he sent me. [43]Why do you not understand what I say? It is because you cannot accept my word. [44]You are from your father the devil, and you choose to do your father's desires. He was a murderer from the beginning and does not stand in the truth, because there is no truth in him. When he lies, he speaks according to his own nature, for he is a liar and the father of lies. [45]But because I tell the truth, you do not believe me. [46]Which of you convicts me of sin? If I tell the truth, why do you not believe me? [47]Whoever is from God hears the words of God. The reason you do not hear them is that you are not from God."

48 The Jews answered him, "Are we not right in saying that you are a Samaritan and have a demon?" [49]Jesus answered, "I do not have a demon; but I honor my Father, and you dishonor me. [50]Yet I do not seek my own glory; there is one who seeks it and he is the judge. [51]Very truly, I tell you, whoever keeps my word will never see death." [52]The Jews said to him, "Now we know that you have a demon. Abraham died, and so did the prophets; yet you say, 'Whoever keeps my word will never taste death.' [53]Are you greater than our father Abraham, who died? The prophets also died. Who do you claim to be?" [54]Jesus answered, "If I glorify myself, my glory is nothing. It is my Father who glorifies me, he of whom you say, 'He is our God,' [55]though you do not know him. But I know him; if I would say that I do not know him, I would be a liar like you. But I do know him and I keep his word. [56]Your ancestor Abraham rejoiced that he would see my day; he saw it and was glad." [57]Then the Jews said to him, "You are not yet fifty years old, and have you seen Abraham?" [58]Jesus said to them, "Very truly, I tell you, before Abraham was, I am." [59]So they picked up stones to throw at him, but Jesus hid himself and went out of the temple.

✦ *Notes:* John 8:31-59

8:31-59 In v. 30 we are told that many believed. Now Jesus directs the introductory statement of this passage to these believers. What follows in 33-58, however, is an unexpected and rather direct indictment of the hearers. The question is: Which sort of pedigree assures a person of acceptance and standing before the God of Israel? The passage is cast in the form of a forensic proceeding in which Jesus will judge these Judeans' presuppositions that form the moorings of their faith in him. The validity of Jesus' judgment was taken up in 8:12-20, but now the tables have turned as the controversy of chapters 7–8 is played out in a trial designed to smoke out pseudobelievers. It may well have derived from the way such pseudobelievers were ferreted out within John's group. Antisocieties always have problems with uncommitted hangers-on.

It is important to note once again John's use of the technique in which Jesus makes a statement, which is misunderstood, leading to an explanation. That pattern appears five times in this short section: 31-37, 38-40, 41-47, 51-55, and 56-58. It is yet another instance of John's concern for identifying the boundary between those inside and outside, those who understand and those who do not. ➪ **In-group and Out-group,** 15:18-16:4a.

8:31b The NRSV (and many other versions) translates here, "*Then* Jesus said . . . ." In so doing, the "resultant" or consequential sense of the Greek particle *oun* is lost (the use of this particle in John is also distinctive). It is better to translate the particle as: "*Therefore,* Jesus said. . . ." It is *because* many believed in him that Jesus now puts the matter to the test. Thus, Jesus takes up the central issue in the trial: the many who believe are indeed truly his disciples if (the statement is conditional) they continue in his word. Whether they do or not is what must now be tested. The issue of being free is quite significant in the ancient agrarian economies of antiquity in which enslavement and slaveholding were part of daily experience. Freed persons were of significantly lower social status than free persons who were never enslaved. To tell free persons that the truth will make them free is rather insulting—and an example of double-meaning phraseology typical of John's antilanguage.

Thus, the judge's (Jesus') introductory statement launches a series of statements (the five misunderstandings noted above) before those on trial. The fact that in each case these "believers" do not understand clearly indicates that they are not really insiders, they are not really in the know, hence, they are not among those who truly believe "into" Jesus.

8:33-37a The first perspective adopted by the accused is that they are indeed Abraham's free descendants. The "logic" of this and the subsequent sections of the trial can only be understood by recognizing the ancient belief that birth determines character, that genealogy is the only significant matrix for (ascribed) honor and status. ➪ **Lineage and Stereotypes,** 8:31-59. The ancients believed that genealogy could be deduced from one's subsequent behavior and character, and that behavior and character offer solid indication of one's genealogy. They believed the dictum, "like father, like son," "like mother, like daughter"; see **Notes** at 8:19. In assuming that Jesus' opening remark implies something about their social status, therefore, the hearers respond quite naturally and immediately by asserting their genealogy. ➪ **Kinship,** 8:31-59.

8:37b-40a In response, Jesus acknowledges their genealogical claim (hence, claim to honor) but then accuses them of the intent to murder. If character bespeaks breeding, their claim to be descendants of Abraham is being undermined. It is questionable whether Abraham is their father at all. Jesus cleverly concludes that they have failed the test because there is no place in them for his word.

8:39 The rejoinder of those being interrogated is to assert with greater vehemence than ever that they are indeed offspring of Abraham. In their minds, the fact of birth should settle the matter, regardless of behavior. However, as all knew, behavior necessarily reveals character and genealogy.

8:40b-42 Jesus raises the issue of Abraham's deeds. He points out that behavior like Abraham's should be quite conspicuous in their conduct. That their behavior does not fit the Abrahamic mold suggests a different lineage than the one they claim.

It is difficult for Westerners to sense the insulting character of Jesus' remark. In a society in which one's honor derived from birth, insults to lineage were the most disparaging insults that could possibly be made. The outburst of the listeners that they are not illegitimate bastards is therefore not surprising. Nor is the way they proceed to up the ante. By claiming descent from God, they ironically claim what John's Gospel claims for Jesus. Character revealed in behavior will determine which genealogical claim is valid.

8:43-47 As the agonistic interaction mounts, Jesus assesses his challengers' conduct and concludes that it bespeaks a genealogy tracing back to "your father the devil." The challenge and riposte now take a decidedly hostile turn. ⇨ **Challenge and Riposte,** 7:14-31. Specifically, Jesus charges his hearers with murder and lying. He echoes precisely the ancient belief that birth determines character ("When he lies, he speaks according to his nature"); see the **Note** above at 8:33-36. In a culture that considers the devil to stand at the opposite pole from God, to call someone the offspring of the devil in an honor and shame society is a truly harsh and demeaning insult.

The "birth equals character" argument is likewise played out in Jesus' remark that if God were the father of his hearers, they would have loved him. Lineage would have guaranteed that. The fact that they do not love him means they could not be the offspring of God.

8:48-50 The reaction of the opponent "believers" consists of slurs on Jesus' lineage and status. The Judeans who have been insulted by Jesus now return the favor. Notice that the insults are again directed at lineage. They charge Jesus with being a Samaritan, assuming that accounts for his behavior. They then up the ante even further by proposing that he is controlled by the power of a hostile spirit.

In his reply Jesus cites his own honorific behavior toward God. The implication is that he, not they, is a true son of the Father, hence his true lineage. Seeking honor for himself would belie that claim, so he does not do it.

8:51-58 With an opening (and closing) word of honor, Jesus now takes up the question of his relationship to Abraham. Their statements reveal that his (now exposed) hearers totally misunderstand (vv. 51, 56). They thus dispel any doubt as to whether they are insiders. While they add the prophets who mediated God's word to their list of ancestors, Jesus, to deflect any claim that he is a disloyal son, reaffirms that he does not seek his own honor. A loyal son always seeks the honor of his father rather than his own.

The closing assertion, coupled with a word of honor, points to Jesus' existence "in the beginning." While Abraham could not make his offspring "children of God," Jesus in fact can and does. This is the burden of the revelation of Jesus to "his own" in the Jerusalem temple: he offers water that assuages all conceivable thirst because he is the light that gives life to all who are born of God.

8:59 At its best the game of challenge and riposte is always a game of wits. An overquick resort to violence is an indication that wits have failed and given way to bully tactics. The notice here that the listeners took up stones against Jesus, attempting to kill him, is the narrator's way of telling us who won this exchange. With the notice that Jesus went out of the temple, this section of the Gospel comes to a close.

✧ *Reading Scenario:* John 8:31-59
Collectivist Personality, 8:31-59

In contemporary American culture when someone asks, "Who are you?" we immediately assume that the questioner wants to know how the person being questioned differs from all other individuals. That is because Americans see each individual as unique, a more or less integrated motivational and cognitive universe and dynamic center of awareness and judgment set over against other such individuals. This sort of individualism has been and is extremely rare in the world's cultures and is certainly absent from the New Testament.

In the world of the New Testament, when someone asked, "Who are you?" he or she normally expected to hear some kind of group identifier like "son of Joseph from Nazareth" (John 1:45) or "descendant *[sperma]* of Abraham" (John 8:33). They saw every person as deeply embedded in a group and therefore assumed that identity is possible only in relation to the others who form this group. For most people this was the family, and it meant that individuals neither acted nor thought of themselves as persons independent of the family group. What one member of the family was, every member of the family was—psychologically as well as in every other way. Mediterranean persons are what anthropologists call "dyadic," or "collectivist"—that is, they are "other-oriented" people who depend on in-group others to provide them with a sense of who they are. Consider the following chart of comparisons between collectivistic (dyadic or strong group) and individualistic (weak group) persons.

COLLECTIVIST	INDIVIDUALIST
1. Much concerned about the effect of one's decisions on one's present standing and future chances.	1. Little concerned about the effect of one's decisions on others (beyond friends and nuclear family).
2. Prepared to share material resources with group members.	2. Expected to provide their own material resources if they are not part of the nuclear family.
3. Ready to share less tangible resources with group members, e.g., giving up some interesting activity for group ends.	3. Generally not expected to and will not share less tangible resources with others, often not even with nuclear family (e.g., time to watch weekend football game).
4. Willing to adopt the opinions of others, especially those highly esteemed in the wider group.	4. Expected to form their own opinion on a range of issues, especially politics, religion, and sex. Expert opinion accepted only in law and health, and this only for oneself and nuclear family.
5. Constantly concerned about self-presentation and loss of face, since these reflect upon the group and one's position in the group.	5. Little concerned about one's impression on others unless others are involved in one's goals. Embarrassment affects the individual (and at times the nuclear family) but not any group at large.
6. Believe, feel, and experience an interconnectedness with the whole group so that positive and negative behavior redound to the group.	6. Act as though insulated from others; actions are not perceived to affect others, and others' actions do not affect them.
7. Sense themselves to be intimately involved in the lives of other group members; contribute to the lives of others in the group.	7. Life is segmented. They feel involved in the lives of very few people, and when they are, it is in a very specific way (e.g., teacher, lawyer, physician, etc.).
8. In sum, collectivists have concern for all in-group members. There is a sense of oneness with other in-group members, a perception of complex ties and relationships, and a tendency to keep other people in mind. The root of this concern is group integrity.	8. In sum, individualists have concern largely for themselves and their nuclear family. They are insulated from other people, sense themselves independent of and unconnected to others, and tend to think of self-reliance alone.

Thus, it is important to identify whether someone is "of Nazareth," "of Tarsus," or wherever. Encoded in these labels is all the information needed to rank any person properly on the prevailing scale of social statuses. ⇨ **Honor and Shame,** 5:31-47. With this information people knew how to interact properly with each other.

Lineage and Stereotypes, 8:31-59

It is characteristic of the Mediterranean world to think in terms of stereotypes. Persons were not known by their psychological personalities and uniqueness, but by general social categories, such as place of origin, residence, family, gender, age, and the range of other groups to which they might belong. ⇨ **Collectivist Personality,** 8:31-59. One's identity was always the stereotyped identity of the group. This meant that the social information considered important was encoded in the labels such groups acquired. Thus, Cretans were always "liars, vicious brutes, lazy gluttons" (Titus 1:12). "Can anything good come out of Nazareth?" (John 1:46). Jesus was a disreputable "Galilean" (John 7:52; Luke 23:6), as was Peter (Luke 22:59). Simon was a "Zealot" (Luke 6:15). Jesus was "Jesus of Nazareth" (John 1:45), while Nathanael was "of Cana in Galilee" (John 21:2), Philip was of Bethsaida in Galilee (John 12:21), and Jesus was also "Joseph's son" (John 6:42).

In John's Gospel, Jesus' opponents feel they know all there is to know about him by simply identifying his lineage: "Is not this Jesus, the son of Joseph, whose father and mother we know?" (6:42). They naturally assume that to know from what family Jesus comes and where the family lives is to know all that is worthwhile to know about him. Note the frequency with which this issue is raised in John's Gospel: 7:27, 34; 8:14; 9:29; 13:36; 14:4; 16:5; 19:9.

Instead of judging people individually and psychologically, then, Mediterranean elites and nonelites alike utilized stereotypical descriptions and explanations. Such stereotypical descriptions are generalizations into which instances of human behavior had to fit. For example, genealogy can be deduced from one's subsequent behavior and character; and behavior and character offer solid indication of one's genealogy. This means that even if one did not know the details of a great person's family background, that background could be readily "provided" on the basis of a person's greatness.

Similarly, social standing necessarily determines one's abilities or lack of them; ability or inability is clear proof of one's social standing. Or again, a person who does something for all humankind must have been born by divine intervention, and therefore birth by divine intervention points to benefits for all humankind. Kings necessarily perform valuable actions of benefit to many; consequently, actions that benefit many point to some royal agent.

On the negative side, magic is effective only among the ignorant and immoral; so one may accurately assume that the ignorant and immoral are addicted to magic. Magicians are fearsome, threatening, and suspicious persons; fearsome, threatening, and suspicious persons are almost certainly magicians. Good and honest persons are preoccupied with continuity and antiquity (they respect the past); hence, those who advocate a break with the past, who advocate something brand new, are rebellious, outsiders, and deviants.

A consequence of all this is that ancient people did not know each other very well in the way we think most important: in terms of psychological development and psychological personality traits. They neither knew nor cared about psychological development or psychological personality traits. They were not introspective at all. Modern comments about the feelings and emotional states of characters in the biblical stories are simply anachronistic projection of our sensibilities onto them. Their concern was how others thought of them (honor), not how they thought of themselves (guilt). "Conscience" was the accusing voice of others, not an interior voice of guilt (note Paul's comments in 1 Cor. 4:1-4).

In the Gospel of John, persons are typically assessed in terms of such stereotypes. That is, individuals are judged in terms of the values ascribed to the categories into which they fall. To find out that someone is "from Nazareth," "from Jerusalem," "a Galilean," "a fisherman," "a Pharisee," "a Sadducee," and the like, is sufficient information to know all there is to know about them. By contemporary U.S. standards, such stereotypical judgments are considered highly inadequate. Yet given the fact that first-century Mediterraneans were not psychologically minded or introspective, stereotypes were the main and preferred way to get to know others and to interact with them safely and predictably.

Here in John 8:31-59 a discussion about political and social freedom puzzles Jesus' hearers (it is not initially clear whether the listeners are opponents or believers). They assert their social identity as politically free people in terms of the group to which they belong: they are descendants of Abraham. They assume that group identification should be enough to indicate that they are and always have been free persons. That is because "everyone" knows the descendants of Abraham are freeborn people. But here Jesus claims (8:37-40) that the usually reliable social compass has gone haywire. He accuses the listeners of being a social anomaly; they do not act as descendants of Abraham would normally be expected to act.

Kinship, 8:31-59

Kinship norms regulate human relationships within and among family groups. At each stage of life, from birth to death, these norms determine the roles we play and the ways we interact with one another. Moreover, what it meant to be a father, mother, husband, wife, son, daughter, sister, or brother was vastly different in ancient agrarian societies from what we know in the modern industrial world. Kinship norms determined one's status, job, marriage prospects, range of relationships, interacting economic partners, the deity (deities) one worshiped, whom one obeyed outside the kin group, and so on. In sum, economics and religion were embedded in kinship (as well as in politics). Economics embedded in kinship meant that "family businesses," "family farms," and the like were the norm; the kinship group constituted both the producing and the consuming unit. Prevailing political systems were hierarchical. Hierarchical society as refracted in kinship meant patriarchy, with the right to employ power in the kinship group reserved to the father or his surrogate. And religion embedded in kinship underscored the role of veneration for the family dead, ancestor veneration (here, emphasis on lineage from the sainted ancestor, Abraham), as well as concern for traditional god(s), such as the God of Abraham, Isaac, and Jacob (or Israel). Kinship provided the roles, statuses, and norms of interaction for all other social institutions.

The demarcation of kinship relations was part of Israel's Torah. Consider, for example, the lists in Lev. 18:6-18 and 20:11-21. By New Testament times these had become lists of prohibited marriage partners. They include a variety of in-laws for whom we do not prohibit marriage today (e.g., see Mark 6:18). More-over, for us marriage is generally neolocal (a new residence is established by the bride and groom) and exogamous (outside the kin group). In antiquity it was patrilocal (the bride moved in with her husband's family) and endogamous (mar-rying as close to the conjugal family as incest laws permitted). Cross-cousin mar-riages on the paternal side of the family were the ideal, and genealogies always followed the paternal line of descent.

Since marriages were fundamentally the fusion of two extended families, the honor of each family played a key role. Marriage contracts negotiated the fine points and ensured balanced reciprocity. Defensive strategies were used to pre-vent loss of males (and females as well whenever possible) to another family. Unlike U.S. families, which are essentially consuming units, the family was also the producing unit of antiquity. Therefore, the loss of a member through marriage required compensation in the form of a bride-price. By far the strongest unit of loyalty was the descent group of brothers and sisters, and it was here that the strongest emotional ties existed, rather than between husband and wife.

Socially and psychologically, all family members were embedded in the fam-ily unit, and the main social goal in life was family integrity. Our individualism and its self-reliance simply did not exist.

CHAPTER VI

JOHN 9:1–10:42
JUDEANS' REACTION TO JESUS' BRINGING LIGHT AND LIFE TO JERUSALEM
Jesus' Rescue of a Man Born Blind Occasions Controversy, 9:1-41

9:1 As he walked along, he saw a man blind from birth. [2]His disciples asked him, "Rabbi, who sinned, this man or his parents, that he was born blind?" [3]Jesus answered, "Neither this man nor his parents sinned; he was born blind so that God's works might be revealed in him. [4]We must work the works of him who sent me while it is day; night is coming when no one can work. [5]As long as I am in the world, I am the light of the world." [6]When he had said this, he spat on the ground and made mud with the saliva and spread the mud on the man's eyes, [7]saying to him, "Go, wash in the pool of Siloam" (which means Sent). Then he went and washed and came back able to see. [8]The neighbors and those who had seen him before as a beggar began to ask, "Is this not the man who used to sit and beg?" [9]Some were saying, "It is he." Others were saying, "No, but it is someone like him." He kept saying, "I am the man." [10]But they kept asking him, "Then how were your eyes opened?" [11]He answered, "The man called Jesus made mud, spread it on my eyes, and said to me, 'Go to Siloam and wash.' Then I went and washed and received my sight." [12]They said to him, "Where is he?" He said, "I do not know."

13 They brought to the Pharisees the man who had formerly been blind. [14]Now it was a sabbath day when Jesus made the mud and opened his eyes. [15]Then the Pharisees also began to ask him how he had received his sight. He said to them, "He put mud on my eyes. Then I washed, and now I see." [16]Some of the Pharisees said, "This man is not from God, for he does not observe the sabbath." But others said, "How can a man who is a sinner perform such signs?" And they were divided. [17]So they said again to the blind man, "What do you say about him? It was your eyes he opened." He said, "He is a prophet."

18 The Jews did not believe that he had been blind and had received his sight until they called the parents of the man who had received his sight [19]and asked them, "Is this your son, who you say was born blind? How then does he now see?" [20]His parents answered, "We know that this is our son, and that he was born blind; [21]but we do not know how it is that now he sees, nor do we know who opened his eyes. Ask him; he is of age. He will speak for himself." [22]His parents said this because they were afraid of the Jews; for the Jews had already agreed that anyone who confessed Jesus to be the Messiah would be put out of the synagogue. [23]Therefore his parents said, "He is of age; ask him."

24 So for the second time they called the man who had been blind, and they said to him, "Give glory to God! We know that this man is a sinner." [25]He answered, "I do not know whether he is a sinner. One thing I do know, that though I was blind, now I see." [26]They said to him, "What did he do to

you? How did he open your eyes?" [27]He answered them, "I have told you already, and you would not listen. Why do you want to hear it again? Do you also want to become his disciples?" [28]Then they reviled him, saying, "You are his disciple, but we are disciples of Moses. [29]We know that God has spoken to Moses, but as for this man, we do not know where he comes from." [30]The man answered, "Here is an astonishing thing! You do not know where he comes from, and yet he opened my eyes. [31]We know that God does not listen to sinners, but he does listen to one who worships him and obeys his will. [32]Never since the world began has it been heard that anyone opened the eyes of a person born blind. [33]If this man were not from God, he could do nothing." [34]They answered him, "You were born entirely in sins, and are you trying to teach us?" And they drove him out.

35 Jesus heard that they had driven him out, and when he found him, he said, "Do you believe in the Son of Man?" [36]He answered, "And who is he, sir? Tell me, so that I may believe in him." [37]Jesus said to him, "You have seen him, and the one speaking with you is he." [38]He said, "Lord, I believe." And he worshiped him. [39]Jesus said, "I came into this world for judgment so that those who do not see may see, and those who do see may become blind." [40]Some of the Pharisees near him heard this and said to him, "Surely we are not blind, are we?" [41]Jesus said to them, "If you were blind, you would not have sin. But now that you say, 'We see,' your sin remains.

✦ *Notes:* **John 9:1-41**

9:1-41 The story of Jesus healing the blind man in Jerusalem parallels the previous healing of the lame man in chapter 5 (see **Notes** to 5:1-47, p. 109). The author of the Gospel situates this incident directly after Jesus leaves the temple area, this time with his disciples. Presumably Jesus' presence in Jerusalem relates to the Feast of Sukkoth and Jesus' revelation to Judeans as the light of Israel. The restoration of sight in this story further underscores Jesus' role as bringer of light/life.

While the blind man receives both physical sight and intellectual insight, in the end the opponents of Jesus will be overcome with darkness and become blind. The two will then have switched positions.

The author tells this story by providing an introduction (vv.1-5) followed by four episodes through which the event unfolds: first the healing (vv. 6-12), then a first interrogation of the newly sighted person (vv. 13-17) followed by the interrogation of his parents (vv. 18-23) and a second interrogation of the healed man (vv. 24-34). The author closes the story with a conclusion (vv. 35-42) matching the introduction.

9:1-5 The notion that sin caused suffering was common in the New Testament period (cf. Luke 13:2; see the debate over this idea in the book of Job). Stereotypical thinking at the time would have Israelites perceive that given the justice of God, suffering could only be the result of some sin, whether conscious or unconscious. As the later Pharisaic tradition put it, "There is no death without sin and no suffering without iniquity" (*b. Shabbath* 55a). Punishment inflicted from birth, however, was a special case. It required a distinct explanation since personal sin on the part of the sufferer appeared to be ruled out. But collectivistic sin was not. Israelite scribal teachers offered two possibilities. On the basis of Exod. 20:5, some argued that the sins of the fathers occasioned the suffering of the children. A child could be *born* blind thanks to his or her parents' misconduct. Much later in the Pharisaic tradition others would argue that it was prenatal sin on the part of the child that brought on such calamities (*Gen. R.* 63.6). If a pregnant woman worshiped an idol, for example, the fetus was said to do the same (*Song of Songs R.* 1.41). In v. 34, then, the opponents assert this connection between sin and blindness, but in 9:3 Jesus rejects such explanations (cf. 5:14). ⇨ **Sin,** 9:1-41.

In antiquity light was "stuff." It was an entity with no source other than itself. ⇨ **Light,** 1:1-18. The light in a human being, which was "living" light as opposed to the light of the sky, derived from the heart and emerged in the eyes in the seeing process. The eyes were made of fire, the "stuff" that causes light, and it was this fire that emanated from the eyes that enabled a person to see. As Aristotle said, "[V]ision is fire" (*Problems* 31.959b); "Sight [is made] from fire and hearing from air" (960a). To be blind was to have eyes from which darkness emanated; darkness was the presence of dark (also "stuff") rather than the absence of light. Blind people were those people whose hearts were full of darkness, hence, from whose eyes "dark" emanated. The blind were often suspected of having the evil eye (Matt. 6:22-23).

Light is also associated with life. The Hebrew of Job 33:30 speaks of the "light which gives life" (also Ps. 56:13). When Jesus says he is the "light of the world," he is saying both that he enables Israel to see the ways things really are and that he is likewise the source of Israel's life.

9:6-12 The author now describes Jesus' healing action. Jesus' behavior here is typical of ancient folk healers. ⇨ **Folk Healers,** 9:1-41. Also ⇨ **Healing/Health Care,** 5:1-18. His use of saliva (also Mark 7:33; 8:23) reflects the widespread belief that saliva afforded protection, especially from the evil eye (which many would have assumed the blind man possessed; see the **Note** above). Even today in Mediterranean societies saliva is often used to protect children from the evil eye.

Many in antiquity believed that sharing saliva was a form of "blood covenant" that could be protective. Pliny reports that spittle from various sources, including humans, had special curative powers (*Natural History* 27.75; 28.5, 48, 61, 77; 29.12, 32; 32.29). Tacitus says that a blind man once sought a cure by applying the spittle of the emperor Vespasian to his eyes (*Hist.* 4.8).

While modern authors note that the explanation of the term *Siloam* as meaning "sent" lacks a clear etymological basis, it serves John's antisocietal purposes well. Fifty-one times in John's Gospel Jesus is said to be "sent" from the Father. This is the language of patron and broker. ⇨ **Patronage,** 5:21-30. Jesus is sent by God to be his broker, and the blind man will soon mediate this information to the authorities.

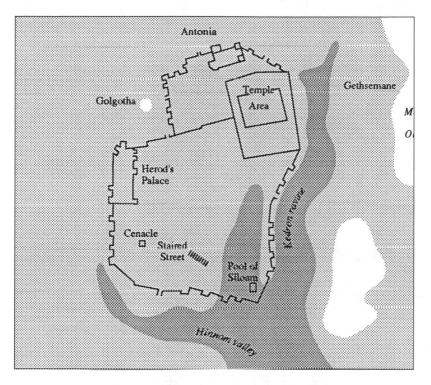

9:7 This map gives an idea of the city of Jerusalem in the time of Jesus. The city was quite small, less than a mile long and slightly over a half mile wide. Cartography by Parrot Graphics.

The first exclamations of surprise in the story come from the healed man's neighbors and those who had seen him begging. Beggars were among the expendables present in every ancient city. Most were forced to live outside the city but came into city streets during the daytime to beg. The disagreement over the identity of the healed man suggests his tenuous ties to the community at large. For a sick man in a similar position, see the **Notes** on 5:1-18. The healed man's acknowledgment that he does not know Jesus' whereabouts indicates that he is not yet part of Jesus' following. All he knows is the name he has heard (presumably) while begging.

9:13-17 The first rather formal interrogation of the newly sighted man is by the Pharisees, who are caught between two important concerns. The first is disregard of the Sabbath prohibition of work (alluded to in vv. 3-4, with the mention that it is the work of God; see **Note** to 5:17). Later in Pharisaic history, Babylonian rabbis argued that one should not anoint an eye on the Sabbath (*b. Abod. Zarah* 28b). Israel's sages recorded in the Jerusalem Talmud (*j. Shabbath* 14d; 17f) argue that one should not put spittle on anyone's eyes on the Sabbath,

9:7 The pool of Siloam was at the far southeast corner of the walled city of Jerusalem in the place where the three valleys met. The pool receives water from the Gihon spring by way of a remarkable tunnel dug through the solid rock to bring water into the city during a siege by the Assyrians around 700 B.C.E. The picture is the pool as it looks today. It still provides water to people of surrounding communities. Photo by Richard Rohrbaugh.

perhaps because no one is to fast on the Sabbath. The other concern is stated by the healed man: "How can a man who is a sinner perform such signs?" According to the ideology of reward and punishment (see vv. 1-2), a sinner should be suffering, not performing signs.

The divided opinion leads to the newly sighted man's next stage of enlightenment: he now identifies Jesus as a prophet. This may be a first stage in recognizing Jesus for the author's group, since it also happens in 4:19; 6:14; 7:40. Here from the initial recognition of Jesus as prophet in Israel, the healed man comes to recognize the Son of Man (v. 35), the "Sky Man" who provides access to the realm of God in the sky (1:51). That persons of the retainer class (Pharisees) would ask one of the degraded class (the blind man) a question of any import is extraordinary indeed. The Greek pronoun in their question ("What do *you* say . . .") is emphatic. The healed man has now begun to play the broker role for which he was "sent" (see the **Notes** above). ⇨ **Pharisees,** 9:1-41.

9:18-23 Now the parents are interrogated. The fear of the parents that they might be expelled is usually thought to be an anachronism from late in the first century, reflecting the debate in that period between the disciples of Jesus and the disciples of Moses (see vv. 28-29). It may also reflect the twelfth of the so-called Eighteen Benedictions that apparently excluded Israelite followers of Jesus from synagogue gatherings. The story in John draws boundaries of this sort and sharply marks off John's antisociety from Judean society.

9:24-34 The newly sighted person now faces a second round of interrogation. One of the primary duties of a client was to praise the patron in public. Public and proper credit was to be given wherever it was due. ⇨ **Patronage,** 5:21-30. In asking the healed man to honor God, and then adding that Jesus is a "sinner," the opponents are asking him to recognize God as his patron but to reject Jesus as broker.

In the question the healed man puts to his interrogators ("Do you also want to become his disciples?"), the Greek implies that he expects a negative answer. The question is thus a sharp public honor challenge. ⇨ **Challenge and Riposte,** 7:14-24. One way of dealing with such challenges, especially if the challenger came from a lower social status, was to pour sarcasm on the challenger and thereby imply that he is not of sufficient station to warrant a direct answer. The Greek term used here *(loidoreo)* means to speak publicly in a highly insulting manner.

See the **Notes** above on drawing boundary lines between the disciples of Moses and the disciples of Jesus. For factional rivalry, ⇨ **Antisociety,** 1:35-51.

The rejoinder of the healed man once more raises the question (frequent throughout John) about where Jesus is "from." ⇨ **Lineage and Stereotypes,** 8:31-59. As we have said repeatedly, to know where a person is from is to know all there is to know about a person. The reply of the healed man is skillfully conceived. It forces recognition of one side of the dilemma posed in v. 16. The healed man clearly wins the honor challenge. The resort to violence ("they threw him out") is always a tacit admission that wits have failed and the challenge is lost.

The healed man's insight develops apace, just as the obstinacy of Jesus' opponents noted above. The healed man is now able to identify that Jesus is from God and is obedient to him, while the blindness of the opponents is growing. They do not know where Jesus is from.

9:35-41 This is a conclusion that brackets the introduction in reverse order (a chiasmus; see the appendix). Jesus' question to the healed man asks if he believes "into" the Son of Man. The idea of believing "into" Jesus, in John's antilanguage, implies loyalty of a high order (see the **Notes** at 6:28-29). In effect Jesus is asking if the man is prepared to be a part of his antisociety. He becomes a full member in v. 38.

When the healed man calls Jesus "Sir" (v. 36), he is recognizing Jesus as his patron. That is repeated in more graphic terms in v. 38, where he not only offers this customary way of addressing a patron, but also offers a traditional patronage gesture. The Greek term *(proskyneo)* translated "worship" by the NRSV is widely used in antiquity to describe the gesture of falling down before a person and kissing the hem of his garment, his feet, or the ground on which he walked. This is what clients did when asking favors of a patron.

The concluding comments of Jesus in the story complete the notion of reversal. The blind see and the seeing have become blind (cf. Isa. 6:10; 42:19-20; John 12:40). When the Pharisees ask if they too are blind, the Greek construction implies that they expect a negative answer. Jesus credits them with enough sight to be accountable.

The term *remain* is the Greek verb *meno*. It is a key term in John, which in the NRSV is sometimes translated "remain" and sometimes "abide." It is most often used to describe solidarity with Jesus and his faction. See the **Notes** at 1:38-39. Its contrary use here draws a sharp distinction between the Pharisees and the followers of Jesus.

✧ *Reading Scenarios:* John 9:1-41
Sin, 9:1-41

Sin is a breach of interpersonal relations. It essentially consists in shaming or dishonoring another person. For clarity's sake, we would like to distinguish three hypothetical degrees. These degrees of dishonor would depend on whether the damage to the offended person's honor is revocable, whether the social boundaries can be readily repaired, and whether the implied or actual deprivation of honor is light, significant, or extreme and total. Transgressions of the boundaries marking off the person run within three degrees.

The first degree involves extreme and total dishonor of another with no revocation possible. This is outrage and would include murder, adultery, kidnapping, false witnessing, theft of vital goods or persons, total social degradation of a person by depriving one of all that is necessary for one's social status. These, in sum, include all the things listed in the second half of the Ten Commandments, for this in fact is what is listed there: outrages against one's fellow Israelite that are simply not revocable but require vengeance.

The second degree would be a significant deprivation of honor, for example, by not allowing others to marry my children if they let my children marry theirs, or by stealing something not necessary to the livelihood of another. In such cases, revocation is possible, for example, by allowing the previously denied marriage, by restoring stolen items, by making monetary restitution for seducing one's unbetrothed, unmarried daughter, and the like.

The third and lowest degree of dishonor would be accidental withholding of the regular and ordinary interactions that require normal social responses, for example, not repaying a gift with one of equal or better value by oversight, or not greeting an equal- or higher-status person due to inattention.

In other words, any implicit or explicit dishonor must allow for satisfaction commensurate with the degree of dishonor present. In the Gospels the closest analogy for the forgiveness of sins is the forgiveness of debts (Luke 11:4; cf. Matt. 6:12), an analogy drawn from pervasive peasant experience. Debt threatened loss of land, livelihood, and family. It was the result of being poor—that is, being unable to defend one's social position. Forgiveness would have had the character of restoration, a return to both self-sufficiency and one's place in the community. Since the introspective, guilt-oriented outlook of industrialized societies did not exist, forgiveness by God meant being divinely restored to one's position and therefore being freed from fear of loss at the hands of God. "Conscience" was not so much an interior voice of accusation as an external one—blame from the in-group, for example, family, friends, neighbors, or authorities (Luke 6:6; John 5:45; 8:10; see also 1 Cor. 4:4). Thus, public accusation had the power to destroy, while forgiveness had the power to restore.

Folk Healers, 9:1-41

Every society has provisions to deal with people who are sick. We call this "the health-care system." The health-care system of antiquity had three overlapping parts: a professional sector, a popular sector, and a folk sector. The professional sector of a health-care system includes the professional, trained, and socially credentialed healers. In the first-century Mediterranean, these were "physicians." Ancient physicians dealt with symptoms of the sick and sought alleviation. Their approach to sickness was philosophical; they studied the behavior of sick people, their symptoms and complaints, and developed theories to explain sickness. They never touched, handled, cut, or otherwise physically ministered to the sick. To this end they used slaves. Should the sick person die, the slave was killed—not the physician.

The popular sector embraces the individual, family, social network, and community and their respective beliefs and activities. The principal concern of the lay, nonprofessional, nonspecialist popular culture is health and health maintenance, not sickness and cure. But this focus on health sensitizes people to notice deviance from the culturally defined norm known as "health." Thus, it is in this popular sector that the deviant condition known as "sickness" is first observed, defined, and treated. The popular sector emphasizes how illness affects and involves everyone in the kinship group and wider community. The consequences of healing therefore affect this wider group as well.

The folk healer is a person who is recognized by people in a community as having the ability to restore people to health. The folk healer's "license to practice" is tacitly granted and acknowledged by each individual sick person and the local community. John's report that some doubted Jesus' abilities as a folk healer and questioned the source of his power (9:18) only highlights the limitations of a folk healer's abilities. As a folk healer, Jesus touches patients (9:6), heals by command (5:8), or heals at a distance (4:50).

Folk healers show the following characteristics:

1. Folk healers share significant elements of the constituency's worldview and health concepts. All the Mediterranean contemporaries of Jesus and his followers believed in the commonly shared explanations concerning the origins of sickness, human and spirit, and proper ways to deal with sickness.

2. Folk healers accept everything that is presented (technically described as behavioral and somatic symptoms) as naturally co-occurring elements of a syndrome. The story of the man born blind (9:1-34) is a good example. That he sat begging where people passed by, that people thought his blindness was due to his own sin (9:34) or that of his parents (9:3), that his parents are constrained to admit his blindness from birth (and hence their probable sin)—these are all so many irrelevancies that a Western diagnostician (other than a psychiatrist) would put aside to focus on the "real" problem, the "alleged" damaged organ of sight. But the folk healer views everything as of equal importance. When John reports that the healed man was sought out by Jesus so that he might "believe in the Son of Man" and not remain blind like the sighted Pharisees (9:40-41), we learn that for John's group part of therapy involved sharing in an attachment to Jesus with the rest of the group.

3. The majority of folk healers treat their clients as "outpatients." As amusing or silly as this self-evident statement might sound to the modern Western reader, it is a key element in the folk-healing process, especially among Mediterranean peasants who are very public people and are much concerned about honor. While, in John, Jesus often does not have a crowd or audience for his healings, John's readers serve this role, thus bestowing honor on the Jesus to whom they are attached. The folk healer is an honorable person but needs to enjoy continuing success to maintain honor. A crowd will always assure this honor because it witnesses the successful venture.

4. Folk healers take the patient's view of illness at face value. In no instance did Jesus ever ignore or correct the "presenting symptoms" as communicated by the sick person or surrogate. Different cultures tend to emphasize one area of symptoms more than others. The pan-Mediterranean emphasis on visual dimensions of existence may explain the prevalence of the blindness and seeing so emphasized in John 9 (blindness) and throughout the Gospel (seeing is believing).

5. The vocabulary folk healers use to describe an illness is invariably associated with the sick person's everyday experience and belief system. Contemporary Western readers who seek to tally and distinguish the various kinds of "diseases" mentioned in the Gospels are likely expecting too much precision from first-century Mediterranean vocabulary.

6. Since folk healers are native to the community and know well its mores, history, and scandals, they make special use of the historical and social context of each illness. While the Gospel narratives often sound as if petitioners meet Jesus for the first time, it is highly probable that his visits and teaching activity in various places provided him with more than a passing acquaintance with many people in the area. For example, Jesus would know the official's son at Capernaum

(4:46) since they lived in the same village; and in Jerusalem the crippled man at the Sheep Gate was a permanent fixture (5:5—thirty-eight years), while the blind man (9:1) made his living by begging; Lazarus was a good friend (11:3).

Thus, just as in the Synoptic Gospels, here in John, Jesus is described as a successful folk healer. Yet John's selection of Jesus' successes highlights truly extreme cases: a boy healed at a distance, a man crippled for thirty-eight years, a man born blind, a person dead and buried for four days.

Pharisees, 9:1-41

The Pharisees were a corporate group of Israelites whose main concern was to fulfill all of God's demands in the Torah, but specifically as spelled out in the Great Tradition of their scribal elders. This tradition laid heavy emphasis on boundary keeping and purity. Thus, in social practice the notable features of Pharisaic ideology were "no-mixture" and "exclusivity." The rule of no-mixture pertained to whatever might enter the social body or the physical body and result in uncleanness. This was all defined by scribal interpretation of Torah directives—no mixture of persons, of foods, of clothing materials, of persons in space, and of persons in time. Avoiding mixture meant that boundaries of both the physical and the social body had to be carefully guarded to ensure ritual purity. Purity, of course, is a matter of having a place for everything and keeping everything in its proper place. ⇨ **Purity/Pollution: Purification Rites,** 3:22-36.

Exclusivity is the other feature of the Pharisaic ideology. Purity plus exclusivity is what defines holiness. For what is holy is what is pure (in the proper place) and exclusive to some person, whether human or divine. Consider the feelings a person has for his or her spouse, children, house, or car should these be damaged by some intruder. The feelings of being bonded to and protective of what is one's own are feelings of holiness and sacredness. When the holy is mishandled by some outsider, one feels profaned, polluted, defiled. These human experiences of the holy were applied by analogy to God. Both God and human beings have exclusive persons, places, objects, times, and places that must be respected by others.

By strict adherence to purity regulations, Pharisees kept themselves exclusively set apart from other groups, especially those marked either by indifference to Torah purity rules or by different interpretations of Torah purity rules. This created special concern for avoiding table fellowship with persons not in their group. As one scholar has pointed out (speaking of the pre-70 Pharisees):

> Of the 341 individual Houses' legal pericopae [i.e., statements], no fewer than 229, approximately 67 per cent of the whole, directly or indirectly concern table-fellowship. . . . The Houses' laws of ritual cleanness apply in the main to the ritual cleanness of foods, and of people, dishes, and implements involved in its preparation. Pharisaic laws regarding Sabbath and festivals, moreover, involve in large measure the preparation and preservation of food. (Neusner 1973, 86)

Pharisees held that even outside of the temple, in one's own home, the laws of ritual purity were to be followed at the table. Therefore, one must eat ordinary, everyday meals in a state of ritual purity as if one were a temple priest.

Such purity concerns regarding the physical body translated into intense concern with the body's physical surface, in particular with its orifices, and especially the mouth. All food is destined to enter the body through the mouth, which is the equivalent of a gate for the social body, the city. As the boundaries of space and time in the social body were to be carefully guarded, so also were the boundaries of the physical body. This also meant substantial concern over the porosity of dishes from which food was consumed and over the washing of the surface of the hands, which convey food to the mouth.

Boundaries and orifices, then, were the chief bodily concerns of Pharisees. This meant care about what and with whom one ate: Unclean people eating unclean foods in an unclean manner threatened the surface, the boundary, or the orifices of observant Pharisees. Care had to be taken so that only clean foods, tithed, properly prepared, served in appropriate vessels, and eaten in clean company entered the physical body by means of hands ritually washed.

Such an ideology of no-mixture protected by no-touching enabled Pharisees to maintain their self-esteem as an exclusive (holy) people. They were to be as exclusive in their affairs as God was with his creation. God expected no less from Israel. In sum, it was exclusivity (holiness) that served as the hallmark of Pharisaism.

Jesus as the Sheep Gate and Good Shepherd, 10:1-18

10:1 "Very truly, I tell you, anyone who does not enter the sheepfold by the gate but climbs in by another way is a thief and a bandit. ²The one who enters by the gate is the shepherd of the sheep. ³The gatekeeper opens the gate for him, and the sheep hear his voice. He calls his own sheep by name and leads them out. ⁴When he has brought out all his own, he goes ahead of them, and the sheep follow him because they know his voice. ⁵They will not follow a stranger, but they will run from him because they do not know the voice of strangers." ⁶Jesus used this figure of speech with them, but they did not understand what he was saying to them.

7 So again Jesus said to them, "Very truly, I tell you, I am the gate for the sheep. ⁸All who came before me are thieves and bandits; but the sheep did not listen to them. ⁹I am the gate. Whoever enters by me will be saved, and will come in and go out and find pasture. ¹⁰The thief comes only to steal and kill and destroy. I came that they may have life, and have it abundantly.

11 "I am the good shepherd. The good shepherd lays down his life for the sheep. ¹²The hired hand, who is not the shepherd and does not own the sheep, sees the wolf coming and leaves the sheep and runs away—and the wolf snatches them and scatters them. ¹³The hired hand runs away because a hired hand does not care for the sheep. ¹⁴I am the good shepherd. I

know my own and my own know me, ¹⁵just as the Father knows me and I know the Father. And I lay down my life for the sheep. ¹⁶I have other sheep that do not belong to this fold. I must bring them also, and they will listen to my voice. So there will be one flock, one shepherd. ¹⁷For this reason the Father loves me, because I lay down my life in order to take it up again. ¹⁸No one takes it from me, but I lay it down of my own accord. I have power to lay it down, and I have power to take it up again. I have received this command from my Father."

✦ *Notes:* **John 10:1-18**

10:1-6 Jesus begins once again by putting his honor on the line ("Very truly, I tell you . . ."). See the **Notes** at 5:19-21. The use of metaphors having to do with sheep and shepherds to describe the roles of central personages has a long history in the ancient Near East. In the Old Testament the metaphor is used theologically. God is frequently said to be the shepherd of his people (Pss. 23:1; 80:2; Isa. 40:11; Jer. 31:9), and God's people are likened to sheep (Pss. 74:1; 79:13; 95:7; 100:3). David, or a Davidic Messiah, is likewise spoken of as a shepherd (Ps. 78:70-72; Ezek. 37:24; Mic. 5:3). Occasionally there is comment about faithless shepherds who injure the flock (Jer. 2:8; 10:20; 12:10; Ezek. 34; Zech. 11:4-9). In Isa. 63:10 Moses, too, is labeled as the shepherd of Israel. Similarly, Egyptian, Babylonian, and Iranian gods were all spoken of as shepherds. So also were Babylonian kings and Greek heroes.

These old traditions account for a certain idyllic quaintness in the use of the metaphor that does not square with the real view of shepherds in Jesus' day. By his time actual shepherds were a despised occupational group. They were generally ranked with ass drivers, tanners, sailors, butchers, camel drivers, and other scorned occupations. Being away from home at night, they were unable to protect the honor of their women; hence, they were presumed to be dishonorable men. Often they were considered thieves because they grazed their flocks on other people's property. ➪ **Shepherd,** 10:1-18.

The first part of the parable (vv. 1-3a) tells of the way to approach the sheep—via the gate—while the second part (vv. 3b-5) comments on the relationship between shepherd and sheep.

The sheepfold envisioned here may have been a yard attached to the house and surrounded by a stone wall topped with briars. The Greek terms for "thief" and "bandit" are not normally synonymous. The former usually refers to a simple robber, the latter to a social bandit or insurrectionist who stole from the elite. For an explanation of the term *gate,* see the **Notes** below.

Calling the sheep by name and having sheep readily follow are common and familiar patterns in Mediterranean shepherding. When asserting that the sheep will not follow another shepherd, the Greek here uses a double negative, hence an emphatic form. Since we learn later that Jesus himself is the shepherd, loyalty to Jesus as the antisociety group leader is intimated. ➪ **Antisociety,** 1:31-51.

10:1 Sheepfold and gate. Photo by Dennis Hamm.

10:6 As frequently in John's Gospel, the failure of a listener to understand Jesus occasions further explanation. Such extended explanations serve to make the audience insiders to the group's talk and thus draw the listeners into the Jesus group.

10:7-10 With another word of honor, Jesus presents another metaphor in which he identifies himself as the "sheep gate." If John's antisociety forms a flock, then Jesus himself is the only access to John's group. Initiation and entry to John's group happens only by means of Jesus himself. Jesus emphatically holds the exclusive role as group executive. He is not only social gatekeeper, but the gate itself. There is no other way into the group.

These verses represent an explanation of the terminology in the first part of the parable above (vv. 1-3a). Explaining and redefining terminology are key features of antilanguage. ⇨ **Antilanguage,** 1:19-28; also the introduction. The term *gate* can now be part of the group's antilanguage.

Group rivalry was extremely common in antiquity; therefore, other group leaders are viewed by John as thieves and bandits. ⇨ **Antisociety,** 1:31-51. Many scholars have seen this as an attack on the Judean leadership, perhaps aimed particularly at the Pharisees, who set social benchmarks for acceptable behavior in Israel.

10:11-14a A second term explained and given particular meaning for the group's antilanguage is "shepherd." Jesus now identifies himself with the shepherd central to the second part of the parable above (vv. 3b-5). John may be alluding to the appointment of Joshua (the Hebrew form of the name Jesus) at the time of Moses' death: "Let the LORD, the God of the spirits of all flesh, appoint someone over the congregation who shall go out before them and come in before them, who shall lead them out and bring them in, that the congregation of the LORD may not be like sheep without a shepherd" (Num. 27:16-17; cf. Mark 6:34). Yet Jesus is far more than Moses in this Gospel. Much of the imagery in this passage also resonates with Ezekiel 34. There it is said that the shepherd will "bring them out from the peoples," an appropriate description of the Johannine antisociety. ⇨ **Antisociety,** 1:35-51. See the **Notes** above for comment on shepherds.

Many commentators have also seen this passage as a further step in the critique of Judean leadership. The imagery of a shepherd protecting the flock from wolves is used elsewhere in the New Testament (Matt. 10:16; Acts 20:28-29). The effect of such language is to warn of dangers and draw boundaries. Imagery of attack from outsiders is common among socially estranged groups grappling with maintaining their boundaries intact over against incursions by the surrounding society. Such imagery is especially common when a group is seeking to keep peripheral members more closely attached and to guard them from the enticements of rival groups.

10:14b-18 This passage describes the close interpersonal, dyadic relationship between Jesus and his Father as well as between Jesus and his own. Though the metaphor here has to do with shepherds and sheep, it is similar in import to the range of antilanguage in the Gospel that highlights interpersonal bonding (believing "into," remaining or abiding in Jesus, vine and branches, and so on). A dyadic relationship of trust and loyalty is a safeguard against attack from outside.

While vv. 14a-18 may comment on the death of Jesus before it happens in the story, they also speak clearly of the depth of loyalty between Jesus and his followers. As John 15:13 asserts, no one has greater love (read, "loyalty") for friends than the one who lays down his life for them.

10:1-6 Shepherd leading his flock. In most sheep-raising countries, the shepherd follows the sheep. In Palestine shepherds still lead their flocks. See Notes 10:1-6. Photo by Avraham Hay.

✧ *Reading Scenario:* **John 10:1-18**
Shepherd, 10:1-18

Jesus describes himself as a capable and concerned shepherd. That analogy would not be lost on his contemporaries, since the breeding and care of sheep was something well known to Israelite peasants. Even in the Middle East today, Arab fellahin classify sheep in a bewildering set of categories, all of significance to the quality of the animal: by gender (ram, ewe, lamb), breeding ability (fertile and barren), age (special word for sheep one to six months old, seven to twelve months old, one to two years old, three years and older), time of birth (Gen. 30:41-42 alludes to early lambs, born in November or December, and summer lambs, born in June; there are also spring lambs, born in February or March), and color (white sheep, black sheep, black sheep with white spots, blue-black–faced sheep, black-faced sheep, white sheep with black face and neck, black-spotted–faced sheep, brown-faced with white nose sheep, brown-headed sheep, brown-and-white-spotted–faced sheep, black-and-brown–faced sheep, grey-headed sheep). There is a different Arabic word for each of these categories. Further, in regard to illness, there are special names for the categories of variously afflicted sheep.

Shepherds contended with heat during the day, cold at night, and frequent sleepless nights (Gen. 31:40). Dealing with wild animals and robbers required special skill in handling sheep and predators. Sheep often injured themselves by getting caught in rocky clefts while foraging. To meet their needs, shepherds carried a scrip, a sling, a club, and a rod (cf. Matt. 10:6-16). Sheep of various flocks often spent the night in common sheepfolds (or caves). In the evening the shepherd used his rod to single out injured sheep from the rest as they passed under his rod into the sheepfold (Lev. 27:32; Jer. 33:13; Ezek. 20:37). The first thing a shepherd did in the morning was to call out and lead his sheep. After calling out his sheep from the sheepfold, the shepherd led the way to pasture in open fields. After the grape harvest, shepherds would lead their sheep through vineyards to eat the remaining foliage (Jer. 12:10).

When the shepherd was not the owner of the flock, he was not responsible for losses caused by predators but had to prove the loss by displaying a piece of the torn animal (Gen. 31:39). Moreover, the hireling was free to use the milk of the flock: "Who tends a flock and does not get any of its milk?" (1 Cor. 9:7). Hirelings were traditionally paid every tenth lamb or kid born in the flock (Gen. 30:28-35).

It was important for the shepherd and his flock to be protected from the range of negative forces that confronted their well-being, from visible thieves and wolves to invisible demons of all sorts. To guarantee security, all sorts of protective measures might be taken. In ancient Israel shepherds were to maintain positive relations with the God of Jacob by offering the firstborn (Num. 3:13; 18:15). Shepherds also attempted to maintain good relations with the protective deity who specialized in sheep. In Israel (and Phoenicia) the protective deity was Ashtarte (identified with the planet Venus). Breeding ewes were called the

"Ashtartes of the flock" (Deut. 7:13; 28:4, 18, 51). The Romans called their traditional protective deity Pales, and on April 21 they celebrated the Parilia to ensure protection. Both the Roman Pales and the planet Venus might be male and female (Venus as morning star is male, as evening star, female). There is extensive information concerning the Roman celebration of the Parilia with parallel behavior in later Christianized Europe.

The point is that here Jesus is the good shepherd who protects his flock with the basic guarantees shepherds sought from protective deities: security, fertility, and provisions. Interestingly, these are the guarantees ancient peoples sought from their kings (⇨ **King of the Judeans,** 18:28—19:16a). Hence, kings were readily described with shepherding metaphors, even though the job of hireling shepherd was considered very low status.

Hanukkah in Jerusalem:
Another Challenge—
Deviance Accusations against Jesus, 10:19-24

19 Again the Jews were divided because of these words. [20]Many of them were saying, "He has a demon and is out of his mind. Why listen to him?": [21]Others were saying, "These are not the words of one who has a demon. Can a demon open the eyes of the blind?"

22 At that time the festival of the Dedication took place in Jerusalem. It was winter, [23]and Jesus was walking in the temple, in the portico of Solomon. [24]So the Jews gathered around him and said to him, "How long will you keep us in suspense? If you are the Messiah, tell us plainly."

✦ *Notes:* John 10:19-24

10:19-21 As the term *again* suggests, divisions of opinion among Jesus' hearers have occurred earlier (7:12, 25-27, 40-41; 9:16). The division here concerns the words Jesus uses. Do they come from the power of evil working in him? Or from the power of good? Someone possessed by a demon would be considered extremely dangerous to the community, especially since most possessed people were also thought to have the evil eye. ⇨ **Demons/Demon Possession,** 10:19-24. Trying to make a label like "demon possessed" stick on a person was a way of destroying honor and ostracizing the person from the community. ⇨ **Deviance Labeling,** 7:19-28.

10:23 The portico of Solomon was the columned porch that ran along the inside of the east wall of the Temple (see diagram at 2:14). It was named after Solomon because the stonework in the outer wall beneath it, visible here on the left of the picture, was known to be much older than the stonework done by Herod's workers, and was attributed, probably correctly, to that done 900 years earlier by Solomon. The picture is another shot of the model referred to at 5:2. Winter is the season of wet and cold in Jerusalem, and so Jesus and his listeners take shelter from the wind and perhaps the rain. Photo by Thomas Hoffman.

10:22-24 The Feast of Hanukkah (Dedication) celebrated the rededication of the altar by Judas Maccabeus (165 B.C.E.) after its three-year desecration by Antiochus Epiphanes (1 Macc. 4:41-61). This festival did not require pilgrimage, but it was nonetheless popular in Jesus' day. It had already come to be known as the Feast of Lights (Josephus, *Ant.* 12.325). It is the last of the great festival scenes in John, which began in chapter 5, and is also the occasion for the last of Jesus' great debates with Judean opponents that form the center of John's Gospel (chaps. 7–10).

The question posed in this section is whether Jesus is or is not the Messiah. Up to this point Jesus had revealed himself to be such only to the Samaritan woman (4:26), even though to maintain belief in Jesus as Messiah with a view to new life is stated as the purpose of the Gospel (20:31). In the Synoptic Gospels the question about whether or not Jesus is the Messiah is put to him by the high priest at the time of his trial.

The question of the Judeans gathered around Jesus is not clear in Greek. A literal translation would be, "How long do you take our life from us?" Ancient evidence for the NRSV translation, "keep us in suspense," is scarce. In modern Greek, however, the phrase is an idiom meaning "provoke us." It should be noted that questions posed in public are always an honor challenge. ⇨ **Honor and Shame,** 5:31-47. The fact that a crowd is "gathered around him" makes this a very public challenge indeed.

✧ *Reading Scenario:* John 10:19-24
Demons/Demon Possession, 10:19-24

The only time demons are mentioned in John's Gospel is in accusations of demon possession aimed at Jesus. There are three occurrences: 7:20; 8:48; and 10:20. In the first two instances the accusation is the response of the Judeans to Jesus' claim that they are trying to kill him. In 10:20 the charge comes up in a dispute among his Judean listeners over Jesus' claim that he lays down his own life voluntarily and not because anyone takes it from him.

In the worldview of the first-century Mediterranean, the cause of events of significance to human beings was always believed to be some person, whether human or nonhuman. Not only was this true at the level of ordinary social interaction, but at the levels of nature and the cosmos as well. Events beyond human control, such as weather, earthquakes, disease, and fertility, were believed to be controlled by nonhumans who operated in a cosmic social hierarchy. Each level in the hierarchy could control the ones below:

1. "Our" God, the Most High God
2. "Other" gods or sons of God or archangels or stars
3. Lower nonhuman persons: angels, spirits, demons
4. Humankind
5. Creatures lower than humankind

Demons (Greek) or unclean spirits (Semitic) were thus personified forces that had the power to control human behavior. Accusations of demon possession were based on the belief that forces beyond human control were causing the effects humans observed. Since evil attacks good, people expected to be assaulted. A person accused of demon possession was a person whose behavior (external symptom) was deviant or who was embedded in a matrix of deviant social relationships. Such a deviant situation or behavior required explanation and could be attributed to God (positive) or to evil (dangerous). Such attribution was something the community would be anxious to clarify in order to identify and expel persons who represented a threat. Possessed persons were excluded from the community. Freeing a person from demons, therefore, implied not only exorcizing the demon, but restoring the person to a meaningful place in the community as well.

In antiquity all persons who acted contrary to the expectations of their inherited social status or role (for example, Jesus and Paul) were suspect and had to be evaluated. Accusations of demon possession such as those leveled at Jesus in John were essentially the judgment that because he could not do what he did on his own power, an outside agency had to be involved. It could be God, as Jesus claimed, or the demonic forces claimed by his opponents. Note that in John's Gospel, even though Jesus does not cast out demons from anyone, he nonetheless trades accusations of demon possession with his opponents (John 8:44-52). For the significance of such name-calling, ⇨ **Deviance Labeling,** 7:19-28.

Jesus' Riposte Nearly Erupts in Violence, 10:25-38

25 Jesus answered, "I have told you, and you do not believe. The works that I do in my Father's name testify to me; [26]but you do not believe, because you do not belong to my sheep. [27]My sheep hear my voice. I know them, and they follow me. [28]I give them eternal life, and they will never perish. No one will snatch them out of my hand. [29]What my Father has given me is greater than all else, and no one can snatch it out of the Father's hand. [30]The Father and I are one."

31 The Jews took up stones again to stone him. [32]Jesus replied, "I have shown you many good works from the Father. For which of these are you going to stone me?" [33]The Jews answered, "It is not for a good work that we are going to stone you, but for blasphemy, because you, though only a human being, are making yourself God." [34]Jesus answered, "Is it not written in your law, 'I said, you are gods'? [35]If those to whom the word of God came were called 'gods'—and the scripture cannot be annulled—[36]can you say that the one whom the Father has sanctified and sent into the world is blaspheming because I said, 'I am God's Son'? [37]If I am not doing the works of my Father, then do not believe me.[38] But if I do them, even though you do not believe me, believe the works, so that you may know and understand that the Father is in me and I am in the Father."

✦ *Notes:* John 20:25-38

10:25-30 The crowd previously challenged Jesus by asking why he continued to provoke the Judean populace. Jesus' riposte to this challenge is to avoid any direct answer to the question. Instead, he points to the works that he says he does in God's name, and claims that his opponents do not believe because they are not part of his group. He then reiterates the earlier part of chapter 10, in which the metaphor of sheep and shepherd was used to articulate the close, interpersonal relationship between Jesus and all those loyal to him. See the **Notes** at 10:1-18.

Throughout the Gospel of John there is much concern to accent the boundaries between insiders and outsiders. ⇨ **In-group and Out-group,** 15:18—16:4a. The Judean opponents here are clearly in the out-group. The twice-repeated claim (vv. 28, 29) that no one will snatch away the sheep from either the hand of Jesus or the hand of God belies an underlying fear of group leaders of having members drawn away from the group.

10:30 This statement has occasioned much comment going all the way back to the early trinitarian controversies (even though the Greek clearly says that Jesus and the Father are one "thing," not one "person"; cf. 14:28). In 17:11 Jesus prays that his followers may be "one" just as he and the Father are "one." In both instances he is speaking of the close, interpersonal relationship of loyalty and trust that John consistently claims exists between himself, God, and his followers. ⇨ **Collectivist Personality,** 8:31-59. See also the **Notes** at 6:28-29.

10:31 Blasphemy means dishonoring another person by means of words. The fact that the Judeans take up stones is usually understood in relation to Lev. 24:16, which provides for stoning any who blasphemes "the Name." ⇨ **Violence,** 10:25-38. While our evidence for what constituted blasphemy in Jesus' day is anything but clear, a later provision in the Pharisaic tradition stressed the importance of pronouncing "the Name" for the charge of blasphemy to be valid: a blasphemer "is not culpable unless he pronounces the name [the Hebrew name of Israel's God, the four letters, YHWH] itself" (*m. Sanh.* 7.5). This Jesus does not do.

Instead, the charge here arises out of Jesus' earlier answer to the query about whether he was or was not the Messiah. His response had been to assert a dyadic unity between himself and God (see the **Notes** above) of the type usually associated with family members. In v. 36 Jesus will acknowledge himself to be God's kin, hence it is this claim of special kinlike unity with God, rather than a formal misuse of the divine name, that gets Jesus in trouble. That had been exactly the issue back in 5:18. And it is this sort of kinlike unity with God that the members of John's group claim to share; thanks to Jesus, they are "children of God."

The fact that Jesus' opponents decide to stone Jesus on the spot rather than (more properly) initiate a judicial proceeding suggests another issue: honor is on the line. Jesus answered the very public challenge to his honor (see the **Notes** above) with a countercharge: his opponents do not believe because they are not insiders, not members of his group. Moreover, they will get none of Jesus' followers away from him because of God's protection. With this response, and with the crowd considering violence, Jesus wins the honor challenge. In any exchange, the first one to resort to violence loses. ⇨ **Honor and Violence,** 10:25-38.

10:32-38 Jesus forestalls the violence by challenging the crowd once again. If they claim one of his works is the basis for their anger, they will have to explain why the works he has done were not good. But of course it is not really the works that are at issue; going back to 5:18, the issue has been that he was making himself God's equal by claiming God as his Father in a context in which God is said to be working even now. That this is a cultivated misunderstanding typical of John's antilanguage is clear from 14:28. As is typical in John's Gospel, misunderstanding becomes the occasion for explanation of the insider view.

187

Jesus makes his argument from Ps. 82:6. There God sits in the divine council and pronounces judgment on those who perform the work of God—the act of judgment itself (Deut. 1:17). There unjust judges are called "gods," presumably because they do this godlike work, but they themselves are judged because they do it unjustly. As the Psalm goes on to say, however, they are clearly mortal and will die like other humans.

Jesus' argument is that if the term *gods* can be applied in this situation without blasphemy, then surely in the case of One whom God has "sent" (see the frequent **Notes** throughout John where this term is used; it implies that Jesus is God's broker), the title "Son of God" (acknowledging kinship but subordination; cf. 14:28) is appropriate. He thus rejects the charge of blasphemy altogether.

In vv. 37-38 Jesus again presses the two major Johannine themes in this passage: (1) his works are the works of God, which his opponents did not deny, and therefore (2) in themselves demonstrate that his claim (vv. 30, 38) to be in a dyadic relationship with God is justified. This is the final argument in the great debates of chapters 7–10 and represents the heart of John's case on behalf of Jesus. It is finally rejected by the Judeans, however, as they seek to arrest Jesus one more time.

✧ *Reading Scenarios:* John 10:25-38
Violence 10:25-38

Violence is about coercing others in a way that social norms do not endorse. The story of Jesus is full of instances of persons, visible and invisible, doing or planning violence toward others in the name of the status quo. These persons ostensibly intend to maintain established values. First, consider the instances of coercion and violence in the Synoptic narratives. In Mark, after his baptism, Jesus is *forced* into the wilderness by the Spirit (Mark 1:12; Matt. 4:11; Luke 4:1). And soon after, Jesus *drives out* an unseen, unclean spirit from a possessed man in the synagogue of Capernaum (Mark 1:25-26; Luke 4:35). The incident implies that unclean and unseen spirits can do violence to humans, and that some humans know how to control them. Then, after the healing of the man with the withered hand, "The Pharisees went out, and immediately held counsel with the Herodians against him, how *to destroy* him" (Mark 3:6; Matt. 9:14; Luke 6:11). Soon after that notice, as crowds gathered so that Jesus and his core group could not even eat, "when his family heard it, they went out to *restrain* him, for people were saying, 'He has gone out of his mind'" (Mark 3:21). Luke, in turn, reports of Jesus' fellow villagers, "When they heard this, all in the synagogue were filled with rage. They *got up, drove him out* of the town, and led him to the brow of the hill on which their town was built, so that they might *hurl him* off the cliff" (Luke 4:28-29). On a whim Herod Antipas could *seize* John the Baptist (Mark 6:17; Matt. 14:3; Luke 3:20). Jesus himself felt free to trespass over presumably well-established social boundaries when "he entered the temple and began to *drive out* those who were selling and those who were buying in the temple, and he *overturned* the tables of the money changers and the seats of those who sold doves; and he would *not allow* anyone to carry anything through the temple" (Mark 11:15-16; Matt. 21:12; Luke 19:45). Jesus' close followers would retaliate for shameless inhospitality with *fire from the sky* (Luke 9:54). As Mark notes, even legitimate authorities (high priests in the temple area) hold back in face of the possibility of *violence* against themselves: "They wanted to arrest him, but they feared the crowd. So they left him and went away" (Mark 12:12; Matt. 21:46; Luke 20:19). Yet Mark would have us believe that the authorities continued in their resolve: "The chief priests and the scribes were looking for a way to *arrest* Jesus by stealth and *kill him*; for they said, 'Not during the festival, or there may be a riot among the people'" (Mark 14:1-2; Matt. 26:4; Luke 22:2). Finally, a crowd came and forcibly *seized* Jesus (Mark 14:43-52; Matt. 26:47-56; Luke 22:47-53).

John, too, knows of such establishment violence. It is directed toward "public sinners," who are to be *stoned* by command of the law of Moses, hence, against Jesus, deemed to fit the divine requirements of such violence (John 10:31-33; 11:8). We are told early on in the narrative that Jesus' opponents sought *to kill* him (John 5:18). Of course, Jesus is well aware of their plans (John 7:19-20; 8:37, 40). John's peculiar account of Jesus' *arrest, torture,* and *crucifixion* are well known (John 18-19).

Similarly, the book of Acts is full of such incidents: the *arrest* of Peter and John (Acts 4:3), *violence* by unseen agents to Ananias and Sapphira (Acts 5:5, 10), the *arrest* of the apostles out of jealousy (Acts 5:18), the council's desire to *kill* them (Acts 6:33), the *vigilante* treatment of Stephen by a provoked crowd (Acts 7:54-60), and so on. For his part, Paul tells us that his fellow Israelites *lashed* him five times, and that he was *beaten* with rods three times and *stoned* once (2 Cor. 11:12).

Finally, when we get to the letter to the Hebrews, we are asked to focus on blood and gore (Heb. 9:7—10:20; 12:4, 24; 13:11-12, 20). This is a community that regales in sacrifice and the endurance of pain. Even God is said to use pain as a "fatherly" device for his sons: "'Do not regard lightly the discipline of the Lord, or lose courage when you are punished by him; for the Lord disciplines those whom he loves, and chastises every child whom he accepts.' Endure trials for the sake of discipline. God is treating you as children; for what child is there whom a parent does not discipline?" (Heb. 12:5-7).

By any reading, this was a violent society with frequent public violence and unsure and explosive crowd reaction. Ordinary persons did not have any rights. There was no universalism in the sense that all human beings were equally human, bearing common human endowments, common human rights independent of individual ethnic origin and social status. Tolerance was an idea whose time would come some seventeen hundred years later! Furthermore, the idea of a plurality of nations endowed with equal rights in the forum of nations was totally absent since there were no "nations" as yet. Neither ancient Israelites, nor ancient Athenians, nor ancient Romans had any idea of juridical relations among broader ethnic groups. In the first century C.E., Roman statesmen dealt with other ethnic groups in terms of good faith based on patron-client relationships. In

Roman perception, Rome was a patron, not a holder of an empire; it wanted persons to behave like clients. To behave otherwise was to be a rebel, an outlaw. Neither persons nor ethnic groups had what we would call "rights."

What modern readers often interpret as rights is political privilege. For example, Roman citizens had preeminence in the *oikoumene* (the inhabited world). To dishonor one Roman was to dishonor, hence challenge, Rome itself. Consequently, Roman citizens were always to be treated honorably by noncitizens; they were not to be flogged publicly, nor were they answerable to any tribunal but that of their own Caesar. Such were the ramifications of the customary values of honor and shame. Since persons and ethnic groups had no rights in our sense, any modern reader's perception of "oppression" in the first-century Mediterranean world would be quite anachronistic.

In short, the Mediterranean world was a violent world, and the Israelite tradition hallowed such violence. Philo, an Israelite Hellenistic philosopher of Alexandria, clearly explains this tradition:

> But if any members of the nation betray the honor of the One, they should suffer the utmost penalties . . . all who have zeal for virtue should be permitted to exact the penalties offhand and with no delay, without bringing the offender before jury or council, or any kind of magistrate at all, and give full scope to the feelings which possess them, that hatred of evil and love of God which urges them to inflict punishment without mercy on the impious. They should think that the occasion has made them councilors, jurymen, nome governors, members of assembly, accusers, witnesses, laws, people, everything in fact, so that without fear or hindrance they may champion respect for God in full security. (*Spec. Leg.* 1.54)

Later, he adds:

> Further if anyone cloaking himself under the name and guise of a prophet and claiming to be possessed by inspiration lead us on to the worship of the gods recognized in the different cities, we ought not to listen to him and be deceived by the name of prophet. For such a one is no prophet, but an impostor, since his oracles and pronouncement are falsehoods invented by himself. And if a brother or son or daughter or wife or a housemate or a friend, however true, of anyone else who seems to be kindly disposed, urge us to a like course, bidding us fraternize with the multitude, resort to their temples and join in their libations and sacrifices, we must punish him as a public and general enemy, taking little thought for the ties which bind us to him; and we must send round a report of his proposals to all lovers of piety, who will rush with a speed which brooks no delay to take vengeance on the unholy man, and deem it a religious duty to seek his death. For we should have one tie of affinity, one accepted sign of goodwill, namely the willingness to serve God and that our every word and deed promotes the cause of piety. But as for these kinships . . . let them all be cast aside if they do not seek earnestly the same goal, namely the honor of God, which is the indissoluble bond of all the affection which makes us one. (*Spec. Leg.* 1.315–17)

He is simply restating the biblical warrant for establishment violence set out in the book of Deuteronomy. (Deut. 13:5, 7-12; 17:2-6, 7, 12; 19:19; 21:21, 22, 24; 24:7).

Honor and Violence, 10:25-38

At its best, the game of challenge-riposte (⊳ **Challenge and Riposte,** 7:14b-18) is primarily a game of wits. The needed skill to defend one's honor was cleverness in repartee. Often that included skill in using the official traditions of the political religion to justify one's position or argument. That is exactly what Jesus demonstrates in 10:34-38.

In situations of challenge-response, however, things could sometimes go too far and result in excessive public damage to the honor of another. Because the honor of a whole family (or a whole group) was at stake in the honor of any one of its members, a whole family's honor could be damaged by a situation that got out of control. The offended family would feel honor-bound to retaliate, which in turn would cause retaliation in response. The resulting blood feuds could result in violence that would disrupt the stability of an entire village. The danger of a resort to violence meant that a family or group would normally restrain its own more volatile members in order to keep them from getting into feuds unnecessarily. It was in everyone's interest to keep violence under control.

In a sense, then, the overquick resort to violence in a challenge-response situation was not only dangerous, it was frequently an unintended public admission of failure in the game of wits. The death of a challenger was sometimes a worthy response to public dishonor, but an overquick resort to violence was an inadvertent admission that one had lost control of the challenge situation. Wits have failed and bully tactics have taken over.

Three times in John we are told that the crowd sought to kill Jesus. In 5:18 they saw Jesus breaking community rules (Sabbath observance) and claiming kinship with God (thereby reaching for an honor status he did not deserve). Jesus' response was to claim that in not honoring the Son, it was they who did not honor the Father. In 8:39-52 Jesus and the Judeans trade insults (accusations of demonic possession), and Jesus ends up calling them liars. He claims it is not he who has honored himself, but it is God who has honored him. The outcome of that exchange is a second resort to violence.

Here in 10:25-38 Jesus insults the crowd (v. 26) and claims a dyadic relationship with God. Unable to respond effectively, they pick up stones to throw at him. Their resort to violence is a tacit admission that their tactics have failed. Their resort to violence indicates that Jesus has won the exchange. (Note that the narrator even adds an insulting touch of his own. He says that the crowd took up stones "again" [8:59], in effect rubbing in the point that they have failed twice to sustain a challenge against Jesus.)

When the dialogue of 10:32-38 resumes, Jesus confounds the crowd with clever use of the official tradition. They again are unable to answer him and again revert to violence. As Mediterranean people heard stories about such behavior, it would be clear to them who has honor and who does not.

191

An Honor Notice about Jesus,
10:39-42

39 Then they tried to arrest him again, but he escaped from their hands.

40 He went away again across the Jordan to the place where John had been baptizing earlier, and he remained there. [41]Many came to him, and they were saying, "John performed no sign, but everything that John said about this man was true." [42]And many believed in him there.

✦ *Notes:* John 10:39-42

10:39-42 The summary the narrator provides here clearly signals the outcome of the escalating debates of chapters 7–10. John had testified (1:34) that Jesus was the Son of God. The debates had reached a crescendo over just that issue (10:36), but the Judean opponents had been unable to win the war of claims and counter-claims. They had resorted to violence (see the **Notes** above) and would do so again at the time of Jesus' death. The public acknowledgment of the truth of John's claims for Jesus is at the same time public acknowledgment of the (honorific) status of Jesus.

CHAPTER VII
JOHN 11:1-54
AS HIS LAST PUBLIC ACT, JESUS BROUGHT
LIFE TO A BELOVED FRIEND (LIKE US)

As we have noted, John's Gospel begins with a wedding and closes with a funeral. Now the special emotion triggered by the funeral of a dear friend sets the mood for this final public scene as well as for events that soon follow. Yet Jesus' raising of Lazarus points to Jesus taking up his own life. These events in the Gospel story provide members of John's antisociety with the awareness that negative events such as funerals can result in radical reversals, from death to life. Feelings evoked by death can be turned into joy for those believing into Jesus; such are the effects experienced by those interpersonally bonded with him.

A Request to Save Lazarus,
a Beloved Friend, 11:1-6

11:1 Now a certain man was ill, Lazarus of Bethany, the village of Mary and her sister Martha. ²Mary was the one who anointed the Lord with perfume and wiped his feet with her hair; her brother Lazarus was ill. ³So the sisters sent a message to Jesus, "Lord, he whom you love is ill." ⁴But when Jesus heard it, he said, "This illness does not lead to death; rather it is for God's glory, so that the Son of God may be glorified through it." ⁵Accordingly, though Jesus loved Martha and her sister and Lazarus, ⁶after having heard that Lazarus was ill, he stayed two days longer in the place where he was.

✦ *Notes:* John 11:1-6

This chapter has a number of surprises. First, we meet a set of persons with whom, we are told, Jesus was quite close: Mary of Bethany, her sister Martha, and their brother Lazarus, highlighted here as Jesus' beloved friend. Second, this family of siblings who live in the vicinity of Jerusalem is formed of parentless Judeans. And third, they appear rather well-to-do. The chapter opens with a request on the part of the sisters for Jesus' help.

The episode of the raising of Lazarus begins with the pattern of dynamic dawdling that occurs in 2:1-11; 4:46-54; 7:2-14; and here; see the chart in **Notes** to 2:1-12 (p. 68). The pattern opens with a request (11:1-3), followed by stalling reluctance (11:4-6) and eventual compliance with the request (11:7-8). While this Gospel has been punctuated with frequent mention of the central feasts of Israel, it is equally significant that, just as Jesus' career opened with a wedding in Galilee, it now closes with a funeral near Jerusalem. In both cases Jesus takes it upon himself to save the families involved from the sanction of shame.

To *have* shame is a good thing. Shame is an expression of commitment to civility, a sign one is both civilized and sensitive to the needs of the community. It is an indication that one knows how to control unwieldy and potentially devastating emotions or actions for the sake of maintaining and preserving good social relations. To *be* shamed, however, is not a good thing. Shameful situations are those that contribute to the breakdown of civilized community. One example is an unneighborly marriage celebration (where wine runs out). Another is an unsatisfying death (being buried without key friends in attendance).

As often in this document, the author presupposes here that his audience knows the story of Jesus. To situate the scene, he refers to Bethany as the village of Mary, who wiped Jesus' feet with her hair, an episode not yet narrated (12:1-7). Furthermore, the author expects us to know Mary's sister Martha, and even Lazarus, since these siblings are presented without introduction. These features point to the audience's prior knowledge of Mary's anointing Jesus and perhaps even the funeral of Lazarus. John will repeat the death story to those who already know it anyway, since he has his own novel way of retelling it (as with virtually all of the stories in his Gospel).

11:1 Hugging the southeastern slope of the Mount of Olives is the tiny village of Bethany. Photo by Thomas Hoffman.

11:1-3 Following the pattern noted above, the sisters here make a request of Jesus. Since Mary and Martha of Bethany are noted as the focal females, with initiative to make rather large expenditures (12:1-7), it is likely that Lazarus of Bethany was a marriageable younger man who died. Given the economic and social position of unattached (we are given this impression) women in antiquity, his loss would have been a terrible blow. He would have been the supporting male in their lives, even when he married. He would be their social security. (His situation is not unlike that of the widow of Nain's son [Luke 7:11-17]. He, too, was an only male support. Expectations for both of these males would have been similar.)

We learn nothing of Lazarus's funeral, only what happened before and after (not unlike the wedding in Galilee, the birth of Jesus in the other Gospels, or the cosmic creative Word in this Gospel). That Jesus dawdled and missed the funeral would look like a dishonor to the Bethany family and may account for a certain testiness in Martha's initial words to Jesus in v. 21.

Commentators have often noted that this story about the raising of Lazarus shares much in common with the story of the Samaritan woman. It is primarily about Jesus' interaction with the women: first, with Martha, and second, with Mary. With the Samaritan woman, the issue was living water as compared to ordinary water; with the Bethany sisters, the issue is living life as compared to ordinary life.

This funeral in Bethany, two miles from Jerusalem (v. 18), is the last public event attended by Jesus before he enters Jerusalem for the last time. That the illness of Lazarus of Bethany was deemed terminal is indicated by the fact that the sisters summon Jesus at all. The author gradually introduces the persons involved in this event: the mortally ill Lazarus, Mary the anointer (in the next chapter), and Martha, all persons for whom Jesus had deep attachment. The accompanying core group around Jesus fades into the background of the action.

11:4-6 Still in keeping with the pattern noted above, Jesus stalls. Jesus loves Martha, Mary, and Lazarus, and yet (or, and therefore) he waits three days before coming to Lazarus's assistance. See the **Note** above on potential dishonor, which the narrator here feels must be explained ("Although he loved him . . . "). People were normally expected to fulfill the symbolic contract implied in friendship by dropping everything and going immediately when summoned. Friends belonged to the in-group of collectivist society. They stood in privileged relationships with other group members and had the "right" to immediate assistance.

In John's narrative the purpose of this stalling reluctance is threefold: to underscore Jesus' ability to overcome death after three days (he arrives on the fourth day), to bring honor to God, and to gain honor for Jesus. The three-day wait is especially important since it points ahead to Jesus' three days in the tomb (20:1ff.; previously alluded to in 2:19-20).

Recall that God's glory (honor) is a central motif in John's Gospel and that the term *glory* is part of his antilanguage. See the **Notes** at 1:14. ⮑ **Antilanguage, 1:19-28**. God's glory is also the interest of Jesus' opponents in 9:24. This divine glory is shared by the Son, God's broker, though his honor is carefully noted as derivative from God's.

Reluctant Compliance:
Jesus Comes to Rescue Lazarus from Death,
11:7-16

7 Then after this he said to the disciples, "Let us go to Judea again." [8]The disciples said to him, "Rabbi, the Jews were just now trying to stone you, and are you going there again?" [9]Jesus answered, "Are there not twelve hours of daylight? Those who walk during the day do not stumble, because they see the light of this world. [10]But those who walk at night stumble, because the light is not in them." [11]After saying this, he told them, "Our friend Lazarus has fallen asleep, but I am going there to awaken him." [12]The disciples said to him, "Lord, if he has fallen asleep, he will be all right." [13]Jesus, however, had been speaking about his death, but they thought that he was referring merely to sleep. [14]Then Jesus told them plainly, "Lazarus is dead. [15]For your sake I am glad I was not there, so that you may believe. But let us go to him." [16]Thomas, who was called the Twin, said to his fellow disciples, "Let us also go, that we may die with him."

✦ Notes: John 11:7-16

11:7 After stalling for several days, Jesus finally complies with the sisters' request. He decides to return to Judea and deal with the matter of Lazarus's misfortune.

11:8 As the pattern we have been describing also suggests, after Jesus has responded to the request, it is not long before the subject of conflict with the Judeans reappears. The mention of stoning here recalls the accusation made against Jesus not long before: blasphemy (10:33, 39). Blasphemy is dishonoring a person by speech. The Judeans perceive Jesus' claim to be Son of God as a dishonor to God, so to defend God's honor, they seek to apprehend him (10:39) in order to stone him. ⇨ **Honor and Violence,** 10:25-38.

11:9-16 Once more the disciples misunderstand what Jesus is up to. In-group readers can see that death is only sleep for believers. Jesus now will demonstrate this so that the disciples might believe it. Nonetheless, the disciples think encounter with Judeans means death for all of them.

11:9-10 The theme of light and darkness, day and night (vv. 9-10), replicates the larger concern about life and death in this chapter. These polar oppositions are part of the antilanguage of John. ⇨ **Antilanguage,** 1:19-28. Note that v. 10 assumes that light is inside persons. As we have noted, ancient people believed that light originated in the heart and shone outward through the eye onto whatever objects the gaze struck; see **Note** at 9:1-5. As an answer to the suggestion that the Judeans are trying to stone Jesus, these verses may also imply that they would not do so openly, in the daylight.

11:11 Lazarus is called "our friend," a relationship Jesus extends to all the disciples during his final words to them (15:14). The word was bound to raise flags of attentiveness among members of John's group since the term *friend* described intense loyalty among social equals. Lazarus is thus designated as a group insider. Throughout John the Jesus group is held together as "friends" by mutual love. ⇨ **Friends,** 14:1—15:17; also ⇨ **Loyalty/Love,** 13:31-39.

11:15-16 Note once again that Jesus' dynamic dawdling is directed to the faith of his disciples ("that you may believe"). The term *believe* is a key piece of anti-language in John's Gospel, standing for loyalty and solidarity with Jesus.

Even though death at the hands of the Judeans is a prospect, Jesus has no fear of dying on behalf of a friend (⇨ **Friends,** 14:1—15:17, and the **Notes** at 15:13). In v. 16 Thomas, the Twin, takes up the fear previously articulated by the disciples in general (v. 8). The explicit theme of death and departure (and the implicit theme of life and presence) permeates this whole section of the Gospel.

Three times (11:16; 20:24; 21:2) John tells his readers that the nickname Thomas means "twin" (it may be a transliteration from the Aramaic or Hebrew root meaning "twin"). The nickname is important: In the ancient Mediterranean world, nicknames were a common means of protection against the evil eye (see also 1:42).

Jesus Rescues Lazarus, the Beloved Friend, from Death, 11:17-44

17 When Jesus arrived, he found that Lazarus had already been in the tomb four days. [18]Now Bethany was near Jerusalem, some two miles away, [19]and many of the Jews had come to Martha and Mary to console them about their brother. [20]When Martha heard that Jesus was coming, she went and met him, while Mary stayed at home. [21]Martha said to Jesus, "Lord, if you had been here, my brother would not have died. [22]But even now I know that God will give you whatever you ask of him." [23]Jesus said to her, "Your brother will rise again." [24]Martha said to him, "I know that he will rise again in the resurrection on the last day." [25]Jesus said to her, "I am the resurrection and the life. Those who believe in me, even though they die, will live, [26]and everyone who lives and believes in me will never die. Do you believe this?" [27]She said to him, "Yes, Lord, I believe that you are the Messiah, the Son of God, the one coming into the world."

28 When she had said this, she went back and called her sister Mary, and told her privately, "The Teacher is here and is calling for you." [29]And when she heard it, she got up quickly and went to him. [30]Now Jesus had not yet come to the village, but was still at the place where Martha had met him. [31]The Jews who were with her in the house, consoling her, saw Mary get up quickly and go out. They followed her because they thought that she was going to the tomb to weep there. [32]When Mary came where Jesus was and saw him, she knelt at his feet and said to him, "Lord, if you had been here, my brother would not have died." [33]When Jesus saw her weeping, and the

Jews who came with her also weeping, he was greatly disturbed in spirit and deeply moved. [34]He said, "Where have you laid him?" They said to him, "Lord, come and see." [35]Jesus began to weep. [36]So the Jews said, "See how he loved him!" [37]But some of them said, "Could not he who opened the eyes of the blind man have kept this man from dying?"

38 Then Jesus, again greatly disturbed, came to the tomb. It was a cave, and a stone was lying against it. [39]Jesus said, "Take away the stone." Martha, the sister of the dead man, said to him, "Lord, already there is a stench because he has been dead four days." [40]Jesus said to her, "Did I not tell you that if you believed, you would see the glory of God?": [41]So they took away the stone. And Jesus looked upward and said, "Father, I thank you for having heard me. [42]I knew that you always hear me, but I have said this for the sake of the crowd standing here, so that they may believe that you sent me." [43]When he had said this, he cried with a loud voice, "Lazarus, come out!" [44]The dead man came out, his hands and feet bound with strips of cloth, and his face wrapped in a cloth. Jesus said to them, "Unbind him, and let him go."

11:38 The entrance to the tomb of Lazarus today. Photo by Richard Rohrbaugh.

✦ *Notes:* John 11:17-44

11:17-19 To explain the Jerusalemite connections of the Judean mourners in the unfolding of this episode, the author states the distance from Bethany to Jerusalem. Along with this space notice, he gives a time notice—Lazarus has been in the tomb four days (repeated in v. 39 and forming an inclusion). Some ancient Israelite scribes believed that a person's life force hovered near the cadaver for three days after death, finally departing on the fourth day. After the fourth day, there was thus nothing of the previous life force around.

It was important to have as many mourners as possible at the time of death, for a large group was an indication of family honor. Mourning usually included loud wailing and beating of the breast (normally a female gesture, but sometimes practiced by men at the time of a death). The sexes walked separately in the funeral procession to the grave. Afterward the women returned home alone to begin the thirty-day period of ritual mourning. During this time women usually sat on the floor.

It is important to note that in many cultures death is a process, not an instantaneous event marked by brain death. In Israel the full death process lasted one year. ✷ **The Meaning of Israelite Burial Customs,** 19:38-42.

11:20-31 Since female family members often stayed home during the mourning period, the notice here that Martha goes outside the village of Bethany to where Jesus was is somewhat unusual. The gossip network, the usual means for news to travel in nonliterate societies, has spread the news that Jesus is in the vicinity. Here Martha professes the traditional faith of Israel as articulated in scribal Pharisaism. In other words, she is not initially a full insider. That will occur in v. 27 when she recognizes that life is in Jesus. ✷ **Life,** 1:1-18.

11:25-27 Jesus articulates the core motive behind the interpersonal bonding with Jesus in John's in-group. Whoever lives now in John's group and believes in Jesus as God's broker will never die; that is why Jesus himself is resurrection and life. When Jesus asks Martha if she "believes," he is asking if she is now understands the antisociety's antilanguage and the group loyalty such understanding implies. ✷ **Antilanguage,** 1:19-28. Martha acknowledges her belief, indicating she is a member of the core group, and goes to fetch her older sister. On the meaning of Jesus as Sky Man from the realm of God ✷ **Son of Man,** 1:35-51.

11:31 The mourners in the house with Mary were undoubtedly women (although on funeral occasions men were customarily permitted to be present); see the **Notes** above at 11:17-19. The entourage thinking to follow her to the tomb would have been largely Judean women.

11:32-34 Mary now goes outside the village of Bethany to where Jesus was.

Mary seems to have been the older sister, properly remaining in the house while the younger runs out to greet Jesus. The fact that Mary disposes of family wealth with such prodigality in the next episode (anointing 12:1-8) may also indicate her elder status.

Mary shares Martha's assessment of Jesus as healer but does not provoke a revelation of Jesus nor take the occasion to show her belief in that revelation. Stereotypically, we would have to say that there is a small hint here of displeasure on Mary's part, because if Jesus were an honorable friend, he would have made a greater effort to be at Lazarus's side. And yet that is difficult to assess. Cultural anthropologists tell us that apart from the sensory experience itself, there is really nothing transcultural about human emotion. Even when things look similar in two different cultures, they are in fact very different. Modern Westerners simply cannot infer the quality and dimensions of the psychological experience that led to the weeping and reactions to it.

Commentators have come up with a variety of theological explanations here for why Jesus was "deeply disturbed" (the Greek term here usually refers to a "display of indignation"). It is likely that Jesus displays indignation and chagrin because Mary has publicly challenged him (⇨ **Challenge and Riposte,** 7:14-24) by questioning whether his actions have been those of a true friend. After all, the mourners are present. See the **Notes** at 11:4-6. Consequently, at this point Jesus appears uninvolved and irritated, unlike Mary and the others who are weeping. But Jesus' demeanor soon changes.

11:34-37 Once more we are told, this time by some Judeans, about "how he loved him"; Lazarus is the only named person in the Gospel described as one loved by Jesus. But note that the Judeans seem to share Mary's question about Jesus' friendship with Lazarus and whether his behavior has been that of an honorable friend. Jesus' indignation in v. 33 seems to have been well placed.

Note the connection between light and life in v. 37; see the **Notes** at vv. 9-10 above. One capable of restoring light to the eyes should be able to maintain life! ⇨ **Life,** 1:1-18.

11:38-44 Jesus now positions himself outside the tomb in which Lazarus was placed. As noted at the beginning of the account, his ultimate purpose in coming to Bethany was to restore life to his dear friend. The earlier notices that Jesus delayed his coming, and then the subsequent displeasure of Mary and the Judean mourners (vv. 32, 37), all build the tension in the story in anticipation of Jesus' rescue of Lazarus.

The scene here is bracketed by the taking way of the stone and the removal of the bandages and cloth. People can now see that where there was death, there is a living being. Such restoration of life is that outward event that reveals something of the honor status of the God of Israel. It also attests to Jesus as God's broker, and we are told that many of the Judeans in Mary's entourage did believe in him.

This belief now specifically entails firm trust in never dying (12:26). The description of this event undoubtedly filled members of John's group with further trust in their undying relationship with Jesus.

11:38-40 The notice that Lazarus had been dead four days is repeated here, thus emphasizing that he was beyond hope; see the **Notes** above at v. 17. Jesus reminds Martha that the glory (honor) of God is his ultimate concern. See the **Notes** at vv. 4-6. "Faith" is the trust of an in-group member. Belonging to the Jesus group will result in seeing God's glory.

11:41-44 This is clear patronage language. ⇨ **Patronage,** 5:21-30. As God's broker, Jesus has complete confidence that the patron will provide. For the sake of those standing around, he makes clear that God is the source of what is provided. In raising Lazarus, Jesus is rescuing Martha and Mary as well. See the **Notes** at vv. 1-3. The dishonor hinted at in vv. 32 and 37 has now been fully overcome. "Life" is also now available to all who believe.

Reaction to Jesus' Raising Lazarus:
A Plot to Kill Jesus, 11:45-54

45 Many of the Jews therefore, who had come with Mary and had seen what Jesus did, believed in him. ⁴⁶But some of them went to the Pharisees and told them what he had done. ⁴⁷So the chief priests and the Pharisees called a meeting of the council, and said, "What are we to do? This man is performing many signs. ⁴⁸If we let him go on like this, everyone will believe in him, and the Romans will come and destroy both our holy place and our nation." ⁴⁹But one of them, Caiaphas, who was high priest that year, said to them, "You know nothing at all! ⁵⁰You do not understand that it is better for you to have one man die for the people than to have the whole nation destroyed." ⁵¹He did not say this on his own, but being high priest that year he prophesied that Jesus was about to die for the nation, ⁵²and not for the nation only, but to gather into one the dispersed children of God. ⁵³So from that day on they planned to put him to death.

54 Jesus therefore no longer walked about openly among the Jews, but went from there to a town called Ephraim in the region near the wilderness; and he remained there with the disciples.

✦ *Notes:* **John 11:45-54**

11:45-46 The first report is one indicating that some Judeans joined the Jesus group. Since "faith" is one of John's antilanguage terms for loyalty, these Judeans are now part of the in-group. As in 5:15, we are left with some ambiguity about those reporting to the Pharisees. It may have been some of the new believers. Nevertheless, the outcome is a negative reaction from the Pharisees and the chief priests. Note also that the pattern cited in vv. 1-16 above is now complete. Hostility with the Judeans is the final event in the cycle.

11:47-48 Here we are informed that the elite leadership of Israel gathers in an attempt to prevent the Romans from doing harm to the Judean populace. This is the first (and only) mention of Romans in the story. Lines are hardening between Judean society and the antisociety of Jesus. ⇨ **Antisociety,** 1:31-51.

11:49-50 Caiaphas's statement about the expedience of executing Jesus is taken by our author to be an oracle bound up with the high-priestly office. Furthermore, he interprets "the whole nation" to include all Israel, whether locally resident or emigrants ("the dispersed children of God").

11:51-54 Once uttered, the high priest's oracle is irrecoverable, inexorable. Plans to put Jesus to death were firm; only the means were to be determined. At least that is what these Pharisees and high-priestly conspirators think. For the author, it was this oracle that determined Jesus' decision not to appear openly among the Judeans anymore. Rather, he joins his core group in hiding in Ephraim. We are not told exactly why or for how long the group remained apart, though there is now a clear separation between the antisociety of Jesus and the dominant society from which his group has withdrawn.

11:54 Ephraim is another of the places that are mentioned only in John. Most modern scholars have located it about fifteen miles northeast of Jerusalem on the edge of the desert of the Jordan valley. See map at 1:28. Photo by Avraham Hay.

A Third Passover Draws Near:
Jesus Is Anointed, 11:55—12:11

11:55 Now the Passover of the Jews was near, and many went up from the country to Jerusalem before the Passover to purify themselves. [56]They were looking for Jesus and were asking one another as they stood in the temple, "What do you think? Surely he will not come to the festival, will he?" [57]Now the chief priests and the Pharisees had given orders that anyone who knew where Jesus was should let them know, so that they might arrest him.

12:1 Six days before the Passover Jesus came to Bethany, the home of Lazarus, whom he had raised from the dead. [2]There they gave a dinner for him. Martha served, and Lazarus was one of those at the table with him. [3]Mary took a pound of costly perfume made of pure nard, anointed Jesus' feet, and wiped them with her hair. The house was filled with the fragrance of the perfume. [4]But Judas Iscariot, one of his disciples (the one who was about to betray him), said, [5]"Why was this perfume not sold for three hundred denarii and the money given to the poor?" [6](He said this not because he cared about the poor, but because he was a thief; he kept the common purse and used to steal what was put into it.) [7]Jesus said, "Leave her alone. She bought it so that she might keep it for the day of my burial. [8]You always have the poor with you, but you do not always have me."

9 When the great crowd of the Jews learned that he was there, they came not only because of Jesus but also to see Lazarus, whom he had raised from the dead. [10]So the chief priests planned to put Lazarus to death as well, [11]since it was on account of him that many of the Jews were deserting and were believing in Jesus.

✦ *Notes:* John 11:55—12:11

The story about Mary anointing Jesus' feet in 12:1-8 is bracketed by two notices (11:55-57 and 12:9-11) of activities among the hostile Judeans. Such bracketing suggests simultaneous action: while the Judeans were looking for Jesus and eventually found him, Jesus was at a meal. Specifically, we are here informed that the Judeans are preparing for Passover (the third Passover mentioned in John), that a good number of Israelites are coming to Jerusalem to purify themselves so as to participate in the Passover Feast, and that Jesus and his program are on their minds. At the same time, the Jerusalem elite, the chief priests and Pharisees, give an order to all under their authority and influence to report Jesus' presence so that they might apprehend him. While this is going on, Jesus comes to Bethany for a dinner.

12:1-2 The dinner scenario opens with precise indication of time, place, and cast of characters. Lazarus is now labeled as "the one whom he had raised from the dead" rather than "the one whom Jesus loved." This new title, repeated in v. 9, has overtones both of Jesus' title as the one whom God had raised from the dead, and of God's self-revelation as he who raised Jesus from the dead. For John's group members, this meal scenario is pregnant with the interpersonal overtones of their relationship to Jesus and to God, perhaps replicated at their own meals.

12:3 Since the streets where people walked were little more than open sewers, and since reclining guests would often be in close proximity to the feet of those near them, it was customary among elites to have slaves wash the feet of guests before a meal. What happens here is another matter. Hosts did not themselves normally deal with the foot-odor problem, nor were feet usually anointed with expensive perfume (the value of the ointment here is nearly a year's wages for a day laborer). This suggests that Mary's action is symbolic.

Aside from grooming, anointing was usually used for rituals of status elevation (anointing the head of one becoming priest, prophet, or king) and status transformation (anointing the whole body of a dead person who moves from the state of family member to ancestor). But here it is neither Jesus' head nor his whole body that is anointed, just his feet. In Israelite society the feet were the body zone symbolizing action; thus, the story points to a ritual of forthcoming transformative action (on the zones of the body, ✿ **Feet,** 13:1-20). Jesus is about to do something of singular significance. As rather wealthy mistress of the house, Mary of Bethany takes it upon herself to acknowledge and affirm Jesus' forthcoming significant action.

Note also that Israelite women did not normally unbind their hair in public, and frequently not even in the home. In Pharisaic tradition, there is mention of a woman who had the high honor of having seven sons become high priest; she explains her good fortune by saying, "The rafters of my house never saw the hairs of my head." (*Lev. Rab.* 188.2)

12:5 The denarius is the most commonly mentioned monetary unit in the Gospels. It was a Roman coin minted of silver and its value is generally given as the equivalent of a day's wage for an unskilled laborer (see Matt. 20:1-16). Hence Philip's estimate of 200 denarii as the cost of bread needed to feed the multitude is translated as "six months' wages" in NRSV (6:7). Oddly, these two references to denarii are the only passages found identically in both the Gospels of Mark and John. Photo courtesy of the British Museum.

12:4-6 As keeper of the group's money, Judas makes a plea for selling the oils used to anoint Jesus, thus putting a halt to the costly social ritual under way. But the narrator brackets Judas's protest with two comments. First, Judas is described again (also 6:64, 71) as "he who was to hand over Jesus." Judas will choose to obey the order of the chief priests and Pharisees—that is, the Judean council (see 11:57 for the order). John knows nothing of the thirty pieces of silver in the Synoptic stories. Second, the narrator notes Judas's propensity to steal from the group's *glossokomon*. The NRSV translates this Greek word here and in 13:29 as "common purse." In fact, it was a coin case or coin box adopted as a security arrangement by Jerusalem pilgrims for transporting temple redemption money, taxes, and alms. Temple expenditures were a major feature of the political nature of money in first-century Israel. Judas was known to divert money from this pilgrimage fund.

12:7-8 Instead of Judas's plans for Mary's oils, Jesus makes known his own: save the oils for Jesus' forthcoming burial. Jesus then rebuts Judas's statement with a proverb from Deut. 15:11 typical of a "limited good" society. In such societies everything that can exist does exist and is already fully distributed. No one can get more unless someone else gets less. The common sentiment was that the current distribution of things should not be altered. The rich will remain rich and the poor will remain poor.

Jesus adds to the proverb a statement that the disciples will not always have him with them. After all the "I am" assurances given by Jesus in the Gospel, including those yet to come, it seems that this statement is to allay the anxiety of John's group members when they no longer experience their Lord in close proximity to them.

12:9-11 Meanwhile, back to the Judeans. Having told us repeatedly of the hostility of the Judeans to Jesus, here John gives us a further update. The crowd of Judeans comes to Bethany both to find Jesus and especially to see "Lazarus, whom he had raised from the dead." Lazarus's presence further complicates the problem of the chief priests, the leadership of the Judeans, since, because of Lazarus, great crowds come to Jesus and believe in him. Hence, Lazarus must die (again) too. This suggests that Judean hostility is aimed not only at Jesus but also at those to whom he has given life.

✧ *Reading Scenario:* John 11:55—12:11

Meals, 11:55—12:11

Meals in antiquity were what anthropologists call "ceremonies." Unlike "rituals," which confirm a change of status, ceremonies are regular, predictable events in which roles and statuses in a community are affirmed or legitimated. In other words, the microcosm of the meal is parallel to the macrocosm of everyday social relations.

Though meals could include people of varying social ranks, normally that did not occur except under very special circumstances (e.g., some Roman *collegia,* or clubs). Since eating together implied sharing a common set of pregnant symbols and values and frequently a common social position as well (cf.13:26), to analyze the significance of a meal, it is important to ask:

Who eats with whom?	Who sits where?
What does one eat?	Where does one eat?
How is it prepared?	What utensils are used?
When does one eat?	What talk is appropriate?
Who does what?	When does one eat what course?

Answering such questions tells us much about the social relations a meal affirms.

There is much evidence from Hellenistic sources of the importance of such matters. In the Hellenistic period it was common for persons to form associations whose members met for table fellowship on holidays, at funerals, and at other times. In Israelite Yahwism the Pharisee group was such a permanent association óf table fellowship formed to keep group members away from any and all out-groups. ➩ **Pharisees,** 9:1-41. To avoid pollution Pharisees would not accept an invitation from ordinary Israelites, whom they labeled as *'am ha-'aretz,* literally "the people of the land"—that is, "the (Canaanite) natives." This out-group of fellow Israelites could not be trusted to provide tithed and consistently pure food. If a Pharisee felt compelled to invite such a person to his own home, he required the guest to put on a ritually clean garment, which the host provided (*m. Demai* 2.2–3). That way he had to wash only the loaned garment, not everything on which the person sat.

In a similar fashion, Roman sources describe meals at which guests of different social rank are seated in different rooms and even served different food and wine depending on their social status (Martial, *Epigrams,* 1.20; 3.60, Loeb 43:201; Juvenal, *Satires* 5, Loeb 69–83; Pliny, *Letters* 2.6, Loeb 109–13). Pliny the Younger offers criticism of socially discriminatory meal practices.

> It would be a long story, and of no importance, were I to recount too particularly by what accident I (who am not fond at all of society) supped lately with a person, who in his own opinion lives in splendor combined with economy; but according to mine, in a sordid but expensive manner. Some very elegant dishes were served up to himself and a few more of the company; while those which were placed before the rest were cheap and paltry. He had apportioned in small flagons three different sorts of wine; but you are not to suppose it was that the guests might take their choice: on the contrary, that they might not choose at all. One was for himself and me; the next for his friends of a lower order (for you must know, he measures out his friendship according to the degrees of quality); and the third for his own freed-men and mine. One who sat next to me took notice of this, and asked me if I approved of it. "Not at all," I told him. "Pray, then," said he, "what is your method on such occasions?" "Mine," I returned, "is to give all my company the same fare; for when I make an invitation, it is to sup, not to be censoring. Every man whom I have placed on an equality with myself by admitting him to my table, I treat as an equal in all particulars." "Even freed-men?" he asked. "Even them," I said; "for on those occasions I regard them not as freed-men, but boon companions." "This must put you to great expense," says he. I assured him not at all; and on his asking how that could be, I said, "Why you must know my freed-men do not drink the same wine I do—but I drink what they do." (Pliny the Younger, *Letters* 2.6)

Table fellowship among Jesus antisociety members is thus a strong reminder of group solidarity.

CHAPTER VIII
JOHN 12:12-50
THE CLOSE OF THE STORY OF JESUS' PUBLIC
OFFER OF LIGHT AND LIFE TO ISRAEL

Jesus Enters Jerusalem and
Is Hailed as King of Israel, 12:12-19

12 The next day the great crowd that had come to the festival heard that Jesus was coming to Jerusalem. [13]So they took branches of palm trees and went out to meet him, shouting,
"Hosanna!
Blessed is the one who comes in the name of the Lord—
    the King of Israel!"
14 Jesus found a young donkey and sat on it; as it is written:
15 "Do not be afraid, daughter of Zion.
Look, your king is coming,
    sitting on a donkey's colt!"
16 His disciples did not understand these things at first; but when Jesus was glorified, then they remembered that these things had been written of him and had been done to him. [17]So the crowd that had been with him when he called Lazarus out of the tomb and raised him from the dead continued to testify. [18]It was also because they heard that he had performed this sign that the crowd went to meet him. [19]The Pharisees then said to one another, "You see, you can do nothing. Look, the world has gone after him!"

✦ *Notes:* John 12:12-19

12:12 Once again, the gossip network kept the festive crowd informed about Jesus' activity. Upon hearing about his availability near Jerusalem, people go out to meet him. ➪ **Gossip Network,** 4:1-42.

12:13-14 The crowd takes up palm branches and chants Ps. 118:25-26 as they go to meet Jesus. However, their intentions are revealed by the addition of the phrase "King of Israel." Note that palms were also a symbol of Israelite ethnicity. They were brought to the temple in Jerusalem at the time of its rededication by Judas Maccabeus after the defeat of the Syrians (2 Macc. 10:7). They also appeared on the Israelite coins minted during the Bar Kochba revolt (C.E. 132–35). In the Testament of Naphtali 5:4, palm fronds are given to Levi as a symbol of power over all Israel. Like the Galilean crowd previously (6:15), now the Judean crowd sees Jesus as King of Israel.

Jesus responds to the acclamation by taking a young ass and sitting on it. The ass was a peaceful mode of transportation, unlike the horse, which was a war animal. Sitting on the young ass would thus signal to the crowds that Jesus would lead no riot; force was not in his repertory for the social change he had in mind.

12:13 Only John mentions the palm (from which the name Palm Sunday derives) as the tree from which the crowd brought branches to welcome Jesus. This picture is of date palms (*Phoenix dactylifera*). The branches are six to ten feet long. It is the only native palm tree in the Holy Land. Actually, it is native only to desert oases, e.g., Jericho, "the city of palms" (Deut. 34:3; 2 Chr. 28:13), but was highly valued for its fruit and transplanted from very ancient times to other sites. Photo by Eugene Selk.

12:15-16 Once more the disciples did not understand what was afoot. The use of Zech. 9:9 to clarify the meaning of the incident comes *after* Jesus is raised, and the disciples receive the spirit of Jesus so that they understand him. In Zechariah 9 the king who comes to Jerusalem will be "humble" and proclaim "peace to the nations." In the Gospel story, every mention of the new understanding available to the disciples thanks to the Spirit given by Jesus makes members of John's anti-society further attentive to the spirit in their midst. It further points to the increasing understanding of Jesus available to them.

12:17-18 Here we are told, specifically, that the crowd that goes out to meet Jesus consisted of those who witnessed his raising of Lazarus plus those who heard about this raising from the witnesses. Both groups believe the sign of the raising of Lazarus, itself a sign of what was forthcoming in the story of Jesus. For John's group, both Jesus' raising of Lazarus and God's raising of Jesus serve as signs of what is in store for those who believe into and abide in Jesus.

12:19 The notice about the Pharisees in this verse picks up from the mention of them in 11:57, where they along with the chief priests issue an order to report on Jesus' whereabouts. The verses also provide a parallel to the chief priests' plan to kill Lazarus in 12:10-11. The Pharisees conclude that it is too late for anything but extreme measures, since "the world"—that is, all of Israel—has gone after him. Further evidence of this is soon to follow in the request of émigré Israelites ("Greeks" at the feast) to see Jesus.

Jesus' Final Public Revelation, 12:20-36

20 Now among those who went up to worship at the festival were some Greeks. [21]They came to Philip, who was from Bethsaida in Galilee, and said to him, "Sir, we wish to see Jesus." [22]Philip went and told Andrew; then Andrew and Philip went and told Jesus. [23]Jesus answered them, "The hour has come for the Son of Man to be glorified. [24]Very truly, I tell you, unless a grain of wheat falls into the earth and dies, it remains just a single grain; but if it dies, it bears much fruit. [25]Those who love their life lose it, and those who hate their life in this world will keep it for eternal life. [26]Whoever serves me must follow me, and where I am, there will my servant be also. Whoever serves me, the Father will honor.

27 "Now my soul is troubled. And what should I say—'Father, save me from this hour'? No, it is for this reason that I have come to this hour. [28]Father, glorify your name." Then a voice came from heaven, "I have glorified it, and I will glorify it again." [29]The crowd standing there heard it and said that it was thunder. Others said, "An angel has spoken to him." [30]Jesus answered, "This voice has come for your sake, not for mine. [31]Now is the judgment of this world; now the ruler of this world will be driven out. [32]And I, when I am lifted up from the earth, will draw all people to myself." [33]He said this to indicate the kind of death he was to die. [34]The crowd answered him, "We have heard from the law that the Messiah remains forever. How can you say that the Son of Man must be lifted up? Who is this Son of Man?" [35]Jesus said to them, "The light is with you for a little longer. Walk while you have the light, so that the darkness may not overtake you. If you walk in the darkness, you do not know where you are going. [36]While you have the light, believe in the light, so that you may become children of light."

After Jesus had said this, he departed and hid from them.

✦ *Notes:* John 12:20-36

12:20 The final event in John's story of Jesus' activity before his arrest is Jesus' reaction to a request by Hellenistic Israelites, Judean émigrés, to see Jesus. This group follows Judean custom by coming up to Jerusalem for the Passover (the Greek verb here, *anabaino,* "to go up," had become a term for pilgrimage; the grammatical form implies habitual behavior).

12:21-22 The action begins when these Hellenists ask Philip, from Bethsaida in Galilee, to see Jesus. The mention of Philip's name and place of origin recall 1:43-44, where we learned Philip was the first disciple sought out by Jesus himself to join his antisociety. Now Philip relays the Hellenists' request to Andrew. Remember that we were previously told that Andrew was the first disciple to recognize Jesus as Israel's Messiah (1:41), and that he too was from Bethsaida (1:44; see the **Notes** at 1:43-46). They both come to Jesus to pass along the Hellenists' request. Note that the chain of access here, really a brokerage chain, from Philip to Andrew to Jesus, indicates the status of those core followers who stand between Jesus and the public.

12:23-28a The coming of the Israelites from abroad to see Jesus triggers Jesus' certainty that the time for him to do what he was always meant to do, the activity marking the culmination of his life's significance, has finally come (as prepared in 7:33-36).

By way of explanation, Jesus prefaces an "unless . . ." statement with his word of honor (NRSV: "Very truly, I tell you . . ."). These "unless . . ." statements in John serve to underscore the increasing requirements of discipleship (see 3:3; 6:53; 12:24; 13:8; 15:4). Here Jesus insists that falling to the ground and dying like a seed will produce much fruit. He clarifies by noting that attachment to life as one now leads it leads to death anyway, while disattachment from living in the present Israelite style (= life in this world) will lead to eternal life. Disciples must give slave service to Jesus by following him in his hour; then God will honor them as God honors Jesus.

By his own admission, the advent of the hour leaves Jesus anxious. Yet, in spite of his anxiety, Jesus embraces the appointed time and what God wills for it. In so doing, he demonstrates his loyalty to and honor of his Father. His firm assent is marked by his utterance: "Father, glorify your name"—that is, "By some outward deed, Father, show everyone how honorable you are!"

12:28b-29 The narrator now informs us that Jesus has an alternate state-of-consciousness experience that involves a sound from the sky. ⇨ **Seeing Jesus: Alternate States of Consciousness,** 20:1-29. Jesus interprets the sound as the voice of God assuring him that God would, indeed, show everyone how honorable God is—just as God has previously done. The crowd, in turn, takes the sky sound to be meaningful thunder or one of God's sky servants, angels, passing by or communicating something. The ancients believed that any event occurring in the sky has meaning for people on the land over which the sky event takes place.

12:30-33 Jesus now explains that the sky sound occurred for the sake of the crowd, since it, too, marks the beginning of the hour: "Now is the judgment of this world." The phrase "to be lifted up" has a well-known idiomatic correlation with crucifixion. The relationship of crucifixion to social elevation was also a commonplace in antiquity. For example, Artemidorus (late second century C.E.)

212

tells us that a crucifixion dream was a good omen for a poor man, "for the cruci-fied is exalted *[hypselos]*"; for a slave it portends freedom, "for those crucified are not subordinate *[anypotaktoi]*"; and a dream of crucifixion in the city "signi-fies a government position *[arche]* corresponding to the place where the cross stood" (*Oneirokritikon* 2.53). Ps-Callisthenes tells how Alexander traps the assas-sins of Darius by his oath to "make them exalted above all men *[periphanestatous . . . pasin anthropois],"* which he does by crucifying them (*Life of Alexander* 2.21).

Note also that "to draw" (all people) is another term with a double meaning; it means both to attract people and to hail persons to court—some for life, others for judgment.

12:34 The crowd cites some unspecified Torah tradition to the effect that Israel's Messiah will not die but will remain forever. After identifying the Messi-ah with the Son of Man, the crowd then claims that Jesus has said the Son of Man must be lifted up, hence be crucified and die. The fact is Jesus said: "I, when I am lifted up from the earth . . ." (v. 31). Thus, while the crowd identifies Jesus as the Son of Man, it concludes its comment with: "Who is this Son of Man?" This is less a question of simple identification (in context it can only be Jesus) than of role, status, and nature.

12:35-36a Jesus' final exhortation to the Judean public is an appeal to join his group. The light (Jesus, "the light of the world") would only be among them for a short while; therefore, they should take the opportunity to become part of the "light" community while it was still possible. ➪ **Light,** 1:1-18.

12:36b With the notice of Jesus' departure and self-concealment, the first half of the Gospel comes to an end. The outstanding feature of this part of the Gospel has been Jesus' self-disclosure in terms of what the author calls "signs." "Signs," as we have repeatedly noted, are events that reveal who Jesus is, hence, events of Jesus' self-disclosure. Yet, as nearly all scholars agree, it is with Jesus' exaltation, his being glorified, that the major self-disclosure occurs. This is what awaits us in the ensuing chapters. Before launching on that central part of his story, however, the author presents a sort of epilogue to explain Jesus' lack of success among Judeans.

The Problem of Judean Unbelief Explained,
12:37-43

37 Although he had performed so many signs in their presence, they did not believe in him. ³⁸This was to fulfill the word spoken by the prophet Isaiah:
"Lord, who has believed our message,
 and to whom has the arm of the Lord been revealed?"
39 And so they could not believe, because Isaiah also said,
40 "He has blinded their eyes
   and hardened their heart,
so that they might not look with their eyes,
   and understand with their heart and turn—
   and I would heal them."
41 Isaiah said this because he saw his glory and spoke about him. ⁴²Nevertheless many, even of the authorities, believed in him. But because of the Pharisees they did not confess it, for fear that they would be put out of the synagogue; ⁴³for they loved human glory more than the glory that comes from God.

✦ *Notes:* John 12:37-43

12:37 After the author has set out the many signs wrought by Jesus in such clear and magnificent fashion, the problem concerning those who did not accept the signs still remains. Why in fact did persons who witnessed the signs not acknowledge Jesus? The Jerusalem crowds, the group Jesus just addressed, had seen such signs "yet they did not believe in him." Why? The author, like the writers who addressed other Jesus groups, turns to the prophet Isaiah for clarification.

12:38-39a The first clarification is from Isa. 53:1, a passage also used by Paul (Rom. 10:16) for similar purposes. The passage from Isaiah implies, as Paul says, that "faith comes from what is heard" (Rom. 10:17a). But so does chosen unbelief! By citing the passage here, John intimates that Judeans "heard," and that the "arm of the Lord" has been revealed to them, yet they have purposefully, actively, and consciously chosen to reject what they have heard and seen. This is what Isaiah intimated, and it had to happen because Isaiah said it. "And so they could not believe" (v. 39a). The argument that follows is quite similar.

12:39b-41 The second clarification comes from Isa. 6:10, a passage also used in the Synoptic tradition (Matt. 13:15; Mark 4:12) to explain why Israel rejected Jesus' proclamation. The mention of the eyes-heart zone in the passage from Isaiah points to emotion-fused thought, to conscience, to choice on the part of those who reject the signs they have witnessed. For the zones of the body, ⊃ **Feet,** 13:1-20. Like Abraham (8:56), Isaiah, too, saw the glory (honor) of the Lord (Isa. 6:1), the author tells us, and spoke of Jesus, the Word made flesh who reveals this glory! However, the reference may be to some tradition such as one finds in the Aramaic version of Isaiah, TgIsa. 6:5: "My eyes have seen the glory of the *Shekhinah* of the eternal king, the LORD of hosts." Here the term *Shekhinah* refers to the presence of God in the sky and on earth; in John's Gospel this presence is the Word enfleshed in Jesus.

12:42-43 After making a generalization about the rejection of Jesus by all Judeans, the author specifies that in fact many authorities believed in Jesus. But they did not talk about it because they were afraid of expulsion and shunning ("to be put out of the synagogue") due to the initiative of the Pharisees. The problem was that "they loved human glory [honor] more than the glory of God." ✩ **Honor and Shame,** 5:16-30. Such ostracism was, of course, a very serious matter in a society in which everything depended on maintaining social networks. The lines between Judean society and the antisociety of Jesus are thus very sharply drawn. ✩ **Antisociety,** 1:35-51. Note that the same critique was leveled against the Pharisees in the Matthean community (the second part of the Sermon on the Mount, Matt. 6).

Conclusion to the Series of Jesus' Self-Disclosures, 12:44-50

44 Then Jesus cried aloud: "Whoever believes in me believes not in me but in him who sent me. [45]And whoever sees me sees him who sent me. [46]I have come as light into the world, so that everyone who believes in me should not remain in the darkness. [47]I do not judge anyone who hears my words and does not keep them, for I came not to judge the world, but to save the world. [48]The one who rejects me and does not receive my word has a judge; on the last day the word that I have spoken will serve as judge, [49]for I have not spoken on my own, but the Father who sent me has himself given me a commandment about what to say and what to speak. [50]And I know that his commandment is eternal life. What I speak, therefore, I speak just as the Father has told me."

✦ *Notes:* John 12:44-50

Before describing Jesus' last day with his inner circle, the author interjects a final public appeal by Jesus that sums up all that has preceded. This final appeal is a recap of themes set forth throughout the whole of the Gospel of John up to this point, from the prologue to the conclusion of Jesus' activities. To reject Jesus—the One sent, the life of the world, the messenger of the Father, the mediator of eternal life—is to reject the Father from whom all these come.

Much of the antilanguage used throughout the Gospel to this point also appears in this summary. ✩ **Antilanguage,** 1:19-28. Note especially the polar opposition between light and darkness being repeated here. This is the language of boundaries—between Judean society and the antisociety of Jesus. ➢ **Antisociety,** 1:35-51. At the beginning (vv. 44-45) and end of the summary (v. 50), special emphasis is also placed on the fact that Jesus is speaking words given to him by his patron, the one who authorizes his brokerage. ➢ **Patronage,** 5:21-30. Jesus concludes, "What I speak, therefore, I speak just as the Father has told me." That is the ultimate justification for everything he has said.

CHAPTER IX
JOHN 13:1–17:26
PASSOVER IN JERUSALEM:
WHAT JESUS SAID AND DID DURING HIS
LAST MEAL WITH HIS FRIENDS (LIKE US)

The prologue to John (1:1-51) introduces readers into the realm of God before creation, only to bring them back into a quite specific time and highly localized place. A series of significant events that disclose who Jesus really is follows the prologue (2:1—12:50) and covers some three years (with three Passovers). In the author's estimation, these include all of the events in Jesus' career of major significance for John's antisociety. With 13:1 we arrive at Jesus' final Passover and consider events that take place in rather rapid succession over a twenty-four-hour period: Jesus' final meal with his in-group, his arrest, sentencing, and death.

Jesus' last day begins with a supper and a final conversation with his disciples. This Gospel's description of Jesus' final conversation with his disciples is a very significant segment of the work. Its structural centerpiece is the new command to disciples to love one another as Jesus has loved them, in 15:12-27. Previously, God's attachment to and concern for Israel ("God so loved the world") was affirmed. When it came to Jesus and his disciples, it was the disciples' relationship to Jesus alone that was in focus. Now, as Jesus approaches his "glorification," he addresses the need for disciples to love one another as he loves them.

Jesus Washes Feet of His Core Group:
Urges Imitation and Mutual Love, 13:1-17

13:1 Now before the festival of the Passover, Jesus knew that his hour had come to depart from this world and go to the Father. Having loved his own who were in the world, he loved them to the end. ²The devil had already put it into the heart of Judas son of Simon Iscariot to betray him. And during supper ³Jesus, knowing that the Father had given all things into his hands, and that he had come from God and was going to God, ⁴got up from the table, took off his outer robe, and tied a towel around himself. ⁵Then he poured water into a basin and began to wash the disciples' feet and to wipe them with the towel that was tied around him. ⁶He came to Simon Peter, who said to him, "Lord, are you going to wash my feet?" ⁷Jesus answered, "You do not know now what I am doing, but later you will understand." ⁸Peter said to him, "You will never wash my feet." Jesus answered, "Unless I wash you, you have no share with me." ⁹Simon Peter said to him, "Lord, not my feet only but also my hands and my head!" ¹⁰Jesus said to him, "One who has bathed does not need to wash, except for the feet, but is entirely clean. And you are clean, though not all of you." ¹¹For he knew who was to betray him; for this reason he said, "Not all of you are clean."

12 After he had washed their feet, had put on his robe, and had returned to the table, he said to them, "Do you know what I have done to you? [13]You call me Teacher and Lord—and you are right, for that is what I am. [14]So if I, your Lord and Teacher, have washed your feet, you also ought to wash one another's feet. [15]For I have set you an example, that you also should do as I have done to you. [16]Very truly, I tell you, servants are not greater than their master, nor are messengers greater than the one who sent them. [17]If you know these things, you are blessed if you do them."

✦ *Notes:* **John 13:1-17**

The first larger segment (13:1-38) of Jesus' final conversation with his disciples is parallel with 17:1-26. ⇨ **Appendix.** ⇨ **Final Words,** 13:1-17. Both segments begin with the author noting that "the hour had come." What characterizes this piece is the repeated word of honor (vv. 16, 20, 21, 38) punctuating the ends of the three pieces that make up the segment: Jesus washes the feet of his core group and urges imitation (vv 1-17); forthcoming proof for Jesus being "I am" (vv. 18-20); Jesus knows of his betrayal and urges mutual love (vv. 31-38).

13:1a "Now before the festival of the Passover." Torah legislation in the book of Leviticus concerning sacrifice and pilgrimage presumes an Israelite populace confined to Judea. And so long as Israel was confined to Judea, pilgrims could share rather uniform and limited expectations of God, similar interests and desires, and a rather common mode of dealing with the meaning of God's commands to Israel. But thanks to emigration from the homeland, pilgrimage feasts now brought together Israelites who held different expectations of the God of Israel, who interpreted the Torah and its practices differently, who spoke different languages and followed varying customs. Philo of Alexandria considered Jerusalem a "mother city" (metropolis; *Flac.* 7.46; *Leg.* 36.281) that has produced a large number of offspring cities—that is, Judean settlements across the Hellenistic Roman Empire. For a list of these emigrants, see Acts 2:9-11, where they are described as "Judeans, devout men from every nation under the sky" (Acts 2:5, literal translation; thus, in Matthew's high-context Israelite setting, Jesus' command "to make disciples of all nations," Matt. 28:19, means to make disciples of Jesus, the Messiah, of Judeans from every nation).

First-century Jerusalem witnessed a wide variety of religious discourses that elite leadership could not absorb and reflect in terms of its local, Judean norms. Pilgrims came with divergent interests and desires, and local Judean elites were unable to cope with the numerous meanings now encompassed by a pilgrimaging Israel from the whole Mediterranean world. The special Roman presence in Jerusalem at pilgrimage times points to this pilgrimage site as an arena of differing interpretations of Torah and conflict concerning Israel's values and hopes. Thus, the continued situations of conflict and social division that pilgrimage provoked required control by Roman power. ⇨ **Pilgrimage,** 2:13-25.

13:1b "Jesus knew that his hour had come." The single day covered by John 13-19 marks the moment toward which all the signs in chapters 2–12 pointed. The first part of that "hour" opens with Jesus' final discourse to his inner circle (chaps. 13–17) and continues with Jesus' "being lifted up" and "giving the Spirit."

13:1c While the return of the Sky Man—that is, the Son of Man—to the Father takes place by his being lifted up by the Judeans in Jerusalem, the vocabulary is one of departure on a horizontal plane, like the Exodus of old. Significantly, in these opening verses of chapter 13 there is no mention of descent and ascent (the vertical dimension symbolizes power: descent is loss of power; ascent is gain of power). Instead, John here speaks of departing to the Father, with the horizontal symbols of coming out and going in. These horizontal symbols signify belonging and solidarity, because he came out of God and goes into God. Horizontal movement is a natural symbol of the interpersonal. This dimension indicates that the emphasis in chapters 13–17 is on the interpersonal in terms of solidarity, loyalty, belonging, and mutual commitment.

We do not find out that an ascent is involved until Jesus appears to Mary Magdalene (20:17). The return of the Sky Man, his being "lifted up," identifies the judgment, the *krisis* of Israel. This lifting up has its initial explanation in 3:14: the bronze serpent is lifted up and heals all who look upon it. Jesus thus "signifies"— that is, gives the meaning behind—what sort of death he was to die (see 8:28; in 12:32 the phrase is identified as crucifixion, realized in 18:32).

So that the reader would not construe the departure of Jesus to mean an end to his solidarity with his followers, the narrator quickly notes that Jesus loves them completely, finally, and forever (Greek *telos*). "Love" is John's term for loyalty and group attachment. ✧ **Love/Hate,** 3:1-21; ✧ **Loyalty/Love,** 13:21-38.

13:2 The role of the devil (= Satan, the accuser) is to test a person's loyalty to God; to this end the devil deceives and lies. Here we learn that Judas Iscariot's loyalty to Jesus is being tested. In v. 27, after being given the morsel by Jesus, Judas succumbs; the fact that he leaves to betray Jesus is proof that he yields to Satan's deceptions. Note that the introduction of Judas's betrayal here connects the foot washing to the issue of group solidarity. For more complete comment on this issue, see the **Notes** below.

13:3-5 Up to this point in the Gospel, emphasis has been on the disciples' relation to Jesus. Now Jesus' behavior and urgings at this final gathering focus on the disciples' relations with one another. This is clearly seen in the foot-washing scene we now encounter.

There are two levels at which to think about this foot-washing scene in John's Gospel. Initially it calls to mind the common practice of washing the feet of guests at a meal, an action usually performed by slaves or low-status servants. It was an onerous and demeaning task because it meant washing off human and animal waste. Human waste was emptied out windows onto the city streets each

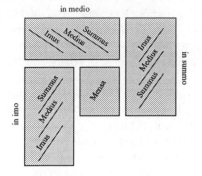

13:3-5 A diagram of the placement of guests at a banquet. In Jesus' day the usual way of dining was to recline on couches or mats. The evangelist assumes an arrangement similar to this in the scenes of the washing of feet and the discussion in 13:23-35, also at the banquet in Bethany (12:3). In the above arrangement for nine guests, the *mensa* is the table. The diners lie on the left side, supporting themselves on the left elbow. Of the three couches or mats, that in the middle (*in medio*) was regarded as the most honorable; of the three places on it, that on the left (the *summus*) was assigned to the guest of highest rank, and no one was reclining behind him on the couch. The couch to his left (*in summo*) was next in dignity; that on the right (*in imo*), being held in lowest esteem, was occupied by the host and his family. These arrangements explain the necessity of refraining from occupying the highest place, which had perhaps been reserved for a "more distinguished" guest (Luke 14:8). Parrot Graphics.

morning, while animal waste was ever-present. Therefore, no matter how well a person bathed, sandals and feet inevitably became smelly and dirty in the process of walking to a meal at another's house. Foot washing was thus a courtesy offered meal guests, though the task itself was performed only by persons of low-honor status. The significance of the interaction in the story depends on the social dynamics of this common custom.

The second level of meaning in the story builds on the first. Here we move from the ordinary use of language and behavior relating to foot washing to the antilanguage and symbolic behavior of the Johannine antisociety. Foot washing becomes a prophetic action that symbolizes forgiveness. The feet (and hands) stand for activity, actions (⇨ **Feet,** 13:1-20). To wash another's feet is to wash away the actions they may have been performed (just as cutting off one's hand is to cease acting in a certain way). Here the foot washing is a parting gesture performed by Jesus and urged upon his disciples; they must forgive one another as he forgives them.

13:6-8a At the first level of meaning (see the **Note** above), Peter is astonished that Jesus would stoop to the role of a servant or slave. As friends, their relationship has been that of social equals. But like Nicodemus (chap. 3), the Samaritan woman (chap. 4), and many others in the Gospel, Peter fails to understand the double meaning in Jesus' words and actions. He does not yet fully understand the antilanguage of Jesus (⇨ **Antilanguage,** 1:19-28), and is therefore not as much an insider to the core group as he imagines (and as the denial mentioned at the end of this chapter clearly shows). The process of being fully engrafted into the core group will not occur for Peter until chapter 21.

Peter is stuck at the first level of meaning: he denies that Jesus will ever wash his feet. In so saying he demonstrates that he does not yet understand the second-level meaning of foot washing at all. Nonetheless, Jesus assures him that he soon will.

3:8b-11 Jesus' reply to Peter is at the second level of meaning. Forgiveness, and the group solidarity it creates, is essential to what Jesus is creating. Yet Peter still misunderstands. Thinking more of a good thing is better than a little, he asks to be washed all over. The response of Jesus cleverly plays upon both the ordinary meaning of language and the antilanguage of John's antisociety. He points out that a dinner guest normally bathes at home, so that only the feet, which have contracted street dirt, need washing. But he then switches immediately to the issue of group solidarity. Note carefully that when Jesus tells Peter "you" are clean, the pronoun in the Greek is plural *(hymeis)*. Here he is talking about the group and the solidarity created by the symbolic act of foot washing, forgiveness. One member of the group, however, is disloyal and will betray Jesus.

13:12-17 This brief statement of Jesus again plays on both levels of meaning in the foot-washing scene (see the **Notes** above). When he talks about servants not being above masters, he is alluding to the ordinary expectations in foot washing: it is done by those of low status for those who are higher. This is a matter of honor (v. 16; "Very truly, I tell you"). His own actions, however, upset that honor expectation, thereby indicating that the values of his antisociety are radically different than those of ordinary society.

✧ *Reading Scenarios:* **John 13:1-17**
Final Words, 13:1-17

The notice in 13:1 that Jesus' "hour had come" indicates that chapters 13–17 present Jesus' final words to his core group before his death. This segment of the Gospel is often called Jesus' final discourse or his farewell speech. In the United States persons about to die are said to see their whole life flash before their eyes. Not so in the Mediterranean world. What is distinctive of final words before death in the Mediterranean (and elsewhere) is that the person about to die is believed capable of knowing what is going to happen to persons near and dear to him or her. Dying persons are prescient because they are closer to the realm of God (or gods), who knows all things, than to the realm of humans, whose knowledge is limited to human experience. Xenophon tells us, "At the advent of death, men become more divine, and hence can foresee the forthcoming" (*Cyrop.* 7.7.21). In the *Iliad* (16.849–50) the dying Patroclus predicts the death of Hector at the hands of Achilles, and the dying Hector predicts the death of Achilles himself (22.325). Similarly, in Sophocles' play *The Women of Trachis,* the dying Heracles summons Alcmene so that she may learn from his last words "the things I now know by divine inspiration" (*Trachiniae* 1148ff.). Virgil finds it normal to have the dying Orodes predict that his slayer will soon meet retribution (*Aeneid* 10.729–41). Plato too reports that Socrates made predictions during his last moments, realizing that "on the point of death, I am now in that condition in which men are most wont to prophesy" (*Apol.* 39c; cf. Xenophon, *Anab. Apol.* 30). Cicero reports concerning Callanus of India: "As he was about to die and was ascending his funeral pyre, he said: 'What a glorious death! The fate of Hercules is mine. For when this mortal frame is burned the soul will find the light.' When Alexander directed him to speak if he wished to say anything to him, he answered: 'Thank you, nothing, except that I shall see you very soon.' So it turned out, for Alexander died in Babylon a few days later" (*De Divinatione* 1.47).

The Israelite tradition equally shared this belief, as is clear from the final words of Jacob (Genesis 49) and Moses (Deuteronomy 31–34); see also 1 Sam. 12; 1 Kings 2:1-17; Josh. 23–24. The well-known documents called "Testaments," written around the time of Jesus, offer further witness to this belief (e.g., Testament of the Twelve Patriarchs, Testament of Moses; see also Jub. 22:10-30; 1 Macc. 2:47-70; Josephus, *Ant.* 12.279–84).

In the United States, with economics as the focal social institution, final words and testaments deal with the disposition of goods. In Mediterranean antiquity, however, with the kinship institution being focal, final words deal with concern for the tear in the social fabric resulting from the dying person's departure. Hence, the dying person will be deeply concerned about what will happen to his or her kin (or fictive kin) group. Before death, the dying person will impart significant information about what is soon to befall the group in general and individuals in the group. This includes who will hold it together (successor) and advice to kin group members on how to keep the group together. Before passing on, the dying person offers good wishes and expresses concern for the well-being of the group. It is within this cultural framework that Jesus' final words and actions need to be understood. The foot washing is a parting gesture; the wealth of information about the future all betokens concern for those given to him by the Father, whom he is about to leave: they are not orphans (14:18), but rather they will have an inheritance with the Father in the place being prepared for them. In the meantime, Jesus and the Father come and make their "dwelling" with them; they continue to have interpersonal relations. Finally, a Paraclete will come to them, whose task it will be to recall and explain the significant items that they missed and to carry on Jesus' work through the disciples.

Feet, 13:1-17

Foot washing was customary behavior on the arrival of guests in the house for a meal. ⇨ **Feasts,** 2:1-12. ⇨ **Meals,** 12:1-8. Since the foot washing in the scene depicted here is not upon arrival, something else is going on. This is a symbolic foot washing. The key to the scenario is the meaning of feet and hence washing the feet.

While some philosophers in the Greco-Roman world thought of the human person in terms of body and soul, traditional Mediterranean persons thought in terms of what anthropologists have called "zones of interaction" with the world around. ⇨ **Word,** 1:1-18. As we previously noted, three such zones make up the human person, and all appear repeatedly in the Gospels: (1) Eyes-heart: the zone of *emotion-fused thought* includes will, intellect, judgment, personality, and feeling all rolled together. (2) Mouth-ears: the zone of *self-expressive speech* includes communication, particularly that which is self-revealing. It is listening and responding. (3) Hands-feet: the zone of *purposeful action* is the zone of external behavior or interaction with the environment. It is the zone of activity—of doing, performing, making.

Human activity can be described in terms of any particular zone, a combination of two, or all three. Here in 13:1-17 a single zone comes into play. The feet serve as a reference for the zone of purposeful action, the zone of behavior and activity. To wash the feet in such a symbolic way points to washing away the effects of one's actions, hence, forgiveness of "trespasses" or "transgressions" (other foot metaphors). Jesus' washing the feet means that he forgives his disciples their "offenses" (another foot metaphor) against him, even forthcoming ones.

As we previously noted, the metaphorical resonance of the "Word" in the opening of the Gospel points to the outcome of a person's mouth-ears. It stands for self-revelation and self-communication. This is what the Word that was with God in the beginning entails—God's self-revelation and self-communication. This Word with God from the beginning is creative and powerful. What God says happens immediately, as we read in Genesis 1. For God, there is no need of hands-feet as is the case with humans and other animate beings, although God does look and pass judgment (the eyes-heart zone).

Finally, when a writer refers to all three zones, we can assume comment is being made about complete human experience. The author of 1 John writes, "We declare to you what was from the beginning, what we have heard, what we have seen with our eyes, what we have looked at and touched with our hands, concerning the word of life" (1 John 1:1). The statement is an expression of total involvement, "body and soul" as we would say. All three zones are likewise present in the Sermon on the Mount: eyes-heart (Matt. 6:19:7-6), mouth-ears (Matt. 7:7-11), and hands-feet (Matt. 7:13-27). The same is true of the interpretation of the parable of the sower in Luke 8:11-15. For additional examples, see Exod. 21:24; 2 Kings 4:34; Prov. 6:16-10; Dan. 10:6.

Jesus Promises Forthcoming
Proof of His Being "I Am," 13:18-20

18 "I am not speaking of all of you; I know whom I have chosen. But it is to fulfill the scripture, 'The one who ate my bread has lifted his heel against me.' [19]I tell you this now, before it occurs, so that when it does occur, you may believe that I am he. [20]Very truly, I tell you, whoever receives one whom I send receives me; and whoever receives me receives him who sent me."

✦ *Notes:* 13:18-20

13:18 This brief, but central, passage calls attention to the significance of disloyalty in John's group. Such disloyalty surrounding events soon to unfold will serve as further basis for believing Jesus is "I am" (v. 19). "To lift the heel" entails showing the sole of one's foot to another. In the eastern Mediterranean world, that is a great insult, expressing the wish to utterly shame another, to step on another's head. The quotation from Ps. 41:9 means: a member(s) of my in-group will utterly dishonor me. The passage undoubtedly is meant to describe Judas's behavior, but perhaps Peter's as well. The repeated "word of honor" in the next segment underscores these personages and their behavior in the unfolding story. The way the author connects disloyalty with the foot washing (both Peter and "he who was to betray him" are singled out) makes clear the symbolic character of the event and the centrality of Jesus' concern for group loyalty and group solidarity.

13:19 Throughout the Gospel, Jesus uses the phrase "I am." This phrase in Greek translated the sacred name of Israel's God, written with the four letters "YHWH," rooted in Moses' burning-bush experience in Exod. 3:13-15. By disclosing himself as "I AM," Jesus claims to be the presence of God in Israel. Jesus' full awareness of forthcoming betrayal will further demonstrate this.

13:20 The concluding word of honor once more underscores the solidarity of those "sent" by Jesus and Jesus' solidarity with God. This is another dimension of being a "child of God," a member of John's group. The concrete referent here is "being received"—that is, being shown hospitality. In fact, 3 John is a letter underscoring the lack of hospitality shown a member of some Johannine group by Diotrephes (3 John 10). The concluding word of honor further intimates that the new values Jesus embodies and articulates here must be the values within the Johannine antisociety (v. 20: "Very truly, I tell you . . .").

Aware of Betrayal,
Jesus Urges Mutual Love, 13:21-38

21 After saying this Jesus was troubled in spirit, and declared, "Very truly, I tell you, one of you will betray me." [22]The disciples looked at one another, uncertain of whom he was speaking. [23]One of his disciples—the one whom Jesus loved—was reclining next to him; [24]Simon Peter therefore motioned to him to ask Jesus of whom he was speaking. [25]So while reclining next to Jesus, he asked him, "Lord, who is it?" [26]Jesus answered, "It is the one to whom I give this piece of bread when I have dipped it in the dish." So when he had dipped the piece of bread, he gave it to Judas son of Simon Iscariot. [27]After he received the piece of bread, Satan entered into him. Jesus said to him, "Do quickly what you are going to do." [28]Now no one at the table knew why he said this to him. [29]Some thought that, because Judas had the common purse, Jesus was telling him, "Buy what we need for the festival"; or, that he should give something to the poor. [30]So, after receiving the piece of bread, he immediately went out. And it was night.

31 When he had gone out, Jesus said, "Now the Son of Man has been glorified, and God has been glorified in him. [32]If God has been glorified in him, God will also glorify him in himself and will glorify him at once. [33]Little children, I am with you only a little longer. You will look for me; and as I said to the Jews so now I say to you, 'Where I am going, you cannot come.' [34]I give you a new commandment, that you love one another. Just as I have loved you, you also should love one another. [35]By this everyone will know that you are my disciples, if you have love for one another."

36 Simon Peter said to him, "Lord, where are you going?" Jesus answered, "Where I am going, you cannot follow me now; but you will follow afterward." [37]Peter said to him, "Lord, why can I not follow you now? I will lay down my life for you." [38]Jesus answered, "Will you lay down your life for me? Very truly, I tell you, before the cock crows, you will have denied me three times."

✦ *Notes:* John 13:21-38

13:21-23 The question of the identity of "the disciple whom Jesus loved" has concerned scholars for many centuries, right up to our own day. In this Gospel the beloved disciple is an anonymous person, never identified. A number of modern scholars identify this disciple as a sort of "Every Disciple." Perhaps this is another double meaning in the story. Yet what of the other referent? The Gospel of John has been largely read in terms of the Synoptics. Given the attribution of this document to "John," this personage was early on identified with John, son of Zebedee. And since the Gospel of John makes no mention of John, son of Zebedee, it was easy to fill out the equation with John, son of Zebedee, being the beloved disciple. Yet, if we adhere to the document and the story it tells, the only referent for the role of beloved disciple up to this point is undoubtedly Lazarus, the only person labeled as "the one whom you love" (11:3) in the story. In 12:2

225

Lazarus is listed as one of those reclining with Jesus at dinner, just as here. And just as Jesus is "in the bosom of the Father" (1:18), so the beloved disciple rests "on the bosom of Jesus" (13:23).

"The disciple whom Jesus loved" is mentioned anonymously here, in 19:25-27 (at the cross), 20:2-10 (at the tomb), 21:1-14 (at the lake fishing), 21:15-23 (question of his death), and in 21:24 as the author of the Gospel. There is also mention of "another disciple" in 18:15-16 (he gets Peter into the high priest's courtyard) and 19:34-35 (witness at the cross); see also 1:35-40. The author explicitly identifies this "other disciple" with "the one whom Jesus loved" in 20:2.

From chapter 13 on, the disciple whom Jesus loved and the other disciple are the same person. Since no name is given to this person, he can only be known from his function. As a rule, in John persons are left anonymous to heighten their typical function. As collectivist personalities, they bear strong and clearly marked qualities of some group. Thus, the mother of Jesus has the qualities of the faithful Israelite community that believes in Jesus; the Samaritan woman has the qualities of schismatic Israel that comes to believe in Jesus. Similarly, the beloved disciple has the qualities of a trusted disciple to whom Jesus reveals himself and who can authoritatively interpret Jesus as witness, evoking loyalty (faith) and attachment (love). Named persons, however, are representative. While they do not bear the qualities of the members of the groups they represent, they do stand for the interests and values of those groups. For example, Nicodemus is representative of official scribal Pharisaism, Caiaphas is representative of chief priests, Pilate is representative of Roman officialdom, and the like.

13:24-30 Persons nearing death were believed by the ancients to be nearer to the realm of God than to the realm of the living. This gave them the power to see from the perspective of God, including to see things about to happen. ⇨ **Final Words,** 13:1-17. Here Jesus knows that Judas will fail the test of loyalty. The disciples, however, not being on the threshold of death, do not understand what is about to happen. Note that this is the third time in this chapter that the betrayal of Judas is brought up. See the **Notes** at 13:2 and 13:18. The symbolic meaning of the foot washing as forgiveness is now beyond question.

The fact that Peter "signals" the disciple whom Jesus loved to ask a question on his behalf may be a status indicator. Josephus indicates that among the Essenes table talk was done in proper order (*War* 2.8.5). Such talk while reclining at table was typical of the Hellenistic symposia. ⇨ **Symposia,** 13:21-38.

13:31-35 Jesus had earlier told the Judeans that where he was going they could not come. See the **Notes** at 7:33-36; 8:22. What is new about the commandment is that it directs disciples toward one another; up until now, it was mutual love between Jesus and the disciples that was underscored. ⇨ **Loyalty/Love,** 13:21-38.

13:36-38 Among the things that Jesus is prescient about is Peter's disloyalty shown in his denial of having been associated with Jesus. ⇨ **Final Words,** 13:1-

17. The exchange between Peter and Jesus also confirms once again that Peter is not yet a fully cognizant member of the group. See the **Notes** at 13:6-8a. To follow (as a disciple) is now understood as "to lay down one's life" if necessary. Going to the Father as Jesus is about to do involves this as well.

✧ *Reading Scenarios:* **John 13:21-38**

Symposia, 13:21-38

Jesus delivers his final words to his friends during a symposium (▷ **Final Words,** 13:1-17). Ancient Hellenistic festive meals consisted of the following: appetizer, main meal, dessert, symposium. The symposium was an after-dinner drinking and discussion session. Consider the following report from the Israelite scribal tradition reflecting Hellenistic custom:

> What is the order of the meal? The guests enter [the house] and sit on benches, and on chairs until all have entered. They all enter and they [servants] give them water for their hands. Each one washes one hand. They [servants] mix for them the cup; each one says the benediction for himself. They [servants] bring them the appetizers; each one says the benediction for himself. They [guests] go up [to the dining room] and they recline, for they [servants] have given them [water] for their hands; although they have [already] washed one hand, they [now] wash both hands. They [servants] mix for them the cup; although they have said the benediction over the first [cup], they say a benediction [also] over the second. They [servants] bring them the dessert; although they have said a benediction over the first one, they [now] say a benediction over the second, and one says the benediction for all of them. He who comes after the third course has no right to enter. (*T. Ber.* 4.8)

This passage provides a typical example of the various implicit rules governing meals. As regards postures, the participants start seated and finish reclining. There are appropriate benedictions (or prayers to the gods) to be said over the first cup of wine, then the second cup follows. A distinction is made between the two washings of hands: the meal begins with a washing of only one hand before the appetizers and is punctuated later with a second washing of both hands before the main course is consumed. Although wine is drunk during the meal, the true drinking comes in the second part of the formal meal, the symposium itself.

During the conversational symposium, the chief guest selects the topic of discussion by his action or by directly asking a leading question(s). At this final meal (13:4), Jesus is chief guest. His action of foot washing begins discussion (13:3-15). He then leads the topics of discussion by making direct statements that provoke varied reactions (13:21: betrayal; 13:33: Jesus' destination; 14:4: the way to that destination; 14:19: Jesus' presence to his own; 16:16: "a little while"; 16:28: clear statement of Jesus' plans). In conclusion, Jesus turns to direct his final words to the Father (chap. 17).

Loyalty/Love, 13:21-38

In the context of the final gathering of Jesus and his core disciples, Jesus' last command to "love one another" is more focused than previous general discussions of love and hate (⇨ **Love/Hate,** 3:1-21). In the Mediterranean world, love always had the underlying meaning of attachment to some group: to one's family, one's village or city quarter, one's ethnic group, one's fictive kin group. The word also could be used of attachment to God. Since in first-century Mediterranean society there was no term for an internal state that did not entail a corresponding external action, love always meant doing something that revealed one's attachment—that is, actions supporting the well-being of the persons to whom one was attached.

The focus here is one of fictive kinship and the friendship it entails. To love one another here is more than general group attachment. It takes on the dimensions of interpersonal attachment, of loyalty, and of the value of reliability revealed in practical actions. Such love is reliability in interpersonal relations; it takes on the value of enduring personal loyalty, of personal faithfulness. The phrase "love one another" presumes the social glue that binds one person to another. That is mutual loyalty (in John's antilanguage it also called *faith, belief, trust,* and the like). This bond of mutual loyalty is the social, externally manifested, emotionally rooted behavior of commitment and solidarity. As social bond, it works along with the value of (personal and group) reliability (translated "faith") and the value of expected (personal and group) allegiance or trust (translated "hope").

In John's story God reveals his abiding loyalty to Israel by sending his only Son so that those Israelites who believe (trust) in him might gain endless life (3:16). And Jesus reveals his abiding loyalty by saving his friends (18:9) and giving his life for them (15:13).

Jesus Gives Reassurance to His Core Group
in Face of His Departure, 14:1-31

14:1 "Do not let your hearts be troubled. Believe in God, believe also in me. [2]In my Father's house there are many dwelling places. If it were not so, would I have told you that I go to prepare a place for you? [3]And if I go and prepare a place for you, I will come again and will take you to myself, so that where I am, there you may be also. [4]And you know the way to the place where I am going." [5]Thomas said to him, "Lord, we do not know where you are going. How can we know the way?" [6]Jesus said to him, "I am the way, and the truth, and the life. No one comes to the Father except through me. [7]If you know me, you will know my Father also. From now on you do know him and have seen him."

8 Philip said to him, "Lord, show us the Father, and we will be satisfied." [9]Jesus said to him, "Have I been with you all this time, Philip, and you still

do not know me? Whoever has seen me has seen the Father. How can you say, 'Show us the Father'? [10]Do you not believe that I am in the Father and the Father is in me? The words that I say to you I do not speak on my own; but the Father who dwells in me does his works. [11]Believe me that I am in the Father and the Father is in me; but if you do not, then believe me because of the works themselves. [12]Very truly, I tell you, the one who believes in me will also do the works that I do and, in fact, will do greater works than these, because I am going to the Father. [13]I will do whatever you ask in my name, so that the Father may be glorified in the Son. [14]If in my name you ask me for anything, I will do it.

15 "If you love me, you will keep my commandments. [16]And I will ask the Father, and he will give you another Advocate, to be with you forever. [17]This is the Spirit of truth, whom the world cannot receive, because it neither sees him nor knows him. You know him, because he abides with you, and he will be in you.

18 "I will not leave you orphaned; I am coming to you. [19]In a little while the world will no longer see me, but you will see me; because I live, you also will live. [20]On that day you will know that I am in my Father, and you in me, and I in you. [21]They who have my commandments and keep them are those who love me; and those who love me will be loved by my Father, and I will love them and reveal myself to them." [22]Judas (not Iscariot) said to him, "Lord, how is it that you will reveal yourself to us, and not to the world?" [23]Jesus answered him, "Those who love me will keep my word, and my Father will love them, and we will come to them and make our home with them. [24]Whoever does not love me does not keep my words; and the word that you hear is not mine, but is from the Father who sent me.

25 "I have said these things to you while I am still with you. [26]But the Advocate, the Holy Spirit, whom the Father will send in my name, will teach you everything, and remind you of all that I have said to you. [27]Peace I leave with you; my peace I give to you. I do not give to you as the world gives. Do not let your hearts be troubled, and do not let them be afraid. [28]You heard me say to you, 'I am going away, and I am coming to you.' If you loved me, you would rejoice that I am going to the Father, because the Father is greater than I. [29]And now I have told you this before it occurs, so that when it does occur, you may believe. [30]I will no longer talk much with you, for the ruler of this world is coming. He has no power over me; [31]but I do as the Father has commanded me, so that the world may know that I love the Father. Rise, let us be on our way."

✦ *Notes:* John 14:1-31

14:1-31 Like its parallel in 16:4b-33, this passage deals with the theme of Jesus' departure. Later, in 16:4b-33, Jesus warns the group of trouble, but here he primarily seeks to offer clarification and encouragement. As in so many other sections of John, this one is structured around a series of questions put to Jesus, followed by answers that are misunderstood, which are in turn followed by additional clarification from Jesus. Using the interpersonal emphases of antilanguage, such conversations function to clarify the values of the antisociety in the face of hostility from the out-group and the insecurity that results from such hostility. ⇨ **Antilanguage,** 1:19-28. ⇨ **Antisociety,** 1:35-51.

The structure of the passage is as follows: the phrase "Let not your hearts be troubled" (followed by reasons) stands at the beginning (vv. 1-4) and end (vv. 27-31) of the piece. It thus brackets off the passage. The body of the segment consists of statements or questions by three interlocutors followed by Jesus' response to each: first Thomas (vv. 5-7), then Philip (vv. 8-21), and finally Judas (not Iscariot; vv. 22-26).

14:1-4 The statement "Let not your heart be troubled" brackets off this segment of John (vv. 1, 27). The "heart" is an important body zone. ⇨ **Feet,** 13:1-20. The term *believe* is a key part of the Johannine antilanguage; it has a special insider meaning for his core group. John's peculiar way of phrasing it—believing "into" Jesus—connotes being completely embedded in the group of which he is the central personage. See also the **Notes** on the term *believe* at 6:28-29.

Another constant theme in this Gospel is where Jesus comes from and to where he is going. See the **Notes** at 6:41-41. ⇨ **Lineage and Stereotypes,** 8:31-59. Both patronage and honor are involved. As God's broker, Jesus claims to have access to the very dwelling of God and to be able to offer the Father's resources (rooms) to his followers. ⇨ **Patronage,** 5:21-30. Moreover, Jesus' access to God is the basis for the claim in 14:6-7. Since God is his "Father" and he is the honored son, to know one is to know the other.

Jesus promises to return after his departure so that the disciples may continue to be with him. It is the fulfillment of this promise that supports the ongoing experience that characterizes life in the Johannine group. For John's audience knows Jesus once left the disciples to go to the Father to prepare a place for them, only to experience him in their midst later (chaps. 20–21), just as John's group does now. It is the current life of the antisociety that is the fulfillment of the promise.

Jesus ends his assertion by affirming that his disciples already know the way to the Father—to where he is going. This assertion provokes a question from Thomas. Thus, we have yet another instance of John's technique of having Jesus make a statement that provokes a misunderstanding, which is then followed by a clarification.

14:5-7 Thomas serves as foil by articulating a misunderstanding of what Jesus is saying. Like other foils in the narrative (Nicodemus, the Samaritan woman, and others), he occasions the clarification the group needs. Note that a narrative of this type would serve to educate and assimilate those coming into the antisociety since new members need to understand its values and language.

Thomas says he does not know where the Father is; therefore, he does not know the way. Jesus, in turn, offers patient clarification. Jesus himself is the way: the truthful way and the living way. To follow Jesus is to go by way of him to the Father. As broker/Son, Jesus provides access to the patron/Father. ⇨ **Patronage,**

5:21-30. Given who Jesus is (as the first chapter has clearly set forth early on), there simply is no other way for Israel. To know Jesus is to see the Father. Yet Jesus' statement leads to another misunderstanding.

14:8-21 Now Philip serves as foil by articulating a further misunderstanding of what Jesus is saying. Jesus just said that he is the way to the Father and that anyone who knows Jesus comes to know and see the Father. But Philip does not get it. So he asks Jesus to show the Father so the disciples might see. Jesus, in turn, offers further clarification, in two parts.

14:9-14 Jesus' first response is, in sum, that he is in the Father and the Father is in him. This assertion of an embedded (dyadic) relationship between Jesus and the Father is critical to the second part of the response. Besides, such an embedded relationship replicates the Johannine antisociety, held together at its core by the close interpersonal relationship between its members and its central personage, Jesus. ▷ **Antilanguage,** 1:19-28. The members of John's group are told that they need no one to show them the Father because they have Jesus in their midst.

The narrator adds that should they have trouble focusing their hearts on Jesus as the presence of God, then they should consider the works of Jesus (presented in the series of events of Jesus' self-disclosure in chaps. 2–12), which are in fact works of the Father.

Mention of works provokes another promise on Jesus' part: the disciples can ask anything in Jesus' name and get Jesus to do it, and thus glorify the Father in their midst, just as happened when Jesus performed his signs.

14:15-21 The second part of Jesus' response is that he is in the Father, the disciples are in him, and he is in them as well. The close interpersonal relationship between God and Jesus includes the disciples.

This second part of the response begins with the mention of love. ▷ **Loyalty/Love,** 13:21-38. It is another Johannine antilanguage term for the close, embedded relationships on which the group depends. This in turn provokes yet another promise. Thanks to Jesus' prayer, the Father will send another Advocate, the Truthful Spirit (literally "Spirit of Truth," as opposed to a lying spirit). The word translated "Advocate" is transliterated from the Greek *parakletos,* as Paraclete. In 1 John 2:1 Jesus is remembered to have been such an advocate, one who stands by the side of a defendant or witness. The other advocate promised here facilitates the continued presence of Jesus (vv. 12, 16), guarantees truthfulness in the antisociety (v. 17; 16:13), and reminds group members of the meaning of what Jesus said and did (v. 26; 16:12-14).

Members of John's group know this Truthful Spirit because it already "abides with you" (v. 17). For the importance of the term *abide* in Johannine antilanguage, see the **Notes** at 1:38-39. Jesus adds that the Truthful Spirit will continue to be "among you" (NRSV "in you" is misleading; the Greek term for "you" here is plural, indicating the group). Thus, vv. 18, 22-23 ("I shall come") do not refer to some final return of the Messiah with power—the parousia of Paul and the other Gospels. Rather, this return of Jesus is a Johannine description of the disciples' altered state-of-consciousness experience. ⇨ **Seeing Jesus: Alternate States of Consciousness,** 20:1-29. That is why they can "see" Jesus after he departs. The "world" (Israelite society) will not be able to see Jesus in this way, but his followers will (v. 19).

See also the **Notes** on chapters 20–21. There, after his ascent to the Father, upon being lifted up and glorified, Jesus comes down repeatedly (three times in chaps. 20–21). The passage closes with the mention of love and the promise of further appearances of Jesus.

14:22-26 This final promise provokes a question on the part of Judas (not Iscariot). He wishes to know why Jesus will be present to his disciples but not to all Israel (the world).

Jesus' response here is that if anyone in Israel seeks to see him, all that person must do is show love for Jesus by keeping his word (presumably all Jesus said in John 2–12). Then the Father and Jesus will "make our home" with them (v. 23). For comment on "abiding" with Jesus, see the **Notes** at 1:38-39. Thus, Jesus manifests himself to Israel (the world). The problem is that "the world" does not love Jesus because it does not keep his word and therefore does not hear the Father who sent Jesus (v. 24).

Now, what about Jesus' word? Jesus concludes with a restatement of his promise that another Advocate, the Spirit of God, "will teach you everything," by recalling to their hearts "all that I have said to you." The disciples will continue to experience the presence of Jesus and understand what the Father is doing.

14:27-31 Jesus once more seeks to allay the anxiety ("troubled hearts") of his disciples, which has been provoked by the mention of his departure. As noted above, these words bracket the discussion of Jesus' departure in 14:5-26. Now Jesus offers a further promise of "peace," a term referring to all that they need for a meaningful existence (v. 27). Here "peace" is a virtual equivalent of "truth," "light," "life," and other terms in John's antilanguage that describe the group's quality of life.

If they love Jesus, if they are truly loyal, embedded members of his group, they should be happy about his departure for Jesus' own sake—he goes to the Father, who is greater than he is (v. 28). For additional comment on where Jesus is from and where he goes, see the **Notes** above at 14:1-4.

Jesus' prediction of his departure should provoke deeper attachment among his disciples. Knowing that he knew he would depart, and that it was not an unplanned disaster, should reassure them. Furthermore, while Jesus foresees death as imminent ("the ruler of this world is coming," v. 30), he does not see death as a force in his life. Rather, he does as the Father wants in order to prove to Israel that he loves the Father.

Jesus is ready to demonstrate what he expects of his followers: obedience to the Father as proof of loving attachment. ⇨ **Loyalty/Love,** 13:21-39. This, of course, is the lifestyle of members of John's group.

This segment ends with Jesus' command: "Rise, let us go hence" (v. 31b). This sentence causes many interpreters to think that the previous passage was once attached to chapter 18, which describes Jesus and the disciples in the Garden of Gethsemane; chapters 15–17 would thus be an insertion by a later editor (perhaps the one who appended chap. 21).

Other interpreters believe Jesus is presented in John as the elusive Messiah who can neither be apprehended nor comprehended by his enemies (here the ruler of this world, Satan, and Israel). Jesus does in fact note that "the ruler of this world is coming" (v. 30). To demonstrate that "he has no power over me" (v. 30b), Jesus is ready to move on at this point: "Rise, let us go hence" (v. 31b).

Solidarity in Jesus' Group, 15:1-11

15:1 "I am the true vine, and my Father is the vinegrower. [2]He removes every branch in me that bears no fruit. Every branch that bears fruit he prunes to make it bear more fruit. [3]You have already been cleansed by the word that I have spoken to you. [4]Abide in me as I abide in you. Just as the branch cannot bear fruit by itself unless it abides in the vine, neither can you unless you abide in me. [5]I am the vine, you are the branches. Those who abide in me and I in them bear much fruit, because apart from me you can do nothing. [6]Whoever does not abide in me is thrown away like a branch and withers; such branches are gathered, thrown into the fire, and burned. [7]If you abide in me, and my words abide in you, ask for whatever you wish, and it will be done for you. [8]My Father is glorified by this, that you bear much fruit and become my disciples. [9]As the Father has loved me, so I have loved you; abide in my love. [10]If you keep my commandments, you will abide in my love, just as I have kept my Father's commandments and abide in his love. [11]I have said these things to you so that my joy may be in you, and that your joy may be complete."

✦ *Notes:* John 15:1-11

The metaphor of the grapevine serves to explain Jesus' relationship with his own group members. In many respects it repeats the theme running throughout these discourses on Jesus' final day: the necessity of close interpersonal relationship between Jesus and group members. See the **Notes** on chapters 13–14.

The four features in the analogy here are: the vine = Jesus, the branches = the disciples, the pruner = the Father, and the fruit = outcomes of the relationship. The theme being underscored is that of enduring relationship with Jesus on the part of each disciple and the joyous outcome of this relationship. Notice how this segment contrasts with 15:18—16:4a, which underscores the opposite themes of hatred and exclusion.

The description here of the disciples' relationship with Jesus clearly bears reference to the enduring experience of Jesus' followers in John's group. The ongoing experience of a close bond with the living Jesus kept the group together after

Jesus had gone away. This same experience became the norm for group members—hence, the mark by which they could be identified. For comment on "abiding" in Jesus, see the **Notes** at 1:38-39. This is a key term in Johannine antilanguage for the critical interpersonal bond between Jesus and his followers. In typical antilanguage fashion, it is used no less than ten times in vv. 4-10.

15:1-6 A well-pruned vine whose branches bear much fruit. Photo by Thomas Hoffman.

The note in v. 6 about persons (branches) not fully engrafted in the vine is a warning about what will happen if the close interpersonal bond is weakened. Such language implies substantial concern among group members that strong boundaries be maintained between fully committed insiders and all others. Only by maintaining the close ties with Jesus and one another (vv. 12-17) will they be safe.

Joy is the fruit of maintaining the close interpersonal bond with Jesus. This contrasts with the hostility so evident in chapters 2–12, and will reassure the community when Jesus is gone. See the **Notes** on 14:1-31 and 16:4b-33.

The metaphor of vine and branches describes a one-to-one relationship between a disciple and Jesus. That is the primary relationship and the basis for the relationships between disciples that flow from it.

Jesus' New Commandment, 15:12-17

12 "This is my commandment, that you love one another as I have loved you.
¹³No one has greater love than this, to lay down one's life for one's friends.
¹⁴You are my friends if you do what I command you. ¹⁵I do not call you servants any longer, because the servant does not know what the master is doing; but I have called you friends, because I have made known to you everything that I have heard from my Father. ¹⁶You did not choose me but I chose you. And I appointed you to go and bear fruit, fruit that will last, so that the Father will give you whatever you ask him in my name. ¹⁷I am giving you these commands so that you may love one another."

✦ *Notes:* John 15:12-17

This is the central segment of Jesus' final conversation with his friends. The passage is marked off by an inclusion in vv. 12 and 17: "This I command you, that you love one another." By its very location, this passage underscores the heart and chief concern of the whole final conversation in chapters 13–17. The main feature of this new command is that the disciples are to be attached to one another as Jesus is attached to them. Hence, more than loving and being attached to Jesus as in the previous metaphor, now Jesus asks that they love and be attached to one another. This command repeats what was said in 13:34. See the **Notes** at 13:31-38. ⇨ **Loyalty/Love,** 13:31-39.

There are several significant features in Jesus' explanation of the new commandment. First, as everyone knew, master and slave (the Greek term here is *doulos,* slave; see the footnote in the NRSV) relationships were one-way: master to slave. But Jesus now calls his disciples "friends." He loves his disciples as friends and expects the same of them toward each other.

The term *friend* was a very significant one in the ancient Mediterranean world. It implied mutual obligations of a high order. Note that what is intended here is fictive kinship, not political friendship. ⇨ **Friends,** 15:12-17. The mutual obligation of this type of friendship involved willingness to defend the friend with one's life, not unlike the willingness expected of close kin to defend family integrity.

Second, Jesus insists that he alone chose his disciples, not vice-versa (v. 16). His group is not a "school" run by a teacher sought out by disciples (or by their parents). Rather, the Jesus group is one chosen by Jesus himself; they are his friends, for whom he is willing to lay down his life (v. 13) and for whom he is willing to procure whatever they ask provided they "bear fruit" as he does (v. 16). Here he offers to be their broker before God. ⇨ **Patronage,** 5:21-30. They must ask in his name—that is, naming him as broker—but the request will be made to the Father, the ultimate patron. What is paramount in this passage is that they demonstrate their attachment to one another; that is Jesus' new and final request.

❖ *Reading Scenario:* **John 15:12-17**
Friends, 15:12-17

The Hellenistic culture of the Roman period witnessed two kinds of friends: political friends and fictive-kinship friends. Political friends were clients who received favors from patrons and in return sought the good reputation of the patron. ▷ **Friend of Caesar,** 18:28—19:16a.

Fictive-kinship friends were persons who treated each other as though they were kin, as members of the same family. In his description of happiness, Aristotle listed: "good birth, plenty of friends, good friends, wealth, good children, plenty of children, a happy old age, also such bodily excellences as health, beauty, strength, large stature, athletic powers, together with fame, honor, good luck and virtue" (Aristotle *Rhet.* 1.5.4). He then further specified what he meant by plenty of friends and good friends. "The terms possession of many friends and possession of good friends need no explanation; for we define a friend as one who will always try, for your sake, to do what he takes to be good for you. The man towards whom many feel thus has many friends; if these are worthy men, he has good friends" (Aristotle *Rhet.* 1.5.16). The chief characteristic of a friend is that he (rarely "she" in the first-century Mediterranean world) seeks the well-being of his friend. And a "good" friend is one who has a recognized honor rating— that is, one who is "worthy." Friendship is a reciprocal affair, with friends mutually seeking the well-being of one another.

In the Roman world fictive-kin friendship could be a hereditary affair. Family members exchanged tokens, which were then passed from generation to generation. If presented to the family with whom some contractual arrangement *(hospitium)* existed, that family was obligated to provide a variety of services to the needy "friend," including a proper burial. Such contractual friendships were usually among social equals.

Here Jesus labels his core group disciples as "friends." The context of a final gathering with final words points to intimates, to fictive kin, rather than political friends. The point is that just as Jesus' friends seek his well-being, so he, too, is totally concerned about their well-being. This undoubtedly is the attitude the members of John's antisociety nourished.

Insiders and Outsiders, 15:18—16:4a

18 "If the world hates you, be aware that it hated me before it hated you. [19]If you belonged to the world, the world would love you as its own. Because you do not belong to the world, but I have chosen you out of the world—therefore the world hates you. [20]Remember the word that I said to you, 'Servants are not greater than their master.' If they persecuted me, they will persecute you; if they kept my word, they will keep yours also. [21]But they will do all these things to you on account of my name, because they do not know him who

sent me. [22]If I had not come and spoken to them, they would not have sin; but now they have no excuse for their sin. [23]Whoever hates me hates my Father also. [24]If I had not done among them the works that no one else did, they would not have sin. But now they have seen and hated both me and my Father. [25]It was to fulfill the word that is written in their law, 'They hated me without a cause.'

26 "When the Advocate comes, whom I will send to you from the Father, the Spirit of truth who comes from the Father, he will testify on my behalf. [27]You also are to testify because you have been with me from the beginning.

16:1 "I have said these things to you to keep you from stumbling. [2]They will put you out of the synagogues. Indeed, an hour is coming when those who kill you will think that by doing so they are offering worship to God. [3]And they will do this because they have not known the Father or me. [4]But I have said these things to you so that when their hour comes you may remember that I told you about them."

✦ *Notes:* John 15:18—16:4a

Parallel to (but contrasting with) the metaphor of the vine and branches (vv. 1-11) and its themes of abiding in the Jesus network and rejoicing in the results of it, comes this segment dealing with the fate of Jesus' disciples "in the world." As throughout most of this document, so especially here there can be no doubt that "the world" is Israel ("their law," v. 25). Those in Israel who reject Jesus as coming from God really do not know God at all. This is the radical theological indictment that John's group presents to Israel. Israel's continued persecution of the group proves the correctness of the indictment.

15:18-21 These verses offer a first explanation of the dominant society's hatred, opening with an "if" clause. If Israel shows hatred for John's disciples, it is because it first showed the same sort of hatred to Jesus. This is only "natural," since as the proverb has it: "A servant is not greater than his master." Israel relates to the disciples both positively and negatively, as it did to Jesus, and this solely "because they did not know him who sent me" (v. 21).

This is as clear a statement of the antisocietal character of the John group as exists in the Gospel. John's term for the dominant society ("world") is used no less than five times in a single verse (v. 19). ⇨ **World/Cosmos = Israelite Society,** 17:1-26. The members of the Johannine group simply do not belong to this dominant society. Having withdrawn their allegiance to it, they are hated in return. ⇨ **Antisociety,** 1:35-51. ⇨ **In-group and Out-group,** 15:18—16:4a.

15:22-25 Here Jesus explains the outcome of the society's hatred, again opening with an "if" clause. "If I had not come and spoken to them, they would have no sin." Those in Israel who showed hatred to Jesus and rejected the witness of his works have sinned because "they have seen and hated both me and my Father."

This, of course, is the supreme indictment of those in Israel who saw and rejected Jesus' signs and his witness to the Father. A quote from the tradition, from Ps. 35:16 (or Ps. 69:4), indicts the opponents of Jesus and of John's group. Their hatred was "without cause."

Such strong oppositional language indicates the magnitude of the breach between the Johannine group and the surrounding society. This type of language abounds in the Gospel (light/dark, above/below, flesh/spirit, truth/falsehood, etc.), of course, but here it reaches a climax. Note carefully that the term *love* means group attachment, whereas the term *hate* means group disattachment. ✷ **Love/Hate, 3:1-21.** Hard boundaries are thus being drawn between those with loyalty to the group and those with none.

15:26—16:4 The author now offers a second comment on the society's hatred. Israel thinks it offers service to God by expelling and killing Jesus' disciples (16:2) and this it does because "they have not known the Father or me" (16:3). Here Jesus further notes the role of these disciples who "have been with me from the beginning" (v. 27); they are his witnesses, just as the Truthful Spirit, the Counselor from God, is. Jesus tells them all about their fate so that when it happened they would endure, abide in Jesus, and thus remain loyal.

✧ *Reading Scenario:* **John 15:18—16:4a**

In-group and Out-group, 15:18—16:4a

Readers of the Synoptic Gospels are familiar with the phenomenon of Jesus giving special information to insiders that is unavailable to outsiders (Mark 4:11-12; Matt. 13:11; Luke 8:10). Equally familiar is the insistence that the world is divided into two groups, those with us and those against us (Luke 11:23). What is true in the Synoptics is even more emphatic in the Gospel of John, as one would expect of an antisociety. Sharp lines are drawn between insiders and outsiders, those with loyalty to the group and those with none. ✷ **Love and Hate,** 3:1-21.

These attitudes are indicative of a fundamental Mediterranean perspective. One of the basic and abiding social distinctions made among first-century Mediterraneans was that between in-group and out-group persons. A person's in-group generally consisted of one's household, extended family, and friends. Yet the boundaries of an in-group were fluid; in-groups could and did change, at times expanding, at others contracting. Persons from the same city quarter or village would look upon each other as an in-group when in a "foreign" location, while in their own city quarter or village, they may be out-groups to one another.

In-group members are expected to be loyal to one another and to go to great lengths to help one another (John 15:13; ✷ **Friends,** 15:12-17). They are shown the greatest consideration and courtesy; such behavior is rarely, if ever, extended to members of out-groups. Only face-to-face groups, in which a person can express concern for others, can become in-groups (15:1-11). Persons interacting positively with one another in in-group ways, even when not actual kin, become "neighbors." The term refers to a social role with privileges and obligations that derive simply from living socially close to others and interacting with them—the same village or neighborhood or party or faction. Neighbors of this sort are an extension of one's kin group (read Prov. 3:39; 6:29; 11:9, 12; 16:29; 25:9, 17, 28; 26:19; 27:10, 14; 29:5). From one perspective, the whole house of Israel were neighbors; hence, the injunction to "love one's neighbor as oneself" (Lev. 19:18) marked a broad in-group, whether the injunctions were carried out or not.

The boundaries of the in-group were shifting ones. The geographical division of the house of Israel in the first century marked off Judea, Perea, and Galilee. What all the residents with allegiance to the Jerusalem temple had in common was birth into the same people, the house of Israel. But this group quickly broke into three in-groups: the Judeans, Pereans, and Galileans. Jesus was not a Judean but a Galilean (7:52), as were his disciples. The Judeans are the main opponents of Jesus in John's Gospel. ⇨ **Jews/Judeans,** 1:19-28. Judeans put Jesus the Galilean to death. Nevertheless, Jesus the Galilean is mockingly called the "king" of the Judeans (19:14-15, 19).

All of these geographically based groups had countless subgroups with various and changing loyalties. To outsiders, such as Romans or Alexandrians, all these in-groups fused into one and were simply called "Judeans." Similarly, the house of Israel could look at the rest of the world as one large out-group, "the [other] nations" (= Gentiles). Paul sees himself as a Judean, coming from Tarsus and living according to Judean customs (called "Judaism") with allegiance to the God of Israel in Jerusalem in Judea. Most such Judeans never expected to move back to Judea. They remained either resident aliens or citizens in the places of their birth. Yet they continued to be categorized by the geographical location of their original ethnic roots. The reason for this was that the main way of categorizing living beings, animals and humans, in the first-century Mediterranean was by geographical origins. Being of similar geographical origin meant to harbor in-group feelings even if long departed from that place of origin. And that place of origin endowed group members with particular characteristics.

In-group members freely ask questions of one another that would seem too personal to North Americans. These questions reflect the fact that interpersonal relationships, even casual ones, tend to involve a far greater lowering of social and psychological boundaries in first-century Palestine than in current U.S. experience. Moreover, in dealing with out-group members, almost "anything goes." By U.S. standards, the dealings of ancient Mediterranean types with out-group persons appear indifferent, even hostile and cruel. Strangers can never be in-group members. Should they take the initiative in the direction of "friendly" relations, only the social ritual of hospitality (being "received" or "welcomed") extended by an in-group member can transform them into "friends" of the group.

The boundaries of in-groups and out-groups are well marked off in the Gospel of John with Pharisees, disciples of John, disciples of Moses, and disciples of Jesus. But by far the most important in-group/out-group distinction is that between the hostile Judeans and the Johannine group who are followers of Jesus. That opposition is nowhere clearer than here in the strongly polarized language of 15:18—16:4a.

Jesus Prepares His Core Group for His Departure, 16:4b-33

4b "I did not say these things to you from the beginning, because I was with you. [5]But now I am going to him who sent me; yet none of you asks me, 'Where are you going?' [6]But because I have said these things to you, sorrow has filled your hearts. [7]Nevertheless I tell you the truth: it is to your advantage that I go away, for if I do not go away, the Advocate will not come to you; but if I go, I will send him to you. [8]And when he comes, he will prove the world wrong about sin and righteousness and judgment: [9]about sin, because they do not believe in me; [10]about righteousness, because I am going to the Father and you will see me no longer; [11]about judgment, because the ruler of this world has been condemned.

12 "I still have many things to say to you, but you cannot bear them now. [13]When the Spirit of truth comes, he will guide you into all the truth; for he will not speak on his own, but will speak whatever he hears, and he will declare to you the things that are to come. [14]He will glorify me, because he will take what is mine and declare it to you. [15]All that the Father has is mine. For this reason I said that he will take what is mine and declare it to you.

16 "A little while, and you will no longer see me, and again a little while, and you will see me." [17]Then some of his disciples said to one another, "What does he mean by saying to us, 'A little while, and you will no longer see me, and again a little while, and you will see me'; and 'Because I am going to the Father'?" [18]They said, "What does he mean by this 'a little while'? We do not know what he is talking about." [19]Jesus knew that they wanted to ask him, so he said to them, "Are you discussing among yourselves what I meant when I said, 'A little while, and you will no longer see me, and again a little while, and you will see me'? [20]Very truly, I tell you, you will weep and mourn, but the world will rejoice; you will have pain, but your pain will turn into joy. [21]When a woman is in labor, she has pain, because her hour has come. But when her child is born, she no longer remembers the anguish because of the joy of having brought a human being into the world. [22]So you have pain now; but I will see you again, and your hearts will rejoice, and no one will take your joy from you. [23]On that day you will ask nothing of me. Very truly, I tell you, if you ask anything of the Father in my name, he will give it to you. [24]Until now you have not asked for anything in my name. Ask and you will receive, so that your joy may be complete.

25 "I have said these things to you in figures of speech. The hour is coming when I will no longer speak to you in figures, but will tell you plainly of the Father. [26]On that day you will ask in my name. I do not say to you that I will ask the Father on your behalf; [27]for the Father himself loves you, because you have loved me and have believed that I came from God. [28]I came from

the Father and have come into the world; again, I am leaving the world and am going to the Father."

29 His disciples said, "Yes, now you are speaking plainly, not in any figure of speech! [30]Now we know that you know all things, and do not need to have anyone question you; by this we believe that you came from God." [31] Jesus answered them, "Do you now believe? [32]The hour is coming, indeed it has come, when you will be scattered, each one to his home, and you will leave me alone. Yet I am not alone because the Father is with me. [33]I have said this to you, so that in me you may have peace. In the world you face persecution. But take courage; I have conquered the world!"

✦ *Notes:* John 16:4b-33

16:4b-33 In this segment of the final conversation, Jesus broaches topics previously noted in the corresponding passage (14:1-31) but in reverse order as befits a chiastic presentation. Jesus prepares his disciples for his departure by specifying a range of benefits that will come to them after he leaves.

16:4b-15 These verses repeat the theme of Jesus' departure and the coming of the Advocate Spirit to the disciples, which was discussed in 14:16, 25-31. While commentators are quick to note that 16:5b contradicts 13:36 and 14:5, the fact is that the ideational dimension (content) of language is not at issue here. Antilanguage is primarily interpersonal rather than ideational. It is repetitive; and it is this repetitiveness rather than content that gives antilanguage its emotional force. ⇨ **Antilanguage,** 1:19-28.

The author is focusing attention on the Spirit's presence among John's group. In doing so, he spells out the function of the Spirit: to convict Israel of three crimes. *Sin* (v. 9) is interpersonal shaming; Israel has shamed God "because they do not believe in me." ⇨ **Sin,** 9:1-41. *Righteousness* (v. 10) is the payment of interpersonal debts of obligation; because Israel has not paid its debt of interpersonal obligation to God in the face of God's countless favors, Jesus will therefore "go to the Father and you will see me no more." *Judgment* (v. 11) is condemnation or negative judgment; Israel is condemned because its ruler is condemned. "The ruler of this world is judged."

The promised Spirit will guide, interpret the meanings of Jesus, and declare things that are forthcoming. Whereas Jesus has been the broker for the community up to this point, now that role will be played by the Spirit (vv. 12-15). The Spirit takes its place in a brokerage chain running from God to Jesus to the Spirit to the disciples. ⇨ **Patronage,** 5:21-30.

16:16-24 As noted above, 16:4b-33 recapitulates the themes of 14:1-31. Here the author returns to the theme of Jesus' departure and quick return to the disciples. This is a rather full elaboration of the "little while" theme of 14:19 in the corresponding parallel panel (the theme was also alluded to in 13:33). See the

Notes at 14:15-21. The "return" of Jesus is the experience of "seeing" Jesus, which recurs in the Johannine community. ▷ **Seeing Jesus: Alternate States of Consciousness,** 20:1-29. This very real experience no doubt puzzled newcomers to the community and required the elaboration John provides.

16:20-22 With a word of honor ("Very truly, I tell you . . ."), Jesus assures his disciples that the sorrow they will experience at his departure will quickly turn to joy, an abiding joy; "no one will take your joy from you" (v. 22). Such undoubtedly was the experience of the members of John's group who "saw" Jesus and thus knew what he meant.

16:23-24 It is a patron's role to meet the needs of clients, yet clients need a means of access to the patron. With another word of honor, Jesus insists that group members make requests of the Father in his name, thereby offering once again to be the broker for the group. As a good friend, his object is the joy of his group.

16:25-33 In keeping with the pattern in this chapter, this segment parallels a like theme in 14:8-11. In these verses Jesus announces that the time is coming when he will speak plainly to his disciples. Curiously, that time arrives only a few moments (sentences) later (v. 29).

What triggers the recognition of plain talk is Jesus' announcement that he came from the Father, came into Israelite society, is now leaving Israelite society, and is returning to the Father. This is very nearly the crux of Jesus' claim to be God's broker. If he is indeed from God and able to return to God, he is clearly a broker with open access to the patron. For the critically important notion of Jesus being from God, see the **Notes** at 6:25-27.

The disciples immediately recognize that this is the heart of Jesus' claim to legitimacy. If he is from God, there are no further questions to be raised. Yet Jesus even now questions whether they really believe this. Recall that the term *believe* in John (antilanguage indicating loyalty and trust, being an insider, being embedded in the group) encapsulates the interpersonal bonding with Jesus that the Gospel is all about (20:31). The disciples think they have fully understood and truly "believe."

16:32-33 With the coming of the hour, the disciples will abandon Jesus and go home, but Jesus will not be alone. As in the parallel segment, Jesus here closes with a wish for peace (see 14:27) and good cheer since he has "overcome the world"—that is, the dominant, hostile society.

Jesus Prays for Honor for Himself and His Followers, 17:1-26

17:1 After Jesus had spoken these words, he looked up to heaven and said, "Father, the hour has come; glorify your Son so that the Son may glorify you, [2]since you have given him authority over all people, to give eternal life to all whom you have given him. [3]And this is eternal life, that they may know you, the only true God, and Jesus Christ whom you have sent. [4]I glorified you on earth by finishing the work that you gave me to do. [5]So now, Father, glorify me in your own presence with the glory that I had in your presence before the world existed.

6 "I have made your name known to those whom you gave me from the world. They were yours, and you gave them to me, and they have kept your word. [7]Now they know that everything you have given me is from you; [8]for the words that you gave to me I have given to them, and they have received them and know in truth that I came from you; and they have believed that you sent me. [9]I am asking on their behalf; I am not asking on behalf of the world, but on behalf of those whom you gave me, because they are yours. [10]All mine are yours, and yours are mine; and I have been glorified in them. [11]And now I am no longer in the world, but they are in the world, and I am coming to you. Holy Father, protect them in your name that you have given me, so that they may be one, as we are one. [12]While I was with them, I protected them in your name that you have given me. I guarded them, and not one of them was lost except the one destined to be lost, so that the scripture might be fulfilled. [13]But now I am coming to you, and I speak these things in the world so that they may have my joy made complete in themselves. [14]I have given them your word, and the world has hated them because they do not belong to the world, just as I do not belong to the world. [15]I am not asking you to take them out of the world, but I ask you to protect them from the evil one. [16]They do not belong to the world, just as I do not belong to the world. [17]Sanctify them in the truth; your word is truth. [18]As you have sent me into the world, so I have sent them into the world. [19]And for their sakes I sanctify myself, so that they also may be sanctified in truth.

20 "I ask not only on behalf of these, but also on behalf of those who will believe in me through their word, [21]that they may all be one. As you, Father, are in me and I am in you, may they also be in us, so that the world may believe that you have sent me. [22]The glory that you have given me I have given them, so that they may be one, as we are one, [23]I in them and you in me, that they may become completely one, so that the world may know that you have sent me and have loved them even as you have loved me. [24]Father, I desire that those also, whom you have given me, may be with me where I am, to see my glory, which you have given me because you loved me before the foundation of the world.

25 "Righteous Father, the world does not know you, but I know you; and these know that you have sent me. [26]I made your name known to them, and I will make it known, so that the love with which you have loved me may be in them, and I in them."

✦ *Notes:* **John 17:1-26**

This chapter has the form of a prayer that Jesus addresses to the Father. It takes up the themes of its parallel panel: 13:1-38. Jesus first of all prays for himself (vv. 1-8), then for his disciples (vv. 9-19), and finally for followers who will believe in Jesus thanks to the word of his present disciples (vv. 20-26). It is important to remember that this prayer forms a conclusion to the final words of Jesus (chaps. 13–17). ⇨ **Final Words,** 13:1-20.

17:1-3 Jesus opens his supper prayer by addressing the Father concerning the issue of honor. Both his own honor ("glorify your Son") and that of the Father ("so that the Son may glorify you") are at issue. Given the fundamental importance of honor in ancient Mediterranean life, Jesus asks for that which is of the highest value. ⇨ **Honor and Shame,** 5:31-47.

In v. 2 Jesus acknowledges his God-given role of broker. He has the authority of the patron and can dispense the resources (eternal life) of the patron. ⇨ **Patronage,** 5:21-30. Note the frequent (forty times) comment in John's Gospel that Jesus was "sent" (3:34; 4:34; 5:23, 24, 30, 36, 37, 38; 6:29, 38, 39, 44, 57; 7:16, 18, 28, 29, 33; 8:16, 18, 29, 42; 9:4; 10:36; 11:42; 12:44, 45, 49; 13:16, 20; 14:24; 15:21; 16:5; 17:3, 8, 18, 21, 23, 25; 20:21). It appears six times in this chapter alone. All of this is patronage language indicating that God is the true source of everything Jesus brought. As John says, eternal life is to experience "the only true God and Jesus Messiah whom you have *sent*" (v. 3).

17:4-8 Jesus has honored God by performing his assigned work, so now Jesus deserves to be honored by God. He prays, "So now, Father, glorify me in your own presence with the glory that I had in your presence before the world existed" (v. 5). This statement recalls the beginning of John's Gospel and the Word, the Lamb of God and the Son of Man—who existed before the world was made. For Jesus, the incarnational interlude is over; his work has been completed. God has been honored in more than creation alone; that is the end of Jesus' career in Israel.

Verses 6-8 offer further indication that Jesus' work is complete: the disciples whom God has given to Jesus (v. 6) now "know" that God is the true source of everything Jesus has. God truly is the patron, and Jesus is indeed his broker. Jesus has completed his revelatory task; hence, the disciples (and John's group members) "believed that God *sent* Jesus" (v. 8).

17:9-19 With the opening phrase, "I pray," Jesus addresses the Father on behalf of "those whom you have given me, for they are yours" (v. 9). What follows are a number of characteristics of Jesus' disciples, features that are very important for understanding the ideology of John's antisociety. As the Father is honored in Jesus, so is Jesus honored in his disciples (v. 10). Thanks to the Father, they are one as the Father and the Son are one (v. 11). They are kept in

God's name (v. 12). They have God's word, and Israel hates them for it (v. 14). Jesus prays to keep them from temptation by the evil one (v. 15). Like Jesus himself, they are not of Israel anymore ("not of the world," v. 16); they are a separate antisociety. Jesus sends them to live in Israel as he did (v. 18), but he wants them to be "consecrated in truth"—that is, to be truly and truthfully set apart, exclusive, without social admixture and contamination—just as Jesus was for their sake (v. 19).

The statement in v. 16 ("They do not belong to the world, just as I do not belong to the world.") is a clear statement of John's antisociety having separated from "straight" society. ⇨ **Antisociety,** 1:35-51. The fact that Jesus acted in this way legitimates this separation for the Johannine group. In v. 18 the brokerage of Jesus is again recognized (see the **Notes** above), but it is now passed on to his followers. Hereafter they will be God's brokers to the world.

17:20-26 With another opening, "I pray," Jesus addresses the Father on behalf of "those who will believe in me through their word" (v. 20). The themes in this segment are very similar to those in vv. 1-8. As in the opening segment, Jesus expresses concern for his honor, now shared with all of his disciples, so that all generations of disciples may abide in unity with one another and in Jesus (vv. 22-23). This is a community of shared honor—Jesus has given them the honor God has given him—much like a fictive kin group in which the honor of one is the honor of all. Shared honor binds them together. ⇨ **Friends,** 15:12-17.

Not only this, but Jesus intends all of them to "be with me where I am, to see my glory, which you have given me because you loved me before the foundation of the world" (v. 24). Again, his statement recalls the beginning of John's Gospel and the Word, the Lamb of God, Son of Man—existing before the foundation of the world. Now, at the completion of his incarnational interlude, Jesus wishes his disciples to experience his precreational, abiding glory. It would seem that this is exactly the experience of members of John's group when they gathered.

In conclusion, Jesus notes that Israel has not known the "righteous Father," but Jesus has, and he has made the Father's name known to these and all other disciples ("I will make it known," v. 26). Thanks to God's love, Jesus may continue to abide "in them."

✧ *Reading Scenarios:* **John 17:1-26**
World/Cosmos = Israelite Society, 17:1-26

"World" is the usual translation of the Greek word *kosmos*. By the Hellenistic period, the term *world* referred to the universe created by God, the earth as opposed to the sky, the inhabited earth, the location of human society, and finally humanity. We continue to use the term *world* in the same ways. For us the "known world" equals the explored universe. We speak of "traveling the world" (as opposed to space). To be in "this world" means where we live, the inhabited world (as opposed to a next or another world). The phrase "the whole world knows" refers to humanity, everybody.

Four times in John's Gospel the "world" refers to God's creation: "light of this world" = the day (11:9), "before the world was made" (17:5), "the foundation of the world" (17:24), and a place for books (21:25). But most often in John the "world" is a subject of personal activity and the object of interpersonal relations. As an entity that personally interacts, it is not inert, material creation. Rather, in all usages in John, apart from the three just cited, "world" refers to humanity, to human beings.

Given John's antilanguage (▷ **Antilanguage,** 1:19-28) and exclusive concern with Israelites, however, this reference to humanity must be confined even further. Note what is said in 18:20: "Jesus answered him, 'I have spoken openly to the world; I have always taught in synagogues and in the temple, where all Judeans come together; I have said nothing in secret." Here the "world" refers to Judeans. They constitute the "world" of John.

When we read that "God so loved the world" (3:16), we should thus assume it means "God so loved the Israelites"—if only because the only begotten Son was given to Israel, "his own," not to all of humanity. Jesus is Israel's Messiah, for "messiah" is a social role that occurs only in Israel or on behalf of Israel. Modern readers who assume "world" refers to all human beings in John are really importing the anachronistic interpretation that comes later in history when Gentile Christians read John in their own ethnocentric perspective. In John's historical circumstances, given John's antagonism to Judeans, "this world" would then refer to "this humanity, this people"—that is, Judeans (8:23; 9:39; 12:25, 31; 13:1; 14:30; 16:11; 18:36).

In sum, in the Gospel of John, "world" refers to three entities: the physical world, Israel as God's chosen humanity, and Judeans as enemies of John's community. What "world" never refers to in John is all human beings, the whole human race.

Prayer, 17:1-26

Prayer is a socially meaningful symbolic act of communication directed to persons perceived as somehow supporting, maintaining, and controlling the order of existence of the one praying. It is performed for the purpose of getting results from or within the interaction of communication. Thus, the object of prayer is a person in charge. The activity of prayer is essentially communication. The purpose of prayer is always to get results. And prayer is always social, rooted in the behaviors of some cultural group.

Prayer to God, religious prayer, is directed to the one ultimately in charge of the total order of existence. Prayer forms directed to God derive by analogy from prayer forms to those in control of the various orders of existence in which human beings find themselves (for example, parents, rulers, social superiors of all sorts). Just as people speak to others with a view to having effect, so too people pray to have effect. Like other types of language, prayer can be:

1. Instrumental ("I want . . ."): prayer to obtain goods and services to satisfy individual and communal material and social needs (prayers of petition for oneself and/or others).

2. Regulatory ("Do as I tell you"): prayers to control the activity of God, to command God to order people and things about on behalf of the one praying (another type of petition, but with the presumption that the one praying is superior to God).

3. Interactional ("me and you"): prayers to maintain emotional ties with God, to get along with God, to continue interpersonal relations (prayers of adoration, of simple presence, of examining the course of a day before and with God).

4. Self-focused ("Here I come; here I am"): prayers that identify the self (individual or social) to God, expressing the self to God (prayer of contrition, of humility, of boasting, of superiority over others).

5. Heuristic ("tell me why"): prayer that explores the world of God and God's workings within us individually and/or in our group (meditative prayer, perceptions of the spirit in prayer).

6. Imaginative ("Let's pretend; what if"): prayer to create an environment of one's own with God (prayer in tongues, prayers read or recited in languages unknown to the person reading or reciting them).

7. Informative ("I have something to tell you"): prayers that communicate new information (prayers of acknowledgment, of thanksgiving for favors received).

While this prayer in John 17:1-26 is in some respects instrumental (asking for something), it is also clearly interactional in intent. It is a prayer asking God to create a shared community of honor between himself, Jesus, and the disciples of all generations. In that sense it shares much with the entire Gospel of John. Throughout the Gospel the focus is on close interpersonal bonds with Jesus and within the Johannine group.

Name, 17:1-26

In the New Testament the word *name* is frequently used to refer to what we call a "person." That is because the first-century Mediterranean world had no distinct term for "person." The Latin word *persona* (and the Greek, *prosopon*) meant mask or face. (The modern connotation of the word *person* [minus the psychology] emerged from the Trinitarian disputes concerning the emperor's divine power in the fourth and fifth centuries C.E. Those disputes led to the conclusion that "person" meant an incommunicable substance [*hypostasis*] of a rational nature, and that there were three such "persons" in the Godhead. It is the quality of incommunicability that eventually developed into our psychological notion of the unique personhood of each individual human.)

In the New Testament, however, the common way to refer to a person is to refer to someone's name. Thus, here in John, to manifest the Father's name is to manifest the Father himself (v. 6), just as to make known God's name is to reveal God (v. 26); it is the same as glorifying the Father's name (12:28). To do something "in my name" (14:13, 14, 26; 15:16; 16:23, 24, 26) is to do something as my representatives, in my stead, as though I were there, and the like."To come in the name of the Lord" (12:13) or "in the Father's name" (5:43) means to come as the Lord's representative, just as to do something "in the Father's name" is to function as the Father's representative (10:25). When Jesus says that he protected the disciples "in your name that you have given me," he means that he has preserved them on the Father's behalf (17:11-12).

To belong to John's group is to "believe in Jesus' name" (1:12; 2:23; 3:18), to believe in and be attached to the person of Jesus, who he really is. And the goal of belonging to John's group is to have life "in his name" (20:31), the life that flows from the person of the exalted Jesus.

CHAPTER X
JOHN 18:1–19:42
JESUS WAS LIFTED UP AND GAVE HIS
SPIRIT TO US: HIS PROCESS OF ASCENT

Like the previous segment, this passage is a well-constructed literary whole. The mention of a garden at the outset (18:1) and the conclusion (19:42) marks off the passage as a literary unit. Some scholars have indicated that these chapters have the formal elements of a Roman trial or of the Hellenistic consecration of a king. The column on the left indicates the formal elements of a Roman trial present in the passage. The column on the right indicates the chief formal elements of a Hellenistic consecration of a monarch. These features will be noted in the comments that follow.

Formal Elements of a Roman Trial		Formal Elements of a Hellenistic Consecration of a King	
1. Arrest	18:4-11	I. Crowning of and Homage to a King	19:1-3
2. Charges	18:29-32	II. Proclamation	19:4-5
3. Exam	18:33-37	III. Acclamation	19:6-7
4. Verdict	18:38-40	IV. Enthronement on Judgment Seat	19:13-16
5. Warning	19:1-3	V. Naming and Title	19:19-22
2. Charges	19:4-8	VI. Royal Burial	19:38-42
3. Exam	19:9-12		
4. Verdict	19:13-15		
6. Sentence	19:16		

The scene before Pilate is the central tableau and focal point of the presentation. The presence of the formal features of a Roman trial, repeated in proper sequence, indicates that the author does in fact see the procedures as a forensic event. However, it is important to realize that the purpose of a trial in the ancient Mediterranean was not to find out the truth and to mete out justice. Rather, as is evident from the rhetorical handbooks of the period, the purpose of a trial among social equals was to dishonor and shame the opponent. By contrast, the purpose of a trial for social inferiors was simply to mete out punishment, to win "satisfaction" for some dishonor to elites. This latter is the situation of Jesus. In the judgment of his accusers, if he were not guilty he would not be presented to the procurator. The fact that he is there indicates that he is guilty. The only real question is what punishment he merits.

The passage unfolds in five major segments: Jesus is arrested in a garden (18:1-11) and in succession is presented before the high priest (18:12-27), before Pilate (18:28—19:16a), and before "this world" (19:16b-37), and finally is placed in a garden tomb (19:38-42). The central scene in the central segment has Roman soldiers declaring Jesus "King of the Judeans" (19:1-3), while at the close of this segment, Pilate himself presents Jesus with the words, "Here is your King!" (19:14), the high point of the whole presentation.

Jesus' Arrest, 18:1-11

18:1 After Jesus had spoken these words, he went out with his disciples across the Kidron valley to a place where there was a garden, which he and his disciples entered. ²Now Judas, who betrayed him, also knew the place, because Jesus often met there with his disciples. ³So Judas brought a detachment of soldiers together with police from the chief priests and the Pharisees, and they came there with lanterns and torches and weapons. ⁴Then Jesus, knowing all that was to happen to him, came forward and asked them, "Whom are you looking for?" ⁵They answered, "Jesus of Nazareth." Jesus replied, "I am he." Judas, who betrayed him, was standing with them. ⁶When Jesus said to them, "I am he," they stepped back and fell to the ground. ⁷Again he asked them, "Whom are you looking for?" And they said, "Jesus of Nazareth." ⁸Jesus answered, "I told you that I am he. So if you are looking for me, let these men go." ⁹This was to fulfill the word that he had spoken, "I did not lose a single one of those whom you gave me." ¹⁰Then Simon Peter, who had a sword, drew it, struck the high priest's slave, and cut off his right ear. The slave's name was Malchus. ¹¹Jesus said to Peter, "Put your sword back into its sheath. Am I not to drink the cup that the Father has given me?"

✦ *Notes:* **John 18:1-11**

18:1-3 This introductory segment presents the location and cast of characters (vv. 1-3) for the action that is to follow (vv. 4-11). The location is a walled garden across the Kidron Valley from Jerusalem. The image is important since it evokes images of the sheepfold of the good shepherd of chapter 10. The cast of characters includes Jesus and his disciples, Judas with a band of soldiers, and some officers from the chief priests and the Pharisees. Judas follows the orders of the chief priests and Pharisees to have Jesus arrested (11:57) rather than abiding in (remaining embedded in and loyal to Jesus and his group) Jesus.

18:4-11 The action that follows allows for a number of interpretations, depending on the perspective of the witness. In this presentation we will postulate two groups of witnesses: those who believe in Jesus and abide in him, and those of "this world" (Judean society) who follow the orders of the chief priests and the Pharisees.

For those of "this world"—that is, of dominant Judean society—the story simply reports events surrounding Jesus' being taken into custody by the representatives of Israel's political-religious institution (the temple). But for those who "believe" (another term for being embedded in and loyal to Jesus and his group), the scene describes three steps in the action, each orchestrated by Jesus himself and not by his opponents. First, Jesus identifies himself as the powerful "I am" (mentioned three times) who knows all that will happen (vv. 4-6); then, like the noble shepherd, he "did not lose a single one" of those whom God had given him (vv. 7-9); and finally, he consciously and voluntarily accepted what God intended for him, his fate symbolized by "the cup that the Father has given me" (vv. 10-11). The shepherd image is evoked by Jesus' behavior at the opening of the garden ("Jesus came forward," v. 4), which is similar to the gate of a sheepfold. Jesus' restrained power is evoked by the soldiers' drawing back and falling to the ground. And his willingness to do what pleases the Father is articulated in his rebuke to Peter, who attempts to have Jesus escape.

In this story of Jesus' arrest, it is Jesus who remains in charge at all times. This is a matter of honor. Only those who are low status or dishonorable are controlled by others above them.

18:1 These ancient stairs are the remains of a main street that led from the western hill down to the city gate into the Kidron Valley to connect to the road to the garden (Gethsemane, see map at 9:7). This was probably the way Jesus walked with his apostles to the garden and the way Jesus was led to the house of the high priest. Both the location of the Last Supper (cenacle) and the houses of Annas and Caiaphas are traditionally located on the western hill. Photo by Avraham Hay.

Jesus before the High Priest;
Peter's Disloyalty, 18:12-27

12 So the soldiers, their officer, and the Jewish police arrested Jesus and bound him. [13]First they took him to Annas, who was the father-in-law of Caiaphas, the high priest that year. [14]Caiaphas was the one who had advised the Jews that it was better to have one person die for the people.

15 Simon Peter and another disciple followed Jesus. Since that disciple was known to the high priest, he went with Jesus into the courtyard of the high priest, [16]but Peter was standing outside at the gate. So the other disciple, who was known to the high priest, went out, spoke to the woman who guarded the gate, and brought Peter in. [17]The woman said to Peter, "You are not also one of this man's disciples, are you?" He said, "I am not." [18]Now the slaves and the police had made a charcoal fire because it was cold, and they were standing around it and warming themselves. Peter also was standing with them and warming himself.

19 Then the high priest questioned Jesus about his disciples and about his teaching. [20]Jesus answered, "I have spoken openly to the world; I have always taught in synagogues and in the temple, where all the Jews come together. I have said nothing in secret. [21]Why do you ask me? Ask those who heard what I said to them; they know what I said." [22]When he had said this, one of the police standing nearby struck Jesus on the face, saying, "Is that how you answer the high priest?" [23]Jesus answered, "If I have spoken wrongly, testify to the wrong. But if I have spoken rightly, why do you strike me?" [24]Then Annas sent him bound to Caiaphas the high priest.

25 Now Simon Peter was standing and warming himself. They asked him, "You are not also one of his disciples, are you?" He denied it and said, "I am not." [26]One of the slaves of the high priest, a relative of the man whose ear Peter had cut off, asked, "Did I not see you in the garden with him?" [27]Again Peter denied it, and at that moment the cock crowed.

✦ *Notes:* John 18:12-27

18:12-16 This segment begins with a new description of the cast of characters, along with a scene change. First comes an opening notice of Jesus being arrested and bound by soldiers and their captain. The NRSV calls them "Jewish police." However, in antiquity there were no police in our sense of the word. Just as the king or emperor had an army at his disposal, so did God in the temple. This temple military served the needs of God by obeying the orders of the high priest, God's majordomo or vizier. ▷ **Temple,** 2:13-25. These are temple soldiers rather than Roman soldiers since they lead Jesus directly to one of the chief priests, Annas. Annas was the father-in-law of the high priest Caiaphas, the one who previously prophesied about Jesus' fate (11:49-50). Then we are told that Simon Peter followed along with "another . . . disciple known to the high priest" (since at 20:2 this "other disciple" is identified with the disciple whom Jesus loved, in the context of the story, this would be Lazarus, a member of the Judean elite living in the Jerusalem suburb of Bethany). Thanks to this other disciple, whose status is reported twice (vv. 15, 16), Peter can enter the courtyard, though he stays outside while Jesus is taken inside. The action that follows is a sort of simultaneous triptych, with Peter outside (vv. 17-18), Jesus inside (vv. 19-24), and Peter still outside (vv. 25-26).

18:17-18 Outside in the courtyard we have a report of Peter's denial that he is Jesus' disciple. This denial, "I am not," corresponds to Jesus' previous avowal, "I am" (also three times in vv. 5, 6, 8).

To "the world"—that is, to Judean society—Peter reveals himself to be without honor, denying his relation to Jesus even to a low-status person like a maid. This in turn dishonors Jesus, who would choose such a disciple and "friend."

To those who "abide" in Jesus, Peter reveals himself as an outsider, standing with the opponents of Jesus (servants and officers), in the cold, warming himself at their fire. While he is not as bad as Judas, who chooses obedience to the high priest and Pharisees over obedience to Jesus sent by God, nonetheless, Peter does reveal his lack of loyalty and shameless character.

18:19-24 Meanwhile, inside, in the high priest's house, Jesus is interrogated about his disciples and his teaching. Mention of the role of "disciple" would have us expect questions about the nature of the way of life Jesus taught. Yet from Jesus' response (vv. 20-21) it is clear the question is about the political import of Jesus' style of teaching: did he teach openly or in secret? Jesus tells his judge to ask the many witnesses about his public teaching "to the world" of Israel, in formal gatherings, in the temple, and wherever Judeans came together.

His question "Why do you ask me?" (v. 21) is taken by one of the temple military officers as an insult to the high priest; the officer honorably steps in to defend the honor of the high priest. To strike someone in the face is an insult and a serious dishonor. The officer further challenges Jesus' honor with a demeaning question (v. 22). ⇨ **Honor and Shame,** 5:31-47.

Jesus ripostes with a question of his own (v. 23), but it goes unanswered. The silence indicates Jesus' acquisition of a grant of honor in the interaction. ⇨ **Challenge and Riposte,** 7:14-24. This central segment concludes with Jesus, still bound, carried off to Caiaphas, the high priest himself.

To "the world" (that is, Israel) Jesus' public teaching indicates open disregard for Israel's traditional, God-appointed authorities—the chief priests and their collaborating Pharisees.

To those who abide in Jesus, his teaching addressed to all in Israel underscores the honorable quality of the way he fulfilled the commission of the Father who sent him. Jesus revealed the Father to one and all in Israel. His ready ability to parry the challenges put to him before Annas further points to Jesus as an honorable person. ⇨ **Challenge and Riposte,** 7:14-24.

18:25-27 Meanwhile, outside in the courtyard, Peter continues his conversation with those standing around the fire, in the cold. To this group, he denies being a disciple of Jesus with another "I am not" (v. 25). See the **Notes** above. And he does so again to an eyewitness who saw Peter trying to help Jesus to escape in the garden (v. 26).

With the mention of the time of morning, the cock crow, the narrator recalls Jesus' words to Peter the previous evening (13:37). The signal indicates that Peter's disloyalty, hence, his dishonor, is complete.

To the dominant society the account of Jesus' avowal and Peter's denial simply shows that Jesus was a rather poor judge of character. Moreover, the dishonor of one member of the group brings dishonor to all. But to those who believe in Jesus, the account confirmed Jesus' full knowledge of what was happening to him and revealed his expectations of Peter (expectations shared, it would seem, by members of John's antisociety). Note that those who challenge Peter— a maid, a crowd, and a slave—are persons of very low honor status.

Jesus before Pilate:
The King of the Judeans, 18:28—19:16a

28 Then they took Jesus from Caiaphas to Pilate's headquarters. It was early in the morning. They themselves did not enter the headquarters, so as to avoid ritual defilement and to be able to eat the Passover. [29]So Pilate went out to them and said, "What accusation do you bring against this man?" [30]They answered, "If this man were not a criminal, we would not have handed him over to you." [31]Pilate said to them, "Take him yourselves and judge him according to your law." The Jews replied, "We are not permitted to put anyone to death." [32](This was to fulfill what Jesus had said when he indicated the kind of death he was to die.)

33 Then Pilate entered the headquarters again, summoned Jesus, and asked him, "Are you the King of the Jews?" [34]Jesus answered, "Do you ask this on your own, or did others tell you about me?" [35]Pilate replied, "I am not a Jew, am I? Your own nation and the chief priests have handed you over to me. What have you done?" [36]Jesus answered, "My kingdom is not from this world. If my kingdom were from this world, my followers would be fighting to keep me from being handed over to the Jews. But as it is, my kingdom is not from here." [37]Pilate asked him, "So you are a king?" Jesus answered, "You say that I am a king. For this I was born, and for this I came into the world, to testify to the truth. Everyone who belongs to the truth listens to my voice." [38]Pilate asked him, "What is truth?"

After he had said this, he went out to the Jews again and told them, "I find no case against him. [39]But you have a custom that I release someone for you at the Passover. Do you want me to release for you the King of the Jews?" [40]They shouted in reply, "Not this man, but Barabbas!" Now Barabbas was a bandit.

19:1 Then Pilate took Jesus and had him flogged. [2]And the soldiers wove a crown of thorns and put it on his head, and they dressed him in a purple robe. [3]They kept coming up to him, saying, "Hail, King of the Jews!" and striking him on the face. [4]Pilate went out again and said to them, "Look, I am bringing him out to you to let you know that I find no case against him." [5]So Jesus came out, wearing the crown of thorns and the purple robe. Pilate said to them, "Here is the man!" [6]When the chief priests and the police saw him, they shouted, "Crucify him! Crucify him!" Pilate said to them, "Take him yourselves and crucify him; I find no case against him." [7]The Jews answered him, "We have a law, and according to that law he ought to die because he has claimed to be the Son of God."

8 Now when Pilate heard this, he was more afraid than ever. [9]He entered his headquarters again and asked Jesus, "Where are you from?" But Jesus gave him no answer. [10]Pilate therefore said to him, "Do you refuse to speak to me? Do you not know that I have power to release you, and power to crucify you?" [11]Jesus answered him, "You would have no power over me unless it had been given you from above; therefore the one who handed me over to you is guilty of a greater sin." [12]From then on Pilate tried to release him, but the Jews cried out, "If you release this man, you are no friend of the emperor. Everyone who claims to be a king sets himself against the emperor."

13 When Pilate heard these words, he brought Jesus outside and sat on the judge's bench at a place called The Stone Pavement, or in Hebrew Gabbatha. [14]Now it was the day of Preparation for the Passover; and it was about noon. He said to the Jews, "Here is your King!" [15]They cried out, "Away with him! Away with him! Crucify him!" Pilate asked them, "Shall I crucify your King?" The chief priests answered, "We have no king but the emperor." [16]Then he handed him over to them to be crucified.

✦ *Notes:* John 18:28—19:16a

As with the previous segments of this trial narrative (see the **Note** at 18:1), this segment begins with a description of the cast of characters along with a scene change (vv. 28-29a). We are abruptly presented with a significant person in the story of Jesus without any further information aside from his name ("Pilate") and where he was situated (praetorium). This is further indication that the author of John presumes that the group for whom he composes his account knows the story of Jesus from elsewhere. His task is to reveal the true meaning of that story.

There is no indication in the story that Caiaphas ever got to see the person about whom he unwittingly prophesied. While Annas sent Jesus to Caiaphas (v. 24), no events are reported there. Jesus is simply led from Caiaphas's house directly to the official Roman residence, the praetorium, early in the morning (of the day before the Passover). Along with this scene change, the author informs us that if Israelites entered the praetorium, they would become unclean and therefore unable to join others celebrating the Passover. ⇨ **Eating the Passover,** 18:28—19:16a. ⇨ **Purity/Pollution: Purification Rites,** 3:22-36.

18:28 Another view of the model of Jerusalem. The picture is of the Palace of Herod the Great (d. 4 B.C.E.). It became the residence of the Roman procurator when he was in Jerusalem. Jesus' trial would have taken place in the spacious courtyard. Photo by Avraham Hay.

To the dominant society, the opening of the scene describes Jesus about to be handed over to the Romans by pious Israelites scrupulously concerned about purity rules so as to please and obey God.

To those who believe in Jesus, the scene links events surrounding Jesus' "lifting up" with the Passover and its lamb and the "Lamb of God" (1:29) who takes away Israel's sin. For them purity concerns are not the issue. ⇨ **Passover Lamb,** 19:16b-37.

18:29-32 In this first scene (of seven) describing Jesus before Pilate and the crowd that led him to the praetorium, the very first thing Pilate does is step outside and inquire about the charges for which Jesus was brought before him. The presumption in the story is that the only reason Judean temple soldiers would lead anyone to the praetorium would be for some sort of forensic action (v. 29). To Pilate's question of charges, Jesus' captors respond that unless Jesus was guilty they would not have brought him to Pilate. The issue is not one of charges, but of proper punishment (v. 30).

To speak here of a "trial" of Jesus, so common in Western scholarly literature, is out of place. Rigidly hierarchical societies such as those under Roman imperial rule in the ancient Mediterranean world do not allow for trials of social inferiors; instead they have accusations and punishments.

Pilate's response that the Judeans should condemn Jesus by their own law allows the real issue to surface. Jesus' captors want to put him to death (v. 31), specifically the form of death meted out by Romans, crucifixion.

For the dominant society, this first scene is a straightforward description of the fact that the high priest and his entourage believed Jesus worthy of death for the sake of the nation.

For those who believe in Jesus, the scene simply portrays what Jesus foretold about the style of his death, "to show by what death he was to die" (v. 32). He will be "lifted up," with all the attendant outcomes.

18:33-37 The second scene would have us imagine Pilate summoning Jesus into Roman space, into the unclean realm of the Roman presence. According to the Roman forensic procedure, the next step after a judge considered the charges was the *"cognitio,"* or judicial investigation by the judge. This is what goes on in this episode.

Pilate's opening question indicates the charges brought against Jesus by the Judeans—a claim to kingship (⇨ **King of the Judeans,** 18:28—19:16a). "Israel" was the in-group name for Judeans, Galileans, Pereans, and their colonials alike. But from the perspective of a Roman, all Israelites were Judeans, since the central temple city of this collectivity was Jerusalem in Judea. ⇨ **Jews/Judeans,** 1:19-28. Jesus answers Pilate's question with a question (as he did the high priest in v. 21). By responding to Pilate's challenge to his honor (outsider questions are always honor challenges) in this way, Jesus offers a riposte befitting an equal. Jesus wants to know whether it was Pilate following Jesus' career himself or whether Pilate was simply repeating the accusation of Jesus' captors (v. 34).

Pilate's return question, "Am I a Judean?" indicates that he was not following Jesus' career, but rather that it was Jesus' fellow Israelites who spied out Jesus as a problem and captured him as a criminal—"your own people and the chief priests handed you over" (v. 35). Pilate, the narrator wishes us to believe, really does not know why Jesus was dumped at the praetorium this fateful Passover eve. So he continues: "What have you done?"

Jesus responds to Pilate's mention of kingship by insisting that his kingship is not "of this world," that is, not of Israelite origin. Otherwise, Israelites would fight and he would not be handed over to his Judean captors (v. 36).

Pilate continues his questioning: "So then you are a king?" Jesus, in turn, offers a response full of meaning for the Johannine group: kingship designations come from "you," from Pilate repeating Judean claims. In fact, Jesus was born and came "into the world" to bear truthful witness. People who are "of the truth," hear and understand what he means. Pilate closes the conversation with his rhetorical question: "What is truth?"

For those "in the world"—that is, in the dominant Judean society—Jesus claimed to be king of Israel. This is a political claim that could only lead to destruction of the people and their chief priests. It would also destroy their existing institutional arrangements with the Romans.

For those who believe in Jesus, Jesus is a truthful witness attesting to what he saw and heard before he was born "into the world" of Israel. Those who hear and understand what he says are those who are "of the truth." Pilate asks the wrong question. His question should be "Who is it that is of the truth?" Then his examination would proceed properly.

18:38-40 In a Roman trial (see above), after the judge's examination comes the verdict. We learn of Pilate's verdict as he leaves the praetorium to announce to the Judeans on the outside: "I find no crime in him." That should be the end of the matter if this were a trial. But that is not what either Pilate or the Judeans have in mind.

To begin with, Pilate describes his willingness to release the innocent Jesus in compliance with a Judean custom of releasing a criminal at Passover. Here the "innocent criminal," Jesus, is put forward by Pilate as "King of the Judeans." With this title, Pilate puts Jesus forward as a challenge to the honor of the Judeans, returning a person they consider a criminal as their actual king.

An additional irony in the story is that Jesus, a *Galilean,* is being put forward as the *Judean* king. Pilate, a Roman, thinks of Jesus, the authorities, the crowd, and everyone involved as Judeans (see above). But the Judeans themselves distinguish Galileans, Pereans, and Judeans. Embedded in Pilate's very broad use of the term *Judean,* therefore, is an insult to the Judean crowd, who would not imagine a lowborn Galilean as their king.

Pilate has thus (wittingly or unwittingly) insulted the crowd. The Judean response is immediate and equally insulting to Pilate. They ask for the release of a social bandit, Barabbas, an enemy of Rome. ⇨ **Social Bandits,** 18:28—19:16a.

19:1-3 Pilate responds to the insult of asking for the release of Barabbas by having Jesus scourged, outfitted like a king, and acclaimed as "King of the Judeans" see chart on page 249: I. Crowning of and Homage to a King). ⇨ **King of the Judeans,** 18:28—19:16a. The scourging is Pilate's warning to Jesus to keep out of trouble. But the soldiers' dressing Jesus up as a king and mocking him is their response to the Judean challenges and insults to Pilate. ⇨ **Challenge and Riposte,** 7:14-24.

This episode marks the central panel in the author's presentation of Jesus' elevation. As these **Notes** indicate, in 18:39—19:3 we have a series of insults traded back and forth between Pilate and the Judeans. Pilate proposes Jesus, a Galilean, as their king and asks if the crowd wishes him released. They reply that they prefer a social bandit, an enemy of Roman order. In defense of Pilate's honor, the soldiers then mock Jesus as the King of the Judeans. This episode bears three distinct meanings.

1. For the Romans: the mocking offer of a lowborn Galilean to Israel as their king is a deep insult to all Israel (whom Romans labeled "Judeans"), a demeaning riposte to the continued Jerusalemite challenge to Pilate's honor (which stands for the honor of Rome).
2. For the Judeans: it is a challenge to their honor since it cast serious doubt on their ability to recognize the quality of divinely appointed, politically oriented

persons in their own midst—they could not tell the difference between a real Israelite king and a pretender even if they tried.

3. For those who believe in Jesus, no matter what the material or social overlay concealing the real nature of Jesus, it is an ironic demonstration that Jesus is in fact the authentic king of Israel, or as the Romans would have it, "King of the Judeans."

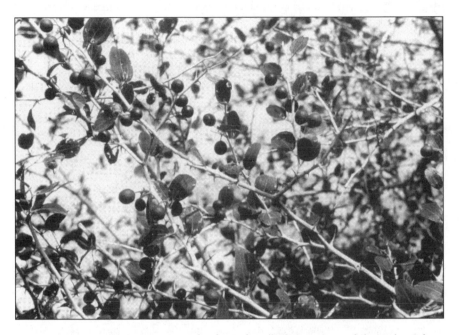

19:2-5 Scholars, preachers, and mystics have described the crown of thorns in various ways. A traditional plant is Christ thorn (*Zizyphus spina-christi*) pictured here. It is a small tree or large bush that is quite widespread in the mountains of Samaria and in the Jordan valley. It has both short hooked spines and straight spines up to an inch and a half long. Photo by Thomas Hoffman.

19:4-8 If a coronation scene (see the chart on page 249: II. Proclamation, III. Acclamation), this would mark the expected proclamation of the king (here by Pilate: "Here is the man!" [v. 5]) and the acclamation by the crowds (here the chief priests and temple military shouting, "Crucify him, crucify him" [v. 6]). These form a rather odd set of proclamation and acclamation statements. But those who see a coronation ritual here would insist these are ironic statements filled with the typical Johannine double meaning.

In a forensic perspective, rather more apparent here, Jesus is declared innocent by Pilate once more: "I find no crime in him" (v. 4). To this end he returns Jesus to the Judean presence. Garbed as a mock king, Jesus is presented by Pilate with the words, "Behold the man!" (v. 5).

With the renewed insistence on Jesus' public and total humiliation by the chief priests and officers, Pilate tells them to crucify Jesus themselves (if they dare, since it would be insulting to Roman authority) and pronounces for the third time a verdict of innocence: "I find no crime in him" (v. 6). In response, the Judeans level a new charge: according to Torah Jesus ought to die "because he has made himself the Son of God" (v. 7) ⊃ **Pretense (False Claims),** 18:28—19:16a. To "make oneself" anything is a challenge to the honor of those denying the claim. But to make oneself "Son of God" is presented here as a challenge to the honor of God himself, which must be properly answered at all costs—with the extremely dishonorable death of the challenger. ⊃ **Challenge and Riposte,** 7:14-24.

Those who believe in Jesus know very well that Jesus does not make himself Son of God, but rather is acknowledged as Son of God by the Father. Regardless of disclaimers by hostile outsiders, their attachment to Jesus as Son is duly warranted and witnessed and is therefore worthy of their ongoing adherence.

This warrant is intimated by the fact that even Pilate becomes "more afraid" (v. 8) to deal with Jesus. Note also that while fear is a shameful response in general, it is especially so for a high-ranking Roman officer, except before superiors and divinities.

19:9-12 Pilate, however, accepts the new charges and opens a new "trial," as is indicated by the way he moves on to another examination of Jesus. This time his concern is with Jesus as "Son of God." Thus, his opening question is one of Jesus' origin: "Where are you from?" (v. 9). As we have noted, the author of this Gospel repeatedly returns to the notion of where Jesus is from. Obviously, the issue is of critical importance to his antisociety; see the **Notes** at 6:25-27. Jesus answers with an insulting silence. Silence is an appropriate response when challenged by an inferior; hence, it is a tacit claim to superiority. In reacting to this claim of Jesus, Pilate points to his own authority to deal with Jesus as he wishes (v. 10). Jesus, in turn, parries directly with reference to God as source of all power and indirectly responds to the question of where he is from as Son of God—that is, he is "from above" (v. 11).

Since God is in charge and Pilate is unwittingly cooperating in the realization of God's will, the person responsible for shaming God ("the greater sin") is "he who delivered" Jesus to Pilate. That is the "they" of 18:28. This includes Annas (one of the chief priests), Caiaphas (high priest), the Pharisees, the temple military, in sum, the establishment of Israel's political religion.

Pilate's preferred verdict is suggested by his intention to release Jesus (v. 12). But the Judeans outside explicitly raise the accusation concerning which Pilate examined Jesus earlier (18:33-38): Jesus claims to be king. To release Jesus would cast doubt on Pilate's allegiance to his patron, Caesar (⊃ **Friend of Caesar,** 18:28—19:16a).

19:13-15 This is a very important scene for the author of the Gospel (see the chart on page 249: IV. Enthronement on Judgment Seat). He clearly notes the name of the place in Greek and in Hebrew. He specifies the date and then explicitly gives the time—about the sixth hour. What is it that is occurring?

Perhaps it is important to note that the Greek grammar of the opening action is not completely clear. It may be understood either as "he brought Jesus out and sat down" or as "he brought Jesus out and sat [him] down" (v. 13). For those reading with a coronation scenario, this scene marks the enthronement of Jesus on the symbol of Roman authority, the judgment seat. Jesus is enthroned with full authority by the legitimate powers in the Mediterranean world. On the other hand, if it is Pilate who takes the judgment seat, this scene marks the sentence meted out on Jesus: "Here is your King!" (v. 14).

Again, from a Roman point of view, this is the supreme put-down to the Judean challenges to Pilate and Roman authority. Jesus is not a pretender, but an actual king—yet a totally humiliated, shameless, degraded, socially insignificant person treated as befits a slave, the lowest social status in society.

From the Judean point of view, Pilate's words are just a further insult in response to their accusation charging Pilate with not being a real friend of Caesar. But for those who believe in Jesus, Pilate's considered judgment is that Jesus is indeed King of the Israelites, not simply one who claims the role. Even a Roman judge can see through the stubborn Judean rejection.

The outcome of the interaction adds insult to injury. For Pilate's insulting question, "Shall I crucify your King?" (v. 15), has the chief priests confessing: "We have no king but Caesar." By Israel's own standards, greater blasphemy than this is inconceivable! Thus, the enemies of Jesus have just shamed themselves in public, insulted the God of Israel in public, and merited God's reprisal. ⇨ **Shame of Crucifixion,** 18:28—19:16a.

19:16a This verse marks the general outcome of the whole foregoing passage. With Pilate's handing Jesus over "to them to be crucified," we come to the sentence—Jesus' total humiliation, or in antilanguage, Jesus' supreme exaltation.

✧ *Reading Scenarios:* John 18:28—19:16a
Eating the Passover, 18:28—19:16a

The Passover meal was to be eaten on the evening of the night when the God of Israel freed enslaved Israelites from Egyptian bondage in order to have them serve him. In Israelite tradition a number of significant events likewise took place on Passover night. These traditions were clustered in the Aramaic version of the Torah reading for Passover. It is useful to keep these traditions in mind as John unfolds his account. Targum Exod. 12:42 reads:

It is a night reserved and set aside for redemption to the name of the Lord, at the time the children of Israel came out redeemed from the land of Egypt. Truly, four nights are those that are written in the Book of Memorials.

The first night: when the Lord was revealed over the world to create it. The world was without form and void and darkness was spread over the face of the abyss, and the Word of the Lord was the Light and it shone; and he called it the First Night.

The second night: when the Lord was revealed to Abram, a man of a hundred years, and Sarah, his wife, who was a woman of ninety years, to fulfill what the Scripture says: Will Abram, a man of a hundred years, beget, and will his wife, Sarah, a woman of ninety years, bear? And Isaac was thirty-seven years when he was offered upon the altar. The skies were bowed down and descended and Isaac saw their perfections and his eyes were dimmed because of their perfections and he called it the Second Night.

The third night: when the Lord was revealed against the Egyptians at midnight: his hand slew the first-born of the Egyptians and his right hand protected the first-born of Israel to fulfill what the Scripture says: Israel is my first-born son. And he called it the Third Night.

The fourth night: When the world reaches its end to be redeemed: the yokes of iron shall be broken and the generations of wickedness shall be blotted out; and Moses will go up from the desert and the king Messiah from on high. One will lead at the head of the flock, and the other will lead at the head of the flock, and his Word will lead between the two of them, and I and they will proceed together.

This is the night of Passover to the name of the Lord: it is a night reserved and set aside for the redemption of all the generations of Israel.

The role of the Word is significant, both at creation, when the Word was Light (as in John's opening segment), and at the final redemption, when the Word is to lead Moses from the desert and the king Messiah from on high. For John, distinctively, Jesus is this Word as well as the king Messiah from on high.

Non-Israelites are excluded: "The LORD said to Moses and Aaron: This is the ordinance for the passover: no foreigner shall eat of it" (Exod. 12:43). ⟡ **Passover Lamb,** 19:16b-37.

Social Bandits, 18:28—19:16a

In John 18:40 we are told that Barabbas was a "bandit." The Greek term used here (*lestes,* meaning thief) is consistently employed by Josephus to describe the phenomenon of social banditry, which played such a pivotal role in the spreading chaos prior to the great revolt of 66 C.E.

Social banditry is a phenomenon that is nearly universal in agrarian societies in which peasants and landless laborers are exploited by a ruling elite that siphons off most of the economic surplus they produce. Persons driven off the land by debt or violence or social chaos of any sort resort to brigandage in which the elite are the primary victims. Recent evidence indicates that the popular legends of bandits who rob the rich and aid the poor frequently have a basis in actual experience. Moreover, such bandits usually have the support of the local peasantry, who sometimes risk their own lives to harbor them. Historically, such banditry increases rapidly whenever debt, famine, taxation, or political or economic crises force marginal peasants from their land.

According to Josephus, social banditry, caused by exactly such conditions, was widespread in Palestine prior to the reign of Herod the Great and again in the mid-first century leading up to the great revolt. In the days of Antipater (father of Herod the Great), Josephus tells how a Hezekiah, "a brigand-chief with a very large gang, was over-running the district on the Syrian frontier" (*War* 1.204). Later he vividly describes the strenuous efforts of Herod to rid the territory of these bandits, who usually hid in the inaccessible wadis and caves of the hill country: "With ropes he lowered (over the cliffs) the toughest of his men in large baskets until they reached the mouths of the caves; they then slaughtered the brigands and their families, and threw firebrands at those who resisted. . . . Not one of them voluntarily surrendered and of those brought out forcibly many preferred death to captivity" (*War* 1.311).

Such gangs of roving bandits formed much of the fighting force in the early stages of the great revolt, and it was they who coalesced with other groups to eventually form the Zealot party after the revolt broke out. While we hear less about such activity during the lifetime of Jesus, it undoubtedly existed, since the conditions that produce it are those pictured in stories throughout the Gospels.

Barabbas plays a key role in the insults being traded back and forth by Pilate and the Judeans in John 18:38—19:16. Pilate insultingly tries to put Jesus, a lowly Galilean, forward as the Judean king. He asks the crowd if they want Jesus released to them as their ruler (18:39). Having been insulted, they return the favor: they ask for Barabbas, a social bandit, an enemy of Rome.

Shame of Crucifixion, 18:28—19:16a

New Testament authors reflect the general perception of crucifixion in the Greco-Roman world as "shame" (Heb. 12:2). As Jerome Neyrey has recently pointed out, the crucifixion process was marked by a progressive public humiliation and deprivation of honor (1994a:113–14):

1. Crucifixion was considered the appropriate punishment for slaves (Cicero, *In Verrem* 2.5.168), bandits (Josephus, *War* 2.253), prisoners of war (Josephus, *War* 5.451), and revolutionaries (Josephus, *Ant.* 17.295).

2. Public trials ("wretched is the ignominy of public judgment," Cicero, *Pro Rabinio* 9–17) served as status degradation rituals, which labeled the accused as a shameful person.

3. Flogging and torture, especially the blinding of eyes and the shedding of blood, generally accompanied the sentence (Josephus, *War* 5.449–51; 3.321; Livy, 22.13.19; 28.37.3; Seneca, *On Anger* 3.6; Philo, *Flac.* 72; Diodorus Siculus, 33.15.1; Plato, *Gorgias* 473bc; Plato, *Republic* 2.362e). Since, according to *m. Mak* 3.12, scourging was done to both the front and back of the

body, the victims were naked. Often they befouled themselves with urine or excrement (3.14).

4. The condemned were forced to carry the cross beam (Plutarch, *Delay* 554B).

5. The victims' property, normally clothing, was confiscated; hence, they were further shamed by being stripped naked and despoiled (see Diodorus Siculus, 33.15.1).

6. The victim lost power and thus honor through pinioning of hands and arms, especially the mutilation of being nailed to the cross (Philo, *Post.* 61; *Somn.* 2.213).

7. Executions served as a crude form of public entertainment, where the crowds ridiculed and mocked the victims (Philo, *Sp. Leg.* 3.160), who were sometimes affixed to crosses in an odd and whimsical manner, including impalement (Seneca, *Consol. ad Marcian* 20.3; Josephus, *War* 5.451).

8. Death by crucifixion was often slow and protracted. The powerless victims suffered bodily distortions, loss of bodily control, and enlargement of the penis (Steinberg 1983:82–108). Ultimately, they were deprived of life and thus the possibility of gaining satisfaction or vengeance.

9. In many cases, victims were denied honorable burial; corpses were left on display and devoured by carrion birds and scavenger animals (Pliny, *Historia Naturalis* 36.107–8).

The real test for the victim, in Mediterranean context, was the *endurance* of pain and suffering as a mark of *andreia,* manly courage. Silence of the victim during torture proved his honor. Yet the loss of honor evidenced by the whole process and inability to defend one's honor were deemed far worse than the physical pain involved.

The Gospels quickly pass over the physical torture of Jesus ("Good Friday" is a medieval Christian invention). Rather, they focus on the various attempts to dishonor Jesus by spitting on him (Mark 14:65; Matt. 26:67; see Mark 10:33-34), striking him in the face and head (Mark 14:65; Matt. 26:67; John 18:22; 19:3), ridiculing him (Mark 15:20, 31; Matt. 27:29, 31, 41; John 19:3), heaping insults on him (Mark 15:32, 34; Matt. 27:44), and treating him as though he were nothing (Luke 23:11; see Acts 4:11).

King of the Judeans, 18:28—19:16a

For most U.S. readers of the Bible, the words *king* and *lord* are perhaps the most difficult New Testament words to appreciate. Most people today simply have no experience of persons embodying these social roles, much less of the social system that supports such roles.

For pre-Enlightenment people (before the eighteenth century C.E.), the king was the author and guarantor of the prosperity of his people—if he followed the rules of justice and obeyed divine commandments. Homer writes (*Odyssey* 19.110ff.): "A good *basileus* [king] who respects the gods, who lives according to justice, who reigns over numerous and valiant men, for him the black earth bears wheat and barley, the trees are laden with fruit, the flocks increase unceasingly, the sea yields fish, thanks to his good government, the people prosper under his rule." This points to the mystical and productive virtue of the king, whose proper function it was to promote fertility about him, both in animals and vegetation. Kings ensured prosperity on land and sea, with abundant fruit and fecund women. Thus, subjects expected peace and prosperity, security and abundance, from their kings.

Defeat or calamity point to ritual death for a king. A Persian prayer from the period of Darius (d. 486 B.C.E.) states: "May Ahuramazda bring me help along with all the others gods and protect this land from the army of the enemy, from bad harvests, from the lie." This prayer alludes to the three divisions of society and what they do: nobles and war, peasantry and cultivation of soil, priesthood and religion. All three are to be guaranteed in their functions by the king, who effects the defeat of enemies, prosperity of the country, and triumph of the spirit of truthfulness in society.

Kings often held scepters. Originally the scepter derived from Hellenic culture, where it was the staff of a messenger who traveled as authorized by someone in power in order to deliver a message. The three qualities of the messenger were: traveler, with authority, and with something to tell. The king, as a worthy messenger of God/gods, delivered his commands with divine authority.

A lord (Latin *dominus;* Greek *kyrios;* Semitic *adon* or *baal*) is a person having the most complete power over persons and things. A lord is the absolute owner of all persons and things in his domain. He has the power to dispose of persons and things as he likes, and he holds this power by a title recognized as valid (by either ad hoc force, custom, or law). This is lordship (Greek *kyriotes,* Latin *dominium*). The lord was entitled to use any thing or person that was his, to enjoy all their products or properties, and to consume entirely whatever was capable of consumption.

Before the ruler of the polis (independent city) of Rome became dictator, the period of the so-called principate, Rome had both a magistrate and an imperator. The magistrate was a person who represented the law of a polis, who said what the law was and who had the power to employ the force the polis placed at his disposal to administer justice. He was invested with legal authority and the sanctions to exercise that authority. The imperator (emperor) on the other hand was a person with the power of using the public forces to ensure obedience to his orders.

With the coming of the imperial system, the principate, the ruler of Rome was in effect lord of the Roman domain, king of the *oikoumene* (the inhabited earth), magistrate of the Roman people. The title "emperor" (Latin *imperator*) means military commander, general. The emperor was in fact a commander in chief, and the empire was a command-in-chiefdom, marked by the presence of the Roman military throughout the inhabited earth. The personal name of Julius "Caesar" was taken to bundle all of the qualities of king and lord together in a single commander-in-chief of the *oikoumene.*

265

Pretense (False Claims), 18:28—19:16a

With Pilate's verdict of Jesus' innocence, the trial should have been over ("I find no crime in him," 19:4, 6). But a new charge is made, which constitutes a new challenge to Jesus' honor: "We have a law, and according to that law he ought to die because he has claimed to be the Son of God" (19:7). The crowds consider this "claim" to be so serious a charge as to warrant the death sentence. And so a new trial ensues to deal with the new charge.

Let us view this new charge from the perspective of honor and shame. In antiquity people were constantly "making themselves" something, that is, claiming a new and higher status or role (Acts 5:36). Hence, the public accusation that Jesus makes himself something functions as a challenge to a perceived empty claim, a common phenomenon in antiquity (see Acts 8:9; 12:22-23; Josephus, *War* 2.55, 60; *Ant.* 17.272, 278). This sort of challenge to Jesus occurred regularly throughout the narrative (1) ". . . making himself equal to God" (5:18); (2) "Who do you claim to be?" (8:53); (3) "You, though only a human being, are making yourself God" (10:33); (4) "He has claimed to be the Son of God" (l9:7); (5) "every one who claims to be a king . . ." (19:12). As Neyrey has noted, in the course of this narrative, the author has consistently dealt with this charge by dividing the charge/challenge: (1) it is denied that Jesus "makes himself" anything, but (2) it is defended that he is such and such (Neyrey 1988:20-23). For example, Jesus claims in 5:19-29 that he is "equal to God." This is no empty claim, for he insists that God has granted him both creative and controlling powers and the honor attached to them. The Father (1) shows him all that God is doing (5:20), (2) has given all judgment to the Son (5:22), (3) has granted the Son also to have life in himself (5:26), and (4) has given him authority to execute judgment (5:27; Neyrey 1988:20–25). Thus, Jesus does not "make himself" anything, for that would be a vainglorious claim and thus false honor. But he truly is "equal to God," "King," and "Son of God," because these honors, roles, and statuses are ascribed to him by God (see the ascribed honor of being "made king" in 6:15).

Moreover, that Jesus himself rarely, if ever, claims to be prophet, Messiah, or King in John, as in the Synoptic tradition in general, is not accidental. These titles tend to be ascribed to him either by God (13:31; 17:5, 24; see Mark 1:11; 9:7) or by others (Son of God—1:34, 49; Messiah—1:41; 10:24; see Matt. 16:16; King—1:49; 6:15; 12:13; Savior—4:42; and Prophet—4:19; 6:14). This traditional perspective steadfastly maintains that Jesus is an honorable person in two respects: he does not seek honor by making vain claims to a given status, but rather he is regularly ascribed great honor by others. The readers and hearers of this Gospel have been schooled in how to interpret this new charge against Jesus. They will reject any sense of a vainglorious claim and thus will affirm the truth of the honor ascribed to Jesus.

Friend of Caesar, 18:28—19:16a

To maintain one's status and survive in a society where the central governing elite were generally totally unconcerned with the populace they governed, people often became embedded in a web of patron-client relationships. Because of receiving goods, influence, or other favors from a patron, a person became a client and then became known as "the friend of so-and-so." In return for favors received, the client owed loyalty and commitment. The accusation against Pilate in John's description of Jesus' degradation ritual makes mention of this feature: "If you release this man, you are not Caesar's friend. Everyone who makes himself a king sets himself against Caesar" (John 19:12). The core of Pilate's identity, then, rests in his being known as Caesar's loyal client—that is, his "friend." His social obligations are to defend Caesar's honor, maintain Caesar's prestige, and work for Caesar's well-being. ⇨ **Patronage,** 5:21-30.

Jesus Is Lifted Up before "This World": His Exaltation (Glorification), 19:16b-37

16b So they took Jesus; [17]and carrying the cross by himself, he went out to what is called The Place of the Skull, which in Hebrew is called Golgotha. [18]There they crucified him, and with him two others, one on either side, with Jesus between them. [19]Pilate also had an inscription written and put on the cross. It read, "Jesus of Nazareth, the King of the Jews." [20]Many of the Jews read this inscription, because the place where Jesus was crucified was near the city; and it was written in Hebrew, in Latin, and in Greek. [21]Then the chief priests of the Jews said to Pilate, "Do not write, 'The King of the Jews,' but, 'This man said, I am King of the Jews.'" [22]Pilate answered, "What I have written I have written." [23]When the soldiers had crucified Jesus, they took his clothes and divided them into four parts, one for each soldier. They also took his tunic; now the tunic was seamless, woven in one piece from the top. [24]So they said to one another, "Let us not tear it, but cast lots for it to see who will get it." This was to fulfill what the scripture says,

"They divided my clothes among themselves,
   and for my clothing they cast lots."

25 And that is what the soldiers did.

Meanwhile, standing near the cross of Jesus were his mother, and his mother's sister, Mary the wife of Clopas, and Mary Magdalene. [26]When Jesus saw his mother and the disciple whom he loved standing beside her, he said to his mother, "Woman, here is your son." [27]Then he said to the disciple, "Here is your mother." And from that hour the disciple took her into his own home.

28 After this, when Jesus knew that all was now finished, he said (in order to fulfill the scripture), "I am thirsty." [29]A jar full of sour wine was standing there. So they put a sponge full of the wine on a branch of hyssop and held it to his mouth. [30]When Jesus had received the wine, he said, "It is finished." Then he bowed his head and gave up his spirit.

31 Since it was the day of Preparation, the Jews did not want the bodies left on the cross during the Sabbath, especially because that Sabbath was a day of great solemnity. So they asked Pilate to have the legs of the crucified men broken and the bodies removed. ³²Then the soldiers came and broke the legs of the first and of the other who had been crucified with him. ³³But when they came to Jesus and saw that he was already dead, they did not break his legs. ³⁴Instead, one of the soldiers pierced his side with a spear, and at once blood and water came out. ³⁵(He who saw this has testified so that you also may believe. His testimony is true, and he knows that he tells the truth.) ³⁶These things occurred so that the scripture might be fulfilled, "None of his bones shall be broken." ³⁷And again another passage of scripture says, "They will look on the one whom they have pierced."

✦ *Notes:* John 19:16b-37

19:16b-18 The introduction to the presentation of Jesus' crucifixion tells of Jesus carrying his cross for himself—that is, for his own purposes. He brings it to a place called Skull Place in Greek, and Golgotha in Hebrew. The actual act of crucifixion itself is quickly passed over in order to note the placement of Jesus' cross, at the center of a crucified threesome. Between two others, Jesus is now lifted up, prepared to draw all people (in John's context: Israel) to himself.

Note that each of the following five scenes is outfitted with some "word" that underscores the meaning of the episode. In the first scene (19:19-22), it is Pilate's unwitting articulation of who Jesus truly is, not unlike Caiaphas's prophecy (11:50). In the second scene (19:23-24), it is the citation from Ps. 22:18 (19:24). In the third and central scene (19:25-27), it is Jesus' own revelation of the relationship of his community and the beloved disciple. In the fourth scene (19:28-30), it is a citation from Ps. 69:22 (19:28). In the fifth and final scene (19:31-37), there are citations from Exod. 12:46 and Zech. 12:10. While for "the world" these five incidents marked Jesus' humiliation, for those who believe in Jesus these same events describe the moment when Jesus was "lifted up."

19:19-22 This first scene notes the *titulus* ("title," Latin for legal charge) specifying the reason for the condemnation. Those who see the story of Jesus' crucifixion as a coronation ritual consider this first scene as the official naming and title of the king. However, as is usual with John, there is much more at issue.

First, the believer in Jesus knows that the reason for the condemnation spelled out here is in fact the revelation of and proclamation of who Jesus of Nazareth really is: Jesus of Nazareth, King of the Judeans (for Romans, "Judean" referred to all Israelites). Note that John gives special emphasis to the origin of Jesus in Nazareth (1:45-46; 7:42, 52; 18:5-7). This marks the lower end of the social scale in the story, the "flesh" that the Word became. "King of Judeans" marks the high end of that social scale, thus, joining opposites.

Second, the title was written in the three languages (and alphabets) known to all Israelites coming to the Passover Feast. "All people" (all Israel) are drawn to the lifted up Jesus as all Israel assembles for that central feast, the Passover. Only John notes that many Judeans read the title, that Jesus was crucified near the city, and that the title was written in Hebrew (that is, Aramaic), undoubtedly for Judeans; in Greek, the international, cultural language; and in Latin, the official, administrative language.

Third, we are told that once again the chief priests wish to manipulate events pertaining to Jesus (v. 21). For the first time Pilate does not give in to the chief priests' demands (v. 22). Actually, that is no longer possible, since Jesus is already lifted up, fully in charge. Authoritatively Pilate states: "What I wrote and stands written [in my declaration], I wrote and continues to stand written [Greek perfect tense]." For those who believe in Jesus, indeed, his kingship continues to stand written.

19:19-20 For more than one thousand years the only translation of the Scriptures wide-ly used in the Roman church was Latin. So Pilate's inscription, IESUS NAZARENUS REX IUDAEORUM, in John's Gospel, abbreviated as INRI, became a part of the traditional representation of the crucified Jesus. The other Gospels each have different versions of the event.

19:23-24 The second scene describes the Roman military custom, given legal basis in Roman law (*Digest* 48:20, "Concerning the goods of the condemned"), of soldiers having the legal claim to the clothing of the condemned person. The scene tells of Jesus' garments, his outer clothing in general, and of his seamless tunic (Greek *chiton*), his inner garment. To explain this event as occurring due to God's will, the author quotes a fulfillment formula and a passage from Psalm 22, an important passage used by early Jesus Messianists to explain events surrounding Jesus' crucifixion.

For those in John's group, there surely must be more to the event (singled out only in John) than soldiers exercising their privileges. Perhaps the meaningful event is the soldiers' unwitting decision to leave the inner garment intact. The tearing of a garment can point to division of a group of men (see 1 Kings 11:30-40, where the prophet Ahijah's garment is torn into twelve pieces, standing for Israel's tribes and their division). Furthermore, the soldiers' term for "tear" (Greek *schizo*) is used in John (7:43; 9:16; 10:19) for a split or schism among people.

In sum, it would seem that the untorn inner garment, left intact by the Roman soldiers, alludes to Jesus' undivided in-group, left intact due to the power of the lifted up Jesus. This unity of John's group was what Jesus prayed for not long before this event (17:11).

19:25-27 The whole Gospel tradition tells of women at the cross; they had access to the cross because they provided no threat to Roman order (unlike a group of males). They are significant in the tradition because they served as witnesses to Jesus' death (Mark 15:40; Matt. 27:55), burial (Mark 15:47; Matt. 27:61), and empty tomb (Mark 16:1.4; Matt. 28:1). However, only John mentions "the mother of Jesus" at the cross. This is the same unnamed character mentioned at the Cana wedding (2:1).

After introducing the women standing next to the crucified Jesus, now lifted up and exalted (v. 25), "the disciple whom he loved" (v. 26) emerges out of nowhere, as though he were somehow attached to "his mother."

As noted previously (13:23), persons are left anonymous in John to heighten their typical function. At Cana the mother of Jesus is a type of the faithful Israelite community that believes in Jesus. She therefore stands for the membership of John's antisociety. The Qumran community contemporary with Jesus similarly believed that it was true Israel that gave birth to the Messiah: "When God will give birth to the Messiah in their [faithful Israel's] midst" (1 QSa 2.11). Likewise, as the Gospel of John amply indicates, the beloved disciple is the trusted disciple to whom Jesus reveals himself and who can authoritatively interpret Jesus. He is a witness, evoking loyalty (faith) and attachment (love) in those who abide in Jesus.

Thus, while the story of Jesus handing over his mother to a disciple is an exemplary piece of behavior, underscoring how a dying son continues to think of his mother to the very end (▷ **Mother/Son,** 19:17-37), for one who believes in Jesus, something quite other is going on.

For the believer, the "hour" of Jesus was likewise the hour when the lifted-up Jesus revealed that the community in which he emerged as God's Son, the community of those who believe in him (the antisociety of which his mother is the type), was now the concern of his beloved disciple. He thus hands over his faithful followers, from whom will emerge further "children of God," to the care of the beloved disciple.

19:28-30 To the casual reader (and observer) this fourth scene reveals the pain of a crucified person asking for some "vinegar," cheap wine serving as painkiller, followed by his death. However, this scene begins and closes with the Greek for "it has been fully accomplished" *(tetelestai).* Immediately after Jesus entrusts those who believe in him to the beloved disciple, we are told that Jesus is aware that everything expected of him by the Father "has been fully accomplished." Now that he has fully performed the "work" entrusted to him, he proceeds to do two more things as he rules with the power of one "lifted up" and drawing all people to himself.

The NRSV and RSV translation, "(in order to fulfill the scripture)," has these significant words in parentheses, like an afterthought. Yet John uses a very odd word for what is here translated "to fulfill." The usual Greek word applied to fulfilling the Scripture is *pleroo*. Instead John uses the Greek *teleioo* (as in 4:34; 5:36; 17:4). The nuance of this latter word is that Israel's Scripture might attain the perfection proper to it, that it might in fact realize what it was intended to realize. It is to this end of having Scripture do what it was intended to do that Jesus says, "I thirst."

The statement "I thirst" and the triple mention of vinegar are an allusion to Ps. 69:22 (English version 69:21). John repeatedly alludes to thirst in this document: 4:13-15; 6:35; 7:37-39. From 7:37-39 we learn that the real thirst quencher offered by Jesus is the Spirit—the entity that interprets and applies what Jesus reveals, that explains and clarifies the truth that Jesus brings and is. In John the thirst quencher is the Spirit! Now what is the outcome of this statement?

In this scene "they" respond by giving Jesus the painkiller of the day, sour wine. But upon receiving the sour wine, Jesus repeats the theme with which the scene opened: Jesus' work "has been fully accomplished." Simultaneously with these words, Jesus bows his head and gives up his spirit. On the surface, he dies, although John's description is quite unusual: literally "he handed over the spirit" (KJV "he gave up the ghost;" RSV "he gave up his spirit"). Yet for those who believe in Jesus, something quite other has happened. When human beings die, while struggling for life to the end, they stop breathing and then their head drops. But here Jesus first bows his head, and only then does he give up his spirit. As a king who was lifted up, he "gives the nod." The act of sanctioning by a king was indicated by a movement of the head; approbation is declared by a sign of the god's head (Latin *nutus,* for example, *ad nutum superioris,* "to give the nod to"). "Zeus gave a sign with his head and ratified his wish" (*Homeric Hymn to Aphrodite,* 222).

After thus ratifying that his purpose has been fully accomplished, Jesus hands over his spirit to those around his cross—the community of those who believe in him, their leader, the beloved disciple and the witnessing women. That this is what the author intends to note is indicated by 7:37-39: "There was yet no spirit, since Jesus was not yet glorified." Now that Jesus has been lifted up, hence, glorified, his spirit comes forth over his own. And in this scene specifically, it is the spirit given by the glorified Jesus that was to be the outcome of Israel's Scripture, the reality it was intended to realize. But only the lifted-up Jesus brought this reality into being. Thus, what pious Pharisees sought in vain by their holiness concerns, and what devoted priestly ranks sought to no avail by their temple ceremonies and rituals, Jesus effects as he is lifted up and exalted.

19:31-37 Even after Jesus' death, the Judeans have plans for him, notably due to their traditions (*halakah,* deriving from Deut. 21:23). They wish to hasten his death and remove him from sight in order to keep holy a "great Sabbath" (a Sabbath on which the Passover falls). They receive Pilate's cooperation, quickly implemented by the soldiers (vv. 31-32). But it is God's will for Jesus that prevails, as the citations from Scripture significantly indicate.

19:33-34 Breaking the legs of a runaway slave or a fugitive was punishment; for a crucified person it was a favor, since it enabled the person to suffocate rather quickly. Here we are told that the soldiers found Jesus already dead, and therefore did not break his legs. Instead, a soldier jabbed his side with a spear (the Greek verb for the action, *nysso,* does not mean to pierce or open; it means to strike or jab). He jabbed it hard enough so that "at once blood and water came out."

19:35 These two features, one negative (did not break) and the other positive (jabbed and immediately water and blood came out) are significant enough for John that he has the event duly witnessed ("he who saw it") and explained as a fulfillment of God's will—that is, a fulfillment of Scripture (vv. 36-37). The purpose for the witness and the quotes is "that you also might believe once-for-all."

✧ *Reading Scenario:* **John 19:16b-37**
Mother/Son, 19:16b-37

A number of commentators have referred to Jesus' behavior here as one of instituting the adoption of his mother by the beloved disciple. The problem with this is that in Israel there was no adoption in any Greco-Roman sense. It would be better to speak of him making his mother the ward of the beloved disciple. But who these personages might actually have been is quite unclear. For John does not seem to know anything of Jesus' Davidic pedigree, and he is equally ignorant of Jesus' actual birthplace (John 7:40-44). Finally, there is no indication that the author of John's Gospel knew the name of Jesus' mother; both here and in the story of the wedding in Cana (John 2:1-4), he simply calls her "the mother of Jesus," which, however, may have been her official Semitic name. Without the Synoptic Gospel tradition, chances are the name of Mary of Nazareth would not be known or remembered at all.

In the Mediterranean world, most sibling relations are rather close. But the mother-son bond is perhaps the closest Mediterranean equivalent (in emotional intensity) to what people in the United States expect in the "love" of a marriage relation. Mother-son relations are a distinctive by-product of Mediterranean child-rearing practices. The heart of the matter is the distinctive Mediterranean male gender-identity ambivalence, revealed in the male's vehement abhorrence or disavowal of everything "feminine." The result is a lifelong defense through honor/shame polarities and prohibitions against unacceptable female identifications.

Mediterranean male gender-identity ambivalence derives from the absence of the father in the family during the boy's early years. In the Mediterranean region, boys are raised under domestic arrangements that exclude the frequent presence of adult males. Thus, boys lack clear male role models during this developmental period. The result is a genuine emotional closeness and affective "symbiosis" of mothers and sons—a pan-Mediterranean trait. Anthropologists studying a variety of Mediterranean countries have reported on this phenomenon. In Portugal the mother-son bond is thought to be the strongest possible bond between two human beings. In Italy this bond is thought to be the primary axis of family continuity. In Greece it is indestructible. Moreover, this uniquely powerful bond originates in a domestic scene in which the boy often perceives the mother—typical in Mediterranean societies—as dominant or "in charge," or as the primary handler of the family's financial resources. Anthropologists have argued, therefore, that these widespread structural features impede the development of a solid male gender identity and promote early psychic identification with the more accessible parent, the mother.

One result of this family pattern is the kind of macho defensiveness about lingering feminine traits that characterizes Mediterranean males after they are thrown out of the women's world and pushed into that of adult males. But another is a lifelong emotional bond between mother and son.

This feature is also rather ancient. For example, after reading a long letter Antipater, his vice-regent, had written in denunciation of his mother, Alexander the Great declared that Antipater did not know that one tear of a mother effaced ten thousand letters (Plutarch, *Lives: Alexander* 39.7.688). It is this Mediterranean value that accounts for the son's concern for his mother in John's narrative. Note, however, that by entrusting his mother to the beloved disciple, Jesus finally channels access to himself by means of the beloved disciple, not through his mother.

Passover Lamb, 19:16b-37

What is at issue with the final scenes of Jesus' exaltation? How does the context of John's account of Jesus' glorification clarify the meaning of these events? Is the author concerned with the simple fact that Jesus did not have his legs broken and that his side was jabbed? Neither of these events is noted in the other Gospels.

Perhaps the first clue to what is at issue is the Scripture quote in 19:36: "Not a bone of him shall be broken." This is a reference to the Passover lamb at the time of the Exodus (Exod. 12:46; Num. 9:12). The number of such references in this account leads to the conclusion that Jesus, the cosmic Lamb of God of chapter 1, has the function of this Lamb's antitype, the Passover lamb, as well.

Note that Jesus' entire last day in Jerusalem takes place within the framework of the Passover celebration. He dies as Passover lambs are being slaughtered in the temple (Day of Preparation, vv. 31, 42). It is because it is Passover Preparation Day that the Judeans want him off the cross and out of sight.

Jesus' openness to his captors in the garden (18:1-10), his insistence that he freely takes the cup offered by the Father (18:11), and his nonresistance to being bound when arrested (18:12) point to Jesus' willingness to submit to slaughter.

All Mediterraneans, Israelites included, attached great importance to the external behavior of a sacrificial victim. Even the slightest sign of resistance was a bad omen. The escape of an animal about to be slaughtered was considered a disaster. Herod's temple had a causeway with a high and narrow embankment leading from the Mount of Olives to the temple so that sacrificial animals might freely walk to the altar to be sacrificed. The point is that everyone at the time knew that a victim had to die willingly in order to be pleasing to the deity(ies). Jesus' willingness to please the Father, like his command of the situation, underscores sacrificial themes befitting the paramount Passover sacrifice.

Jesus is bound when arrested (18:12), just like the only begotten Isaac, another person ready to be sacrificed by his father (Genesis 22). In Israelite lore, all sacrifices offered on Jerusalem's altar get their merit from the binding of Isaac (see *Tg. Neofiti Gen.* 22). Further, in that story we learn that while God told Abraham he would provide a lamb (Gen. 22:8), God in fact provided a ram (Gen. 22:13). In Israelite scribal lore, since Moses says that God said he has a lamb to give Abraham, yet in fact gives Abraham a ram, then that lamb must still be with God, having been created before the foundation of the world. After all, God exists in the seventh day of creation now; he does not work (something Jesus disputes in this Gospel). Hence, God's lamb was still with God in the sky, the Lamb of God.

Bound, Jesus was brought to the high priest in that condition for examination, and on to Pilate (18:28), where Jesus' captors stopped outside the praetorium "so that they might not be defiled, but might eat the Passover" (18:28). So Pilate comes out, marking the beginning of the process that is really directed by the chief priests, and this leads to Jesus' death. Throughout John's account it is the high priest and other chief priests who orchestrate Jesus' death; it is the priest's paramount function to serve God in God's special place, the temple, by offering sacrifices (vv. 18:3, 13, 15, 16, 19, 22, 24, 35; 19:6, 15, 21).

Mention of hyssop in the previous scene likewise recalls the Exodus (Exod. 12:22), at which time hyssop was used to sprinkle saving blood on the doorposts.

Finally, the mention of blood and water points to "mixed blood," noted in the Talmud as the blood of a crucified person (for example, *b. Oholoth* c.3, 5, Soncino 122). The significant feature here in John is the witness's attestation that the blood and water "came out immediately"—that is, it spurted. This is an allusion to scribal Pharisaic requirements for the "kosher," or "fitness," quality of an animal to be slaughtered when it just died or was at the point of death. If blood "spurts forth" when it is found dead or on the point of death, it is "fit" (*m. Hullin* 2.6). Jesus on the cross is still quite "kosher"!

The point of all this is that John's group is to believe that Jesus, the cosmic Lamb of God, has become enfleshed and ended up as the Passover Lamb of God, who takes away the sin of the world (that is, Israel's dishonoring of God) as befits the cosmic Lamb of God. ⇨ **Lamb of God,** 1:29-34. Yet, a fitting Passover Lamb, he can now nourish and protect those who acknowledge him, as the Passover Lamb did in the Exodus (see Exod. 12).

In v. 37 there is an additional quote from Scripture. Zech. 12:10 reads in full:

"And I will pour out a spirit of compassion and supplication on the house of David and the inhabitants of Jerusalem, so that, when they look on the one whom they have pierced, they shall mourn for him, as one mourns for an only child, and weep bitterly over him, as one weeps over a firstborn." The passage in Zechariah continues, noting that while Judeans and all the land duly mourn, "On that day a fountain shall be opened for the house of David and the inhabitants of Jerusalem, to cleanse them from sin and impurity" (Zech. 13:1). The spirit breathed out by the exalted Jesus along with this newly open fountain, with water spurting from Jesus' side, relates to birth from water and spirit referred to in 3:5. Thus, the final outcome of looking on him whom they pierced, if they could only perceive it, is the same as that performed by the cosmic Lamb of God. This is the restoration of honor status before God through the eradication of Israel's sin. At least for the "children of God," John's community, this is the outcome of Jesus' being glorified.

Conclusion:
Jesus' Burial in a Garden, 19:38-42

38 After these things, Joseph of Arimathea, who was a disciple of Jesus, though a secret one because of his fear of the Jews, asked Pilate to let him take away the body of Jesus. Pilate gave him permission; so he came and removed his body. [39]Nicodemus, who had at first come to Jesus by night, also came, bringing a mixture of myrrh and aloes, weighing about a hundred pounds. [40]They took the body of Jesus and wrapped it with the spices in linen cloths, according to the burial custom of the Jews. [41]Now there was a garden in the place where he was crucified, and in the garden there was a new tomb in which no one had ever been laid. [42]And so, because it was the Jewish day of Preparation, and the tomb was nearby, they laid Jesus there.

✦ *Notes:* John 19:38-42

For those who see a coronation ritual in John, it is odd to have this ritual end abruptly in a royal burial. Two representative disciples, Joseph of Arimathea and Nicodemus, see to Jesus' burial. Joseph was previously unmentioned, so the author tells us that for fear of the Judeans he remained a secret disciple. He was of sufficient status to approach Pilate and have Pilate accede to his wishes. He was joined by the scribal Pharisee, Nicodemus, noted in 3:1-15. Now that Jesus has been exalted and glorified, these disciples are quite fearless.

Nicodemus provided enough embalming material for a royal funeral (v. 39). He and Joseph prepare Jesus' body in Judean fashion (v. 40) and place him in a brand-new tomb that is untouched by any other dead person (v. 41). ✪ **The Meaning of Israelite Burial Customs,** 19:38-42. We soon learn that the tomb was a room of sorts (20:6), with a small, low entryway (20:5), sealed with a large rolling stone (20:1). All this happened because the Passover Sabbath would soon begin (v. 42).

✧ *Reading Scenario:* John 19:38-42
The Meaning of Israelite Burial Customs, 19:38-42

Archaeological evidence and later scribal Pharisaic documents disclose to us the meaning of Israelite burial customs at the time of Jesus. Israelites regarded death as a lengthy process, not a moment in time. In elite circles in Judea, between the last breath and sundown, the body would be laid out on a shelf in a tomb carved into limestone bedrock outside Jerusalem. Mourning rites would commence, continuing throughout the year as the body underwent decomposition. The rotting of the flesh was regarded as painful, but also expiatory for the dead person. One's evil deeds were thought to be embedded in the flesh and to dissolve along with it.

After a year, the mourning ritual concluded. In the first century, people thought that the bones retained the personality, and that God would use them to support new flesh for the resurrection. After this year of purification and putrefaction, the bones of the deceased were often collected and placed in an ossuary or "bone box," which was in fact a second burial casket. This process was called the *ossilegium,* "the collection of bones." The ossuary was designed like a box for scrolls, just long enough for the thigh bones to be laid in like scroll spindles awaiting a new hide and new inscription by the divine hand. In an alternate image, the bones could also be regarded as loom posts made ready for God to weave a new body. In keeping with these views on the character of resurrection, inkwells and spindle whorls have been found in excavated tombs.

This day of second burial marked the end of the family's mourning and its turn toward the hope of reunion and resurrection. Obviously, then, the disappearance or loss of a body after death would be experienced as a greater calamity than the death itself because the family would be unable to prepare the bones for resurrection.

Legally, even the bones of an executed criminal were supposed to be returned to the family after being held in custody of the Sanhedrin during the yearlong period of atoning putrefaction. In effect, capital punishment included the loss of life, the suppression of mourning, and the imposition of supposedly painful but purifying disintegration of the flesh overseen by the court in a special tomb maintained for that purpose. When the flesh was gone, the sentence was completed, the debt was paid, and the bones became eligible for resurrection.

These cultural beliefs and practices provide the context for understanding the claims of the first generations of Jesus' followers about the resurrected Jesus. In John's account, Jesus dies condemned by the Judean populace, leaders and crowds alike (although at the hands of the Romans). Then a ranking Judean,

Joseph of Arimathea, takes his body into custody. It is laid in a separate tomb, to begin to serve the sentence of decay in order to atone for its sins.

It is precisely this penal/atonement process that is interrupted if the tomb is suddenly discovered to be empty. To say that Jesus was raised is to say that God overturned the judgment of Israel's chief priests and the Judean populace, the judgment that Jesus needed to rot to prepare for resurrection. Instead, God supposedly took Jesus directly from last breath to resurrection because there had been no guilt in his flesh. God intervened before the rotting started, hence God overturned the death sentence.

The claim that Jesus is raised by God is a claim of divine vindication for the deeds and words of Jesus. His life has been that of the Word made flesh in Israel, and God preserves its fleshly record intact.

Taken in its cultural context, the claim of resurrection for Jesus asserts that his death was wrong and has been overturned by a higher judge. This cultural interpretation of the death of Jesus contrasts sharply with the theological one: that Jesus' death was right and necessary and required by God "to take away the sin of the world." The Synoptics juxtapose the two interpretations in a smooth narrative sequence, with Jesus even predicting three times that he will die and be raised. But John has none of this. Thus he spares us the dissonance between the two interpretations, or the artistry of the Gospel author who blended them. This dissonance is generally not recognized by Synoptic readers, who often read the Synoptic perspective into John. John does not share these two strands, cultural and theological, in his presentation of Jesus' exaltation. Only one view makes sense and is definitive for the faith of his antisociety. For John, Jesus calamitously died due to the intransigence of the Judeans, but God rescued and vindicated him because Jesus was in fact the mediator of life itself. The other tradition, that Jesus died deliberately because God wanted him dead for the benefit of others, is not in John.

(For further information on Israelite burial customs, see: Rahmani, L. Y., "Ancient Jerusalem's Funerary Customs and Tombs." Part One: *Biblical Archaeologist* [summer 1981]: 171–77; Part Two: *Biblical Archaeologist* [fall 1981]: 229–235; Part Three: *Biblical Archaeologist* [winter 1981]: 43–53; Part Four: *Biblical Archaeologist* [spring 1982]: 109–19.)

CHAPTER XI
JOHN 20:1-31
GOD'S VINDICATION OF JESUS:
JESUS ASCENDS TO GOD AND
DESCENDS TO HIS FRIENDS

Jesus Completes His Ascent
and Descends Twice, 20:1-29

20:1 Early on the first day of the week, while it was still dark, Mary Magdalene came to the tomb and saw that the stone had been removed from the tomb. ²So she ran and went to Simon Peter and the other disciple, the one whom Jesus loved, and said to them, "They have taken the Lord out of the tomb, and we do not know where they have laid him." ³Then Peter and the other disciple set out and went toward the tomb. ⁴The two were running together, but the other disciple outran Peter and reached the tomb first. ⁵He bent down to look in and saw the linen wrappings lying there, but he did not go in. ⁶Then Simon Peter came, following him, and went into the tomb. He saw the linen wrappings lying there, ⁷and the cloth that had been on Jesus' head, not lying with the linen wrappings but rolled up in a place by itself. ⁸Then the other disciple, who reached the tomb first, also went in, and he saw and believed; ⁹for as yet they did not understand the scripture, that he must rise from the dead. ¹⁰Then the disciples returned to their homes.

11 But Mary stood weeping outside the tomb. As she wept, she bent over to look into the tomb; ¹²and she saw two angels in white, sitting where the body of Jesus had been lying, one at the head and the other at the feet. ¹³They said to her, "Woman, why are you weeping?" She said to them, "They have taken away my Lord, and I do not know where they have laid him." ¹⁴When she had said this, she turned around and saw Jesus standing there, but she did not know that it was Jesus. ¹⁵Jesus said to her, "Woman, why are you weeping? Whom are you looking for?" Supposing him to be the gardener, she said to him, "Sir, if you have carried him away, tell me where you have laid him, and I will take him away." ¹⁶Jesus said to her, "Mary!" She turned and said to him in Hebrew, "Rabbouni!" (which means Teacher). ¹⁷Jesus said to her, "Do not hold on to me, because I have not yet ascended to the Father. But go to my brothers and say to them, 'I am ascending to my Father and your Father, to my God and your God.'" ¹⁸Mary Magdalene went and announced to the disciples, "I have seen the Lord"; and she told them that he had said these things to her.

19 When it was evening on that day, the first day of the week, and the doors of the house where the disciples had met were locked for fear of the Jews, Jesus came and stood among them and said, "Peace be with you." ²⁰After he said this, he showed them his hands and his side. Then the disciples rejoiced when they saw the Lord. ²¹Jesus said to them again, "Peace be with you. As the Father has sent me, so I send you." ²²When he had said this, he breathed on them and said to them, "Receive the Holy Spirit. ²³If

you forgive the sins of any, they are forgiven them; if you retain the sins of any, they are retained."

24 But Thomas (who was called the Twin), one of the twelve, was not with them when Jesus came. [25]So the other disciples told him, "We have seen the Lord." But he said to them, "Unless I see the mark of the nails in his hands, and put my finger in the mark of the nails and my hand in his side, I will not believe."

26 A week later his disciples were again in the house, and Thomas was with them. Although the doors were shut, Jesus came and stood among them and said, "Peace be with you." [27]Then he said to Thomas, "Put your finger here and see my hands. Reach out your hand and put it in my side. Do not doubt but believe." [28]Thomas answered him, "My Lord and my God!" [29]Jesus said to him, "Have you believed because you have seen me? Blessed are those who have not seen and yet have come to believe."

20:1 Side view of an ancient tomb in the Holy Land. It shows the use and large size (four to five feet in diameter and nine to ten inches thick) of the stone used to close the entrance. It was set in a slot that allowed it to be opened and closed, but it would have required several men to do so (see Mark 16:3). Photo by Thomas Hoffman.

✦ *Notes:* **John 20:1-29**

This passage is the concluding chapter of John's Gospel, as the epilogue (vv. 30-31) indicates. The next passage (chap. 21) is an addendum of sorts.

20:1-2 This introduction to the events that follow again sets the time and place of the activity along with the principal personages. First, there is Mary Magdalene. She was introduced into the account as one of the women standing beside the cross. Who she might have been and what might have been her reasons for being with the crucified Jesus are not mentioned. All we know is that she witnessed Jesus being "lifted up," and now on the first day of week, early, while it was still dark, she came to the tomb and saw the stone rolled away.

Her reaction is to run immediately to the other principals, Peter and the other disciple. Here we are explicitly told that the other disciple is "the one whom Jesus loved." Mary Magdalene presumes that "they" stole the body and adds that "we" do not know where they took it. The language reflects typical in-group and out-group boundary marking.

20:3-10 While both of the disciples run to the tomb after hearing Mary's report, the beloved disciple defers to Peter (vv. 4-5), whom he allows to enter first. Although Peter sees, it is the beloved disciple who sees and believes (v. 8) that God did something with Jesus, even though neither knows how to clarify the meaning of the empty tomb with the help of the Scripture (v. 9). ✿ **The Meaning of an Empty Tomb,** 20:1-29. Consequently, the author would have us understand that Peter did not consider the option of God interrupting the dying-burial process with a resurrection (see the **Notes** at 19:38-42; also ✿ **The Meaning of Israelite Burial Customs,** 19:38-42), although the beloved disciple "believes." This is not surprising if the beloved disciple were Lazarus, since Jesus intervened to have God interrupt the dying-burial process in his case.

Upon viewing the empty tomb, the disciples return home, presumably someplace in or near Jerusalem, since Mary Magdalene has ready access to them.

20:11-18 This segment opens with Mary weeping in the garden and stooping to look into the tomb once more. This second look results in a vision of two sky beings, one at the head, the other at the foot of where Jesus was laid. The tomb, then, was a sort of *arcosolium* (vv. 11-12).

To the question put by the two sky servants as to why Mary is weeping, she answers that it is because Jesus' body was stolen and she does not know where it is. She wishes to have it continue in the dying-burial process (see the **Notes** at 19:38-42; also ✿ **The Meaning of Israelite Burial Customs,** 19:38-42). Like Peter she does not consider the option of God interrupting the dying-burial process with a resurrection. But upon giving her response to the sky servants, she turns and has a vision. She sees Jesus, whom she does not recognize (vv. 13-14).

To the question put by the unrecognized Jesus, she answers by asking about the body of Jesus, thinking the object of her vision is a gardener. Jesus then says her name, and she turns and answers in Aramaic, *Rabbouni* (literally "My Great One"), which the author translates as "Teacher" (vv. 15-16).

In return, Jesus reveals his status: he does not want Mary to touch him because the process of his ascent to God has not been completed. Jesus' comment about "my Father and your Father, my God and your God" reminds the reader of Jesus' prayer that the disciples, he, and the Father may all be one (17:21). Mary is directed to give the news of Jesus' ascent to the disciples (see 3:13), now raised in rank to brothers of Jesus. She tells the disciples she has had a vision of the risen Jesus and gives them his message (vv. 17-18). ➪ **Seeing Jesus: Alternate States of Consciousness,** 20:1-29.

20:19-23 Unlike Jesus' secret disciples, Joseph of Arimathea and Nicodemus, Jesus' Galilean core group members are still in fear of the Judeans as they gather behind closed doors on the evening of the day Mary and the two disciples discovered the empty tomb. Jesus suddenly appears to the group with the traditional greeting: "Peace be with you." Jesus then shows them his hands and side. This first appearance of the risen Jesus presumes Jesus has descended, since he offers himself for examination (vv. 19-20). This is the first descent of the risen Jesus.

With another wish for peace, Jesus now sends out his core group as the Father previously sent him from the sky, breathing his spirit on them as he previously did on the women and the beloved disciple at the cross. Finally, he explicitly corroborates his disciples in their choice to forgive or not forgive offenses against their in-group, John's antisociety (vv. 21-23).

20:24-29 The next episode involves the disciple Thomas. We are told he was not with the group that experienced Jesus' first appearance. When the disciples bear witness to the event, he rejects their testimony. Instead, he wants to touch Jesus as proof that Jesus descended from the realm of God.

A week later the disciples gather once more, this time with Thomas, and the doors are closed. Apparently, they still fear the Judeans. Once more Jesus descends, suddenly appearing to the group, greeting them with "Peace be with you" (vv. 24-26).

A conversation between Jesus and Thomas follows. First, Jesus reveals that he knows what Thomas is up to, and he invites Thomas to touch him—proof that Jesus has ascended to the Father and has now descended to appear to his disciples (v. 27). Thomas responds with a statement acknowledging the risen Jesus, a statement that serves also as an acclamation expressing his submission to Jesus' authority (v. 28). Jesus concludes with an affirmation of the honor that belongs to those who believe even though he has not yet appeared to them (v. 29). That would include many of those in the Johannine group as well as all who subsequently hear the Gospel read and come to believe.

✧ *Reading Scenarios:* John 20:1-29

The Meaning of an Empty Tomb, 20:1-29

To understand the sort of problem that finding Jesus' empty tomb might provoke, consider the first-century ordinance (said to be found near Nazareth) promulgated by the Roman emperor:

> Ordinance of Caesar: It is my pleasure that graves and tombs—whoever has made them as a pious service for ancestors or children or members of their house—that these remain unmolested in perpetuity. But if any person lay information that another either has destroyed them, or has in any other way cast out the bodies which have been buried there, or with malicious deception has transferred them to other places, to the dishonor of those buried there or has removed the headstones or other stones, in such a case I command that a trial be instituted, protecting the pious services of mortals, just as if they were concerned with the gods. For beyond all else it shall be obligatory to honor those who have been buried. Let no one remove them for any reason. If anyone does so, however, it is my will that he shall suffer capital punishment on the charge of tomb robbery. (SEG 8.13 Nazareth [?] first century C.E., Metzger 1980, 77)

If this ordinance was in fact published in Galilee some time prior to the death of Jesus, then at the time of Jesus' resurrection there was in force a severe law against tampering with buried bodies. An empty tomb would entail capital punishment for Jesus' "friends." As Metzger notes, "The panic-stricken disciples are very unlikely to have braved" the consequences of infringing on such an ordinance (Metzger 1980: 90-91).

Seeing Jesus: Alternate States of Consciousness, 20:1-29

In the Gospel of John (as in Paul), Jesus himself is the revelation of God. The experience of Jesus raised by God was a crucial event for Jesus' followers in the postapostolic generations. When the risen Jesus appears, he is generally not immediately recognized. This is normal in descriptions of alternate reality. Moreover, both in the Synoptic Gospels and in John, there are accounts of the appearances of the resurrected Jesus to the core group of disciples that describe the incident in a rather straightforward manner, much like previous events in the story. The disciples, gathered as a group, gradually come to recognize the resurrected Jesus and interact with him; he appears just as they knew him before the crucifixion: physical, touchable, sharing food with them. We might categorize such accounts as a "group appearance" type. By contrast, there are also accounts in which Jesus appears in a sudden and unexpected manner to one or two individuals who are somewhat distraught, and he addresses them so that eventually they come to recognize him (for example, Mary Magdalene in John 20:14-18; the Emmaus disciples in Luke 24:13-35). We label these accounts as a "singular appearance" type. Such singular appearances of the Gospel tradition are like those appearances to Paul (Acts 9:3-7), Stephen (Acts 7:55-56), and the astral prophet John (Rev. 1:10-18). In the New Testament, when such singular appearances occur, generally after Pentecost, Jesus appears from or in the sky in brilliant light and is perceived through some alternate mode of perception (see Acts 7:55-56; 9:7; 22:9) including an ecstatic condition (Acts 10:10; Rev 1:10).

It was the group appearance type that was recognized and required in those groups that succeeded the Jesus movement as the basis for apostolic authority, with apostolic significance: normative, legitimate, legal. Paul, of course, did not experience such an appearance of Jesus; his were rather the singular type of vision(s). The type of singular appearance in a vision later became common among Gnostics for establishing their authority in face of competing apostolic claims wielded by non-Gnostic bishops. Gnostics claimed continuing revelations of Jesus through visions. To eliminate Gnostic claims to authority based on such visionary experiences, yet to include the letters attributed to Paul and the book of Revelation among traditionally valid, authoritative witness to Jesus, non-Gnostic leadership set up a canon, or norm, of Scripture for Jesus groups. Henceforth no other visions of Jesus could bear meanings of public import for the membership of Jesus groups, especially if the message of these visions deviated from the one in the collection of normative writings, the New Testament canon.

Interactions with the risen Jesus as described in various early Jesus groups can best be explained in terms of experiences generally unavailable to human perception in a culture such as ours. In other words, during the centuries before and after the Gospel of John was written, countless persons reported a range of visions and appearances involving celestial entities. There is no reason not to take the experiences of these persons seriously, at their word, and to interpret what they have to say within the framework of *their* own culture (rather than ours). Mainstream U.S. culture frowns upon and even denies the human capacity for ecstasy and experiences of alternate realities. We are very curious about nonrational dimensions of human existence but tend to label all such occurrences as irrational (see the anthropologist Goodman 1988, 1990; and especially Pilch 1993). John Pilch cites the work of Erika Bourguignon, who compiled a sample of 488 societies in all parts of the world, at various levels of technological complexity, and found that 90 percent of these societies evidence "alternate states of consciousness." Her conclusion: "Societies which do not utilize these states clearly are historical exceptions which need to be explained, rather than the vast majority of societies that do use these states" (cited by Pilch 1994). Thus, it would be quite anachronistic and ethnocentric to take our post-Enlightenment, post-Industrial Revolution, technologically obsessed society as normative for judging anyone other than ourselves. For most of the world, even today, a report of alternate states of awareness would be considered quite normal.

The variety of persons witnessing appearances of Jesus raised from the dead suggests an experience of an alternate state of awareness. This may be difficult for us to believe because we have been enculturated to be selectively inattentive to such states of awareness except in dreams and under the influence of controlled substances. Pilch (1994:233) has noted:

> The physician-anthropologist Arthur Kleinman offers an explanation for the West's deficiency in this matter. "Only the modern, secular West seems to have blocked individuals' access to these otherwise pan-human dimensions of the self." What is the Western problem? The advent of modern science in about the seventeenth century disrupted the bio-psycho-spiritual unity of human consciousness that had existed until then. According to Kleinman, we have developed an "acquired consciousness," whereby we dissociate self and look at self "objectively." Western culture socializes individuals to develop a metaself, a critical observer who monitors and comments on experience. The metaself does not allow the total absorption in lived experience which is the very essence of highly focused ASCs (= alternate states of consciousness). The metaself stands in the way of unreflected, unmediated experience which now becomes distanced.

If we recognize that "objectivity" is simply socially tutored subjectivity, we might be more empathetic with persons of other cultures who report perceptions that we find incredible just because they are socially dysfunctional for us.

Be that as it may, John reports the appearances of Jesus as witnessed events, with a further witness attesting to the initial witnesses. How are we to assess John's statements? Felicitas Goodman is an anthropologist who has studied persons who have perceived alternate realities like those reported by the disciples. She observes that it is not difficult to teach individuals how to become sensitive to alternate states, such as falling into trance states, but that such experiences are generally empty unless filled with culturally significant and expected scenarios.

What this means is that if disciples witness to having repeatedly experienced the risen Jesus, it is undoubtedly because they were culturally prepared to have such experiences. Hence, any interpretation of their experiences requires the interpreter to delve into the available reports in Israel's tradition that tell about events that took place in an alternate dimension of reality and that involved people or beings who straddled the two dimensions. Ezekiel, Zechariah, Daniel, and the book of Enoch are excellent examples of available reports. Furthermore, Goodman lists four things common to persons whom she has studied who have alternate states of consciousness experience: (1) The visionary needs to know how to find the crack between the earth, ordinary reality, and the sky on the horizon, the alternate reality. (2) Since the human body is an intruder in that alternate reality, some bodily preparation (posture, heavy exertion, sleeplessness, and the like) is necessary for the visionary to tune the physical self to the alternate reality. Only in this way can he or she properly perceive it. (3) The visionary needs the readily learnable proper angle of vision. (4) The event perceived in the experience of the alternate reality is sketched out very hazily. What this means is that ASCs must be recognized by means of the general cultural expectations (as well as any specific, local beliefs) (Goodman summarized by Pilch 1994).

Thus, reports of appearances of the risen Jesus are not a distinctive feature of John's Gospel. We have similar reports in the Synoptics (transfiguration accounts, Mark 9:2-8; Matt. 17:1-8; Luke 9:28-36) and the writings of Paul (Gal. 1:12; 2 Cor. 12:2-4). Such experiences were widely known in ancient Mediterranean culture and are best understood in terms of that culture's expectations. However, what is distinctive to John's Gospel is the assessment of these appearances as descents from the sky, the realm of God. In John's antisociety, the perspective adopted was that the Word of God once descended from the sky and was enfleshed in Israel, only to be lifted up and raised from the dead so as to undertake an ascent to the realm from which he came. After that initial ascent to the Father, this Son of God continues to descend and appear in the midst of the Johannine "children of God." The Gospel of John is the story behind these ongoing descents.

Epilogue:
Purpose of the Gospel Is to Maintain Life, 20:30-31

30 Now Jesus did many other signs in the presence of his disciples, which are not written in this book. ³¹But these are written so that you may come to believe that Jesus is the Messiah, the Son of God, and that through believing you may have life in his name.

✦ *Notes:* John 20:30-31

20:30-31 The NRSV adopts the perspective of those who would hand out the Gospel of John, considering it to be a self-authenticating writing that would win conversions. So these translators think the Gospel was "written so that *you may come to believe* that Jesus is the Messiah, the Son of God, and that through believing *you may have life* in his name" (italics ours). Thus, the document's purpose was to generate belief. However, given the boundary concerns of John's group and Jesus' concerns in the Gospel to preserve those given to him, it would seem that the single Greek verbs behind the translation here would better read: "so that *you may continue to believe . . . may continue to have life.*" Both versions do justice to the Greek grammatical form. But the high-context quality of ancient communication plus the social situation of the Johannine group in which the communication occurs have to be taken into account to express the meaning realized in the grammar (see Introduction).

These verses constitute the formal conclusion to the document called the Gospel of John. The first point stated is that the foregoing document presents only a selection of Jesus' significant and witnessed deeds. The second point is that the selection narrated here has been presented for two related reasons: so that members of John's group may continue to believe that Jesus is the Messiah—that is,

Israel's Redeemer, the Son of God, the divine Sky Man; further, by such belief they will maintain "life in his name." This, of course, is their life as "children of God." This Gospel has been written to mediate and maintain life in John's antisocietal group and to whomever this group might include within its membership. This theme has been articulated right from the outset, in the first chapter of the work. ⇨ **Life,** 1:1-18.

CHAPTER XII
JOHN 21:1-23
ADDENDUM: ANOTHER DESCENT AND
APPEARANCE OF THE RISEN JESUS
Third Appearance of the
Risen Jesus, 21:1-14

21:1 After these things Jesus showed himself again to the disciples by the Sea of Tiberias; and he showed himself in this way. ²Gathered there together were Simon Peter, Thomas called the Twin, Nathanael of Cana in Galilee, the sons of Zebedee, and two others of his disciples. ³Simon Peter said to them, "I am going fishing." They said to him, "We will go with you." They went out and got into the boat, but that night they caught nothing.

4 Just after daybreak, Jesus stood on the beach; but the disciples did not know that it was Jesus. ⁵Jesus said to them, "Children, you have no fish, have you?" They answered him, "No." ⁶He said to them, "Cast the net to the right side of the boat, and you will find some." So they cast it, and now they were not able to haul it in because there were so many fish. ⁷That disciple whom Jesus loved said to Peter, "It is the Lord!" When Simon Peter heard that it was the Lord, he put on some clothes, for he was naked, and jumped into the sea. ⁸But the other disciples came in the boat, dragging the net full of fish, for they were not far from the land, only about a hundred yards off.

9 When they had gone ashore, they saw a charcoal fire there, with fish on it, and bread. ¹⁰Jesus said to them, "Bring some of the fish that you have just caught." ¹¹So Simon Peter went aboard and hauled the net ashore, full of large fish, a hundred fifty-three of them; and though there were so many, the net was not torn. ¹²Jesus said to them, "Come and have breakfast." Now none of the disciples dared to ask him, "Who are you?" because they knew it was the Lord. ¹³Jesus came and took the bread and gave it to them, and did the same with the fish. ¹⁴This was now the third time that Jesus appeared to the disciples after he was raised from the dead.

✦ *Notes:* John 21:1-14

This addendum to the Gospel of John records a third descent of Jesus in the midst of his disciples. The significant feature now is that he is not only seen and touched, but even eats with his own. Furthermore, Jesus' appearances are not confined to Jerusalem or Judea, since here Jesus reveals himself to his followers in Galilee, at the Sea of Tiberias.

21:1-2 Verse 1 is repeated in v. 14, thus bracketing off this segment. At the outset we are told where and to whom Jesus revealed himself this third time. Although the Gospel does mention "the Twelve" in the previous chapter (20:24; note also 6:67, 70, 71), here only seven disciples are mentioned, three by name.

This is the first and only mention of the sons of Zebedee in the whole Gospel. Hence, it is only at this point that we learn that they were among Jesus' disciples. Furthermore, the fact that neither of these sons is explicitly connected with the "other disciple" or "the disciple whom Jesus loved" should warn against reading John's story of Jesus in the light of traditions set forth in the Synoptics. The significant Synoptic trio of Peter, James, and John simply does not figure in this version of the Jesus tradition, just as Nathanael, Andrew, Philip, Thomas, and Lazarus, "whom Jesus loved," have no salience in the Synoptics.

21:3 At Peter's suggestion, the seven return to fishing. ➪ **Fishing,** 21:1-14. Compared to the role of the "Twelve" in Acts and the commissioning of the "Eleven" in Matthew, these seven are rather sedentary, transformed by their experience of Jesus but living an ordinary life. The only extraordinary feature of their life now is their repeated experience of the risen Jesus. Perhaps this is a depiction of the new life in John's antisociety.

21:4-14 Jesus appears on the beach, duly unnoticed by the disciples. He now calls to them with a new designation: "Children," perhaps indicating their new status as "children of God" (the burden of the prologue to the whole Gospel; see 1 John 3:1 and passim, and the frequent title in 1 John 2:1, 12, 18, 28). Jesus asks about fish, and they respond that they have none. Jesus gives directions from the shore, they obey, and the result is extraordinary.

The disciple whom Jesus loved is the first to recognize Jesus, this time as "Lord." ➪ **King of the Judeans,** 18:28—19:16a. Peter takes his witness and responds to it by donning appropriate clothing and rushing to Jesus. The disciples could not drag in the net full of fish by themselves. They see a fire, presumably prepared by Jesus, with fish and bread, reminiscent of the incident of the loaves and fishes that also took place here during Jesus' initial descent when they were "the Twelve" (6:67,70,71).

Jesus now asks for some of the recently caught fish. He offers the disciples breakfast, and they all recognize the Lord even though they are too frightened to say so. Jesus then distributes bread and fish. The author of the addendum duly notes this was the third time that Jesus was revealed, hence, descended.

This first part of chapter 21 is clearly reminiscent of chapter 6, the story of the loaves and fishes that led the Galilean crowd to recognize Jesus as a prophet and to desire to make him king. Jesus is now unquestionably the risen "Lord." His appearance is as it was "after he was raised from the dead" (v. 14). To the ongoing Johannine group, this is how Jesus will now be seen. This is how they will be fed.

✧ *Reading Scenario:* **John 21:1-14**
Fishing, 21:1-14

Increasing demand for fish as a luxury item in the first century led to two basic systems of commercialization. In the first, fishermen were organized by either royal concerns or large landholders to contract for a specified amount of fish to be delivered at a certain time. Compensation was either in coin or in kind (processed fish), and papyri records indicate that complaints about irregular or inadequate payment were not uncommon. Such records also indicate that this system was highly profitable for estate managers or royal coffers. The fishermen themselves got little.

The second system made fishing part of the taxation network. Fishermen leased their fishing rights from the toll collectors of the New Testament times for a percentage of the catch, which could go as high as 40 percent. The remaining catch could be traded through middlemen who both siphoned off the majority of profits and added significantly to the cost of fish in elite markets. Legislation in Rome early in the second century sought to curtail rising costs by requiring that fish be sold either by the fishermen themselves or by those who first bought the catch from them. Such tax fishermen often worked with "partners," a term used in Luke 5:7. The fishing done by Peter, the sons of Zebedee, and the others mentioned here may have been of this second type. This descent of Jesus at the shore assures them abundance.

Tying Up Loose Ends in the Story,
21:15-23

15 When they had finished breakfast, Jesus said to Simon Peter, "Simon son of John, do you love me more than these?" He said to him, "Yes, Lord; you know that I love you." Jesus said to him, "Feed my lambs." [16]A second time he said to him, "Simon son of John, do you love me?" He said to him, "Yes, Lord; you know that I love you." Jesus said to him, "Tend my sheep." [17]He said to him the third time, "Simon son of John, do you love me?" Peter felt hurt because he said to him the third time, "Do you love me?" And he said to him, "Lord, you know everything; you know that I love you." Jesus said to him, "Feed my sheep. [18]Very truly, I tell you, when you were younger, you used to fasten your own belt and to go wherever you wished. But when you grow old, you will stretch out your hands, and someone else will fasten a belt around you and take you where you do not wish to go." [19](He said this to indicate the kind of death by which he would glorify God.) After this he said to him, "Follow me."

20 Peter turned and saw the disciple whom Jesus loved following them; he was the one who had reclined next to Jesus at the supper and had said, "Lord, who is it that is going to betray you?" [21]When Peter saw him, he said to Jesus, "Lord, what about him?" [22]Jesus said to him, "If it is my will that he

remain until I come, what is that to you? Follow me!" [23]So the rumor spread in the community that this disciple would not die. Yet Jesus did not say to him that he would not die, but, "If it is my will that he remain until I come, what is that to you?"

✦ *Notes:* John 21:15-23

21:15-23 The second part of the addendum consists of two of Peter's conversations with the risen Jesus that wind up loose ends in the story of Jesus and his disciples. These particular features must have been of specific interest to John's group. The first conversation deals with Jesus' relationship with Peter. Peter denied Jesus, not once, but a number of times. Such disloyalty normally required satisfaction on the part of the one dishonored. What sort of satisfaction did Jesus take? Did the two ever become reconciled? This first conversation provides an answer to such questions. The passage is marked by three successive questions that parallel the three denials of Peter. Peter is appropriately shamed ("Peter felt hurt," v. 17). In conclusion Jesus gives his word of honor about Peter's fate, thus also intimating reconciliation. Death for members of John's group is another way of "glorifying God."

The second question relates to the beloved disciple. Early in the story the beloved disciple does not appear at all. But from the time of the funeral in Judea, all the clues in the story indicated that the beloved disciple, the one whom Jesus loved, was Lazarus, but not univocally. For Lazarus was representative of a person restored to living wholeness by Jesus, while the beloved disciple was a type of every Johannine disciple. But if, as we suggest, Lazarus is identified as the beloved disciple, then this incident ties into the Gospel story. For Jesus resuscitated Lazarus after he lay dead for four days. There seems to have been a belief in the gossip network of John's group that Lazarus, now also known as the beloved disciple, would not die, since he had already died once. The final conversation in this addendum is to put that rumor to rest. ➪ **Gossip Network,** 4:1-42.

CHAPTER XIII
JOHN 21:24-25
EPILOGUE: GROUP ATTESTATION TO
THE AUTHOR'S VERACITY

24 This is the disciple who is testifying to these things and has written them, and we know that his testimony is true. 25But there are also many other things that Jesus did; if every one of them were written down, I suppose that the world itself could not contain the books that would be written.

✦ *Notes:* John 21:24-25

21:24-25 This conclusion states that the disciple referred to in the previous conversation is the witness and author of what has been written in the Gospel of John. The extant John group, expressed here with an anonymous "we," attests to his veracity. This conclusion again acknowledges the selective character of the information previously presented. The final comment about the "many other things which Jesus did" undoubtedly points to various descents of Jesus—that is, the appearances John's group continued to experience at least up to the time this work was completed.

Later Insertion:
Jesus Rescues a Woman Caught in Adultery
(7:53—8:1-11)

53 Then each of them went home, 8:1 while Jesus went to the Mount of Olives. 2Early in the morning he came again to the temple. All the people came to him and he sat down and began to teach them. 3The scribes and the Pharisees brought a woman who had been caught in adultery; and making her stand before all of them, 4they said to him, "Teacher, this woman was caught in the very act of committing adultery. 5Now in the law Moses commanded us to stone such women. Now what do you say?" 6They said this to test him, so that they might have some charge to bring against him. Jesus bent down and wrote with his finger on the ground. 7When they kept on questioning him, he straightened up and said to them, "Let anyone among you who is without sin be the first to throw a stone at her." 8And once again he bent down and wrote on the ground. 9When they heard it, they went away, one by one, beginning with the elders; and Jesus was left alone with the woman standing before him. 10Jesus straightened up and said to her, "Woman, where are they? Has no one condemned you?" 11She said, "No one, sir." And Jesus said, "Neither do I condemn you. Go your way, and from now on do not sin again."

✦ *Notes:* John 7:53—8:11

This passage is considered an insertion into the final form of the Gospel of John largely because it is not found in the most ancient manuscripts (it is lacking in P66, P75, and all the major codices except D) and is unattested in ancient versions apart from Latin ones. But since it is found in the ancient Latin and in Jerome's Vulgate, most Western church traditions consider it canonical, authoritative for Christian theology and worthy to be read as Scripture.

8:1-5 The opening of the passage fits very well into the context of Jesus' teaching in the temple during the Feast of Sukkoth. As Jesus taught, "the scribes and the Pharisees" challenge Jesus with a hostile question. ✷ **Challenge and Riposte,** 7:14b-18. These are Jesus' usual opponents only in Matthew (Matt. 5:20; 12:38; 23:13, 15, 23, 25, 27, 29).

8:3-5 In this high-context passage, the author presupposes his readers know about the social meaning of marriage and its dissolution, divorce. Marriage in the first-century Mediterranean was the union of two families both for their mutual benefit and for the social security of the couple through offspring. One of the major roles of women was to unite two families through males; she links her father and her family of origin with her husband and his family. Marriage took place in stages, one of which was betrothal, later followed by the taking of the wife into the house of the husband.

At issue in this passage is the required treatment of an adulterous woman by nonfamily members of Israelite society. Since it is Jesus' honor that is on the line, and not the full social dimensions of adultery for the families in question, there is no mention of the adulterer and no mention of the offended male. As far as the families are concerned, adultery refers to dishonoring a male by having sexual relations with a woman embedded in his honor, whether a betrothed female or a married wife. Both betrothal and marriage required a divorce for the dissolution of the union (as is well known, for example, from Matt. 1:18-19). By custom, a male dishonored by another male in this way is required to defend his honor by challenging the offending male and taking his life. In usual circumstances, both males are collectivistic persons with ties to larger kinship groups that inevitably get involved in defending the family's honor. The result is a feud. (Note that the purpose of the final six prohibitions of the Ten Commandments is to guard the community from feuds that hopelessly damage the social fabric through murder, adultery, false witness, kidnapping, and theft.)

As a community response serving as a sort of further hedge to prevent such feuding, the woman in question is to be killed. Since the woman ties two groups together through their prominent males, her sexual relations with another male is an anomaly with regard to this social connection. Her death severs all ties, legal and illegal, and life can go on. Deut. 2:23-24 decrees stoning for a betrothed virgin who had committed adultery; but for an adulterous wife, Lev.

20:10 and Deut. 22:22 prescribe death without specifying the manner of execution. Later scribal tradition recommend that adulterous wives be strangled. Unless we are to presume the woman in question is betrothed, the issue would be which specific manner of execution Jesus would choose. The test is about what sort of Torah interpretation he will choose: death as Moses prescribed or life, which is against Moses' prescription.

8:6 There can be no doubt that this is a challenge to Jesus' honor, since his opponents' purpose is "to test him" (v. 6)—that is, test his loyalty to God. Again, this is a frequent ploy in the Synoptic story of Jesus (Matt. 16:1; 22:18, 35; Mark 8:11; 10:2; 12:15; Luke 10:25; 11:16). It is not otherwise found in John's Gospel. Here Jesus' opponents use the woman's loss of her shame to ensnare Jesus' honor. ⇨ **Honor and Shame,** 5:31-47.

8:7-10 In any event, given the nature of the interaction, Jesus chooses to defend his honor by dishonoring his challengers. Sin is a breach of interpersonal relations relative either to God, one's in-group fellows, or both. ⇨ **Sin,** 9:1-41. Matthew 23 presents a list of typical sins of "scribes and Pharisees." The unwillingness of Jesus' opponents to have their sins paraded in public leads them to abandon the confrontation. After all, it was to dishonor Jesus that they came, not to carry out the law of Moses!

8:11 With no official witnesses against the woman, Jesus cannot condemn the woman to death either. Instead, he closes the case with an admonition that she henceforth live honorably. The incident suits the thrust of John's Gospel, for it underscores Jesus' bringing of life in face of death. But the style and implied high context of the passage poorly fit the antilanguage of John's antisociety. Some ancient manuscripts put the passage after Luke 21:38.

APPENDIX
GOSPEL NOTATIONS

People remember how to perform a piece of music by using musical notations on a scale. A similar solution to the problem of remembering how to perform a piece of dance has been solved with the use of Labanotation. In antiquity, it seems most written documents were intended to be read aloud, hence to be performed. The purpose of writing was to facilitate remembering how the document went when one recited it aloud. But how did one make paragraphs or mark off units in a document read aloud? It seems that the main way to mark off a unit was to use repetition of words and/or phrases at the beginning and end of a unit, either alone (as in Matt. 5:3, 10: ". . . for theirs is the kingdom of heaven") or in parallel bracketing fashion (as listed below for John 1:18). The Greeks called such parallel brackets a *chiasmos,* after one half of the Greek letter "Chi" (our X), thus ">". In this appendix we present a reconstruction of such a bracketing analysis of the Gospel of John that accounts for the way we have outlined the document into smaller units. Such analysis is well known; for an application of it to John, see Stibbe 1993.

I. Prologue: Presenting Jesus, Israel's Messiah—The Source of Light and Life That Makes Us Children of God (1:1-18)

1:1-18   A Poem about the Messiah's Cosmic Status and Mission to Israel
A   1:1-5 The creative Word = Life and Light
B   1:6-8 John the witness
C   1:9-11 The Light in Israel, rejection
D   1:12-13 Children of God (new life)
C'   1:14 The Word in Israel, acceptance
B'   1:15 John the witness
A'   1:16-18 The life-mediating, light-revealing Son

II. *Presenting Jesus of Nazareth, Israel's Messiah (1:19-51)*

1:19-28 The Witness of John the Prophet about Himself
A Theme The testimony of John
 1 1:19 Priests and Levites sent from Jerusalem to John
 2 1:20-21 Not Christ . . . Elijah . . . the prophet
 3 1:22 Let us have an answer
B 1:23 I am Voice: Prepare the way of the Lord (Isa. 40:3)
A' Theme The expectations of John
 1 1:24 They were sent from the Pharisees
 2 1:25 Neither the Christ nor Elijah nor the prophet
 3 1:26-28 John answered: The one who comes after me

1:29-34 The Witness of John the Prophet about Jesus
A 1:29-30 He saw + Title: Lamb of God
B 1:31 I myself did not know him
C 1:32 John bore witness: I saw . . .
B' 1:33 I myself did not know him
A' 1:34 Have seen . . . Title: Son of God

1:35-51 The Origins of Jesus' (Our) Antisociety

1:35-42 Jesus' First Invitation
A 1:35-36a John + two disciples
B 1:36b Title: Behold the Lamb of God
C 1:37 Two heard and followed (Jesus)
D 1:38-39 Invitation:
 a Jesus saw and said: What do you seek?
 b They said: Rabbi, where are you staying?
 b' Jesus said: Come and see
 a' They saw and stayed
C' 1:40 One of those who followed (John)
B' 1:41 Title: Messiah (which means Christ)
A' 1:42 Jesus + two disciples

1:43-51 Jesus' Second Invitation
A 1:43-44 In Galilee: Jesus finds Philip: Follow me
    —note Philip, Andrew, Peter, all of Bethsaida
B 1:45 Philip finds Nathanael
   Title: He of whom Moses wrote in the Law
   He of whom the Prophets also wrote
   Jesus of Nazareth, son of Joseph
C 1:46-48 Invitation
 a Nathanael says, Philip says: Come and see

        b   Jesus sees and says
        a'   Nathanael says, Jesus answered: I saw you
    B'   1:49 Nathanael answers:
                  Title: Son of God, King of Israel
    A'   1:50-51 Jesus answers Nathanael: See . . . believe . . . see
                      —Jesus' first word of honor: They will see the open sky and
                      Son of man as access for sky servants!

III. Jesus Began Bringing Life to Israel: From Galilee to Jerusalem and Back (2:1—4:54)

2:1-12 A Wedding in Galilee: Jesus' Initial Self-Disclosure
    A   2:1-2 Third day
        1   Marriage at Cana
        2   Mother
        3   Jesus
        4   Disciples
    B   2:3-4 Mother said to Jesus
    C   2:5 Mother said to servants
    D   2:6 Six stone jars for purification
    C'   2:7 Jesus said to them (servants)
    B'   2:9 Steward said to bridegroom
        1   2:11-12 Jesus at Cana (first sign)
        2   Mother
        3   Brothers
        4   Disciples
    A'   Few days

2:13-25 First Passover: Jesus' Opposition to the Temple System Elicits Belief
    A   2:13 Passover . . . Jerusalem
    B   Prophetic symbolic action
        1   2:14 In the temple
        2   2:15 Out of the temple
        3   2:16-17 Scriptural quote to explain, his disciples remembered
    C   2:18 Judean request for prophetic sign
    B'   Divine symbolic action
        1   2:19 Destroy this temple + three days
        2   2:20 This temple + three days
        3   2:21-22 Jesus' intention, his disciples remembered
    A'   2:23 Jerusalem . . . at the Passover

3:1-21 Jesus' Conversation with Nicodemus Signals the Coming Opposition between Believers Who Have New Life and Unbelievers Who Do Not

A   3:1-2a   Occasion: Pharisee Nicodemus, official + Jesus at night
           3:2b   Address to Jesus: Rabbi
           3:2b   Claim: We know you are a teacher come from God

B   3:3   Word of honor . . . born anew . . . enter the kingdom of God
           3:4   Misunderstanding: Born . . . womb . . . born

C   3:5   Word of honor . . . born of water and spirit . . . enter the kingdom of God
           3:6-7   Clarification: Born of flesh . . . born of spirit . . . born anew
           3:8   Reply #1: Spirit . . . comes and goes . . . born of Spirit
           3:9   Misunderstanding
           3:10   Reply #2: Reference to 3:2, teacher in Israel

B'   3:11   Word of honor: Know . . . bear witness, have seen . . . testimony

A'   3:12   Conclusion: Earthly . . . celestial

Addendum 3:13-21
    3:13-15   Theme 1: Son of Man
    3:16-18   Theme 2: Son
    3:19-21   Theme 3: Light

3:22-36 John's Affirmation of Jesus' Superiority Signals Coming Opposition Between Believers Who Have New Life and Unbelievers Who Do Not

Transition 3:22-24

A   3:22   Jesus in Judea . . . baptized

B   3:23a   John baptizing at Aenon near Salim

A'   3:23b-24   People came . . . baptized + reason (John not imprisoned yet)

A   3:25-26a   Occasion: John's disciples + Judean over purifying
           3:26b   Address to John: Rabbi
           3:26c   Claim: He to whom you bore witness is baptizing + gaining all

B   3:27   Reply: Everything from the sky

A'   (John and Jesus)
     1   3:28   I am not the Christ, but sent before him
     2   3:29   not the bridegroom but friend of the bridegroom
     3   3:30   He must increase; I must decrease

Addendum 3:31-35
3:31   Theme 1   What comes from the sky
3:32-33   Theme 2   Jesus' witness
3:34-35   Theme 3   The Son
Conclusion 3:36   Belief in Son = eternal life, otherwise wrath of God

4:1-42 On the Way Back to Galilee: Jesus Encounters a Samaritan Woman
Transition summary 4:1-4
Introduction: Time and place 4:5-6

Theme 1 Water
A   4:7 Draw water
B   4:7b+8 Give me a drink + reason for talking with her
C   4:9 Question: How is it . . .
D   4:10 Living water
D'   4:11 Living water
C'   4:12 Question: Are you greater than our father Jacob?
B'   4:13-14 Drinks . . . drinks
A'   4:14b Water . . . water

Theme 2 Husbands
A   4:15 The woman said to him
B   4:16 Your husband
C   4:17a I have no husband
C'   4:17b I have no husband
B'   4:18 Not your husband
A'   4:19 The woman said to him

Theme 3 Worship
A   4:20 Our fathers worshiped on this mountain
B   4:20b To worship
C   4:21 Worship the Father
D   4:22a You worship what you do not know
D'   4:22b We worship what we know
C'   4:23 Who worship will worship the Father in spirit and truth
B'   4:23b To worship
C"   4:24 Who worship . . . worship in spirit and truth
A'   4:25-26 The woman said to him, "I know that Messiah is coming (he
      who is called Christ); when he comes, he will show us all things."
      Jesus said to her, "I who speak to you am he."

Theme 4 The Christ?
A   4:27 Disciples
B   4:27b They marveled
C   4:28-29 Woman to people: . . . Can this be the Christ?
B'   4:30 They went out
A   4:31 Disciples

Theme 5 Harvest
A   4:32 Jesus said . . . food
B   4:33 Disciples said . . . food
C   4:34 Jesus said . . . my food
B'   4:35 Do you (disciples) not say . . . (food) harvest
A'   4:35b I (Jesus) tell you . . . harvest
D   4:36 Reaps
E   4:36b Sower and reaper
E'   4:37 One sows and another reaps
D'   4:38 To reap

Theme 6 Outcome
A   4:39 Many Samaritans believed
B   4:39b Woman's testimony
C   4:40 Samaritans came to him . . . asked
C'   4:41 Many more believed because of his word
B'   4:42 Woman . . . your words
A'   4:42b We believe . . . savior of the world

4:43-45 Jesus' Honor in Galilee
A   4:43a Time + he went
B   4:43b-44 Into Galilee: A prophet has no honor in his own country
B'   4:45a Into Galilee: The Galileans welcomed him
A'   4:45b He went + time (feast)

4:46-54 A Healing in Galilee: Jesus' Second Self-Disclosure
A   4:46 Cana in Galilee, mention of water into wine, first sign
B   4:46b Son was ill
C   4:47 Come down . . . death
D   4:48 Unless you see sign you will not believe
E   4:49-50a Come down before my child dies. Go, your son will live
D'   4:50b The man believed
C'   4:51 Going down . . . living
B'   4:53 Son will live
A'   4:54 Second sign, Galilee

IV. Jesus' Bringing Life to Israel Provoked Controversy in Jerusalem and Galilee (5:1—6:71)

5:1-20 A Feast in Jerusalem: Controversy over Jesus' Rescue of a Lame Man

A   5:1   Feast of Judeans . . . Jesus
B   5:2-3   Location and people
C   5:5-6a   Jesus saw him
D   5:6b-8   Dialogue: Jesus and sick man
E   5:9   Healing, proof + it was Sabbath
D'   5:10-13   Dialogue: Judeans and formerly sick man
C'   5:14   Jesus found him
B'   5:15   Left the location and people
A'   5:16   Judeans . . . Jesus

Addendum 5:17-20
Theme   Why the Son heals on Sabbath: The Father is working still
A   5:17   Father is working
B   5:18   Called God Father . . . equal with God
B'   5:19   Word of honor: Son can do . . . only what he sees Father doing
A'   5:20   Father . . . is doing

5:21-30 Jesus as God's Honored Broker

A   5:21a   Father raises dead
B   5:21b   . . . gives life . . . Son gives life
C   5:22   Father . . . given judgment to the Son
D   5:23   Honor the Son as they honor the Father
E   5:24   Word of honor: He who hears my word . . . has eternal life
E'   5:25   Word of honor: Dead will hear . . . voice . . . will live
D'   5:26   As Father has life, so he has granted the Son to have life
C'   5:27   Given him authority to execute judgment
B'   5:28-29a   All in tombs . . . resurrection of life or
A'   5:29b-30   Resurrection of judgment . . . my judgment is just

5:31-47 Legitimation of Jesus' Brokerage

Theme 1   Witnesses to the Son 5:31-40
A   5:31   If I bear witness to myself . . . testimony
B   5:32-33   Another bears witness . . . John has born witness
C   5:34   Testimony not from man
D   5:35   (John) was lamp . . . light
D'   5:36   Testimony is greater than John
C'   5:36b   The works of the Father which I do bear witness
B'   5:37-38   The Father . . . has borne witness
A'   5:39-40   Scriptures bear witness to me . . . source of life

Theme 2 The Father's Honored Son and Unbelief (5:41-47)

A   5:41-42 I do not welcome glory from men . . .

B   5:43 I have come in my Father's name . . . another comes in his own
       name

C   5:44a You have glory from one another

C'   5:44b Do not seek glory that comes from the only God

B'   5:45-46 Accuse you to the Father . . . Moses . . . if you believed Moses

A'   5:47 How will you believe my words?

6:1-15 Second Passover, in Galilee: An Outdoor Meal of Bread and Fish

Introduction 6:1 Sea of Galilee, which is Sea of Tiberias

A   6:2-3 Signs . . . mountain
       6:4 Passover, feast of Judeans, at hand

B   6:5-7 So that people may eat . . . two hundred denarii

C   6:8-9 One of his disciples . . . barley loaves and two fish

D   6:10 Sit down . . . sat down . . . about five thousand

E   6:11a Jesus took loaves and after . . . given thanks

D'   6:11b Those who were seated . . . as much as they wanted

C'   6:12-13a Told his disciples . . . twelve baskets from five barley loaves

B'   6:13b Those who had eaten

A'   6:14-15 Sign . . . mountain

6:16-23 Jesus' Power over the Sea

A   6:16 Disciples went down to the sea

B   6:17a Got into a boat

C   6:17b Across the sea to Capernaum

D   6:17c-18 It was now dark—no Jesus—sea rose—strong wind

E   6:19 Jesus walking on the sea . . . they were frightened

E'   6:20-21a It is I; do not be afraid . . . then they were glad

D'   6:21b Immediately the boat was at the land

C'   6:22a On the other side of the sea

B'   6:22b Jesus had not entered the boat

A'   6:22c Disciples had gone away alone

Conclusion 6:23 Boats from Tiberias to where Jesus had given thanks (6:10)

6:24-59 Jesus Talks with the Crowd about Bread of Life

6:24-31a Seeking Jesus: A Challenge to Jesus at Capernaum on the Other Side of the Sea

A   6:26a Jesus' word of honor

B   6:26b Not because you saw signs but because you ate

C   6:27 On him has God the Father set his seal

D   6:28 To do the works of God

D'   6:29a This is the work of God

C'   6:29b Believe in him whom he has sent
B'   6:30 What sign do you do . . . what works do you perform
A'   6:31a Israel's tradition

6:31b-59 Jesus Explains the Passage Cited from Exodus 16 by His Challengers

Introduction 6:31b
A   6:32 Word of honor
      —explanation that Moses did not give bread but my Father gives bread
A'   6:47 Word of honor
B   6:48 I am the bread of life
C   6:49-50 Your fathers ate . . . and died; a man eats bread of heaven and does not die
      —explanation that a man eats bread and does not die—central word of honor
C'   6:58 Father ate and died; he who eats this bread lives forever
Conclusion 6:59

6:60-66 Insider Talk Unmasks Antisociety Disloyalty

A   6:60a Many of his disciples
B   6:60b Saying
C   6:61 Disciples murmur
D   6:62 You see
E   6:63a Spirit that gives life
E'   6:63b Spirit and life
D'   6:64a You do not believe
C'   6:64b Those (disciples) that did not believe
B'   6:65 He said
A'   6:66 Many of his disciples

6:67-71 Reaction of the Twelve

A   6:67 The Twelve
B   6:68 Simon Peter
C   6:69 You are the Holy One of God
C'   6:70 One of you is a devil
B'   6:71a Son of Simon Iscariot
A'   6:71b One of the Twelve

V. Jesus Brought Light and Life to the Jerusalem Temple (7:1—8:59)

7:1-9 Around the Feast of Sukkoth in Galilee: A Challenge from Jesus' Brothers

A	7:1	Galilee
B	7:2	Feast of Sukkoth
C1	7:3	His brothers
C2	7:3	Show yourself to the world
C'1	7:5	His brothers
C'2	7:7	The world
B'	7:8	Feast . . . feast
A'	7:8	Galilee

7:10-14a Around the Feast of Sukkoth in Jerusalem: Divided Public Judgment about Jesus

A	7:10	The feast
B	7:11	Judeans
C	7:12	Judgment split on Jesus
B'	7:13	Judeans
A'	7:14a	Feast

7:14b—8:59 At Sukkoth: Jesus Teaches in the Temple

John tells us that about the middle of the feast Jesus emerges in the temple teaching (7:14). The whole block of teaching is marked off by mention of Jesus going into the temple (7:14b) and leaving the temple (8:59). The pattern of the whole seems to be as follows, with emphasis on the center panel and Jesus' proclamation of himself as light of the world.

I	7:14b	Jesus went up into the temple and taught
II	7:28	Jesus proclaimed as he taught in the temple
III	7:37	Jesus proclaimed in the temple: If anyone thirst
IV	8:12	Jesus again said to them: I am the light of the world
V	8:20	He spoke in the treasury as he taught in the temple
VI	8:59	Jesus went out of the temple

Opening Marker I: Jesus went up into the temple and taught 7:14b

7:14b-18 Sukkoth in Jerusalem: Initial Challenge to Jesus about His Authority to Teach and Interpret Scripture

A	7:15	Learning without study
B	7:16	My teaching . . . his who sent me
B'	7:17a	Teaching is from God
C	7:17b	Speaking on my own authority
C'	7:18a	Speaks on his own authority
D	7:18b	Seeks his own glory

D   7:18c Seeks the glory of him

7:18d Him who sent him

7:18e Is true, in him is no falsehood

7:19-28 Jesus' Riposte: Moses Gives the Law, but You Do Not Observe It

A   7:19-20 Why do you seek to kill me?

B   7:21 I did one deed

C   7 22 Moses gave you circumcision

D   7:22b You circumcise on the Sabbath

D'   7:23a If on the Sabbath a man is circumcised

C'   7:23b Law of Moses

B'   7:23c On the Sabbath I made a man's whole body well

7:24 You judge by appearances, not with right judgment

A'   7:25 The man whom they seek to kill

Epilogue

A   7:26 Do the authorities really know this is the Messiah?

B   7:27a We know where this man comes from

B'   7:27b No one will know where the Messiah comes from

A'   7:28 You know me and you know where I come from?

Marker II: Jesus proclaimed as he taught in the temple 7:28

7:29-36 Second Challenge in Jerusalem: Attempts to Arrest Jesus

A   7:29 I come from him and he sent me

B   7:30 They sought . . . to arrest him

C   7:31 People: Will Messiah do more signs than this man?

B'   7:32 Pharisees, priests and Pharisees . . . arrest him

A'   7:33 I go to him who sent me

Comment

A   7:34 you will see me and you will not find me; where I am you cannot come

B   7:35 Judeans: Where does he intend to go (dispersion among Greeks)?

A'   7:36 you will see me and you will not find me; where I am you cannot come

Central Marker III: Jesus proclaimed in the temple: If anyone thirst, let him come to me and drink! 7:37-39

7:40-52 Opponents' Controversy over Jesus' Status and Role

A   7:40   This is really the prophet
B   7:41   Is the Christ to come from Galilee?
C   7:42   Has not the Scripture . . . ?
D   7:43-44   People and outcome of discussion
E   7:45   Chief Priests and Pharisees
F   7:46   Officers: No man ever spoke like this man!
F'   7:47   Pharisees: Are you led astray?
E'   7:48   Authorities and Pharisees
D'   7:49-50   Crowd and outcome of discussion
C'   7:51   Does not our Law . . . ?
B'   7:52a   Are you from Galilee too?
A'   7:52b   No prophet is to rise from Galilee

Central Marker IV: Jesus again spoke to them saying, "I am the Light of the World" 8:12

8:13-19 Opponents' Controversy over Jesus' Testimony

A Witness
     a 8:13a   witness to yourself (positive)
       b 8:13b   your testimony is not true (negative)
     a' 8:14a   If I do bear witness to myself (positive)
       b' 8:14b   my testimony is true (positive)
A1 Qualifications
         c 8:14c   I know whence I come and go (positive)
         c' 8:14d   you do not know whence I come and go (negative)
B Judging
           d 8:15a   you judge according to the flesh (positive that is negative)
             e 8:15b   I judge no one (negative that is positive)
             e' 8:16a   even if I judge it is true (positive)
           d' 8:16b   (we judge) I do not judge alone; I and he who sent me
                 (positive)
A' Witness
       b" 8:17   testimony of two is true (in your Torah) (positive)
     a" 8:18   I bear witness and the Father who sent me (positive)
A1' Qualifications
         f 8:19a   You know neither me nor my Father (negative)
         f' 8:19b   If you knew me, you would know my Father (positive)

Marker V: He spoke in the treasury, as he taught in the temple 8:20

8:21-30 Jesus Uses a Riddle as a Counterchallenge

8:21-24a First Gambit
A 8:21a You will seek me and die in your sin
B 8:21b Where I am going, you cannot come
B' 8:22 Where I am going, you cannot come?
C 8:23a You are from below, I am from above
C' 8:23b You are of this world, I am not of this world
A' 8:24a I told you that you would die in your sins

8:24b-30 Second Gambit
A 8:24b Unless you believe that I am he
B 8:25-26a Who are you? . . . I told you from the beginning
C 8:26b But he who sent me is true
D 8:27 Father
E 8:28 When you have lifted up the Son of man, then you will know that I am he
D' 8:28b Father
C' 8:29a And he who sent me is with me
B' 8:29b He has not left me alone, for I always do what is pleasing to him
A' 8:30 Many believed in him

8:31-59 Controversy over Kinship with Abraham
Introduction 8:31-32 Statement triggers controversy

8:33-37a Abraham's Free Descendants
A 8:33 Descendants of Abraham
B 8:33b You will be made free
C 8:34 Slave to sin
D 8:35a Slave does not continue in house
D' 8:35 Son continues forever
C' 8:36 Son makes you free
B' 8:36b You will be free indeed
A' 8:37a Descendants of Abraham

8:37b-40a Abraham Your Father?
A 8:37b You seek to kill me
B 8:38 Seen with my Father
C 8:38b Heard from your father
C' 8:39a Abraham is our father
B' 8:39 If you were Abraham's children
A' 8:40 You seek to kill me

8:40b-42 Abraham's Deeds

A 8:40b I tell what I heard from God
B 8:40c (You do) not what Abraham did
C 8:41a You do what your father did
D 8:41b We were not born of fornication
C' 8:41c We have one Father, even God
B' 8:42a If God were your Father
A' 8:42b I came forth from God

8:43-47 Your Father the Devil

A 8:43a Why do you not understand?
B 8:43 Hear my word
C 8:44a Your father the devil
D 8:44b He was a murderer
E1 8:44c Nothing of the truth
E2 8:44d There is no truth in him
D' 8:44e He is a liar
C' 8:44f The father of lies
E1' 8:45 I tell the truth
E2' 8:46 I tell the truth
B' 8:47a Words of God
A' 8:47b You do not hear . . . you are not of God

8:48-50 Slurs on Jesus' Lineage and Status

A 8:48 You are Samaritan and have a demon
A' 8:49a I do not have a demon
B 8:49b I honor my Father
B' 8:49c You dishonor me
C 8:50a I do no seek my own glory
C' 8:50b One seeks it and judges

8:51-58 Before Abraham, I Am

A 8:51 Word of Honor: He will never see death
B 8:52 Judeans said . . . Abraham died
C 8:53 Our father Abraham
D 8:54 If I glorify myself, my glory is nothing
D' 8:55 If I said I do not know him, I should be a liar like you
C' 8:56 Your father Abraham
B' 8:57 Judeans said . . . have you seen Abraham?
A' 8:58 Word of Honor: Before Abraham was, I am

Closing Marker V: Jesus went out of the temple (as they attempted to kill him!)
8:59

VI. *Judeans Reaction to Jesus' Bringing Light and Life to Jerusalem (9:1—10:42)*

9:1-41 Jesus' Rescue of a Man Born Blind Occasions Controversy
Introduction 9:1-5 (forms bracket with Conclusion 9:35-42)
A   9:1-2   Man blind from birth . . . who sinned?
B   9:3   That the works of God might be made manifest
C   9:4-5   Work the works of him who sent me, while it is day . . . I am the light of the world

Episode I: Healing
A   9:6-7a   Eyes . . . Siloam
B   9:7b   Came back seeing
C   9:8   Is not this the man
D   9:9a   Some said, It is he; others said, No, but he is like him. He said
C'   9:9b   I am the man.
B'   9:10   Eyes opened
A'   9:11   Eyes . . . Siloam
      9:12   They said to him, Where is he? He said, I do not know

Episode II: First Interrogation
A   9:13-14   Blind . . . opened his eyes
B   9:15a   Pharisees
C   9:15b   Eyes . . . see
B'   9:16   Pharisees
A'   9:17   Blind . . . opened your eyes
      9:17b   He said, He is a prophet

Episode III: Interrogation of Parents
A   9:18   Parents
B   9:19   Blind . . . see
A'   9:20a   Parents
B'   9:20b-21a   Blind . . . sees
C   9:21b   Ask him, he is of age
A"   9:22a   Parents
D   9:22b   If anyone should confess him to be Christ, he was to be put out of the synagogue
A'''   9:23a   Parents
C'   9:23b   He is of age, ask him

Episode IV: Second Interrogation
A   9:24 Sinner
B   9:25-26 Blind . . . eyes
C   9:27 You would not listen
D   9:28 Disciples of Moses
E   9:29a We know God
F   9:29b We do not know where he comes from
F'   9:30 You do not know where he comes from
E'   9:31a We know that God
D'   9:31b If any one is a worshiper of God and does his will
C'   9:31c God listens to him
B'   9:32 Eyes . . . blind
        9:33 If this man were not from God, he could do nothing
A'   9:34a Born in sin
        9:34b And they cast him out
Conclusion 9:35-42 (forms bracket with Introduction 9:1-5)
C'   9:35-38 You have seen him
B'   9:39 Judgment . . . those who do not see may see and those who see become blind
A'   9:40 We see . . . your guilt remains

10:1-18 Jesus as the Sheep Gate and Good Shepherd
Introduction (Word of Honor) Truly, truly, I say to you,
A   10:1a He who does not enter the sheepfold by the door but climbs in by another way (negative)
B   10:1b That man is a thief and a robber
C   10:2a But he who enters by the door (positive)
D   10:2b The shepherd of the sheep
E   10:3a The sheep hear his voice, and
D'   10:3b He (shepherd) calls his own sheep by name
C'   10:4 Sheep follow . . . know his voice (positive)
B'   10:5a Stranger
A'   10:5b Not follow . . . not know the voice (negative)
Conclusion 10:6 They did not understand this figure

Introduction (Word of Honor) Truly, truly, I say to you
A   10:7 I am the door of the sheep
B   10:8 Thieves and robbers; but the sheep did not heed them
A'   10:9 I am the door; if any one enters
B'   10:10a Thief comes only to steal and kill and destroy
A"   10:10b I came that they may have life . . .

Introduction 10:11a I am the good shepherd

A   10:11b The good shepherd lays down his life for the sheep

B   10:12 Hireling not a shepherd, (he) whose own the sheep are not

C   10:12b Sees the wolf coming and leaves the sheep and flees

C'   10:12c And the wolf snatches them and scatters them

B'   10:13 Hireling cares nothing for the sheep

A'   10:14a I am the good shepherd

Introduction 10:14b I know my own and my own know me

A   10:15 As the Father knows me and I know the Father; and I lay down my life for the sheep

B   10:16a Other sheep, not of this fold; I must bring them also

B'   10:16b They will heed my voice: One flock, one shepherd

A'   10:17a For this reason the Father loves me, because I lay down my life

C   10:17b That I may take it again

D   10:18a No one takes it from me, but I lay it down of my own accord

D'   10:18b I have power to lay it down

C'   10:18d And I have power to take it again

A"   10:18e I have received from my Father

10:19-24 Hanukkah in Jerusalem: Another Challenge—Deviance Accusations against Jesus

A   10:19 There was again a division among the Judeans because of these words

B   10:20 Many of them said, He has a demon, and he is mad; why listen to him?

B'   10:21 Others said, These are not the sayings of one who has a demon. Can a demon open the eyes of the blind?

C   10:22 It was the feast of the Dedication at Jerusalem

C'   10:23 It was winter, and Jesus was walking in the temple, in the portico of Solomon

A'   10:24 So the Jews gathered round him and said to him, How long will you keep us in suspense? If you are the Christ, tell us plainly

10:25-38 Jesus' Riposte Nearly Erupts in Violence

Introduction 10:25a I told you, and you do not believe

A   10:25b-27 Works . . . Father's name . . . but you do not believe + reason

B   10:28-29 And no one shall snatch them out of my hand . . . out of the Father's hand

C   10:30 I and the Father are one

D   10:31 To stone him

A'   10:32 Works from the Father . . . stone me?

D'   10:33a Stone you

C'   10:33b Blasphemy because you, being a man, make yourself God

E   10:34 In your law, I said, you are gods?

E'   10:35 He called them gods (and scripture cannot be broken)

B'   10:36 Blasphemy because I said, I am the Son of God?

A"   10:37-38a Works of my Father, then do not believe me . . . believe the works

Conclusion 10:38b The Father is in me and I am in the Father

10:39-42 An Honor Notice about Jesus

Introduction 10:39 Again they tried to arrest him, but he escaped from their hands

A   10:40a He went away again across the Jordan to the place where

B   10:40b John at first baptized, and there he remained

C   10:41a Many said, John did no sign

B'   10:41b But everything that John said about this man was true

A'   10:42 And many believed in him there

VII. As His Last Public Act, Jesus Brought Life to a Beloved Friend (Like Us) (11:1-54)

11:1-6 A Request to Save Lazarus, a Beloved Friend

A   11:1 Certain man was ill

   a Lazarus

   b Mary

   c Martha

B   11:2a Mary who anointed the Lord

C   11:2b Whose brother Lazarus was ill

D'   11:3 Whom you love is ill

C'   11:4 Illness not unto death

B'   11:4b Son of God be glorified

   c' 11:5 Martha

   b' Sister

   a' Lazarus

A'   11:6 When he heard that he was ill

11:7-16 Reluctant Compliance: Jesus Comes to Rescue Lazarus from Death

A   11:7 To disciples: Let us go into Judea again

B   11:8 Disciples say: Are you going there again

C   11:9-10 Jesus answered: Day and light

D   11:11 Fallen asleep . . . sleep

D'   11:12-13 Fallen asleep . . . death . . . in sleep

C'   11:14 Jesus told them plainly: Lazarus is dead

B'   11:15 Jesus says: Let us go to him

A'   11:16 To disciples: Let us go that we may die

11:17-44 Jesus Rescues Lazarus, the Beloved Friend, from Death

Introduction 11:17-19 Time, place, cast of characters

A   11:20-31 With Martha outside the village

B   11:32-37 With Mary outside the village

C   11:38-44 With Lazarus outside the tomb

11:45-54 Reaction to Jesus' Raising Lazarus: A Plot to Kill Jesus

A   11:45-46 The reaction of the Judeans to Jesus

B   11:47-48 The gathering of the Sanhedrin

C   11:49-50 Caiaphas's prophecy

B'   11:51-53 The gathering of the children of God

A'   11:54 The reaction of Jesus to the Judeans

11:55—12:11 A Third Passover Draws Near: Jesus Is Anointed

Introduction 11:55 Many went up: Passover time . . . Jerusalem, purpose

  a 11:56 They (many) look for Jesus

  b 11:57 Chief priests and Pharisees

A   12:1-2 Exact time, place, cast of characters, scenario
Lazarus, whom he had raised from the dead

B   12:3 Mary of Bethany performs a symbolic action

C   12:4-5 Disciple Judas's protest

D   12:6 Explanation: Judas's motivation

B'   12:7 Jesus said: Explanation of symbolic action

C'   12:8 Jesus' rebuttal of Judas's position

  a 12:9 Great crowd of Judeans seek Jesus and

A'   Lazarus whom he had raised from the dead

  b 12:10 Chief priest

Conclusion 12:11 Many Judeans were going away

VIII. The Close of the Story of Jesus' Public Offer of Light and Life to Israel (12:12-50)

12:12-19 Jesus Enters Jerusalem and Is Hailed as King of Israel

A   12:12 Great crowd: For feast in Jerusalem

B   12:13-14 Outside Jerusalem: Acclamation King of Israel, seated on young ass

B'   12:15-16 Scriptural quote to explain, his disciples remembered

A'   12:17-18 Crowd: Motivated by sign and witness to sign of Lazarus
          12:19 Pharisees (see 11:57): The world has gone after him

12:20-36 Jesus' Final Public Revelation

Introduction 12:20 Hellenistic Israelites: For feast

A   12:21-22 Hellenists to Philip, Philip and Andrew say to Jesus

B   12:23 Jesus says: Hour has come for the Son of man to be glorified

   a 12:24-25 Word of honor: If it dies . . . eternal life

   b 12:28 Serve and be honored

   c 12:27-28a Hour . . . glorify

B'   12:28b God says: Sky voice: Assurance of glory

A'   12:29 Crowd says: Thunder or sky servant

B"   12:30-31 Jesus says: Son of man to be lifted up and draw all men

A"   12:34 Crowd says: Son of man not be lifted up

B'''   12:35 Jesus says: Choice: Walk in light or be overtaken by darkness

Conclusion 12:36 Jesus departed and hid himself from them

12:37-43 The Problem of Judean Unbelief Explained

A   12:37 Problem: Jesus did many signs, but Jerusalem crowd did not believe

B   12:38 Solution: Because Isaiah said, they could not believe

B'   12:40 Solution two: Isaiah also said because he saw the glory of the Word and spoke of him

A'   12:42-43 Problem two: Fear of Pharisees and of expulsion

12:44-50 Conclusion to the Series of Jesus' Self-Disclosures

A   12:44 Believes . . . him who sent me

   a 12:45 Sees . . . him who sent me

   b 12:46 Light into the world

B   12:47 Hears . . . not to judge the world but to save the world

B'   12:48 Reject and does not receive . . . word is judge on last day

A'   12:49 The Father sent me . . . commandment what to say and to speak

   b 12:50a I know his commandment is eternal life

   a 12:50b I say as the Father has bidden me

*IX. Passover in Jerusalem: What Jesus Said and Did During His Last Meal
with His Friends (Like Us) (13:1—17:26)*

A 13:1-38 Jesus Washes Feet of Core Group: Urges Imitation and Mutual Love

Themes of glorification and love

    a 13:1-17 Foot washing (forgiveness); Jesus urges imitation
      b 13:18-20 Forthcoming proof for Jesus being I am
    a'1 3:22-38 Aware of betrayal, Jesus urges mutual love

B 14:1-31 Jesus Gives Reassurance to His Core Group in Face of His Departure

Themes of Jesus' departure and the encouragement of the disciples

    a 14:1-4 Let not your hearts be troubled + reasons
      b 14:5-7 Thomas says and Jesus answers
        c 14:8-21 Philip says and Jesus answers
      b' 14:22-26 Judas (not Iscariot) says and Jesus answers
    a' 14:27-31 Let not your hearts be troubled + reasons

C 15:1-11 Solidarity in Jesus' Group

Themes of abiding and joy

    a 15:1 I am the true vine, and my Father is the vinedresser
      b 15:2 A branch that bears no fruit
        c 15:2b Branch that does bear fruit he prunes, that it may bear more fruit
          c' 15:3 You are already made clean by the word which I have spoken to you
        d 15:4a Abide in me, and I in you
      b' 15:4b As the branch cannot bear fruit by itself
        d' 15:4c Unless it abides in the vine, neither can you, unless you abide in me
    a' 15:5a I am the vine, you are the branches

Introduction 15:5b-6 He who abides in me, and I in him or not abide

    a 15:7 If you abide in me, my words abide in you
      b 15:8 By this my Father is glorified
      b' 15:9 As the Father has loved me, so have I loved you; abide in my love
    a' 15:10 If you keep my commandments, you will abide in my love
      b" 15:10c Just as I have kept my Father's commandments, abide in his love

Conclusion 15:11 For joy

D 15:12-17 Jesus' New Commandment

Theme: Love one another

  a 15:12 This is my commandment, that you love one another as I have
  loved you

    b 15:13 Friends

    b' 15:14a My friends

  a' 15:14b What I command you

      c 15:15 Servants

      c' 15:15b The servant

    b" 15:15c Friends

        d 15:15d My Father I have made known to you

          e 15:16 Choose me, but I chose you . . . bear fruit and fruit . .
          abide

        d' 15:16b The Father in my name, he may give it to you

  a" 15:17 This I command you, to love one another

C' 15:18-16:4a Insiders and Outsiders

Themes of hatred and exclusion

  a 15:18-21 First explanation of world's hatred

    b 15:22-25 Result of world's hatred

  a' 15:26—16:3 Second explanation of world's hatred

B' 16:4b-33 Jesus Prepares Core Group for His Departure

Themes of Jesus' departure and warning to the disciples

  a 16:4b-15 Jesus' departure and the disciples

    b 16:16-24 Jesus' departure and return to the disciples

  a' 16:25-33 Jesus' revelation and the disciples

A' 17:1-26 Jesus Prays for Honor for Himself and His Followers

Themes of glorification and love

  a 17:1-8 Jesus prays for himself

    b 17:9-19 Jesus prays for his disciples: I pray

  a' 17:20-26 Jesus prays for the world: I pray

X. Jesus Was Lifted Up and Gave His Spirit to Us: His Process of Ascent (18:1—19:42)

A 18:1-11 Jesus' Arrest
Introduction In the Garden
    18:1-3 Cast of characters
    18:4-11 Action: Jesus loses none given to him

B 18:12-27 Jesus before the High Priest; Peter's Disloyalty
    18:12-16 Cast of characters; scene change
    a 18:17-18 Peter's first denial—outside
      b 18:19-24 Jesus before Annas: Teacher and Revealer—inside
    a' 18:25-27 Peter's Second and Third Denial—outside

C 18:28—19:16a Jesus before Pilate: The King of the Judeans
    18:28 Introduction; general scene change
    a 18:29-32 First scene—outside: Theme is crucifixion and death
      b 18:33-37 Second scene—inside: Theme is power of Jesus
    (Jesus is king of truthfulness, as revealed on the cross)
        c 18:38-40 Third scene—outside: Theme is kingship of Jesus
        (Jesus' innocence declared, but first rejection of it)
          d 19:1-3 Central scene—no motion: Theme is Jesus declared
          King of the Judeans
        c' 19:4-8 Fifth scene—outside: Theme is Behold the Man
        (Jesus' innocence declared and rejected second and third time)
      b' 19:9-12 Sixth scene—inside: Theme is power of Pilate
    a' 19:13-15 Seventh scene—outside: Theme is crucifixion and death
    19:16a Conclusion: General outcome of the whole scenario

B' 19:16b-37 Jesus is Lifted Up before "This World": His Exaltation (Glorification)
    19:16b-18 Introduction: Place of action emphasized
    a 19:19-22 First scene: Title on the cross and reaction to it
    b 19:23-24 Second scene: Jesus' clothing
    c 19:25-27 Third scene: Jesus' mother at the cross
    d 19:18-30 Fourth scene: Jesus' work completed
    e 19:31-37 Fifth scene: The piercing of Jesus
      1 19:31-32 Man's decision
      2 19:33-37 God's will

A' 19:38-42 Conclusion: Jesus' Burial in a Garden

XI. *God's Vindication of Jesus: Jesus Ascends to God and Descends to His Friends (20:1-31)*

20:1-31 Jesus Completes His Ascent and Descends Twice

A   20:1-2 Prologue

B   20:3-10 Peter and beloved disciple at the tomb

     a   20:3 Two disciples run to tomb

       b   20:4-5 Beloved disciple comes first, does not enter

         c   20:6-7 Peter arrives second, enters first and sees

       b'   20:8-9 Beloved disciples enters second and sees

     a'   20:10 Two disciples leave tomb

C   20:11-18 Mary Magdalene sees the raised Lord

     a   20:11-12 Mary sees two sky servants at the tomb

     b   20:13-14 Question-answer-turning

     b' 20:15-16 Question-answer-turning

     a' 20:17-18 Mary is told to announce the news

C'   20:19-23 Jesus descends: First appearance of the risen Jesus

     a   20:19-20 Jesus says, shows: Disciples see and rejoice

       b   20:21-23 Jesus says, breathes on "them"

B'   20:24-29 Jesus descends again: Second appearance of the Raised Jesus

     a   20:24-25 Thomas and question of unbelief

       b   20:26-27 Jesus says, shows; Thomas touches

     a'   20:28-29 Thomas and issue of belief

A'   20:30-31 Epilogue: Purpose of the Gospel

XII. *Addendum: Another Descent and Appearance of the Risen Jesus (21:1-31)*

21:1-14 Third Appearance of the Risen Jesus

A   21:1-2 Jesus revealed himself (= appeared) to disciples (list added)

B   21:3 Simon Peter said: I am going fishing

C   21:4 Jesus on the beach; the disciples did not know

D   21:5 Jesus said: Children have you any fish?

E   21:7 Peter dressed up and jumped into the sea

F   21:8 Net full of fish

G   21:9 They saw a charcoal fire there, with fish lying on it, and bread

F'   21:10 Jesus said: Bring some of the fish

E'   21:11 Peter went aboard

D'   21:12 Jesus said: Come and have breakfast

C'   21:12 None of the disciples dared

B'   21:13 Jesus took bread and fish

A'   21:13-14 Third time Jesus was revealed (= appeared) to disciples

21: 15-23 Tying Up Loose Ends in the Story

Theme 1: Reconciliation conversation with Peter 21:15-18

A   21:15a Introduction: Time notice, Jesus to Peter

  1 21:15b Jesus' first question and Peter's first answer

  2 21:16 Jesus' second question and Peter's second answer

  3 21:17 Jesus' third question and Peter's third answer

A'   21:18 Conclusion: Jesus' word of honor about Peter's fate

Theme 2: About the fate of the beloved disciple 21:19-23

A   21:19 To Peter, Jesus' command: Follow me

B   21:20 Beloved disciple + supper description: Follows them

C   21:21 To Jesus, Peter asks of beloved disciple's fate

D   21:22a Jesus' statement: If it is my will . . .

A'   21:22b To Peter, Jesus' command: Follow me

B'   21:23a Brethren's opinion about the beloved disciple

C'   21:23b What Jesus did not say about the beloved disciple's fate

D'   21:23b Jesus' statement: If it is my will . . .

XIII. Epilogue: Group Attestation to the Author's Veracity (21:24-25)

Later Insertion: Jesus Rescues a Woman Caught in Adultery (7:53—8:1-11)

BIBLIOGRAPHY

Introduction

Ashton, John
1991   *Understanding the Fourth Gospel.* Oxford: Clarendon.
Brown, Raymond
1979   *The Community of the Beloved Disciple.* Mahwah, N.J.: Paulist.
Fowler, Roger
1981   *Language as Social Discourse.* Bloomington: Indiana University Press.
Giblett, Rodney
1991   "Childhood Secret Languages as Anti-language." *Neophilologus* 75:1–10.
Giles, Howard, and John M. Wiemann
1987   "Language, Social Comparison and Power." Pp. 350–84 in Charles R. Berger and Steven H. Chaffce, eds., *Handbook of Communication Science.* Beverly Hills: Sage Publications.
Giles, Howard, et al.
1987   "Speech Accommodation Theory: The First Decade and Beyond." Pp. 13–48 in Margaret L. McLaughlin, ed., *Communication Yearbook 10.* Beverly Hills: Sage Publications.
Halliday, Michael A. K.
1976   "Anti-languages." *American Anthropologist* 78:570–84.
1978   *Language as Social Semiotic: The Social Interpretation of Language and Meaning.* Baltimore: University Park.
Harris, Grace Gredys
1989   "Concepts of Individual, Self and Person in Description and Analysis." *American Anthropologist* 91:599–612.
Kress, Gunther
1978   "Poetry as Anti-language: A Reconsideration of Donne's 'Nocturnall Upon S. Lucies Day.'" *P[oetry and] T[heory of] L[iterature]: A Journal for Descriptive Poetics and Theory* 3:327-44.

Malina, Bruce J.
1985   *The Gospel of John in Sociolinguistic Perspective* (48th Colloquy of the
        Center for Hermeneutical Studies, ed. Herman Waetjen). Berkeley: Cen-
        ter for Hermeneutical Studies.
1994   "John's: The Maverick Christian Group: The Evidence of Sociolinguis-
        tics." *Biblical Theology Bulletin* 24:167–82.
Malina, Bruce J., and Richard L. Rohrbaugh
1992   *Social-Science Commentary on the Synoptic Gospels.* Minneapolis:
        Fortress Press.
Miller, Gerald R.
1987   "Persuasion." Pp. 446–83 in Charles R. Berger and Steven H. Chaffee,
        eds., *Handbook of Communication Science.* Beverly Hills: Sage Publi-
        cations.
Mol, Hans
1976   *Identity and the Sacred: A Sketch for a New Social-Scientific Theory of
        Religion.* New York: Free Press.
Urban, Greg
1981   "Review of Language as Social Semiotic: The Social Interpretation of
        Language and Meaning, by M. A. K. Halliday." *American Anthropolo-
        gist* 83:659–61.

Commentary

Ashton, John
1991   *Understanding the Fourth Gospel.* Oxford: Clarendon.
Brown, Raymond E.
1979   *The Community of the Beloved Disciple.* New York: Paulist.
Derrett, J. Duncan M.
1993   *The Victim: The Johannine Passion Narrative Reexamined.* Shipston-on-
        Stour, Warwickshire, U.K.: Drinkwater.
Ford, Josephine Massyngbaerde
1995   "Jesus as Sovereign in the Passion According to John." *Biblical Theolo-
        gy Bulletin* 25:110–17.
Giblin, C. H.
1980   "Suggestion, Negative Response, and Positive Action in St. John's Por-
        trayal of Jesus (2:1-11; 4:46-54; 7:2-14; 11:1-44)." *New Testament Stud-
        ies* 26:197–211.
Goodman, Felicitas D.
1988   *Ecstasy, Ritual and Alternate Reality: Religion in a Pluralistic World.*
        Bloomington: Indiana Univ. Press.
1990   *Where the Spirits Ride the Wind: Trance Journeys and Other Ecstatic
        Experiences.* Bloomington: Indiana Univ. Press.
Hanson, K. C.
1994   "'How Honorable! How Shameful!' A Cultural Analysis of Matthew's
        Makarisms and Reproaches." *Semeia* 69:81–111.

1997   "The Galilean Fishing Economy and the Jesus Tradition." *Biblical Theology Bulletin* 27:99–111.

Hanson, K. C., and Douglas E. Oakman

1998   *Palestine in the Time of Jesus: Social Structures and Social Conflicts.* Minneapolis: Fortress Press.

Kysar, Robert

1976   *John: The Maverick Gospel.* Atlanta: John Knox [rev. ed. 1993].

Malina, Bruce J.

1985   *The Gospel of John in Sociolinguistic Perspective,* (48th Colloquy of the Center for Hermeneutical Studies, ed. Herman Waetjen), Berkeley: Center for Hermeneutical Studies.

1993a   *New Testament World: Insights from Cultural Anthropology.* Rev. ed. Louisville: Westminster/John Knox.

1993b   "Apocalyptic and Territoriality." Pp. 369–30 in Frederic Manns and Eugenio Alliata, eds., *Early Christianity in Context: Monuments and Documents. Essays in Honour of Emmanuel Testa.* Jerusalem: Franciscan Printing Press.

1994   "The Book of Revelation and Religion: How Did the Book of Revelation Persuade?" *Scriptura* 51:27–50.

1995   *On the Genre and Message of Revelation: Star Visions and Sky Journeys.* Peabody, Mass.: Hendrickson.

1996   "Christ and Time: Swiss or Mediterranean?" Pp. 179–214 in Bruce J. Malina, *The Social World of Jesus and the Gospels.* London and New York: Routledge.

Malina, Bruce J., and Jerome H. Neyrey

1988   *Calling Jesus Names: The Social Value of Labels in Matthew.* Sonoma, Calif.: Polebridge.

Malina, Bruce J., and John J. Pilch

1993   *Biblical Social Values and Their Meanings: A Handbook,* Peabody, Mass.: Hendrickson.

Malina, Bruce J. and Richard L. Rohrbaugh

1992   *Social Science Commentary on the Synoptic Gospels,* Minneapolis: Fortress Press.

Metzger, Bruce M.

1980   "The Nazareth Inscription Once Again." In *New Testament Studies: Philological, Versional, and Patristic.* New Testament Tools and Studies, 10. Leiden: Brill.

Münderlein, G.

1980   "chelebh." *Theological Dictionary of the Old Testament* IV:391–97.

Neusner, Jacob

1973   *The Idea of Purity in Ancient Judaism.* Studies in Judaism in Late Antiquity, 1. Leiden: Brill.

Neyrey, Jerome H.

1988   *An Ideology of Revolt: John's Christology in Social-Science Perspective.* Philadelphia: Fortress Press.

1994a   "What's Wrong with This Picture? John 4, Cultural Stereotypes of Women, and Public and Private Space." *Biblical Theology Bulletin* 24:77–91.

1994b   "Despising the Shame of the Cross: Honor and Shame in the Johannine Passion Narrative." *Semeia* 69:113–37.

1996   "The Trials (Forensic) and Tribulations (Honor Challenges) of Jesus: John 7 in Social Science Perspective." *Biblical Theology Bulletin* 26:107–24.

OGI   *Orientis graeci inscriptiones selectae.* 2 vols. ed. Wilhelm Dittenberger. Hildesheim: G. Olms, 1960 (reprint).

OTP   *Old Testament Pseudepigrapha.* 2 vols. ed. James Charlesworth. Garden City: Doubleday, 1983, 1985.

Pilch, John J.

1992   "Lying and Deceit in the Letters to the Seven Churches: Perspectives from Cultural Anthropology." *Biblical Theology Bulletin* 22:126–35.

1993   "Visions in Revelation and Alternate Consciousness: A Perspective from Cultural Anthropology." *Listening* 28:231–44.

1995   "The Transfiguration of Jesus: An Experience of Alternate Reality." Pp. 47–64 in Philip F. Esler ed., *Modelling Early Christianity: Social-Scientific Studies of the New Testament in its Context.* London/New York: Routledge.

1996   "Altered States of Consciousness: A 'Kitbashed' Model." *Biblical Theology Bulletin* 26:133–38.

Rogers, Everett M. with Lynne Svenning

1969   *Modernization among Peasants: The Impact of Communication.* New York: Holt, Rinehart and Winston.

Rohrbaugh, Richard L., ed.

1996   *Using The Social Sciences in New Testament Interpretation.* Peabody, Mass.: Hendrickson, 1996.

Stibbe, Mark W. G.

1993   *John.* Sheffield, U.K.: JSOT.

INDEX
READING SCENARIOS